Women Can't Hear What Men Don't Say

"Shocking and provocative. Warren Farrell has the gift of compelling us to look at old problems with new eyes. He challenges countless popular assumptions with a devastatingly persuasive picture of reality. Most important, he points the way to urgently needed solutions."

—Nathaniel Branden, author of *The Six Pillars of Self-Esteem*

"Warren Farrell has given us a gift by writing *Women Can't Hear What Men Don't Say*. He points us to the only way to end the battle of the sexes in the 21st Century."

—Karen DeCrow, attorney and former president, National Organization for Women

"You can hardly read a sentence in this fascinating book without thinking: 'Really? I didn't know that!' Warren Farrell is a true pioneer."

—Bernard Goldberg, Reporter, CBS News' *48 Hours*

"Bursting with provocative data. . . . Farrell's specific prescriptions for better communication make it must reading."

—Howard M. Halpern, Ph.D., former president, American Academy of Psychotherapists and author of *How to Break Your Addiction to a Person*

"An amazing piece of work. *Women Can't Hear What Men Don't Say* is a great contribution to communication between men and women. It substitutes illumination for emotional and careful research for skewed statistics. It is my hope that the law will hear what men don't say in time for our children to reap the benefit."

—Norman Vroman, District Attorney, Mendocino County, California

"Dr. Warren Farrell is one of the most original thinkers of our time."

—Nancy Friday, bestselling author of seven books, including the recent *Our Looks, Our Lives*

"For women and men who want greater effectiveness at the office and more love at home. Perceptive . . . Outspoken . . . Courageous."

—Martin Edelston, President, Boardroom Inc., and Editor, *Bottom Line/Personal*

Women
Can't Hear What Men
Don't Say

Women Can't Hear

What Men Don't Say

DESTROYING
MYTHS,
CREATING
LOVE

Warren Farrell, Ph.D.

JEREMY P. TARCHER/PUTNAM
a member of PENGUIN PUTNAM INC. *New York*

Most Tarcher/Putnam books are available at special quantity discounts for bulk purchases for sales promotions, premiums, fund-raising, and educational needs. Special books or book excerpts also can be created to fit specific needs. For details, write Putnam Special Markets, 375 Hudson Street, New York, NY 10014.

Jeremy P. Tarcher/Putnam
a member of
Penguin Putnam Inc.
375 Hudson Street
New York, NY 10014
www.penguinputnam.com

Library of Congress Cataloging-in-Publication Data

Farrell, Warren.
    Women can't hear what men don't say / by Warren Farrell.
       p.   cm.
    Includes index.
    ISBN 0-87477-988-X
    1. Man-woman relationships.   2. Interpersonal communication.
    3. Communication in marriage.   I. Title.
    HQ801.F355   1999   99-16286 CIP
    306.7—dc21

Printed in the United States of America
10   9   8   7   6   5   4   3   2   1

This book is printed on acid-free paper. ♾

BOOK DESIGN BY MAUNA EICHNER

ACKNOWLEDGMENTS

I am uncertain whether it is age or maturity that allows me to appreciate more deeply with each book the love my family provides. As my dad, Tom, approaches his nineties, I feel blessed at the balance, wisdom, and foresight he has modeled. My "new" mom, Lee, has been a thirty-year blessing, as is her relationship with my dad. Lee and my sister, Gail, are always present with their thoughtfulness. As Gail shares her experience teaching both gifted and special education students, I admire her intuitive understanding of what makes children tick. I hope some of my family's gifts have been accurately reflected in this book.

Joyce McHugh, who has been with me full time or part time for much of the past eighteen years, has brought her competence to this book, her administrative skills to the office, and her quick wit to my everyday life. She has known early mornings, late nights, and weekends to help me keep the book in this millennium's publishing schedule. That staff help was rounded out by additional competent assistance during portions of the past five years, especially from Sophia Ruiz and Susan Engbring, as well as Alexa Deere (especially on the housework chapter), Michael Estes (domestic violence), and Ethan Michaels, Zia Bhaisa, Jeff Seeman, Ravi Vora, and Alison Poggi.

This book began in the competent hands of Marilyn Abraham at Simon & Schuster. When she retired, it experienced, shall we say, some post-traumatic stress syndrome (about which you will read). Jeremy Tarcher, a man who I held very dear largely as a friend, then became my publisher. He is a man who understands my vision and was thus able to choose for it an extraordinary editor, Mitch Horowitz. Mitch's intellect has stimulated my thinking, and his availability, balance, and devotion have nurtured the book to its completion.

Writing is lonely and people help sustain a writer in ways that reflect their gifts. I have felt especially sustained by the love of Nathaniel and Devers Branden, Liz Dowling, and Erin and Alex Blanchard, as I have by the friendship of Greg Dennis, and the unique contributions to my life of Grainger Weston, Lydia Colocho, Francisco Velasquez, Erick Hornak, Carey Linde, Nancy Friday, Norm

Pearlstine, Lindsay Kenny, Joseph McCaffrey, Doug McKegney, Robert Olson, and Riki Robbins.

This manuscript was built on a base of information that was not gathered by me alone, but required the sharp eyes and devotion of Stuart Pedersen, Steve DeLuca, Norman Black, Ron Henry, Jimmy Boyd, David Dinn, Howard Hayghe, Robert Keith Smith, and Hugh Nations—each of whom made my mail carrier and fax machine feel needed.

A woman friend once told me that when I shopped with her and she tried on clothes, she felt very vulnerable, since her final selection was designed to cover up the flaws I was seeing. As authors, Steven Collins, Martin Fiebert, and Nathaniel Branden saw all my flaws as they read the entire first drafts. And, when someone reads only a few chapters, I feel as vulnerable as I feel when someone walks into a speech late and leaves early, which reflects the trust I feel for these colleagues, who fulfilled with care that request to review a few chapters: Eugene August, Art Barker, Devers Branden, Armin Brott, Ellen Brown, Greg Dennis, Liz Dowling, Martin Fiebert, Suzanne Frayser, Bernard Goldberg, Steven Holzner, Helena Lea, Cindy and Robert McNeely, R. L. McNeely, Linda Nickell, Kay Schwartzberg, Judith Sherven, Jim Sniechowski, and Hans-Günther Tappe.

Finally, this book rests in part on the dream of empowerment feminism shared by the late Wilma Scott Heidi, former President of NOW, and sustained to this day by a later NOW President, Karen De Crow. That dream felt alive in the everyday life of a beloved friend I dearly miss, Shari Lewis.

To Dad, Mom, Lee, Gail, and Wayne

CONTENTS

Introduction

A lie can travel halfway around the world while the truth is putting on its shoes.   MARK TWAIN

MY PERSONAL JOURNEY

In my first book, *The Liberated Man,*[1] I shared my feelings about the importance of independent women for secure men and the contribution of the women's movement in fostering women's self discovery. My mother's death, prior to the women's movement, was due, in part, to not living at a time in which she was encouraged to explore all aspects of herself. And her death was doubtless part of the motivation that led me to spend three years on the board of directors of the National Organization for Women in New York City, an experience that deepened my excitement about women's potential. That was in the '70s.

As the women's movement moved from mocked to mainstream, I increasingly sensed an anger toward men that permeated our culture as unnoticed as bacteria in water. Women were asking, "Why are men such jerks?" and "Why are men afraid of commitment?" and men were confused: Why would a woman want commitment from a jerk?

As women spoke, they wondered, "Why can't men listen?" As they pleaded for intimacy, they feared men cared only about sex. The 600 or so men's and women's groups I had formed helped me to hear what was behind women's anger and what men could barely say. The findings took the form of *Why Men Are the Way They Are,*[2] written to answer women's questions about men in a way that rang true for men. That was in the '80s.

I felt mixed emotions about these decades . . . as if they were the best of times and the worst of times between the sexes. The sexes have never communicated as much, nor have they ever divorced as much; they have never known so much about raising a child's self-esteem and never left their children so destabilized. The male role (mostly) has never been so successful at expanding

1

women's life expectancy (by over 50 percent in the twentieth century), yet never been so blamed for its neglect of women.

In retrospect, I saw the '50s as the decade of the family; the '60s, as the decade of men (sex without marriage; freedom; questioning authority); and the last three decades of the millennium, the decades of women. Unfortunately, while the decade of men also released women (birth control, professional choices, sexual self-discovery), the decades of women are in many ways a dark age for men.

Since the beginning of the women's movement, the suicide rate for women has *decreased* by about a third, while the suicide rate for men has *increased* by about 15 percent,[3] yet we've focused only on the damage to women's self-esteem. Something was going on . . .

By the late '80s, the anger toward men had become institutionalized. It was dividing families and poisoning love. The newest dirty word was not a four-letter word, it was a three-letter word: men. The women's movement had done a wonderful job of freeing women from sex roles, but no one did the same for men. The more women gained advantages, the more its movement went from favoring equality to fearing equality. Big feminism became like big labor: Both started by correcting an imbalance; both became so preoccupied with getting protection that soon everyone near them needed protection from them.

I began to feel that as women spoke up and men didn't, men and masculinity were becoming demonized and the baby was being thrown out with the bathwater. Soon I began distinguishing among the feminism I loved (what I now call empowerment feminism) and the two forms of feminism I feared (victim feminism and competitive feminism).

Empowerment feminism empowers a woman by encouraging her to develop all of her potential without regard to gender. It is the feminism I shall always support. *Victim feminism* focuses on how men and society systematically view women as second-class citizens and incapable, and any accomplishments a woman achieves are despite these barriers. *Competitive feminism* does not stop with saying women have it bad: It says that women have it *worse* than men; women's victimhood was *caused* by men. It arrives at these conclusions by exaggerating women's burdens and understating men's. Competitive feminism creates a male catch-22: If he says nothing, he looks like a deadbeat or oppressor; if he points out the exaggeration, he appears to be anti-woman.

Both Parts II and III are rife with examples of victim and competitive feminism, but with solutions as to how they can become empowerment feminism. If victim and competitive feminism have resulted in the last third of the twentieth century being dark ages for men, they haven't done so without men being a co-conspirator.

For six years I sorted out my feelings on these issues and worked to make The Myth of Male Power a new paradigm of men and power, and a more progressive male-female dance. I had come to feel that men's traditional definition of power did not give men real power. **Men had come to define power as feeling obligated to earn money that someone else spends while he dies sooner.** That felt to me like a better definition of obligation and responsibility. The Myth of Male Power redefined "power" as controlling one's own life.

The research on The Myth of Male Power helped me ferret out what I came to feel was the biggest misunderstanding in my thinking as a feminist—my failure to understand that, historically, neither sex had power; both sexes had roles. Our fathers and mothers had responsibilities, not rights; they had obligations, not options. Women were obligated to raise children; men were obligated to raise money. Earning money was not male privilege, it was male obligation. Privilege was about options, like the option to raise children or raise money; it was the option to spend money. . . . That was in the '90s.

However, the breadth of The Myth of Male Power—explaining perhaps a hundred myths about men that created the larger myth of male power; explaining how our genetic heritage had come into conflict with our genetic future; proposing not a women's movement condemning men or a men's movement condemning women, but a gender transition movement—neglected to counter some myths in enough depth to expect social change. And it neglected a method of communicating about these myths that could increase love without sacrificing honesty to do it. Myths first . . .

Some of the myths were so ingrained that thoughtful people could not be expected to drop them in response to a few paragraphs of explanation. For example, a conscientious feminist running a battered women's shelter would fear subjecting vulnerable women to a new treatment plan based on a few paragraphs explaining why their treatment program was based on false assumptions about men. She would need more depth before she could make responsible changes.

In-depth redefining is important, but women can't hear what men don't say partly because of the way men say it. And partly because it's so difficult to listen to anything we don't really want to hear.

So Women Can't Hear What Men Don't Say has to be about more than the substance of myths. It has to also be about process. The process of communicating difficult feelings; the process of listening to difficult feelings.

If I were to choose for myself a heritage of teaching men and women everything there is to understand about each other, or teaching men and women how to understand, I would choose the latter. The process is more important than the substance. The process is like learning to ride a bicycle or use a computer: The process will be useful even when the substance changes. The process is Part I.

The substance of *Women Can't Hear What Men Don't Say* will put the process to the test. All of us give lip service to having an open mind. The substance of this book will ask us to put our money where our mouth is, so to speak. That's Part II. More on that later.

Part I, then, is about the process it takes to understand someone who has a different perspective, be that person a husband or wife, a parent or a child, an employer or employee, a brother or sister, a Conservative or Liberal. . . . And even more important, it is about the ability to not only handle personal criticism, but to create a safe environment for it.

My feelings that political agreement was less important than listening skills emerged in the late '60s and early '70s when I was in college (at Montclair State University in New Jersey) and during graduate school at UCLA and NYU. I was one of those Vietnam War protestors who was a civilian, a Civil Rights advocate who was white, a gay rights supporter who was straight—someone your dad probably wanted to wrap up in a Soviet flag and burn. It was no surprise to anyone that by 1970, right after the women's movement surfaced in 1969, I was a male on New York City's board of directors of the National Organization for Women.

To my liberal friends, I was a certified liberal; to my conservative friends, I was a *hopeless* liberal. But to me, liberalism was never the issue—listening was. When, instead of listening, we pigeonholed feminists as "bra burners," slandered African-Americans as "niggers," branded war protesters as "commies," and derided gays as "queers," I felt sad. It seemed to me that labeling was the lobotomy of our soul.

The gap between my friends' and my desire to hear everyone's story left my liberal friends aghast when I argued that even those on our enemy list deserved an equal-opportunity ear. But this time the equal-opportunity ear was not to hear the story of the gay black Communist Vietnamese female—it was to hear the straight white European-American male . . . , er, me. (Oh, my. Wasn't "he" the oppressor? Weren't we defending the oppressed?)

The problem was that listening to myself required more confrontation of self than did listening to the perspectives of gays, blacks, women, and Vietnamese Communists. Which made it deliciously tempting to indulge our standard escape from listening to men: "Haven't we been listening to men's stories for thousands of years?"

But among those men was my own dad. When all was optimal, dad left home at 7 to 8 A.M. and returned at 6 to 7 P.M. That optimal work week—of fifty-five hours—was when he didn't work overtime. Or have to take a second job. Or

4

go to school at night. Often, though, my dad, and many of the dads in our neigh- borhood, put in a total of sixty to eighty hours per week, with that combination of work, overtime, school, and commuting. Sometimes our home must have seemed less his castle than his mortgage.

Eventually dad got his reward—managing a company in Holland. The company moved our family of five to Holland. Mom, though, found Holland too rainy and lonely. Dad responded by putting his company on notice, moving the family back to the United States, and staying alone in Holland until he could join us. Once back in the United States, though, his age—and having just quit his last job—kept him from finding a job managing another company. He was soon selling Fuller brushes door to door so my sister Gail and I could go to college where, ironically, I would learn why he should be on my enemy list.

For years, I never asked my dad how he *felt* selling Fuller brushes. But once, he did tell me how empty he felt walking the street, banging on doors, persuading some woman it was worth it to buy a brush from him at twice the price of a supermarket; and how bad he felt that the promises to Mom (his reasons for coming home late at nights and working weekends) had amounted to nothing. These realities were in such stark contrast to my theories of male privilege that it stopped me in my tracks.

And then I saw Mr. Longson, our next-door neighbor, die of a heart attack in his fifties. I began to wonder about calling it male power when he fulfilled his obligation to earn money his family spent while he died early. I realized that Mr. Longson and my dad had not had their internal stories and fears expressed, only repressed. To this day, I hear the stories of the women on my staff, but not those of the men who collect my garbage.

Removing my blinders, though, also removed my feminist support system. It was sad to feel that their support was dependent on my blinders. Feminists brought me not only my nurturance—my psychological support—but also my financial support. Removing my blinders severely damaged my financial success, but it deepened my soul as it forced me to confront the self-righteousness that sometimes seeped in as I viewed myself as "more enlightened," "unique," and "sensitive" for being "one of the few men" who could hear the perspectives of women. Hopefully, via that confrontation, it deepened those qualities in reality. And it certainly helped me distinguish between friends and political allies: Friends valued my integrity; political allies valued my agreement. It helped me understand that everyone had moccasins that needed a little wearing—even men.

IF MEN HAVE PROBLEMS, WHY AREN'T THEY SPEAKING UP?

Sharing fears and feelings will happen more slowly for men than with any other group, because although men, like women, received love by solving problems for others, the process it took for men to solve problems involved a more complete repression of his own problems. A man didn't tell his sergeant in the army that he, too, had some perspectives and problems the sergeant should consider . . . That would not have led to the man becoming the officer and the gentleman, but a failure and a reject, and he didn't notice many women rushing to a movie called *A Failure and a Reject.*

For men, success has always been the best preventive medicine to avoid the cancer of female rejection (. . . as well as everyone else's). Success came from repressing feelings, not expressing feelings. For women, expressing weakness and fear attracted a savior; for men, expressing weakness and fear attracted contempt. Hearing a man complain makes a woman feel like a mother, not a lover. Complaining was part of women's evolutionary heritage; for men, complaining is an evolutionary shift.

Women will not respect men until they speak up. But this does not mean women will respect men as soon as they speak up. The reason women *ultimately* respect a man who speaks up is because he must jump over hurdles, and his willingness to do it shows he cares, and his ability to do it earns respect. For example . . .

Some women say, when a man speaks up, that he must be a woman hater. That's one of the hurdles. For a man, that's perhaps the most painful one because he is speaking up so his love for a woman can be more genuine. He feels like he's been hit below the belt, like women wanting to hear his feelings is a fraud. But for some women, criticism does feel like hatred. She has just expressed her feeling.

The first part of this book is about helping both sexes know how to take potentially destructive mutual misunderstandings like that and turn them into love. Ultimately, this book is about both sexes speaking and both sexes listening in a radically different way. But prior to the "ultimately," there are reasons men are the silent sex, and men need to let women know their intent when they make a transition from suppression to expression.

For example, a man needs to let a woman know that his intent in speaking up is to have a more intimate relationship with an *equal* partner—that to not speak up is to treat her like a child.

If a man is not speaking up out of a need to protect, he is creating something worse than a parent-child relationship. He becomes like a permissive parent who soon finds himself needing protection from the child who knows no one's perspective but her or his own. This is what men's silence has created both individually and socially.

It is not the men who confront women directly that women need to fear; it is the men who fear confronting women because they don't think there's any hope, they "know" she'll never understand, or they're unwilling to risk the possibility she will call him "woman hater." When men do not speak up it demonstrates a blend of fear of women and contempt for women with a lack of courage. That cannot coexist with truly loving a woman as an equal partner.

In contrast, a man who speaks up is engaged. A man who is engaged cares. He has hope. He is risking for the hope of intimacy. But a man needs to let a woman know that is his intent. She'll recognize the truth in it. On some level she already knows it. *She just needs to know he knows it,* and that that's where he's coming from. She needs that assurance.

Another hurdle: When Dr. Laura (Schlessinger) researched *Ten Stupid Things Men Do to Mess Up Their Lives,* she "asked my male listeners to write or fax me suggestions for the stupid things men do. I got thousands of responses of the most moving, vulnerable, meaningful material. But women have not been open to hearing it. . . . Women feel angry and threatened by men's feelings. They don't really want men to be sensitive, just sensitive to *their* (women's) feelings."[4]

Both sexes fear confronting their partner. When I first became involved with the National Organization for Women, women would invite me for dinner and ask me to share my feminist perspectives with their husband so they could be shielded from his response. Similarly, men who are honest often find the honesty costs more than it was worth. A single man or woman can afford to weed out of their lives someone who cannot handle who they are. But for couples with children it's more complex.

Some of America's most powerful men have personally shared with me how their own life matches the experiences about which I write, but they shudder with the thought of sharing this with their own wives—"If I disagree with her, it'll just cause trouble . . . I can't just consider myself; we have children too." When the world's opinion leaders feel they cannot differ with their own wives . . .

Fortunately, many women feel supported when men speak up. And many women are feeling so strongly about the need to create a better world for children that they are speaking up even when men are silent. The man in charge of the 1-800-FATHERS hotline told me more than half the calls they received were made by women.[5] Often the woman was a second wife who saw how much her new husband loved his children. She was angry at him for placating his ex and shocked that the system could allow his ex to prevent him from being with the children. In many cases she felt that she and her new husband could provide more balance for the children than could a single mom. This woman is perhaps the first to experience how the Second Wives' Club loses when the First Wives' Club wins.

Millions of women will be second wives. And millions more won't because the man they love is still in shock at his last transition from husband to a member of the men's auxiliary of the First Wives' Club.

FEELINGS AND DATA

I like feelings a lot more than data. Yet there's a lot of data in this book. Many women will be tempted to say, "Why can't you just tell me how you feel—I can listen to that. That means more to me than a statistic."

How men feel is crucial; but if a man said, "I just don't feel men are more violent to women than women are to men," most women would just say, "Sorry, you're wrong," and dismiss him as an ignorant chauvinist.

Without responsible, concrete information, we get stuck in the quicksand of self-fulfilling prophecies. When the society has no awareness that men are battered by women in significant numbers, we don't develop hotlines, so we don't hear men's feelings; we don't develop shelters, so we don't hear men's feelings; we don't train social workers to be sensitive to men who get hit first, so they develop treatment programs based on what they can see. Without responsible new information neither sex nor any social workers can be asked to alter a working paradigm. And that only occurs if we care enough to let it in.

The best hope of knowledge is the creation of caring. Until Rachel Carson wrote *Silent Spring*, we didn't have enough knowledge to care about the insecticides that poison our food. *Women Can't Hear What Men Don't Say*, which is about the "silent sex," provides the knowledge to care about the myths that are the insecticides that poison our love for men. It will succeed only if it inspires others to share their stories. The numbers help men know they are not alone; they help women know that these are not just my opinions. It takes the personal stories and the numbers for a critical mass to care. And care creates the search for solutions.

Anger toward men is perpetuated as much by men's blindness as by women's. If a person doing a survey on housework asks a man what housework he has done in the past week, and he has just remodeled the house, he may say "none" because he doesn't consider remodeling the house to be "housework." If a man had just come back from a camping vacation and he drove the family everywhere, and the person doing the housework survey asked him about his contributions during the week, chances are he would not mention his time driving, setting up the tent, packing the car, or organizing the trip. He'd be as likely to say, "None—we were on vacation." As men learn to explain their contributions, women see how men contribute, feel more like a partner than a slave, feel less used and more loved.

The hope of this book (if a book can have hope) is that by doing the hard work of gathering, documenting, double-checking, publishing, and publicizing data that has fallen short of the public consciousness, millions of men will not fear being thought of as fools when they share what they would otherwise fear might be an isolated observation. And millions of women will discover who men are. A woman who understands her dad discovers she was loved more than she knew, which allows her to love her husband more fully and nurture her son more completely.

THE GOALS OF PARTS I, II, AND III

Our poor socialization to effectively give and receive personal criticism does more to destroy families than any other weakness. Why? Handling criticism is the Achilles' heel of us mortals. The more we love someone the more difficult it is to handle criticism from them because we fear it means losing their love. Ironically, when we can't hear criticism from them, we lose their love; when we can, we strengthen their love. This book seeks to strengthen that skill so there will be stronger marriages and fewer divorces.

Am I being redundant when I say stronger marriages *and* fewer divorces? No. Many marriages that are legally together "for the children" are minimum security prisons for the parents. Togetherness is usually better for the children than divorce, but "minimum security–prison togetherness" is still an inferior role model for teaching children to love. Strengthening our skills at giving and receiving personal criticism creates *both* stronger marriages *and* fewer divorces. And better parenting.

I have put more emphasis in Part I on hearing personal criticism well than on giving it well because therapists are good at helping people give criticism effectively, but have spent less time helping people handle criticism that is badly given. Many therapists are by nature sensitive and oriented toward protection, so guiding people to be sensitive in the way they criticize comes more naturally than teaching people to handle criticism given badly. Problem is, almost anyone who is criticized tries to "kill" the criticizer before they are killed by the criticism, so criticism is almost always given *back* badly even if it's given out sensitively. In Part I, I will explain why that is true and what to do about it.

Part I's real goal, though, is to do more than refrain from killing the criticizer. It is to feel genuine compassion for the person doing the criticism. No. It is more than that. It is to *predictably* feel genuine compassion for the person doing the criticism. So the person criticizing can *depend* on a safe environment. Your incentive? You give this to a partner who is giving it to you—so your incentive is also receiving a safe environment for expressing your most upsetting fears.

You'll notice that the fourth chapter is about how to get men to express feelings. This chapter will surprise you with the confluence of contradictory messages we send men about feelings: the number of ways we undermine men expressing their feelings even though we say we want men to express feelings. It is the first chapter that makes clear how men's external world affects men's internal world. It makes clear what we can do about it personally, and, because the influences are also external, politically.

Most books dealing with relationship or personal issues steer clear of political issues. The assumption underlying *Women Can't Hear What Men Don't Say* is that *that* is a cop-out. When we learn to communicate at home by talking while others are talking, or debating more than listening, we tend to become politically more rigid—we develop a "hardening of the categories" and are attracted to political ideologies and religions that make us right and others wrong.

Even more important to this book, politics and social attitudes affect our personal relationships. If you have a dad who grew up during the Depression, you know he still has a thing about saving money, and that affects his relationship with your mom. A woman growing up in the fifties was much less likely to even think of becoming a corporate executive than if she grew up just twenty years later. And that difference affects her selection of a husband and the way she and her husband raise children.

The difference in politics and attitudes facing a soldier returning from Vietnam than that facing a soldier returning from World War II affected these men's attitudes toward themselves and everyone in their lives. And the everyday personality of millions of men (in contrast with their female peers) was molded by the political decision to require only men to be drafted or become conscientious objectors, thus forcing every eighteen-year-old boy into either interpreting patriotism as requiring his disposability, or experiencing a crisis of conscience that would pit him against the U.S. government. That choice between disposability and powerlessness was called a rite of passage into manhood. That same choice still exists only for our eighteen-year-old sons (who must still register for the draft or pay a quarter-million dollars and be barred from federal employment for the rest of their lives).

Today we have a social and political attitude toward men. Or, as our kids would put it, when it comes to men we have an "attitude." Part II shows how that political attitude affects our personal lives. How, for example, as it exposes us to headlines about women doing more housework, but not men doing more remodeling, painting, or gutter cleaning, a woman becomes resentful as she picks up

10

his underwear. Because she sees no headline saying *she's* not doing half the painting, gutter cleaning, or repairs (*e.g.,* "Study Finds Women Complain, Men Repair"), nothing modulates her resentment. As she hears men's perspective and also understands the underlying process that has cut her off from men's perspective, she has the opportunity to deepen her love for men and raise her son more effectively.

Part II does more than give us examples of myths that create anger toward men—it makes us aware of what we need to ask before we can determine whether we are being told the full truth when we hear the news. Why, for example, do we believe that men batter women more than women batter men when we've had extensive research to the contrary for a quarter century? Clarifying these myths is like cleaning filters, allowing us to breathe the air but not the pollution, like the thresher that separates the wheat from the chaff.

Part III allows us to see the results of that anger in the form of man bashing, and the biases of the institutions that disseminate it: what I will call "The Lace Curtain."[6] The Lace Curtain is the tendency of most major institutions to interpret gender issues from only a feminist perspective, or from a combination of feminist and female perspectives. As we look closely at the anger, it is apparent what women are angry about and what we can do about it so our children don't inherit it.

In brief, *Women Can't Hear What Men Don't Say* is asking men to take the primary responsibility for, first, doing the hard work it takes to get in touch with their feelings, then for speaking up in the first third of the twenty-first century just as women did in the last third of the twentieth century. But it suggests there are powerful reasons men have difficulty revealing their real vulnerabilities to the women they love—reasons powerful enough to make it predictable men would reach the moon before they expressed their feelings. Until we understand the relationship between the personal, social, political, and biological wires, we won't be able to disentangle them for our sons or ourselves. Fortunately, we don't need perfect answers to make progress.

It is my hope to strengthen our resolve to destroy man hating before it destroys our sons' and daughters' relationships, and the lives of their children. It is not my hope to make man hating politically incorrect, but to add the information and emotional perspectives we need to dissolve the hatred that creates it.

It is my hope that by both exposing the myths about men and exposing the process that creates those myths, I will contribute to stopping a process that is leaving our children without fathers and our sons without self respect; that is dividing the sexes and poisoning love.

It is my hope that by making the environment safe for men to speak up, men will be inspired to be in touch with their feelings, do their homework, learn to speak with love, and then speak. As for me, I will do this less than perfectly. I will be just like the men you love.

Nothing helps my ability to communicate more than hearing from my readers. Write me, teach me, grow me. Write to me at:

PMB #220
103 N. Highway 101
Encinitas, CA 92024-3252

and check out:
www.warrenfarrell.com

The Secret to Being Loved:

How to

Communicate

with Anyone,

Anywhere,

Anytime

The Most Important Thing to Understand About Men... In Fact, About Anyone

There will always be a battle between the sexes because men and women want different things. Men want women and women want men.
GEORGE BURNS

NO ONE'S EVER TOLD ME, "I WANT A DIVORCE, MY PARTNER UNDERSTANDS ME"

The most important thing to understand about men is their desire to be understood. In fact, it is the most important thing to understand about *anyone*. In more than thirty years of conducting workshops, no one has ever said to me, "Warren, I want a divorce—my partner understands me."

What is so precious about being understood? First, it is rarer than a diamond. Often, when we explain a problem to our parents, they problem-solve. Or they criticize. Or they reassure ("You don't really need to feel that way because . . ."), thus discounting the pain. Or they say "I understand," but we don't feel their compassion. We wish they would let us know *what* they understand. When we hear someone tell us, "I understand what you're saying," we often feel our feelings are being dismissed rather than elicited.

Conversely, if we are parents, being truly understood by our children rarely precedes the birth of grandchildren. Young children are too needy to think of anyone but themselves. Teenagers are too concerned with their own identities. Adults without children are focused on careers or the problems they imagine their parents to have created. When it comes to being understood, the best hope of a parent is becoming a grandparent.

Most of us don't try to understand our partner, we try to explain our partner. Which is a polite way of saying we try to analyze their faults. Yet, in those same thirty years of conducting workshops, I have never heard anyone say, "Warren, I want to remain married—my partner has such an accurate analysis of my faults." An analysis of our faults may help someone else feel *they* understand us, but it does not leave *us* feeling understood.

With about 50 percent of marriages ending in divorce, the fact that any one characteristic is associated with marital survival is astonishing. And survival isn't the only victory. People in relationships in which they feel understood usually *want* to be there. That's in contrast with many marriages in which a couple is legally married but psychologically divorced. What I call "Minimum Security–Prison Marriages."

On the surface, it seems men should feel understood. After all, as corporate heads and "heads of households," don't men have the power to explain themselves and speak up about whatever they think? Yes . . . about whatever they *think,* but not about whatever they *feel.* **A man becomes successful by repressing his feelings, not expressing his feelings.**

It used to be that women didn't speak up either. Especially around men. They became passive-aggressive (*e.g.,* passively agreeing to do something, but then not doing it; or agreeing with the man to his face and expressing their real opinion to their women friends). Especially around men. Today, men are the passive-aggressive sex. Not only individually (April: "Sure I'll fix the faucet, honey"; May: "Sure I'll fix the faucet, honey"), but collectively (which is what this book is about).

ISN'T IT NATURAL FOR MEN TO EMOTIONALLY WITHDRAW . . . INTO THEIR "CAVES"?

We often hear that it is natural for men to withdraw into their caves.[1] Natural? Maybe. Functional? No. When either sex suppresses the expression of feelings, it is almost always because they don't feel there is a safe environment to express them. Many men fear that expressing feelings will lead to conflict. His wife is usually more articulate, so he often loses; but if he "wins," she may withdraw emotionally. Or sexually, into her cave. Either way he loses. Cave is safer.

Withdrawal into a cave is almost always a sign that the environment outside the cave is not safe; withdrawal is usually an unconscious calculation that outside the cave the potential for loss exceeds the potential for gain. The remote control is his security blanket. Unfortunately, what gives him control makes him remote. There is little incentive for a man to remain closed up if he feels understood when he opens up.

It works the same with our kids. Two friends with a teenage daughter complain that she never shares her feelings with them. When I was at their home for dinner, though, I overheard her talking with a friend on the phone nonstop about her feelings. Why? One day, she tells her parents that the guy she's dating is moving too quickly toward sex. The next day, she has a curfew. Or a lecture. It seems like the feelings she expresses one day are used against her the next. It's natural for anyone to withdraw when the environment for expressing feelings is unsafe. It is more functional, though, to have a safe environment.

Are so many men afraid of expressing feelings because they are afraid of intimacy? No. **A man fears that conflict with his wife will lead to less intimacy, not more intimacy.** He suppresses the expression of his feelings because he fears destroying the intimacy they do have. Men and women both fear the loss of intimacy, but he fears discussion will leave him losing and, therefore, he'll lose intimacy, while she feels discussion will bring them closer. And even when it doesn't, her hope triumphs over her experience. From her perspective, the more he withdraws, the more alienated she feels, thus the more convinced she is that he doesn't want intimacy with her, or doesn't want intimacy, period. So depriving our partner of a safe environment to express feelings makes both sexes feel intimacy is hopeless.

Providing a safe environment to express feelings is *not* the best way to get a man to express feelings. The best way is to choose a man who already expresses them! **Our choice of partners is perhaps the clearest single statement of our choice of values.** Therefore, when we blame our partner for anything, we should really be confronting ourselves. Not as in, "Yes, I made a bad choice," but as in, "How does this choice reflect my values?"

Most women genuinely feel they value a man's feelings—if she could have those feelings without making herself less secure (either emotionally or financially). But if she values security more, she often chooses a man who is successful at work. The problem is that the process required to succeed in most high-paying careers is inversely related to the process it takes to be vulnerable. If she likes his success but deplores his capacity for intimacy, she should be looking within herself, not blaming him. Similarly, if he's forty and marries a beautiful twenty-year-old but then blames her for being immature and entitled, he should be confronting his own values, not hers.

While most of us can agree that our choice of partners is the best statement of our choice of values, men continue to choose sex objects and women continue to choose success objects, and then both sexes claim to want what's missing! Put another way, **why do both sexes fall in love with the members of the other sex who are the least capable of loving?**

For millions of years, women have biologically selected men who were heroes and rejected the other men—the "losers." So their children had heroes' genes. But think of a hero's feelings. You can't? That's the point. The very word "hero" is derived from the Greek word *"serow,"* from which we get our words for "servant," "slave," and "protector."[2] Servants and slaves were not expected to express feelings, but to repress feelings. Just like heroes. Just like corporate executives. Just like surgeons, engineers, CEOs. Our genetic heritage—the socialization process that led to women marrying killer/provider men and men marrying beautiful women, thus selecting genes from which the next generation of children were born—is still with us. If we have integrity about our desire to support men to express feelings, every institution and attitude between the sexes will require questioning and adjusting. That's what I'll investigate in chapter 4 on supporting men to express feelings.

IF UNDERSTANDING EACH OTHER IS SO VALUABLE, WHY HAVEN'T WE LEARNED IT ALREADY?

Throughout history, we learned to survive by killing people who didn't understand us—we called them "the enemy." Compassion for the enemy was not a top priority because **survival was more dependent on combat than on compassion.** In fact, compassion for the "other side" was called treason. In the 1950s, even one positive statement about Communists would elicit the beginnings of ostracism ("You Commie!"). In brief, humans have spent tens of thousands of years learning to fight and debate with the other side, and almost no time learning to listen and empathize.

Haven't women, though, spent their lifetimes learning compassion? Yes, when someone is on their side. But neither sex learned compassion for people who argued with them. At the time of divorce, women are not more compassionate to men than men are to women. Under adversarial conditions, both sexes have learned much better debating skills than listening skills. Just go to a divorce court and see if anyone is listening.

There's one downside to understanding someone. Almost as soon as we do, we expect understanding in return. We up our ante. It's easy to still be unhappy by increasing our expectations faster than our partner's ability to respond. When we do, we paralyze our partner with unrealistic expectations. And then, although we are deepening our love on one level, we are also destabilizing the relationship. If we don't get the understanding we expect in return, then we expect some-

18

thing else. Like a new car. The good news is, we will usually receive it. Understanding is that powerful of a gift. The bad news is that if we don't receive even more understanding, the material girl is as unhappy as the material guy.

IF I REALLY WANT TO BE UNDERSTOOD, WHAT DO I DO?

Give up. (Just kidding!)

If communicating effectively were easy, we'd already be doing it. I often joke that when I decided to focus my life on getting women and men to understand each other, at least I knew I'd always be employed! Before you assume the effort is more than it's worth, let me tell you how much it's worth.

Imagine having one relationship tool that would, more than any other, make your partner less likely to want to divorce or break up with you. Spend one moment thinking about the costs of a divorce—not only economically, but psychologically; not only to you, but to your children . . . and their children.

Now imagine this same relationship tool being almost as likely to improve your relationships with your children, your parents, your employer, and your employees. If it took you as much time to learn this relationship language as it takes most people to learn computer language, wouldn't it be worth it?

I often see couples in my workshops afraid to understand their partner's point of view partly because they fear they will have to give in or compromise. The fact is that when we do not understand our partner, we wind up giving in a lot more. A man who wants more time watching sports on TV will be less interested in it the moment he feels more understood at home; a woman who wants a new necklace or ring is a lot less interested in it when she is encircled with understanding. People who cannot offer understanding will find themselves paying for more and receiving less.

The good news about the first four chapters is that, as with a computer, learning even a little will bring some success. The benefit of computer language is that it opens us up to options that our parents couldn't have dreamed of fifty years ago; the benefit of relationship language is that it opens us up to a type of love no one could have imagined fifty years ago. And, as with a computer, every option becomes usable through learning something new and practicing it frequently. As with computers, our children will sometimes be able to learn it faster than we, but we old dogs can learn.

If you're overwhelmed, remember, if we give to our partner nothing more than a few of the steps that follow, we'll be giving more than 95 percent of what couples give their partner. We will have made love . . . from a new position.

2

How To Give Criticism So It Can Easily Be Heard

The practical steps to giving criticism—the focus of this chapter—contain the underlying assumption that criticism should be given. But should it—does it help or hurt relationships? And if it should, how much and in what way? Do men and women have different approaches to giving criticism and expressing anger?

ARE CRITICISM AND ANGER GOOD OR BAD FOR A HAPPY MARRIAGE?

Common wisdom seems divided. Some feel it's better to get criticism and anger out; others feel that what you say, especially in anger, can never be taken back. The truth? Both. Studies of happy marriages find that anger and criticism are expressed, not repressed . . . up to a point. And they find that the way they are expressed does count.[1]

In marriages that ended in divorce, it was more likely that the ex-wife expressed *a lot of* anger, sadness, disgust, and fear, was often belligerent, contemptuous, defensive, was domineering, and frequently whined and stonewalled her husband. The husband was more likely to have been belligerent, defensive, and contemptuous.[2]

Do Women Have More Difficulty Expressing Anger?

Books like Harriet Lerner's *The Dance of Anger,* articles in women's magazines, as well as TV talk shows and assertiveness training classes, all tell us that women are socialized to be uncomfortable with anger, especially toward men.[3] This leaves us with the belief that expressing anger is difficult for women, but the one emotion that is easy for men.

What's true is that *everyone* is uncomfortable with expressing anger and being critical. Anger and criticism generate rejection. And everyone hates rejection. Men do learn to express anger and criticism toward other men, but when it comes to women, men are socialized to protect women, not attack them. They are socialized to argue outside the home (with men), not inside the home (with women). The research bears this out.

Researchers find that when only one sex expresses argument-provoking feelings, it is likely to be the wife—by a ratio of almost *six* to one (85 percent vs. 15 percent). When both sexes participate but one dominates, women are about twice as likely to dominate.[4] Overall, women are more willing to initiate conflict, more willing to escalate conflict, better able to handle it when it occurs, and, when they have initiated it, are quicker to get over it.[5]

These findings come from numerous sources.[6] They are found among couples of high, medium, and low socio-economic status.[7] They are found using a variety of methodologies: The couples themselves acknowledge this gap,[8] and, much more reliably, researchers who systematically observe couples verify the couples' own assessments.[9]

Probably the most respected researcher in the field is John Gottman at the University of Washington. He records pulse rates, heart output, skin conductance, and other indicators of stress. Then he videotapes the couples to observe facial expressions and body language. He does not ask the couples to fight, since that would be artificial. Instead, he basically works with a couple and when a major area of disagreement naturally evolves, he asks them to discuss it and attempts to resolve it. When a fight naturally occurs, the equipment is there to record it.[10]

Gottman found that men are more intimidated by angry women than women are by angry men. Men are more stressed by marital arguments, while women are more comfortable with emotional confrontation and are better at it.[11]

Even in the feminist movement, the medium is the message: Feminists express anger even as the message is that women cannot express anger; men repress anger even as they are judged to be the sex that has no problem expressing it! We often hear we have a battle of the sexes when, in fact, we have a war in which only one side has shown up.[12] (Men put their heads into the sand and hope the bullets will miss!)

Withdrawal is not the way men do battle with men. It is the way men do battle with women. Because the purpose of doing battle with men was to prepare men to protect women from conflict, not to be the source of conflict.

The job of this book is not to create an affirmative action plan for men's anger to be equal to women's. It is to create a method of communicating that transforms anger in the way a solar panel transforms heat—by taking intense heat that would normally leave us hot one moment and cold the next, and transforming it into energy that keeps us warm all the time.

IF WOMEN EXPRESS ANGER MORE EASILY, WHY DO WE THINK MEN DO?

A nine-month-old infant was crying. In a scientific experiment, observers who were told the infant was a boy were much more likely to say "he" was expressing "anger"; observers told the identical infant was a girl were more likely to say "she" was expressing "fear."[13] One reason we think men express more anger is because we tend to interpret as "anger" in a man what we would call "fear" in a woman. We can see why we do this when we look at the effect it has.

When we interpret a woman's emotion as fear, two instincts are set into motion: the instinct to protect any woman, and the instinct to protect someone who is afraid. A woman in fear is assumed to be a woman in jeopardy, and this generates a double dose of our protector instinct. When the identical emotion (e.g., the crying) is expressed by a man, but we interpret it as anger, we want to fight back or run away.

When a woman appears to express fear, we cannot assure her without at least releasing her from responsibility; when we interpret the same emotion in a man as anger, we want to blame him and be certain he acknowledges responsibility. We want to find her guiltless; we want to find him guilty.

Once this double standard is woven into our mindset, it translates into our feelings about how to criticize a woman vs. a man: When a man criticizes a woman, it makes us fear for her; when a woman criticizes a man, it makes us cheer for her. Either way, we're on her side. Emotionally, we experience her as a damsel in distress and, if we're a man, we feel summoned to compete for her love by protecting her. When then Vice President Candidate George Bush was campaigning against Geraldine Ferraro in 1984, he and his advisers realized they could not criticize her the way they would a man and expect positive voter reaction, which is one reason they focused on her husband's finances, as did Dianne Feinstein's opponents when she ran for U.S. Senate in California.

This is no one's fault. The difference has evolved from our genetic heritage (the socialization process that led to women marrying killer/provider men and men marrying beautiful women, thus selecting genes from which the next generation of children were born). A nineteenth-century "gentleman" carried a sword with which he was expected to avenge an insult to a woman, even if it cost him his life. Criticism of her meant possible death to him. This heritage makes it difficult for all of us to accept even today a man whose feelings about a woman are critical.

WHY BEING CRITICIZED FEELS LIKE BEING KILLED

While anger and criticism need outlets for expression, using them to clear the air of problems is a bit like using insecticide to clear the air of bugs: Both can pollute the air to clear the air. Criticizing and complaining create negative energy before they create positive energy. And they don't always create positive energy. Why not?

Being criticized feels like being "killed." A woman friend of mine told me, "I remember when my third grade teacher criticized me in front of the class. I disintegrated. And when *you* criticize me, it feels like you're putting a knife into my heart."

My woman friend may have been more literally accurate than she knew. The *New England Journal of Medicine* reports that speaking about one's faults creates abnormalities in the pulsation of our heart. Tiny abnormalities? No. Abnormalities as great as those produced by riding a stationary bicycle to the point of either exhaustion or chest pain.[14]

Why does being criticized feel like being stabbed in the heart? Why are we tempted to stab back, even though we know intellectually it's the worst thing we could do? **Historically, criticism could lead to ostracism, which could lead to death.** The word "ostracism" itself comes from the Greek word *ostrakon,* meaning "tile." The *ostrakon,* or tile, was the ballot cast by the community to decide whether or not to ostracize someone. If there were more *ostrakons* in the "yea" group, she or he was ostracized. To ostracize someone meant to not speak with them, trade with them, or in any way deal with them. So if you were a doctor, for example, and you were ostracized, you would have no patients—you couldn't support your family. Being the subject of criticism could mean your family starving.

Criticism feels like it will kill us, then, because it could lead not only to our own death, but to our family's deaths. And to parents, a child's death is more to be feared than their own. Thus **our genetic heritage made it functional to kill the criticizer before the criticizer killed us.** If you're the one contemplating criticism, that doesn't create much incentive to be honest. And today, with our partner able to leave us, perhaps the incentive is even less. So we became approval seekers.

Put another way, we are the offspring of approval seekers. We want approval so badly that we vacillate between conforming to get it and standing out (being outstanding) to get it. Even the rebel, whose defiance may create the illusion of not caring about approval, secretly nurtures the hope of being admired (awaiting the day when they are ultimately seen to be right while everyone else is seen to be wrong).

Many of us can't even go to a party without first finding out how most of the guests will be dressed; without checking our appearance in the mirror half a dozen times; without mentally rehearsing how we will respond when we meet someone who matters. . . .

Our need for approval comes in many forms for our children, too. One boy will join a gang, where having a "rep" is just another way of saying he wants love, respect, and approval. A boy in my high school joined the Marines because he wanted to prove himself, which is just another way of saying that he wanted approval, respect, and love. He risked his life for it, and was killed. At least a hundred women in my workshops have said that they knew before their wedding that getting married wasn't right for them, but they were afraid to back out because "the invitations had already gone out." All these men and women risked their lives for fear of criticism.

If criticism is ranked next to death and worse than taxes, is it possible to provide a safe environment against being, well, killed? Yes—it *is* possible. The process begins with mastering the "Rules of the Game" to giving criticism.

FIVE RULES OF THE GAME

It is the responsibility of the criticizer or complainer (or the person who is upset) to abide by five Rules of the Game.

1. *Tone of voice is more crucial than words.* Words don't hold a candle to the tone of our voice and the look in our eyes. Try using the words "I love you" in a malicious tone of voice to a baby or a puppy dog and watch it withdraw; yet say in a loving tone of voice "dumb doggie" or "smelly baby" and watch it be responsive. If the tone and the look reflect respect, appreciation, even a touch of admiration, well, you'll melt any iceberg! Studies find that although a wife is more likely than her husband to complain, a marriage is significantly more likely to be stable and happy if she softens her complaints with positive affect (e.g., humor, affection, interest, agreement, approval, smiles, positive physical contact, laughter).[15]

2. *Don't complain too often.* How often is too often? Rule of thumb: "Complaining every day keeps your lover away." If complaints come too often or you feel like you're walking on eggshells, group your complaints as I suggest in the Plan Ahead Method below. Turn the rest of the week into a "Complaint-Free Zone."

3. *Never criticize someone who has just criticized you.* Wait until that person says she or he has felt heard.

4. Ask *the listener to just "play listener."* If you have the listener's "buy in," you have a partner; if you don't, you have an opponent. Make sure the timing is right.

5. *Try not to cross-examine the listener with questions* that require an explanation for her or his behavior ("Tell me, *why* did you do that?"). Explain to the listener that if you slip up and ask for an explanation, the request should be treated as rhetorical.

If there are two iron rules of criticizing they are tone of voice is more crucial than the words and don't complain too often.

Sometimes criticism will come from us like the spontaneous combustion of a sneeze. To get a handle on criticism though, it's better to control it rather than have it control us. If you're going to use a knife, it's better to think ahead before the sharp edge that's cutting for you is cutting into you. (No, that's not something my mom told me!)

THE "PLAN AHEAD METHOD" OF GIVING CRITICISM SO IT CAN BE EASILY HEARD

STEP 1: WRITE DOWN YOUR NEGATIVE FEELINGS

I like it best in my personal life when I arrange with my partner to write complaints on a piece of paper or an index card and put them in a little box. I find that the mere act of writing them down releases much of the negative energy.

It also helps me sort out which ones are worth bringing up. Harry Truman used to say, "When notice of an emergency arises, I stuff it in a drawer. At the end of the week, I open the drawer. If it's still an emergency, I take care of it." I try to take care of complaints the same way.

STEP 2: CREATE A PREDICTABLE TIME IN WHICH TO SHARE NEGATIVE FEELINGS—ONCE EVERY WEEK OR TWO

The best way to take care of complaints is to create a predictable time to do so every week or two—a "sharing and caring" evening. Harry and Sally illustrate why.

After Harry met Sally, they moved in together (they didn't tell you that in the movie; you learn these things from books). It was about seven P.M. and they were running late for a play at eight. They had tickets to the play for more than a month and Harry especially was looking forward to the evening. The phone rang. It was Sally's sister. Sally always got caught up in long conversations with her sister, and Harry was pacing before her, catching her eye, pointing to his watch. Finally, Sally got off the phone and exploded, "You've never liked my sister. I really felt controlled. You don't give me the freedom to make my own judgments. So what if we are a little late to the play?"

Now Harry was doubly impatient. He wanted to tell her that he wished she would have let the answering machine pick it up, but he was afraid she'd have a response and they'd miss the play altogether. His face showed impatience that her "ranting" was making them even later. Sally picked up on his impatience and hammered the nail into the coffin, "Now you're impatient that we're talking about this. What's more important—one stupid play or our relationship?"

Harry sensed the question was a bit biased. Nevertheless, he didn't want to miss the play. So he responded, "Can we put this on hold, and discuss it after the play?" "No," Sally said, "I have these feelings *now*; I've had them before and we never talk about them. I can't enjoy the play with all this swimming around in my head."

Who's right?

They both are. Fortunately, there's a win-win solution.

Sally needed some assurance that feelings that had cropped up repeatedly would not, once again, get postponed. She needed a security blanket. Harry had been looking forward to the play for more than a month and, from his perspective, there was no need to sacrifice either the relationship or the play. This was a play that he, more than Sally, had been looking forward to, and he felt that she would not now be bringing up this relationship issue if they were on their way to one of Sally's beloved operas. To him, Sally was either being manipulative or having problems setting boundaries.

If Harry and Sally had created a predictable time to share negative feelings—say, seven on Sunday evening (*60 Minutes* will kill me for this)—Sally would have had her security blanket. And Harry would have had his play. And both would have had time to discuss their underlying feelings.

Back to the "sharing and caring" evening.

At the end of the week, then, about an hour before the planned meeting time, review the cards and choose between three and six issues that still retain some negative energy. Harry Truman might have called these the "emergencies."

Once there's a predictable time each week, turn the rest of the week into a "no-complaint zone." At least no complaints that our partner has to hear. In some ways this is easier said than done; in other ways it is easier to do than it appears because the process of writing the complaint down releases our need to keep reviewing it in our mind; and the security of knowing we'll have a predictable time to discuss it releases the anxiety that comes when we feel we have to keep bringing it up in order for it to be attended to. In brief, don't dismiss this before you try it.

Applying the Predictable Time Approach to direct complaining and criticism strikes a good balance between two extreme ways of dealing with potential conflict: The "stuff it" extreme and the "clear the air *now*" extreme.

The "stuff it" extreme first. People who stuff their feelings eventually find them popping up in two other forms; Attacking and/or Avoiding—what might be called the Double-A responses to stuffing feelings. The Attack substitute for complaining and criticism may surface in the form of little digs, sarcasm, put-downs, backstabbing in the presence of company, or the *worst infidelity:* talking to our friends about our partner, behind our partner's back.[16] The Avoidance substitute for complaining and criticism may come out in headaches, hiding behind a sports event, gambling, drinking, or preoccupation with work, church, children, or a cause. The Avoidance list is endless.

The Predictable Time Approach works because predictability fosters security. When our security needs are met, the vacuum of neediness is filled. A baby breast-fed at predictable intervals needs to be fed much less than the baby who cannot count on when it will next be fed. Without predictability the baby becomes anxious, needy, and has to be fed much more to be equally secure. In all of us there is that baby.

STEP 3: SHARE AT LEAST FOUR POSITIVE FEELINGS WITH EACH NEGATIVE

Then comes the tough part: making the transition from negative feelings to a positive event. This is the part we even look forward to. Couples who are happy give each other between four and four hundred positive strokes for each criticism. So, I find this works best when my partner and I create at least four things we appreciate about the other for each problem area. We require ourselves to give specific examples. Instead of, "I like how thoughtful you are," we'd write, "I liked it when you noticed we were running low on fresh-squeezed orange juice, volunteered to pick some up, and asked me if there was anything else I needed while you were at the store. I felt so nurtured." To each of the examples we tried to add the positive feeling or feelings it created. In this case, feeling nurtured.

By requiring ourselves to create four positives for each criticism, and allowing ourselves only an hour for review before meeting time, we found ourselves making positive notes throughout the week, which also meant we didn't begin the pre-meeting review hour with a flood of negative feelings. It remained easy to see the positives in the relationship. This worked well for a number of reasons, but my favorite was the incentive we gave ourselves to do the positive notes ahead of time.

We could get double-duty out of these positive notes by writing a version of them on a Post-It that we might leave immediately on the other's steering wheel, or on a card with a fresh-cut flower from the garden on each other's pillow, or E-mail. By doing them ahead of time, then, four positives could be turned into eight or twelve. Cheating? No one complained.

What the positive notes really created was (no, not writer's cramp!) but a "muscle"—the "muscle" of pro-actively looking for the positive.

Step 4: Incorporate Humor and Romance into the "Feelings" Evening

For me, humor might take the form of mocking what I do. For example, one of my criticisms might say, "Sometimes I question your judgment. How can you be in love with a relationships manual?" Humor glues souls, reminding us that we're on the same team.

And so does romance. I like lighting candles, cutting flowers, turning on Enya-type music. My woman friend loves the candles and the flowers, but is ambivalent about my turning on Enya.

We sit eye to eye. One of us starts by sharing our positives and then one criticism. Then we hold each other, in part for nurturance, in part for congratulations. (Or maybe it's relief.) Then we alternate. That's one round. We continue until we complete between three and five rounds. Hopefully three.

Sometimes we feel so understood that we want to make love. We allow that. But if we do that before we complete the process, we *always* return to complete the process. And that last point is crucial. Otherwise the lovemaking becomes an escape from the process, then the security blanket disappears, things start getting brought up midweek, and the rest of the week as a no-complaint zone disintegrates.

When I bring up this last point in workshops, I am sometimes asked whether lovemaking should be saved until afterward, as sort of a reward. The value of being spontaneous is that it doesn't create performance pressure at the end of the process. Also, men, in particular, will sometimes keep from being fully honest if they feel it may deprive them of sexual intimacy; so if you want to encourage honesty, allow yourselves to make love when it comes naturally. Having said this, if you try a lovemaking break but don't return to complete the process, then next time save the lovemaking until the end.

The "Spontaneous Method" of Giving Criticism So It Can Be Easily Heard

It's ideal to give criticism in the Plan Ahead Method mode. But we don't live in an ideal world. Sometimes we feel critical about a decision that we feel has to be made right there and then. So the following steps are useful both when we're being spontaneous, *and also as ingredients that should be incorporated into the criticisms we share in the Plan Ahead Method.*

Step 1: Identify Your Loved One's Best Intent—the Best Spirit of Her or His Strongest Argument, Without Distortion

Mom yells at her daughters, "Alex and Erin, no, you can't take your bikes to the 7-Eleven by yourselves—and if you keep pestering me, you won't be able to ride your bikes at all."

WHAT DAD IS THINKING

Dad feels that Alex and Erin should be able to take their bikes to the 7-Eleven. He feels the road isn't that dangerous, and that he and his wife have given Alex and Erin plenty of instruction and watched them—now it's time to wean them. He feels it's more important for Alex and Erin to learn to depend on themselves, become responsible, and not be so protected. He feels his wife's propensity to protect the girls is part of what is making them so anxious, so afraid of taking risks, making mistakes, and making transitions. He's worried for them, worried about the child psychologist bills he and his wife are paying to alleviate the girls' anxiety, and worried about his wife always worrying about everything Alex and Erin do. Finally, he feels his wife winds up exhausted, which impacts their relationship, which requires more counseling . . .

Because Dad feels this way, he's also thinking there's no reason for Alex and Erin to be hollered at. And of course, no reason for the girls to be threatened.

Because Dad has thought all this before, virtually all of this occurs to him in just a few seconds—triggered by the hollering.

DAD'S MOST LIKELY RESPONSE

Dad's gut instinct is to holler, "For heaven's sake, let them go," but he knows better. He quietly tries to explain his perspective. He feels this is a big improvement over his gut instinct.

THE PROBLEMS WITH DAD'S "QUIET EXPLANATION" RESPONSE

When Dad does not first create the conditions to help Mom feel heard, Dad's "quiet explanation" response leaves Mom thinking about what Dad is *not* taking into account. Until he hears Mom completely, she will feel minimized and, in this case, feel the children are being minimized (since only one mistake at a dangerous intersection could lead to Alex's and Erin's deaths).

Once Mom feels minimized, she's on a roll . . . she knows Dad can't guarantee that Alex and Erin are as capable of avoiding mistakes now as they will be in a year or two. So Mom's thinking, "What's the big deal in waiting a year or two? Aren't you being irresponsible? Can I really trust you? Can I leave the house, put you in charge, and be sure Alex and Erin will both be safe? This makes me feel I don't really have a partner who can share with me the task of raising our children. It's what makes me feel like a prisoner of my home and my children."

Mom does not say these things aloud, so on the surface, Mom may even appear to be listening. In reality, she is "self-listening"—listening secondarily to Dad, primarily to herself; listening to Dad just enough to be able to formulate the best possible response as he is talking. This is not a female problem—it is a two-sex problem, indigenous to anyone who does not first feel completely heard.

Second, Dad is not really explaining his perspective, he is reiterating his perspective. Why? Because he didn't feel it had been heard before. He is right. **Dad's perspective wasn't heard because few people hear anything that conflicts with their mindset until they feel completely heard themselves.** So most of us find ourselves saying the same things over and over again to our loved ones. And that, of course, just makes our partner tune out, which just encourages more repetition. The repetition breeds angst, which further alienates our partner and, well, you've got the picture.

The problem is, the more powerfully Dad feels he has something to contribute, the more likely he is to feel too impatient to first "endure" all five steps of understanding that follow. Every ounce of him wanted to jump in to explain why Alex and Erin should be permitted to take risks.

Dad has some choices. He can use the "quiet persuasion in private" approach and elicit defensive self-listening, or he can see past his wife's less-than-perfect behavior (hollering) and identify her best intent.

DAD'S IDEAL FIRST RESPONSE

Dad's ideal first response would be something like, "I know you didn't let Alex and Erin ride their bikes to the 7-Eleven because you didn't want them crossing that dangerous road by themselves. You're wise enough to know it takes only one mistake on a dangerous road to lead to Alex's and Erin's deaths. And you know the girls will be more capable of avoiding mistakes in a year or two—so why risk their lives?"

WHY DAD'S IDEAL FIRST RESPONSE WORKS

Now Mom doesn't feel defensive because her strongest arguments have been articulated by Dad—*without distortion.* Dad has understood her best intent.

Strongest arguments first. Most of us are afraid to articulate our partner's strongest arguments out loud. It is as if we fear that the moment we do, our partner will say, "Now that you understand, do it my way." What is more likely to happen is that it releases the energy our partner puts into trying to feel understood.

Imagine it this way. Imagine our partner's energy focused on their mouth, constantly trying to explain it better and better until we understand it. But the second we've articulated their *strongest* arguments back to them, the energy no longer needs to focus on the mouth. It can transfer to the ear. **As we articulate our partner's strongest arguments, we free them to transfer their energy from their mouth to their ear,** so to speak.

Note that articulating our partner's strongest argument means acknowledging their deepest fear. In this case, Dad articulated Mom's fear of the possible deaths of Alex and Erin. This, at least, was the deepest fear she expressed.

A more typical response to Mom would have been, "You have to take risks in life—getting out of bed is a risk." Had Dad said this, Mom would have doubled the intensity of her focus on the dangers—she may have started cutting out newspaper clippings of children who had died crossing streets, picked out lectures of TV shows. The moment the dangers are acknowledged, she becomes free to make a transition. She may reiterate another time or two, but usually the energy will be much less intense, and with patience, the transition will be enough that the ears become clear.

Second, **without distortion.** I emphasize the "without distortion" because, well, suppose Dad had said the following—see if you can spot the distortion: "I know you're afraid to let Alex and Erin go anywhere by themselves because you think they could get hurt or killed."

Try the word "anywhere." Guaranteed, the moment Mom heard the word "anywhere," she would be thinking, "Not true. I've let them go to school by themselves, to Ashley's by themselves, to Sarah's by themselves, to . . . I let them go *every*where that doesn't put their lives in danger. I'm not overprotective, I'm reasonably protective."

The problem is not just that everything Dad said during that period of time would have been wasted. It is that **the moment Mom feels her best intent is dismissed or belittled, there is a decrease in trust.** When her best intent is heard, there is an increase in trust and a deepening of love.

Third, **looking past the less-than-perfect.** Dad didn't feel there was a need for Mom to holler at Alex and Erin, or to threaten the girls with not being able to use their bikes. But if Dad had said, "You're always hollering at Alex and Erin—you're just getting them to tune you out," Mom would have become defensive ("I wouldn't holler if they'd listened to me the first time"). Had Dad not looked past Mom's less-than-perfect style, chances are that Mom and Dad would never have discussed the issues—of safety and risk taking. It is, of course, fine to discuss the style, but if Dad's goal is to address the issue, he'd better start out by looking past the imperfections in the style. In other words, choose your battle . . . er, your priority.

If all this sounds overwhelming, remember that most of it boils down to attitude. If our binoculars search for our partner's best intent, it will usually be found. And if we miss it, we'll be close enough to the bull's-eye to maintain trust. Our attitude will compensate for our inaccuracy. Few people ever told a divorce judge, "Your Honor, my spouse's empathy was slightly off the mark."

STEP 2: IDENTIFY YOUR PARTNER'S *DILEMMA* OR STRUGGLE

If Dad goes beyond identifying Mom's best intent and also identifies her dilemma, he deepens Mom's feelings of being understood. For example, Dad might say, "I imagine you felt caught between, on the one hand, your desire to allow Alex and Erin to be independent, explore, and also please them; and, on the other, your desire to make sure they're alive."

Some of us fear this will just encourage our partner to focus on their struggles. In the extreme, that's true. But as a starter, it does the opposite. Mom now feels she has a partner to help share the burden. She feels lighter, more secure, more capable of handling the burden. It helps Mom to *transfer her energy away from a focus on her struggles, to get on with it.*

STEP 3: IDENTIFY THE *FEELING* BEHIND YOUR PARTNER'S DILEMMA

If Dad goes beyond identifying the dilemma, to identifying the feelings the dilemma might create, he takes Mom's degree of feeling understood—or loved— to an even deeper level. In this situation, he might say, "It must feel terrible to have to play the role of bad mom and police woman. And when I get to be their advocate even though I spend less time with them, it must make you feel unappreciated."

How does a guy dig all this up? Can a guy—the "unempathetic-and-inarticulate-about-feelings" sex—really be expected to do this? Yes. Here's why.

Any guy who's played team sports has practiced a skill I call "team-sport empathy": He's practiced focusing on anticipating the other team's moves. That means figuring out their way of looking at the situation. He does this by focusing on their perspective—by walking a mile in their moccasins. When he does this well, we call him a good competitor. True. But he's also developed skills of empathy. Now he just has to apply them to his partner, and to remember, it's only getting out there and doing it that develops confidence. With confidence comes articulateness.

Being a good competitor, then, involves empathy. **Empathy for women is an attribute of masculinity.** When men play the protector role they are trying to save a woman from grief or pain. If they had no glimpse of her grief or pain, they wouldn't know when to protect.

When he focuses on her feelings (or when she does this for him), he'll sometimes uncover for her feelings she didn't even know she had. When we do this for our partner, we give them one of the greatest gifts.

Suppose Dad is wrong? Suppose he's identifying feelings she doesn't feel? Well, if Dad can imagine her feeling fearful of being seen as a policewoman, but she has, in fact, remained free from of those feelings, that can make her feel she's avoided a possible pitfall. And that feeling creates strength. And remember, few people protest empathy, even misplaced empathy.

STEP 4: IDENTIFY THE POSITIVE *CHARACTER* TRAITS YOUR PARTNER EXHIBITED IN HER OR HIS HANDLING OF THIS SITUATION

Dad added, "it takes a lot of courage to follow your gut, a lot of strength of character to handle the disapproval of your daughters."

This is an important one because, remember, Dad disagrees with what Mom is doing. It never occurs to most of us at a moment of disagreement with our partner to take the time to appreciate our partner's positive character strengths *as reflected in a stance we disagree with.* When we do that, it allows our partner to know that no matter which decision she or he makes, our trust in their underlying character is never in question. It turns every disagreement into a potential gift of love. Because it is a gift so few people give, it is precious.

Dad's hesitation to do this, though, was that it would reinforce Mom's protective behavior toward Alex and Erin. Instead, it further softened Mom's need to fight for her position. Unconsciously, part of Mom's defensiveness came from defending against not being respected, as being seen as a bad Mom for being overprotective. When Dad made it clear he saw her strength of character in her willingness to incur her daughters' disapproval, Mom could release yet another layer of defensiveness.

Dad's trust in Mom allowed Mom to see Dad did understand the strength it took to restrict and protect. And that freed Mom to trust Dad. When we give trust, we receive trust. And people who trust us pay attention to us.

Suppose you're reading this and you say, "My God, I should have done that during my last disagreement—I wish I had." Forget the regrets. Would you mind someone bringing up something that happened a week ago and acknowledging the positive character traits they felt your perspective reflected—a perspective with which they had disagreed? Would you mind if it was a year ago? It's a present that, in some ways, ripens with age.

STEP 5: RECALL RELEVANT *PAST* CONVERSATIONS AND USE THEM TO MAKE YOUR PARTNER FEEL MORE UNDERSTOOD

Dad remembered a past incident of a similar nature in which Alex and Erin had shouted, "All the other parents let their children go to the 7-Eleven by themselves." He could have used this to argue his own point ("The other parents agree with me. You're turning Alex and Erin into outcasts."). Instead, he added, "And I admire your courage in deviating from the other parents to do what you think is right for Alex and Erin without regard for whether or not you've won a popularity contest." In doing this, Dad showed that he wants to use their history—their past shared experiences—to support his wife rather than as ammunition against her.

Notice that this is a reversal of the normal method of most couples—tossing in everything but the kitchen sink to win an argument, only to discover that the more they throw in, the more they lose; that even if they've won the battle, they've lost the love. And to what end?

THE QUICKIE REVIEW TO GIVING CRITICISM SO IT CAN EASILY BE HEARD

Notice that I am not calling this section "The Quickie *Guide* . . ." It's useless as a guide; but as a review, it can serve as a trigger to recall the chapter . . .

PLAN AHEAD METHOD: STEPS	PLAN AHEAD METHOD: EXAMPLES
Step 1: Write down your negative feelings	"I really felt abandoned when you couldn't help me plan for Jeff and Sarah's anniversary."
Step 2: Create a predictable time in which to share negative feelings—once every week or two.	"Does it work for you if we schedule a 'caring and sharing' evening around five P.M. every other Sunday ?"

PLAN AHEAD METHOD: STEPS	PLAN AHEAD METHOD: EXAMPLES
Step 3: Share at least four positive feelings with each negative	"I really felt appreciated when you took Kris to get a haircut and left me time to soak in my bubble bath."
	"I was very relieved when you cut short the phone call with your sister so we could make the play on time."
	"I felt very loved when you left the rose on the passenger seat of my car . . ."
Step 4: Incorporate humor and romance into the "feelings" evening	". . . and very relieved that the rose was on the *passenger* side—until I saw you even picked off the thorns!"

SPONTANEOUS METHOD: STEPS	SPONTANEOUS METHOD: EXAMPLES
Step 1: Identify your loved one's *best intent*	"I see that you're trying to prevent an accident."
Step 2: Identify your partner's *dilemma* or struggle	"I imagine you feel caught between wanting to give the girls freedom and wanting them to live."
Step 3: Identify the *feeling* behind your partner's dilemma.	"It must feel terrible to have the kids look at you like you're the enemy."
Step 4: Identify the positive *character* traits your partner exhibited in her or his handling of this situation.	"It takes a lot of courage to stand by your decision despite the kids' feeling differently."
Step 5: Recall relevant *past* conversations and use them to make your partner feel more understood.	"I remember the neighbors were telling their kids they can go, and you let our kids know you were there for them, not for popularity."

If all this seems a bit overwhelming, not to worry. You're not alone. Start with the Plan Ahead Method. And don't expect to do it alone. Get the support of a professional to work with you. If you were learning to program, you'd take computer science classes. And you're not only learning to program, you're learning to reprogram—that's a lot harder.

TOWARD A SOLUTION

During what years should a child be introduced to better ways of giving and receiving criticisms—to what I call "relationship language"? Before school age. The best teacher? Parents. *Parade* magazine's national survey discovered that daughters who had infants out of wedlock had one thing in common: not being able to talk to their parents.[17] Think of relationship language as your child's most important insurance policy—guaranteeing a role model, reducing the risk of you being divorced, as well as the risk of your teenager creating a pregnancy out of wedlock. If you wish to give a gift to the next generation that was not available to us, help bring this into local school systems—once you've become reasonably proficient yourself.

How would relationship language change the priorities in our schools? Schools currently excel in encouraging children to express opinions, but are deficient in encouraging children to say, for example, "Oh, that's different from my perspective—tell me more."

Schools internationally teach debate, but debating skills tend to reward listening for the purpose of uncovering the other team's faulty analysis. What's wrong with that? Uncovering our partner's faulty analyses is to a relationship what a termite is to wood: a little adds to the character; a lot, well, you know. Remember my mentioning that in my workshops I never heard someone say, "I want to stay married; my partner has such an excellent analysis of my faults"? Anyone who believes that analyzing faults creates a healthy marriage has a faulty analysis!

This doesn't mean there's no place for debating. There is. Listening skills should not replace debating skills, they should add to them. But **teaching children to debate without teaching children to listen is divorce training.** It is preparing our children for out-of-wedlock children and drugs. It is child abuse.

Why were both sexes poor listeners? In Stage I families (defined as families in which survival was the primary focus), a parent needed to be a problem solver.[18] Fathers, in particular, needed to "tough it out" by denying the feelings created by seeing his best friend's head split apart by a bullet before his eyes. A father learned to teach his children the survival skills of arguing, debating, and persuading, the skills that had made him "eligible" for a wife and children. Since they were a prerequisite for all his relationships, these skills were his relationship language. Problem is, "toughing it out" fed his loved ones' mouths, but didn't nurture his loved ones' souls.

In Stage II families (defined as families in which survival is mastered enough so that self-fulfillment is at least of equal concern), we can afford to strike a balance between survival skills and relationship skills. And that implies a "relationship language" that nourishes the soul, not just survival skills that nourish the body.

How likely is it that we can teach ourselves a new relationship language? Well, our grammar schools are teaching a whole generation *computer* language to adjust to the technological needs of a Stage II society. The next step is teaching a whole generation relationship language to address the social and psychological needs of a Stage II society.

Should we teach this just to our children? Is it too late for adults? No. Close to half of senior citizens are now learning computer language. And relationship language requires parental involvement even more than computer language. A parent who doesn't learn computer language may actually help a child feel good about knowing something about which his parents are ignorant; with relationship language, a child who learns to listen in school but faces shouting at home might feel more abused than he or she previously would have exactly because the child is now aware of what should be happening at home. Put another way, computer language without parental involvement can enhance a child's self-esteem, but relationship language without parental involvement can damage a child's self-esteem.

Relationship language is the best hope of restabilizing the family that technology has destabilized. Before the era of technology, couples could not afford to divorce; therefore, marriages without emotional understanding felt like *maximum* security prisons. Since then, couples have been able to afford divorce, so marriage has become a choice. **Once staying married became a choice, people could have partners who didn't understand them** and marriages without understanding became *minimum* security prisons.

When couples have the option to leave their minimum security prisons, relationship language becomes the new security. In marriage and love, we have upped the ante from desiring to be understood to requiring to be understood. Without relationship language, technology will destabilize marriage or make us desire to return to the old days of maximum security–prison marriages. In brief, relationship language stabilizes the family that technology destabilized.

3

How To Hear Criticism So It Can Easily Be Given

Some people feel they are good at communicating because they are in touch with their feelings and express them well. But that's the easy side of communication. The hard part is hearing criticism so it can be easily given.

Imagine being able to share criticism with your partner—or your parents—and knowing they will respond by providing a supportive and safe environment for you doing that and that they will genuinely appreciate your efforts to be closer to them. It would probably revolutionize your relationship. Normally, though, we neither receive that nor give that.

Here's a questionnaire to help you evaluate whether or not you usually provide a safe environment. Take it now and take it again once a week after you finish this chapter until you get where you'd like to be. Don't answer what you'd *like* to do, but what you *actually* do most of the time. Take a "tough love" approach to yourself. It's the first step in the process of turning the criticism we hear into the love we desire.

WHEN MY PARTNER CRITICIZES ME OR GETS ANGRY, I AM MORE LIKELY TO:

1. ___ (a) point out my partner's equivalent shortcomings ("Well, you often interrupt me"), *or*

___ (b) share with my partner what I heard her or him say (with empathy in my eyes, love in my voice, and all that positive attitude stuff).

2. ___ (a) criticize the style (e.g., "The sarcasm in your voice made me tune out"; "You *always* exaggerate!"), *or*

___ (b) look beyond the style to my partner's best intent.

3. ___ (a) criticize the demeanor ("You look so angry, it scares me"; "As soon as you shout, I tune out"; "You're hypersensitive."), *or*

___ (b) be compassionate no matter what his or her demeanor.

4. ___ (a) look for the flaw in the accuracy of the criticism, *or*

___ (b) look for the germ of truth.

5. ___ (a) distort what my partner said until I create something I can effectively debate, *or*

___ (b) search for my partner's most valid point and acknowledge it.

6. ___ (a) sidestep my partner's deepest underlying concern and, while my partner's blabbing on, figure out what I have the best response to and focus on that, *or*

___ (b) deal directly with my partner's deepest concern, even if it puts me in a bad light.

7. ___ (a) feel impatient (as in "I know what you mean; shut up already"), *or*

___ (b) be genuinely patient (out of an understanding that the more your partner feels it's safe to express negative feelings to you, the closer she or he will feel to you).

8. ___ (a) say some version of "If you really feel that way, then it's hopeless," *or*

___ (b) say some version of "Your willingness to express feelings gives me more hope for intimacy."

9. ___ (a) cry, *or*

___ (b) be genuinely joyful (out of an understanding that this means my partner trusts me enough to know I won't counterattack).

10. ___ (a) wait for my partner to apologize first, *or*

___ (b) apologize first.

11. ___ (a) hold a grudge, *or*

___ (b) let it go.

12. ___ (a) emotionally withdraw, *or*

___ (b) become more caring.

13. ___ (a) sexually withdraw, *or*

___ (b) sexually open up.

The "b" answers are ideal only if you eventually also have an opportunity to offer your own response. Without that, we're speaking of the repression of feelings as the cost of peace. Not a good trade-off. When you know you'll have a chance to respond, then each partner has an opportunity for the full expression of feelings without the anxiety of being "killed" in the process.

If you still think the "b" answers are a bit much to ask for, review the questionnaire once more. This time ask yourself, "Which answer would I prefer *from* my partner?" Would you want your partner to find flaws, interrupt, hold a grudge, sexually withdraw, criticize your style and demeanor (the "a" answers), or give you supportive eye contact and look for the germ of truth in what you're saying (the "b" answers)?

When we are asked what we want *from* our partner, the "b" answers are so obvious that the question seems rhetorical; when asked what we could be expected to give *to* our partner, the "b" answers seem a bit much to ask for.

WHAT IS YOUR SAFE ENVIRONMENT QUOTIENT?

A "safe environment" is not just an ecological issue. Think of the "b" answers as your starting point toward creating a safe environment for intimacy. You might call it your Safe Environment Quotient.

If you've got guts, do a reality check. Ask *your partner* to check off which behaviors she or he thinks are most common for you when you encounter criticism or anger.

For an even deeper reality check, *discuss* those points in which your partner evaluated you less positively than you evaluated yourself. By the way, during that discussion, did you respond receptively or defensively?

IF YOUR SEQ IS LOW, DON'T FEEL BAD, BECAUSE . . .

- We are *all* gifted of the mouth, retarded of the ear.

- The first instinctive response to any criticism is a defensive response (the quicker the response, the more defensive).

- All defensive responses to criticism are natural (it is natural to think of our own perspective before someone else's).

IF IT'S SO NATURAL TO RESPOND DEFENSIVELY, SHOULD WE REALLY BE FOOLING WITH NATURE?

Yes. In nature, killing leads to survival of the fittest. Exactly because it is so natural, we have to create strict laws where we no longer feel it is functional. Similarly, in the past, when criticism could lead to ostracism, which could lead to poverty and therefore death, killing the criticizer was a natural survival skill. But we are discovering it is more functional to communicate than to kill. Shouting back at someone who is criticizing us is natural, but dysfunctional. Listening that empathizes with the criticizer is *un*natural, but a lot less likely to end in domestic violence.

Killing the criticizer, then, is part of our evolutionary past; listening in response to criticism is part of our evolutionary future. Listening in response to criticism mandates a shift in our internal psyche that marks perhaps the most important single evolutionary shift humans can make.

Listening is self-empowerment via the empowerment of others. But listening to empower, like playing the piano, takes practice. The more it is mastered, the more it plays music to the souls of all who experience it. Listening in response to criticism is "good karma."

How To Prepare Our Children To Succeed in Work and Love

The ability to handle criticism has traditionally been a prerequisite for success, helping someone become a human "doing," but has also involved disconnecting a person from their feelings, thus hurting a person's progress as a human being. How, then, do we create the ability to endure criticism and at the same time prepare our children to fully love and be in touch with their feelings? It begins by looking at criticism in a different way.

People attracted to the profession of therapy tend to be sensitive and, therefore, oriented toward protecting sensitive people from abuse or discomfort. Perhaps as a result, therapists have made strides helping people *give* criticism in kinder and gentler ways, but not nearly as much helping people *receive communication given poorly.* Instead of working almost exclusively with the bad communicator as the only one who can be changed, suppose we also work on the receiver.

The out-of-the-box question then is, "Can we think of verbal abuse as we do a virus and develop psychological vaccines strong enough to prevent the virus from creating damage?" If the verbally "abused" no longer experiences himself or herself as abused when subjected to the same virus that formerly would have been experienced as negative, we have, ironically, protected the abused even more.

Obviously I share the ideal of giving criticism well. That is what the previous chapter is about, and that leaves fewer people hurt and leaves everyone happier because the criticism is more easily received. And if criticism always happened in this ideal way, this chapter would be helpful, but not necessary. In reality, though, even the best of us has been verbally abusive (via shouting, put-downs, name calling, and lying).

If we are to prepare our children to be pioneers of political, social, or scientific change, we have to do more than protect them from criticism, verbal abuse, and neglect: We have to prepare them to experience it as a growth opportunity. We can read the biography of almost anyone we wish our children to have as a role model and be astonished at the amount of criticism they endured in their time. Try Jesus, Gandhi, Darwin, or Sir Thomas Moore; Lincoln, FDR, or King; Socrates, Galileo, or Copernicus; Elizabeth Cady Stanton or Susan B. Anthony; Einstein or the Wright Brothers; Kinsey or Freud. Learning to handle criticism is a prerequisite to success.

While these pioneers all endured criticism that would have defeated most of their colleagues, still others endured childhoods that were textbook examples of abuse and neglect. And some, like Charles Dickens, actually used the abuse, neglect, and rejection of their growing-up years as the very fuel for their success. Significantly, Dickens didn't ask for self pity, but pioneered reform based on empathy for his characters, such as David Copperfield and Oliver. What allowed these leaders to succeed while others with similarly abusive backgrounds sank? They learned to use criticism, abuse, neglect, and rejection to create fires they controlled rather than be consumed by the fire in their soul.

If you've had an adolescent son (or been one), you've doubtless seen this process in progress. Unless you've been very protective, you've probably overheard him exchanging wit-covered put-downs with his friends. I'd go so far as to say that the commerce of male adolescence is the trading of wit-covered put-downs. You've probably noticed he does this the most with boys he calls his "best friends." Why? **Wit-covered put-downs are boys' way of teaching each other to handle the criticism they will have to handle if they are to become a success.** It is also boys' way of teaching each other to handle the rejection that comes with still being the gender *expected* to take the sexual initiatives and to handle the failures should they risk business ventures, or becoming an inventor, or the personal attacks should they risk running for political office.

In concrete terms, boys learning to associate criticism (even public criticism) with friendship is part of what allows two male lawyers to go at each other in court one day and talk as friends on a golf course the next day, or allows candidates Bush and Gore to criticize candidates Reagan and Clinton, respectively, in the primaries only to have Reagan and Clinton ask their critics to be their vice presidential partners for the next four years.

That's the upside of knowing how to endure criticism. But it left two crucial unresolved problems. First, notice that most people who endure public criticism are men. Second, these men often paid a severe price—the price of disconnecting from their feelings to handle criticism. Or, perhaps even worse, becoming so proficient with their defenses, in the form of wit, social criticism, or leadership skills, that sometimes unhealthy defenses evolved into a primary source of praise. And this left many of these men ineffective in their love relationships. (The qualities it takes to succeed are often inversely related to the qualities it takes to love.[1] Put another way, the qualities it takes to succeed in life are often inversely related to the qualities it takes to love your wife.)

How, then, do we create the ability to endure criticism, even use it as the fuel for success, and at the same time prepare our children to fully love and be in touch with their feelings? My goal in this chapter is to offer my reader a vaccine against the virus of criticism that allows us to succeed in love, succeed in life, and still be in touch with our feelings.

THE FOUR CONSTANTS

I call the four points below "constants" because they work only if they are constantly kept in mind (during the process of listening to criticism or anger). Again, if this feels overwhelming, remember, even a little listening, like a little smile, is better than none. Toward the end of the chapter, I provide a Starter Kit with the essentials, but it's best to have the larger picture in mind first.

THE "CINEMATIC" APPROACH AS INSURANCE POLICY

Because criticism feels like being killed, we're not going to be open to it unless we have a bullet-proof vest. The "cinematic" approach is that vest.

You can probably recall watching a film in which your gut was in turmoil. I felt this watching *Saving Private Ryan*. I had to keep assuring myself, "It's only a film, I can *choose* to let it get to me or realize it's just images on a screen." Similarly, when I feel criticism is getting to me, I **imagine the criticizer being on a movie screen,** and my having the choice to "take it in" or listen with the fascinated, but removed, interest of someone watching a film. In Hinduism, the person doing this is called the "witness."

This "cinematic" approach is also Buddhist in its orientation, seeing life as a play and seeing ourselves as playing roles. As Shakespeare would put it, "All the world's a stage" and we are but players making our entrances and exits. The "cinematic" approach keeps our ego from preventing us from viewing the situation as other's would view it.

Think of criticism as the sun and our ego as a magnifying glass. When the sun is directed through the magnifying glass it burns, it doesn't nourish. When criticism comes through the magnifying glass of our ego, we're more likely to get a sunburn than a tan. Our job is to let the sun nourish as it was intended to nourish, not burn by putting our ego between it and us.

The paradox of the "cinematic" approach is that because we know we can temporarily remove our egos, we become free to involve ourselves. When we see our partner's story in the same way we would see a character on the screen's story as his or her story, the threat is gone and we can focus on their story.

Become a master of the "cinematic" approach. Begin by renting a video of a murder mystery; when you get to a scene you can't handle, keep replaying it until you can choose at will to alternate between full-ego involvement and cinematic-witness–type ego involvement. When you've mastered that, then purposely discuss politics or religion (or whatever pushes your buttons), with a friend.

Let the cinematic approach be triggered the second you experience any feeling of discomfort, especially anger, during a conversation (especially with a loved one). But remember, it is only a positive because you will have your turn to express your feelings. And it is only necessary because no human being can be supportive of someone "killing" them if they actually experience the knife going in. You are not missing what your loved one is saying, you are just removing your ego enough so you don't overwhelm your defenses and trigger a nuclear attack.

I mentioned that the paradox of the "cinematic" approach is that because we know we can remove ourselves, we become free to involve ourselves in our loved one's story. How?

KEEPING THE ENERGY ON OUR PARTNER'S STORY

The second core ingredient to providing a safe environment for our partner's criticism and anger is keeping our energy on our partner's story rather than on our defenses.

Why a "story"? Once we look at our partner's experience as a story it is easier to remember because our unconscious has been programmed to remember stories better than abstractions or facts. By story, I don't mean fiction. I mean their version, their mini-bio if you will. But you're listening to it as you would listen to a story, with one event evolving naturally from the other, as she or he sees and experiences it.

Most people, when confronted by criticism, self-listen rather than listen to their partner. The self-listening is pretty all-consuming because the self-listener not only has to prepare defenses in response to everything their partner is saying, but modify the defenses to adjust to each new criticism. If someone is busy ducking bullets, they are not going to be looking at the point of the bullet.

For example, when Janet complained that her husband often drifted off in conversations, her husband, Jim, "self-listened"—he listened to himself create defenses such as, "When I drift off, it's because I'm tired and need some time to relax first," or "I'm in the middle of something and you interrupt. If you'd wait till I finish, or just give me a half hour of peace and quiet after I come home, I'd be ready to pay attention. But you never give me that."

Jim self-listened, then counterattacked. Which created for Janet a dangerous environment for the expression of feelings: Instead of being heard, she was attacked. Note that what Jim said might be true, and that his solution might be valid. But everything has its season. A peach picked before it is ripe is a stone.

Jim's primary job is to *focus on Janet's version of herself.* When Jim wants to hear Janet like a child wants to hear the next sentence in a bedtime story, then Janet will want to share her feelings like a parent wants to tell a bedtime story. We love telling bedtime stories to our children as much as children love to hear them in part because the child is not building defenses as the bedtime story is being told. The child's energy is with the story. The child is not looking for flaws in the story.

Jim's job is to want to hear Janet with the anticipatory enthusiasm of an Archimedes who knows he's on the verge of another "Eureka!" He *is* on the verge of a "Eureka!"—he is discovering his loved one. Jim's job, then, is to get *into* Janet's emotions and needs. Jim's job is to get into Janet's story. He can do this because his ego is not involved with himself. And once, of course, he can do it with Janet, he can do it with his parents, children, employer . . .

When Jim kept the energy on Janet's story, Janet's body language softened. She felt heard. She became loving. She stopped repeating her story. Jim no longer saw Janet as a nag. Janet no longer saw Jim as a . . . (some things are better left unsaid).

SEARCH OUT YOUR PARTNER'S BEST INTENT; AVOID THE GREAT TEMPTATION OF DISTORTION

You'll need a focal point as you're tracking your partner's "story line." Make the focal point your search for your partner's best intent: the best spirit of your loved one's strongest argument.

In every good story there is a villain—a devil, if you will. The devil in most people's criticism is distortion. It is the Great Temptation—tempting us to lose our ability to search out our partner's best intent, and if it has its way, tempting us to lose focus on our partner's story altogether.

Each time you hear your loved one distort your perspective, think of it as a challenge to leap over, duck under, or dance around. Why? Distortion usually derives from misinformation or pain (pain that may surface as malice, but underneath, pain). If it's misinformation, well, a critic's fear of retaliation leaves her or him with a one-track mind; when misinformation is coming one way on one track, new information cannot go the other way on the same track without a train crash. So step aside.

And as for pain, it is best resolved by empathy. So either way, avoid the great temptation of being pushed off your track of searching out your partner's best intent rather than his or her story.

BE ABSOLUTELY CERTAIN YOUR PARTNER CARES

I can rail on *ad infinitum* that if someone cares enough about you to risk being emotionally "stabbed" by you in order to get closer to you, well, that's a lot of caring, but chances are you're a bit skeptical about your partner's criticism being a sign of your partner's caring. And since you can't get to Step 1 of providing a safe environment for feelings—giving supportive eye contact that's genuine—unless you genuinely believe your partner cares, let's see how we can be sure your partner does care.

It's almost impossible to think of someone as caring when they are lashing out at us. Some of us lived in the era when a child being spanked was part of being a good parent ("Spare the rod, spoil the child") rather than a reason to call 911. Nevertheless, few of us believed it when our parents said, "This hurts me more than it hurts you." We didn't believe caring and lashing out at us could be connected until we became parents—until we reversed roles. So I'll ask you to reverse roles, but with your partner.

Think of the last time you felt critical of your partner. Did you fear bringing it up? Did you feel you were walking on eggshells? Did you think of yourself as trying to "get up the courage" to bring it up? Did it require courage because you were risking being "stabbed"?

If you finally got up the courage, was your willingness to risk being "stabbed" a reflection of your caring enough about intimacy to take that risk? If you believe that's true for you, could it also be true for your partner? If you're sure your partner doesn't care as much as you do, tell me, what are you doing with your partner?

The resistance to becoming convinced that our partner really cares is that the conviction implies our shifting from "the problem with our partner" to our own responsibility.

Okay, so exactly what is the best way to give supportive eye contact while our partner appears to be engaging in unilateral guerrilla warfare?

EIGHT STEPS TOWARD PROVIDING A SAFE ENVIRONMENT FOR YOUR PARTNER'S CRITICISM AND ANGER

These eight steps are all important to have in the back of your mind, but remember to begin with the Starter Kit at the end of the chapter, otherwise you'll be overwhelmed.

GIVE YOUR PARTNER SUPPORTIVE EYE CONTACT

You are free to give your partner supportive eye contact that's genuine because your ego is not in fear of being sliced and diced, and you know your partner cares. (That's what your supportive eye contact is supporting—being cared for.) Look into your loved one's eyes, repeating in your mind's eye, "His/her best intent is to be closer to me." Your eyes of love are your partner's greatest incentive to open up. They signal your willingness to provide a safe environment for your partner's criticism or anger. With that safety signal comes a responsibility to keep your partner safe.

Your eyes are also expressing a relaxed eagerness to hear what's on your partner's mind. This might be expressed by a nod of receptivity, or just eyes of receptivity.

Suppose your partner challenges you, "*Why* did you . . . ever do that?" Just tell your partner, "At this point, just let me hear you out." The moment you say *why* you did it is the moment you transfer the energy from your partner to yourself; you lose your ability to focus all your energy on your partner's story. You lose your supportive eye contact.

GIVE YOUR PARTNER VERBAL SUPPORT

Draw your partner out by saying, for example, "Tell me more about that . . . ," "Yes, I see . . . ," "Would you explain . . . ," "Mmm . . ." But no more than a few words. Never transfer the energy from your partner to yourself.

NOW THE BIG ONE: SHARE WITH YOUR PARTNER YOUR UNDERSTANDING OF WHAT SHE OR HE SAID

Focus first on the main points, always incorporating the specific examples that generated upset for your partner. You do this not by saying "I heard you," but by saying *what* you heard. Not by saying, "I see you're upset," but by being specific about what upset your partner. "Getting it" means going beyond the bottom line to the specific incidents and feelings that add up to the bottom line.

Do not offer assurances, but describe the specific feeling your partner said it created. (When your partner has described a feeling, do a best guess.)

Since you've searched out your partner's best intent, this is the time to let your partner know your understanding of his or her best intent.

Whatever you do, do not problem solve. That's for the end, and only if asked. Quick problem solving is usually premature problem solving. It is only telling your partner you are smarter than she or he is—you can figure out in a minute what your partner couldn't figure out at all.

When I brought up the problem with premature problem solving at a workshop at Esalen (in Big Sur, California), one of the women in the workshop, Liz, shared the following experience.

Liz had two children and ran a small public relations business out of her home. We had spent the morning on criticizing and listening skills, when Liz said she'd been trying to share something with her husband, Bob, and she felt he had tried to help but she didn't feel satisfied.

Liz explained, "I told Bob that when the children come home at three thirty, I feel bad when I'm talking to a client and the kids have to slip me a note. I promise myself I'll fix something healthy for them before they get home, but I don't usually get around to it. Then I feel guilty if I let them have junk food and guilty if I don't."

"When I mentioned this to Bob, he volunteered that he would prepare them a snack the night before. I really appreciated that, so I'm mad at myself for not feeling, well, satisfied with the conversation. Is something wrong with me or does it have to do with what you're calling premature problem solving?"

After Bob took a ribbing about his being a "premature problem solver" (which gave me a minute to think of how I wanted to handle this), I responded, "Pretend it's a month ago, and you're at that moment when Bob came up with the solution. Pretend he didn't. Role play from that moment on, as if you were having that conversation then—a month ago." Liz and Bob both agreed. She and Bob sat across from each other.

"Yesterday Erin's lunch got wet, so I fixed her something when she came home, but then I forgot a telephone appointment with a client and got a 'what type of business is this?' message on my answering machine from a new client. God, Bob, that made me feel like a fraud—trying to compete with the big guys out of my home."

Bob looked at her with a bundle of love in his eyes, "Honey, you're not a fraud, you're saving your client overhead and you're brighter and more experienced than all those inexperienced college grads who know more about footnotes than public relations."

Liz appreciated his confidence in her, but she still did not have a look of complete satisfaction. Bob complained, "I can't seem to please her. Why?" They both looked at me.

"Bob, you're supportive, and that's great; you're tracking, and that's great. And I'm sure Liz feels your love. But you're still problem solving, just in a different way—via assurance."

"Okay, so I should reflect back what Liz says." Bob stopped, got his act together, and said, "What I hear you saying is that you feel overwhelmed by the demands of work both outside and inside the home."

At first this left Liz frustrated. "Bob does seem to understand the essence, but I can't honestly say I feel understood."

"So what do I do?" Bob asked.

"Bob, you're giving Liz the bottom line, not the feelings that lead to the conclusion. She wants to know you understand her journey, not just where she ended up. **When you are specific, she knows you carry in your mind the same visual pictures she carries in hers. This is what makes her feel understood.**"

Bob paused, "That's clearer . . ."

Sensing "clearer" wasn't clear enough, I asked Bob what he did for a living. He said he was a construction contractor.

"Bob, would you feel more understood by Liz empathizing that you had a tough day, or by her letting you know how frustrating it must have been when one of your subcontractors didn't show up for the second day in a row, how that was going to prevent the drywall from being added for a week because the drywaller was scheduled today, and that was making the customer not trust you . . . ?"

Bob brightened. I saw the lightbulb go off in the form of a Cheshire cat's grin. "I got it. That's the first time it's become really clear."

After some discussion, I decided to take it to the next level. "What's clear thus far is that Liz would like specifics, but something else also happened when you gave Liz assurance."

Bob and Liz and everyone looked blank. "Okay, we need a break. Dance music on. Ten minutes. Forget the question. I'll repeat it when we return."

After the break, Liz immediately volunteered, "I don't know if this is what you have in mind, but I have to admit that at the time I did feel interrupted."

"That's exactly what I had in mind. No one who is interrupted feels satisfied she or he is really being heard."

"Let me assure you," Bob said. "Liz usually isn't shy about objecting to being interrupted."

Liz had a different take, "Actually, Bob, you hear about it when I object, but not when I keep it to myself. I wonder what makes me object sometimes, but not others."

"When we get interrupted by someone offering assurance or help, it is the most difficult to complain because we appear to be an ingrate. It's like filling the pitcher of a hungry person with milk and the hungry person feeling awkward explaining they don't like milk." Another workshop participant chimed in, "So, Liz, if you hadn't been interrupted, what would you have said?"

Liz looked both fearful and grateful at the opportunity to continue. "Well, I felt terrible yesterday when, once again, I had to rely on Judy to take Alex to soccer and Erin to baseball—I'm *so* overdue. And even though Judy took them, I got involved in a conference call and didn't have time to prepare a decent dinner.

And after dinner, although you helped with the homework and cleaned the dishes, Bob, and I appreciated that, I couldn't ignore the kids' questions. By the time we tucked them in, I had no time to prepare adequately for a presentation to obtain a new client."

Liz paused.

Bob, with a very positive attitude, began, "What I hear you saying is—"

I was hesitant to stop Bob, but the point was crucial. "Bob, I love your willingness to get right in there, but the reason I ask the listener to wait until she or he is asked to speak is because sometimes the most difficult things are saved for last, when we're on a roll and our not being interrupted makes us increase our trust enough to share them."

I could see now that there was a part of Liz that wished I had just let Bob jump in, and a part that was relieved. I could feel Liz's mind moving at a vertiginous pace with both a need to share and a fear of sharing. I encouraged her to continue.

"Oh, boy . . . Well, I was so tired last night, and when I felt pressure from you to make love, then anger and rejection when I felt too tired, that turned me off even more. Emotionally I felt I had another kid on my hands." Liz lightened it up by joking, "I just need a thirty-six-hour day," but Bob was already crushed.

Later Bob told us he normally would have responded either defensively about his sexual needs or told Liz he understood her by discussing the equal but parallel pressures he endures (thus transferring the energy from Liz to him), or problem solved: even offering Liz the option of not working, or working part-time, while he assumed the financial burden. He acknowledged that all these responses crossed his mind—no, they actively tempted him—but he was clear that none of these responses left Liz feeling understood. So he kept focused on Liz's story.

As Bob put it, "It reminded me of when I played end in sand-lot football—someone waving his hand in my face trying to distract me, and me trying to remain focused on the ball."

Liz looked at Bob and said, "Keep practicing that football. I can't remember when I've felt closer to you, Bob."

We took another break. Liz and Bob took a longer one.

EXPAND ON YOUR PARTNER'S BEST INTENT BY SHARING YOUR OWN NEW INSIGHTS—INSIGHTS YOU BELIEVE WOULD INCREASE YOUR PARTNER'S FEELINGS OF BEING UNDERSTOOD

When Jim told Janet he was upset about her drifting off when he was speaking with her, Janet, after a lot of discussion in our workshop, eventually responded, in effect, that, "When I drift off, you must feel like I don't respect you. I guess you probably feel taken for granted."

That came fairly easily from Janet. But as I asked Janet to really get into Jim's feelings (as best as she could imagine them), she came out with, "On some level you must feel like you are being set up to have an affair—if just to meet some woman who will pay attention to you." When Jim felt Janet's generosity, he responded, "I hadn't quite thought of it that way, but I guess you're right. Ironically, when you're so generous, it makes me feel loved, and that makes me not even want to think about an affair."

I then asked Janet to see if she could connect Jim's feelings to any other feelings Jim had been having. Suddenly Janet had a little epiphany, "No wonder you say that sometimes when we make love, I seem like I'm doing it for you, not for me. That's the way my drifting off feels at those moments, yes?"

Jim's body language softened. He smiled, took Janet's hand, and pulled her toward him for a long hug. Janet seemed pretty focused.

Ask Your Partner To Clarify Anything You May Have Misinterpreted or Omitted

After the clarification, share your new understanding with your partner. Repeat the process until your partner feels completely heard.

Take a Brief Break

Take a brief break, especially if getting to this point has been exhausting. Hold each other. It's okay to allow this to drift into lovemaking, but *only if you return to the listener's response.* I emphasize this because as a rule women are more likely to register complaints and men are more likely to want sex and, if a man thinks listening without giving his response won't get her upset and, therefore, will lead to sex, then not responding is a big temptation. Since most women don't like to listen to men complaining or expressing anger, it's tempting to strike a nonverbal, perhaps even unconscious, bargain of his listening to her but not responding with his perspective. But that bargain is truly a Faustian deal for both sexes because, if the process stops without the man having an opportunity to clarify perceived distortions, then he'll build up anger that will surface as sudden outbursts, drinking, flirtations, or affairs. Eventually there is less intimacy and less sex.

Respond by Reversing Roles

Now (finally!) explain your perspective. It is fine to clarify what you feel are distortions. Do not, though, bring up new issues. Bring up only the issues that are directly related to the ones already brought up by your partner. Even though you are responding, you are still focusing on your partner's initial source of complaint or upset.

You and your partner reverse roles—your partner plays listener in the same way you played listener. That is, your partner reflects back to you what you say, asks you if there are any distortions, and you both continue until you feel well represented and understood. And most important, your partner does all this within the framework of the four constants (the "cinematic" approach; energy on you; searching out your best intent; and certainty that you care).

GIVE THE PERSON WHO DID *NOT* BRING UP A COMPLAINT AN OPPORTUNITY TO DO SO

The first time or two you go through these steps, you may have only enough energy to handle one complaint by one person. If that's the case, schedule a specific time for the other person to register her or his complaint, then reverse the process, with the complainer following the guidelines in chapter 2 (on giving criticism) and the listener following the guidelines in this chapter.

As you become more proficient, you'll be able to schedule the sharing and caring evenings and go through two to four complete rounds. In the process of becoming proficient, though, pay attention to these four caveats.

FOUR CAVEATS

The first two of these areas—the way we offer physical support and the tendency to make promises to change our behavior—can undermine our effectiveness as we execute the Eight Steps; the second two—rising expectations and self-righteousness—can undermine our effectiveness even when we've done virtually everything right.

PHYSICAL SUPPORT

The best way to support your partner by physical touch is to ask your partner what feels most supportive. Many people don't want any physical touch when they are criticizing—they want space.

If your partner prefers no touching, fine; but before you label your partner as anti-touch, ask your partner, "When I touch you while you're making a point, do you sometimes feel controlled by the way I touch?" For example, Sam noticed that Susan often took his hand when she wanted to interrupt. He experienced the touch not as an act of intimacy, but as an act of control.

Sam also noticed Susan withdrew her hand when he said the "wrong" thing and returned when he said the "right" thing. From his perspective, then, touching was not an act of intimacy, but a reward and punishment system that made him feel like a behavior-modification experiment in Pavlov's lab.

Assuming our touch is not masking a need to control, then the form of physical support most frequently appreciated is being touched *very lightly* on the foot, shoulder, or knee (depending on your position vis-à-vis your partner). The emphasis here is on "very lightly" because virtually any other touch feels controlling to the criticizer.

Of course, once your partner is satisfied that she or he has been fully heard, the issue isn't as "touchy," so to speak. Then holding your partner is more likely to signal acceptance and support. Hold each other in silence for ten to twenty seconds. Spend part of it giving each other appreciative eye contact.

Avoid Promises To Change

Men tend to be problem solvers and especially prone to listening to women for the purpose of getting to the bottom line so he can figure out a solution while she's elaborating. Therefore, when this process is finished, he's likely to be tempted to be spontaneously generous, promising a change in his behavior, or to rescue her in some other way (get married, have a child, get a new home). Hold off on the promise of a behavior change—especially if you're a man. It's a shock for many men to discover that a woman who feels heard, listened to, and respected feels so well-cared for that her needs for change in behavior are significantly reduced. It's usually better to wait a few days to see if the real behavior that needed change was the expression of compassion. On the other hand, if the behavior change is simple, inexpensive, and can be done quickly, go for it.

Rising Expectations

Every change comes with shadow sides—that is, a cost, downside, trade-off, or a more selfish motive than has been openly acknowledged. One shadow side is common to every positive change in human behavior: rising expectations. Our partner changes, but we want even more, faster. So we're no happier than we were before.

For a society, rising expectations have a positive value—they avoid complacency and stimulate us to make the next layer of improvement—but they are damaging to individual happiness. And whenever, as an individual or as a society, we raise our expectations faster than we raise our level of change, we defeat happiness and therefore defeat the purpose of change.

Self-Righteousness

A second shadow side is one common to virtually every stage of psychological growth: self-righteousness. It grows out of our belief that we have changed more than our partner. Why? We're aware of all of our efforts, but we see only our partner's outcome. Their efforts are usually invisible. The problem is, our partner sees all of his or her efforts and only your outcome. So both of you become self-righteous. And angry at not being acknowledged for our efforts. Moreover, self-righteousness is worse than the problem it replaces. Even defensiveness is not as ugly as self-righteousness.

Because self-righteousness makes us both angrier and uglier, thus defeating our efforts to be happier and more loving, having a way to avoid it is important. The first way is to be aware that the real issue we are dealing with is feeling unloved. That is, **when we do not see our partner's efforts clearly, we unconsciously believe that they are not making as much effort as we are because they love us less than we love them.** What we're really shouting when we tell them about all the changes we've made, is, "I'm afraid I love you more than you love me. It makes me afraid of rejection. It makes me scared. I feel like a little child."

The solution? First, just share that; share your fear of not being loved. Sharing your fears makes you endearing; a litany of your efforts makes you a braggart.

Second, search for the efforts. A woman friend of mine had a habit of being late. When I told her she had kept me waiting and the sacrifices I had made to get there on time myself, her natural response was defensiveness. When I spent just a second imagining the efforts she had made to get there on time, I was almost always able to come up with something, to the effect of, "How are you? You must have had a load on your hands finishing your workday, getting dinner ready for the children, and dealing with their complaints about being left alone for the evening." When I chose that route, she felt seen and usually began by volunteering an apology. The result was appreciation from her, a hug, and me experiencing her love. And that was what I wanted.

A QUICKIE REVIEW

Before we look at the Starter Kit, let's get a quick review of everything we've been through. Remember, this is not a guide, but a review.

A QUICKIE REVIEW TO PROVIDING A SAFE ENVIRONMENT FOR YOUR PARTNER'S CRITICISM AND ANGER

THE FOUR CONSTANTS

- *The "Cinematic" Approach as Insurance Policy.* Imagine the criticizer being on a movie screen. You have the choice to "take it in" or listen.

- *Keeping the Energy on Your Partner's Story.* Don't be thinking of your possible response.

- *Search Out Your Partner's Best Intent.* Avoid the great temptation of distortion.

- *Be Absolutely Certain Your Partner Cares.* Do this by recalling how much you care when you criticize your partner.

EIGHT STEPS TOWARD PROVIDING A SAFE ENVIRONMENT FOR YOUR PARTNER'S CRITICISM AND ANGER

- *Give Your Partner Supportive Eye Contact.* This can only be genuine if it emanates from all four constants. These eyes of love are your partner's greatest incentive to open up. With them comes a responsibility to keep your partner safe.

- *Give Your Partner Verbal Support.* Like, "Tell me more."

- *The Big One: Share with Your Partner Your Understanding of What She or He Said.* Give specific examples that illustrate those points so your partner knows both your hearts share the same "visual picture."

- *Expand on Your Partner's Best Intent.* Now that you know your partner's story, what feelings must she or he have that have not been expressed directly yet.

- *Ask Your Partner to Clarify Anything You May Have Misinterpreted or Omitted.* Repeat this process until your partner agrees that you both share the same perception of the complaint.

- *Take a Brief Break.* Be certain you return to the process of the listener having a chance to clarify perceived distortions. Men: Beware of the Faustian deal of silence for sex. In the long run it means less intimacy and less sex.

- *Respond by Reversing Roles.* Time for your perspective, but not your own issues yet. Stick with the issues your partner presented. Your partner follows the steps to providing a safe environment.

- *Give the Person Who Did Not Bring up a Complaint an Opportunity to Do So.* It's the listener's turn to bring up whatever is bothering him or her.

THE STARTER KIT

The Quickie Review can still overwhelm—it's still a twelve-step program. When we're beginning it's often better to try the essential steps, experience some satisfaction, then add on. Besides, anger and criticism usually erupt too spontaneously to have the time to read a chapter to discover the appropriate response. And when we're hurt so much, we don't even *want* to do that. The best we can hope for is a willingness to glance at a Starter Kit once our nervous system no longer feels like it's being struck by lightning.

So here's a Starter Kit . . .

THE STARTER KIT TO PROVIDING A SAFE ENVIRONMENT FOR YOUR PARTNER'S CRITICISM AND ANGER

THE TWO ESSENTIAL CONSTANTS

- *The "Cinematic" Approach as Insurance Policy.* Imagine the criticizer being on a movie screen. You have the choice to "take it in" or listen.

- *Focus Your Energy on Your Partner's Story.* Don't be thinking of your possible response.

THE FOUR STARTER STEPS

- *Give Your Partner Supportive Eye Contact.* This can be genuine if it emanates from the Constants. These eyes of love are your partner's greatest incentive to open up. With them comes a responsibility to keep your partner safe.

- *The Big One: Share the Main Points of Your Partner's Best Intent.* Also include the examples that illustrate those points so your partner knows both your hearts share the same "visual picture."

- *Ask Your Partner to Clarify Anything You May Have Misinterpreted or Omitted.* Repeat this process until your partner agrees that you both share the same perception of the complaint.

- *Respond by Reversing Roles.* Time for your perspective, but not your own issues yet. Stick with the issues your partner presented. Your partner follows the steps to providing a safe environment.

I suggest using the Starter Kit at least the first few times you try this. However, even if you're a woman who does provide a safe environment in these ways, you can be even more helpful encouraging your partner or son to open up by becoming aware of the forces that surround us everyday that reward men for repressing feelings even as we ask them to express feelings.

4

How To Help Men Express Feelings

When a friend of mine read the title of this chapter, she asked, "If men want help expressing feelings, why don't they just get help—go to a therapist, form a support group, talk with each other—do what women do when they need help?" I asked her to imagine a man in the 1950s saying, "If women want to own companies, why don't they just start one, like men do?"

The belief that men don't need help is part of the problem. In contrast, we have helped women make transitions to traditional male skills by using virtually every major institution of society and billions of dollars (math and science programs only for women, affirmative action programs, minority status, special scholarship funds, self-esteem courses, a women's movement, professional associations for women in every profession, associations of university women, women's magazines, TV talk shows, all-female schools). In this deeper respect, neither men nor women have changed: Men are still playing protector of women's transitions, and both sexes expect only men to make transitions on their own.

Helping men express feelings starts with understanding why men don't express them. Do we give lip service to wanting men to express feelings and reward men for repressing feelings? Yes. Who's the "we" who does this? The family, the workplace, the church, the government, the education system. Here's how.

WHY CAN'T MEN EXPRESS THEIR FEELINGS?

Many people believe men communicated better before industrialization because, for example, they taught their trade to their sons. But working together is communicating about performing, not communicating about feelings. Sharing *instructions* about how to perform better for *others* is very different than sharing *feelings* about life experiences that make *us* happy or sad.

The nature of men's responsibilities distanced men from feelings, whereas the nature of women's responsibilities encouraged the expression of feelings. Men's pay paid women to love and nurture, to connect and feel. To be nurturer-connectors. In contrast, men received their pay by being some form of killer-protector. By becoming a human doing (a captain or a coal miner), not a human being (a person who feels happy or sad). Why?

Societies in which men are unwilling to dispose of themselves in war were societies that usually got disposed of. Societies that were protected were pro-tected by killers, which is why I call the traditional role of men the role of killer-protector. Killers, like people who got killed, could not be in touch with their feelings. Killers could not be nurturer-connectors.

Both sexes had an unconscious investment in keeping men from expressing feelings of fear and vulnerability. Why? Both sexes wanted a cadre of people al-ways available to protect them. This is why no legend told its children of beauti-ful princesses falling in love with conscientious objectors.

Historically, then, a man being a human being was dysfunctional. A human being in touch with his feelings would value himself too much to want a bullet to go through his head in war or to be coughing up coal dust deep in a mine. If we taught men to repress feelings and rewarded him instead for being a captain he might be willing to die to protect us; if we paid him enough to feed his family if he worked in a coal mine, he might be willing to die sooner to keep us warm. But all that required him to forfeit his feelings—his power as a human being—and substitute it for "power" as a human doing: feeling obligated to earn money some-one else spent while he died sooner.

Becoming a human doing was exactly what society needed. But for an indi-vidual man, becoming a human doing was his undoing.

All of this is man's genetic heritage. However, man's genetic heritage is in conflict with his genetic future. In the past, socializing men to become the best killer-protectors led to the survival of the "fittest." In the future, with nuclear technology, training killers is more likely to lead to the destruction of everyone. And in the future, women will increasingly want men who can nurture them and connect with them. In the future, women will increasingly want nurturer-connectors, since part of what he will be nurturing is her ability to protect herself.

In order to connect and nurture, it is not just helpful to be in touch with feelings, it is necessary. So man's first job—his next evolutionary strategy—in-volves being in touch with his feelings. Because both sexes have an investment in this type of man, the path to changing this is difficult for both sexes.

DILBERT *by SCOTT ADAMS*

Prior to the past thirty years, neither sex spoke very much to the other sex about what bothered them. Both sexes became passive-aggressive in different ways. Men got drunk and women got headaches. However, during the past thirty years, the women's movement has supported women to express virtually every feeling women felt. To other women. To men. To society. Women's feelings became course curriculum, women's studies, TV specials, talk shows, and Lifetime cable. Women's feelings were called both education and entertainment. Men's were repressed until they were called ulcers.

Because men complained less, we made the false assumption that the complaints women experienced were only women's complaints and, therefore, only women's problems. Which created the rationale for women's problems to be solved—or at least addressed—by public policy.

Unfortunately, the conversations of the great majority of men are still focused on one or more of what I call the "Five Male Crutches."[1] They are:

- Business

- Women, as beauty or sex objects

- Issues

- Sports

- Equipment (computers, cars, stereos, tools, guns, etc.)

How is it that during thirty years of "liberation," men have made so little progress expressing their feelings, and most of the time when they do, it's at the behest of women? The truth is that virtually everything conspires against men expressing their feelings. Each internal and external influence tightens the grip of the vise, keeping him emotionally constipated.

Let's start with the family, since the process of keeping men as human doings (rather than human beings) deadens our sons and leaves our daughter walking down the aisle on her wedding day to be transferred from the arm of one human doing to another.

61

THE FAMILY

THE "FATHER'S CATCH-22"

When the main purpose of the family was survival, its main method of survival was the division of labor. And this created a division in the way fathers and mothers loved their family. **A father's traditional role prepared him to love his family by being away from the love of his family.** Before the industrial revolution, a boy had to prepare to be away from his family in war, to hunt, and, to a lesser degree, in the field. After the industrial revolution, this intensified: The better a man was at supporting his wife and children, the more disconnected he was from the support of his wife and children. That was the Father's Catch-22.

The opposite was true of a mother. A mother's role prepared her to love her family by being *with* the family she loved.

We think of the division of labor as being outdated, but in fact it has reemerged. In the early '80s, a mother was 43 times more likely than the father to leave the workplace for family responsibilities;[2] more recently, a mom is 135 times more likely to leave the workplace for family responsibilities.[3]

Dad's paycheck is still much more likely to pay Mom to love. And in poor families, where the government becomes a substitute husband, pay is given to mothers to love, but fathers in poor families rarely get paid to love. Whether rich or poor, it is rare for men to be paid to love. And the paychecks that pay women to love are the paychecks that take men away from love.

It is still rare for us to financially support men who provide love; we still love men who provide support.

A HUSBAND'S EMOTIONAL INVESTMENT

Women are socialized to take advantage of four informal options for emotional support: husbands, women friends, children, and parents. Men are socialized to take advantage of only one of these informal options: their wife or woman friend. Since men tend to put all their emotional eggs in the basket of their wives (or women friends), it is difficult for a man to communicate feelings of disappointment to his wife because, if she withdraws, it feels to him like his entire emotional support system has collapsed.

After a conflict, women are not only more likely to turn to other women friends for support, but are nine times more likely to be with their children should conflict become divorce. She is also much more likely to reconnect with her parents, both emotionally and financially. (A woman living with her mother has limited freedom; a man living with his mother has limited freedom and limited respect.) For most men, the vacuum (of no support system) is so devastat-

HOW TO HELP MEN EXPRESS FEELINGS

ing, they'd rather agree with their wife than express their feelings and risk emotional withdrawal.

DIVORCE

After divorce, women's biggest fear is economic deprivation; men's biggest fear is emotional deprivation. Divorce laws have given women some economic support after divorce; no laws have given men emotional support after divorce. Men are required to continue their obligations to their exes in the form of alimony or child support; women are not required to continue their obligation to their exes in the form of homemaking or nurturing. At a point in history in which about 50 percent of men are eventually deprived of marriage's emotional support, we are compounding that deprivation by depriving men of other forms of emotional support.

We had affirmative action programs to help women help themselves economically. Is it now time for affirmative action programs to do for men's feelings what the government did for women's economics? Instead of outlawing men's organizations, should it be part of the government's affirmative action programs to sponsor and encourage all-male groups to help men teach themselves emotional responsibility?

Unlike affirmative action programs aimed at helping women, which are paid for more by men, men's groups nurturing men would *relieve* women of providing emotional support to men. All-male groups can help men teach themselves emotional responsibility without taxing women.

CHILDREN OF DIVORCE

Divorce has had an exceptionally difficult impact on boys expressing their feelings. It has left millions feeling abandoned by the person most eligible to be their role model. A boy brought up by his mom, then thrust into a 90 percent–female child-care environment and then an 85 percent–female elementary school system has virtually no male role models.

The result has been severe damage to a large portion of a whole generation of boys. Some join gangs for some male-male identity. A large study of urban children found that children from poor and wealthier families had equal crime rates if they both had dads. **The difference in crime rate could be predicted only by comparing the children without fathers at home to the children with fathers at home.**[4]

As for suburban boys, the six shootings in 1998–'99, from Springfield, Oregon, to Littleton, Colorado, have been by boys in suburban public schools. Coincidence or significant? What has been the relationship of these boys to their dads? If such studies have been done, they are not part of the public conscious-ness, and therefore not molding public policy. When we care more about our sons, there will be fewer teenage graves for both our daughters and sons.

In academic subjects, students coming from father-present families score higher in math and science *even when they come from weaker schools*. (The poor educational performance in the United States in the past twenty years, especially in math and science, might have more to do with the absence of fathers than with the quality of schools.)[5] The deprivation of male role models is so pervasive and the impact so powerful that recent studies show that even when income was the same, *both* the *boy* and the *girl* child did better brought up by a single dad than a single mom.[6]

Organizations like Boy Scouts and Big Brother are more vital than ever if we want fewer gangs and more positive male role models to teach our sons and daughters intelligent risk taking. For example, team sports provide dozens of ar-eas not just of physical tension and conflict, but also of emotional tension and conflict. Our children need to experience many more male role models helping them translate what just happened on the playing field into what happens in their everyday life.

We need, though, to introduce into organizations like Boy Scouts, Boys Clubs, and Big Brother discussions of ethics, values, relationships, and commu-nication, conducted by men of all ages, so that boys see men not only as physical adventurers but as emotional adventurers as well. These new male skills, mod-eled by men, should not substitute for the more traditional contributions men's organizations have brought to boys. Rituals like taps, flag folding, marching, awards ceremonies—rituals that are repeated in predictable intervals—create feelings of security and stability on a deeply emotional and psychic level that are even more important in a culture of divorce than in a culture of intact families.

When rituals are conducted in the presence of men or boys, it connects that security and stability to the men and boys. Boys miss this from a female parent, no matter how loving or conscientious she is, as virtually every single mother I know is.

Should groups like Boy Scouts include girls? Some male and female groups can be integrated, but there is also a value to single sex groups if we wish both sexes to express the full range of their feelings. Boys' socialization to perform for girls and to protect girls inhibits boys from expressing feelings of vulnerability in front of girls, and girls are less open and more in conformity with what they think will bring them the approval of boys when boys are present. That said, it is also important for our sons and daughters to spend *most* of their time with the other sex, since childhood is preparation for life with both sexes.

THE WORKPLACE

Hasn't men's emotional support system been the workplace? Mostly no. For many reasons the workplace is a far more precarious place for most men to express feelings than for most women.

Since a woman is still 135 times more likely than a man to leave the workplace for family reasons,[7] her husband is still much more likely to be providing for the family, therefore more likely to be repressing feelings of personal vulnerability for fear of increasing his family's vulnerability. In contrast, this woman is more likely to be developing friends who cannot hire or fire her, which allows her to express her feelings without fear.

In addition, his and her style of seeking support are likely to be different. Imagine this couple getting into a conflict, both needing support. She picks up the phone, calls her woman friend, and spends an hour reconstructing the conflict—what she said, he said, her response—all from her perspective. She expects from her woman friend compassion ("Yes, he seems more interested in the sports pages than in you. You must feel lonely even when he's there."). Her woman friend is expected to share a similar story. Ultimately, she may get some advice, some of it even from the man's perspective, but compassion is expected to precede advice. As it should.

With him, it's different. Men develop fewer men friends. This tendency is magnified by the fact that if he's an assistant vice president of a bank and he tells the bank vice president about the conflict, he's allowed, at most, a three-minute window of opportunity to share his story. No protector instinct is stimulated by the vice president toward a man. So after that three-minute window, he notices the bank vice president's eyes glaze over, as if to say, "Okay, then, I've heard you, you've had your opportunity to cry in your beer, now get back to work."

If he violates that three-minute window, well, when the next opportunity for promotion comes, the vice president will recommend someone else "who's less disturbed." So **the price to him of revealing his vulnerability is greater vulnerability.** And if he's supporting a wife and children, that's a vulnerability he feels he has *no right* to expose.

Is this different with the full-time working woman? Yes and no. Even when women work *full-time,* they average ten hours less in the workplace than full-time men because they have more responsibilities at home.[8] Therefore he still tends to be more colleague-as-friend dependent.

A characteristic of jobs held mainly by women versus jobs held mainly by men is that jobs held by 80 percent or more women are often extensions of their maternal role, such as teacher, nurse, or social worker, while jobs held 90 percent or more by men are likely to offer very little nurturance, such as a truck driver, garbage collector, welder, roofer, or engineer.

Human Resources Development (HRD) divisions of companies would ideally provide an outlet for men's workplace frustrations and anger. Instead, though, a man who gets angry about a failed sexual relationship at work or a failure to be promoted is seen as losing control, whereas a woman is seen as a victim of discrimination. Her anger becomes a lawsuit; his becomes an ulcer. It is rare for HRD divisions to pro-actively seek out men's feelings in these areas despite the fact that the expression of men's feelings would be a perfect affirmative action program for a sex that has become successful via the repression of feelings.

In brief, men have learned that expressing vulnerabilities at work is a hazardous job. Thus, the larger the family a man supports with that job, the more a wife who provides a safe environment for him to express feelings of vulnerability is uniquely treasured.

THE CHURCH

The church is the only worldwide institution to pro-actively invite all men to ask for help, to "let go, let God." On the other hand, the people in most churches who are most respected are men who are giving help, not asking for help. And the women come to see the problem solvers, not the men asking for help.

Christ himself was the ultimate problem solver—he died to save us from our sins. Christ, like most religious leaders, listened to those who asked for help and created miracles to solve their problems. It was for his invulnerability that he was worshipped. Thus, just as the family creates for men the Father's Catch-22, so the church creates for men the Religious Catch-22: we tell him to ask for help to preserve himself, even as we worship a man who disposed of himself.

In contrast, both female socialization and the church encourage women to ask for help. Church, therefore, creates no conflict between female socialization and religion, as it does for men. Thus **traditional churches are divided into mostly females praying to have their problems solved, and mostly males hired to solve their problems (ministers, rabbis, priests).** Similarly, nontraditional spirituality is divided into mostly females seeking help and mostly male gurus competing to give it.

A women without a man in her life, then, can choose among the church-as-substitute father, the government-as-substitute-husband, and the guru-as-substitute-mentor without any conflict with her female socialization. For men, the government does not play the role of substitute wife and the church or guru as substitute parent or mentor creates greater conflict with the message to men that real respect comes with being the mentor, not asking for one.

The church reinforces this conflict among its potential male followers every day. Even though the church is dominated by women seeking help, which would logically suggest the need for special outreach programs for men, we nevertheless find there are women's associations of Methodists, but no men's associations of Methodists; there are Young Women of the Church of Jesus Christ of Latter Day Saints, but no young mens. . . .

The one Christian church organization aimed at men—Promise Keepers— also continues this contradiction. On the positive side, it supports men to express feelings, discuss family, and meet in small groups—an extraordinary positive contribution that again separates out the church as the one institution to offer men pre-crisis support. On the other hand, its emotional support comes with pressure on men to play the role of provider, the role that creates the Father's Catch-22: providing for the family he loves by being away from the family he loves.

In brief, the church's message to women is consistent—love your children by being *with* the children you love; the church's message to men is conflicting— love your children by being *away* from the children you love. In the secular world, a woman who asks for help attracts a savior; a man who asks for help attracts no one. Thus for women there is no role conflict in attending church; for men there is considerable role conflict in attending church, asking for help, expressing vulnerability.

THE GOVERNMENT-AS-SUBSTITUTE-HUSBAND

The feminist movement, while helping many women become independent, has also given millions of women the option of dependency. It has done this by pressuring the government to play a role—the role of government-as-substitute-husband.[9] The government-as-substitute-husband has been easy to create because it appealed to both the protector instincts of the mostly male legislators and the "protect us" instinct of almost every female legislator.

The issue here is not government-as-*protector*, but the government legislating protection for women more than for men even in those areas in which women are less vulnerable. For example, 85 percent of the street homeless are men,[10] yet many more special accommodations are open only to homeless women (with or without children); men are more than twice as likely to be murdered, but we have only a Violence Against Women Act; women receive 23 percent more bachelor's degrees,[11] yet there are affirmative action privileges and scholarships for white women that are not available to white men in any case, or to any man in many cases; and, as chapter 7 explains, men are as likely to be battered, yet there are shelters and hotlines only for battered women.

Women are the exclusive recipients of all of these governmental protections, whereas there is no legislation focused exclusively on protecting men—emotionally, financially, or physically. What the government finances exclusively for men is more likely to put men at risk: male-only draft registration and the subsidizing of athletic programs that include football. The result? If men do have feelings of great vulnerability, there are few places to go—no battered men's shelters, no suicide hotlines, no programs to help men obtain access to their children, no men's bureau in the department of labor, no office of men's health.

THE EDUCATION SYSTEM

During the '60s and '70s the Free Speech Movement led to students saying so much their parents thought they'd never shut up. Today, speech codes have replaced free speech. I will look in depth in chapter 8 (on the Lace Curtain: "It's Men in the News . . .") at how and why the entire education system has turned into hostile territory for our sons' feelings. I explain there why, especially in top universities in the social sciences, your son will be expected to treat women as equals unless something he might say or feel will offend them. He may be confused.

What might confuse your son more is that the censorship of his feelings has an ideological basis. Feminism, mostly Marxist feminism, although evolving from the social sciences, defines gender politics university-wide. If your son is dating, his feelings of confusion and growth will be much less free than your daughter's to evolve, be experimental, and question. In universities, women don't hear what men don't say because it is clear that should the silent sex decide to take its head out of the sand and speak it can jeopardize its career as well as its self-esteem. I'll leave the evidence for that to chapter 8, but suffice it to say here, I am not aware of any point in human history in which the need for a safe environment for men to relax and "let their hair down" has been greater.

Instead of safe environments for the expression of feelings, even private men's clubs have been disappearing as women's appear.

MEN'S CLUBS OUT; WOMEN'S CLUBS IN

The alternative to men's organizations is men becoming even more dependent on women for all their emotional support. Yet instead of creating men's organizations, we are destroying them: It used to be that most clubs we could think of— Elks, Kiwanis, Rotarians—were men's clubs. Now, when we search the

Encyclopedia of Associations for organizations or clubs that are exclusively men's vs. women's, **there are more than *twenty* women's organizations and clubs for each *one* men's club or organization.**[12]

Similarly, we are now integrating YMCAs, but not integrating YWCAs, allowing women to join men's sports teams in high school and junior high school, but not allowing men to join women's sports teams. Where women need help to bond and network, the government is giving it to them and the Supreme Court is sanctioning it.[13] Where men need help to bond and network, no one is giving it to them. Even the Boy Scouts are being sued for not including women.

In the last third of the twentieth century, women's support systems increased and men's decreased to such a degree that there are now approximately 400 to 500 women's professional organizations versus virtually no men's professional organizations or associations. The *Encyclopedia of Associations* does list a few men's professional organizations, but with very few exceptions the encyclopedia described them as "defunct."

Are women's organizations more common because women are more likely to be in the minority in more professions? Not quite. Nonuniversity educators are mostly women, but there is no Association of Male Nursery School Teachers or Association of Male Elementary School Teachers. Overall, there are approximately five times as many women's *professional* organizations as there are all men's organizations put together.

It is tempting to say that the pendulum has swung from a propensity for men's clubs to a propensity for women's. But that misses the fact that both sexes had places where they could "let their hair down" without the other sex around. While men had clubs, bars, and sports, women could get together over garden fences or at garden clubs; in clubs of their own, or in auxiliaries of men's clubs; for quilting bees or shelling peas; and always, for tea and sympathy. Thus in the past, both sexes had an opportunity to discuss their frustrations in a safe environment. The pendulum swung from equal to less-than-equal for men.

Sometimes a man wants his own space because he feels, rightly or not, that as soon as something is made to accommodate both a woman and a man, her needs dominate. She walks in, he can't swear too much or talk too much about sex. Similarly, in his own space, a men's room, he has urinals. A home, built for both sexes, has a toilet seat like a woman's room does, but no urinal like a men's room does. And then that toilet seat, which can be used by both of them with a little adaptation, is required to be left in that position that never requires any adaptation on her part, only on his. If he doesn't obey, he's called insensitive.

Some men sense these things, but fear a woman's reaction enough to not say them to a woman; other men try not to even think them, lest they say something and get in trouble. In truth, a man could care less about the toilet and doesn't mind adapting to women's toilet seat needs, but he does mind it when the woman he loves says he's insensitive and can't adapt even as he's adapting.

TRADITIONAL MEN'S ORGANIZATIONS

While many women can see the value of men getting together in the type of nontraditional, introspective men's support groups I have formed during the past thirty years, they have more trouble with traditional men's groups like the Elks. But traditional men's groups provide the traditional man's equivalent of tea and sympathy or the garden fence. They serve some of the same functions for the traditional man that the church provides for the traditional woman, for the reasons mentioned just above.

Neither sex feels there is a safe environment to talk about certain types of feelings with the other sex. A woman who goes out on a first date and fantasizes marriage within ten minutes of meeting the man doesn't usually feel comfortable talking with him about it, but her woman friend will immediately identify. A man who goes on a first date and fantasizes sex within ten seconds of meeting her doesn't usually feel comfortable talking with her about it (!), but his buddy will immediately identify. When both are disappointed, both sexes find it easier to share their frustrations with the same sex. At a point in history when the male bashing I cite in chapter 7 is called humor and female bashing is sexism, women have a public outlet for what must increasingly be kept private among men.

Men with deep male-male friendships are less likely to become self-destructive during crises such as death and divorce. When a woman dies, her husband is ten times as likely to commit suicide as is a woman when her husband dies.[14] This leaves his entire family in grief over both her death and his suicide; it leaves other widows without men to marry or love.

Why are men so much more self-destructive in response to the loss of love? Scene One: husband dies. The widow is crying, her friends see she needs help, they call, arrange to drop by, *invite* her to call at 3:00 in the morning. Exactly because she has cried she needs less help—friends respond and people even become friends by responding; and the tears clean out impurities, leaving her with a stronger immune system.

Scene Two: wife dies. He represses his tears. His men friends *do* ask if he needs help, but he often says, "Thanks, Jack. Really appreciate it. This is really hard. But I'll be okay. Thanks." He signals less need for support and therefore receives less support. The result? **He may feel no one loves him or needs him—the two characteristics most associated with suicide.** And that's where male-male friendships are crucial—he has a support system he knows loves him and needs him.

My eighty-nine-year-old dad belongs to a men's organization called Activities Unlimited. The male friendships he has developed through that group have supported him through my mom's bouts with cancer and through his heart surgery. My mom, sister, dad, and I all know that the chances of his being alive, no less anticipating next ski season, would be much less were it not for the phone calls, hospital visits, dinner invitations in which someone picked him up so he didn't have to drive at night, admiration, respect, and love he receives from many of those men, and now, many of their wives.

More traditional men's groups—be they football teams, Boy Scouts, or Elks—prepare each other to be protectors. The Elks provide a fascinating example of this. They support female organizations like Girls State and Girl Scouts, not just boys' organizations. Their symbol, the antlers, is a symbol of protection. But interestingly, the antlers of the elk also symbolize the *burden* of protection: An elk that does not rub its heavy antlers against a tree to shed them when it no longer needs them to protect others makes itself more vulnerable to death—the antlers also prevent the elk from fleeing from its predators. Note that the antlers made the elk more vulnerable to fleeing from predators all along, but he was willing to die as long as he could protect his family doing it. It is a perfect metaphor for the challenge traditional men's groups face—helping its members know when to shed their antlers so men's symbols of strength do not remain men's weakness.

If traditional men's groups introduce more introspection, sharing of feelings, encouragement of vulnerability, questioning, and the understanding of trade-offs, they will combine the best of both worlds. Although they currently do not do that, the friendships formed in traditional men's groups, and the ritual that catalyzes these friendships, do provide a crucial source of emotional support in times of crisis—emotional support that is greater exactly because the men are around men who are like themselves.

NONTRADITIONAL MEN'S GROUPS

Nontraditional men's groups encourage men to share their fears with those who share their fears. A man who does this is better able to share his fears with his wife because he doesn't think there is something uniquely wrong with him.

Like women, when a dream falls apart, men also feel that something is wrong with them. For men, these feelings are especially potent when they face downsizing or demotion, conflict at work or with their spouse, a boring sex life, or rejection every night and special-occasion "mercy sex"; divorce, and especially custody battles that involve denial of joint custody or visitation, false accusations, or their feeling that their ex is bad-mouthing him to the children.

The value? A man who doesn't know that other men also share his problems and feelings disappears. He may disappear into a bottle (hopefully to come out at an AA meeting) or into work, behind a newspaper or in front of the TV ("the one thing I can turn on"), behind a mouse or behind a remote ("where my input at least registers"). He seeks excitement in the victories of a local sports team, one that is the winner he never was, the winner he fears he will never be. Today's anxiety becomes tomorrow's ulcers, cancer, or heart attacks. A men's group often turns a dead end into a T intersection.

Ironically, the most common discovery related to identity in all men's groups is "I'm not alone," "I am not unique"—but that creates positive identity because enormous self-doubt is engendered in men who believe their fears and failures are shared only by men who are wimpy, fearful failures.

On an everyday level, how do we know that people with common fears feel more comfortable expressing those fears in front of those who share the fears? Just think how your adolescent daughter opens up when she talks to her girl-friend on the telephone. Remember how her tone of voice changes when Mom or Dad walks in? She shares with her adolescent girlfriend a common set of fears. She still needs time in her life to communicate with boys and parents, but needs some separate space to share her fears with those who share her fears. As do parents. As do women. As do men.

The obligation to provide and protect is the heritage common to all men. The fear of not fulfilling that obligation is also a heritage common to all men. But in these all-male settings, men discover that even when they do fulfill these obligations, they face a catch-22: If he provides well financially, he hasn't had enough time for his family, leaving both them and him unnurtured. On the other hand, if he has been close emotionally, he fears he has not provided adequately financially. That's why each man shares the fears of other men.

As one man after the other speaks of his experience, he begins to understand that the qualities it takes to be successful at work are often inversely related to the qualities it takes to be successful in love; why becoming a killer-protector is inversely related to being a nurturer-connector.[15] Each man gets a sense of the ways in which his own life is out of balance. Men's groups allow men to follow like a pilot; each man who speaks serves as a gauge, helping him see the adjust-ments he needs to make on his journey.

In some men's groups, the importance to men of sharing feelings is symbol-ized by using a talking stick—a vine-wrapped stick similar to the caduceus, the ancient medical symbol that symbolizes healing. Why? Talking about feelings is healing; and feeling heard heals even more.

But same-sex groups have limitations. When I set up men's and women's support groups, I encourage them to meet separately for a period of three months and then meet alternately together and separately after that. I find that if either sex did not first meet separately, they were often afraid to discuss deeper fears honestly; but if they met separately for too long, they began to think their problems were only women's problems—or only men's problems—and were caused by the other sex.[16]

This structure also allowed me a chance to observe the differences between the way men communicated in a single-gender vs. a mixed-gender group. When women were present, men were more likely to compete with each other to be the best problem solver for problems women brought up. In groups in which sensitivity was the biggest virtue, men just competed to be the biggest jock in the sensitivity group! In other words, when women are present, men perform. Just as women do when men are present.

What gets neglected with women present is men's willingness to go deeply inside of themselves to explore territory they fear will make them look like losers in front of women. Since most men's emotional eggs are all invested in the basket of women, they fear questioning in front of women the success that brings them the love of women. A doctor is afraid to explore becoming a nurse and working half the hours, or writing a novel that may not sell. Introspective men's groups help men make a transition between their current life choices and future ones. Instead of doing it with a Corvette, a bimbo, and their genitals, they do it with six men, their head, and their heart.

The path to helping men help themselves, though, is rife with irony and paradox.

"YOU'RE SO IN TOUCH WITH YOUR FEELINGS—I WISH GARY COULD BE LIKE YOU"

I was facilitating a workshop, helping a woman uncover her feelings and suddenly she stopped and said, "I wish Gary could be like you—you're so in touch with your feelings." I thanked her, but reminded her that I had not shown any sign of being in touch with my feelings—I had been in touch with *her* feelings.

The distinction is important because Ginger had blamed Gary for not being in touch with his feelings; she had also felt bad about "needing more than a twenty-four-hour day just to have time to talk together." She had not appreciated that as a result of Gary not expressing his feelings she had almost 100 percent of the free time to air hers. When we put someone in touch with their feelings, they have the air time; we don't. They may have less time to hear us, understand us. Which is why we haven't rushed to reexamine the structures of our lives that keep men emotionally underground.

Among these structures are the helping professions. As we've already seen among clergy, men who are workshop facilitators and therapists are experts at lis-

Nicole Hollander, *Sylvia*, Rockport, Maine

tening to others, but rarely experts at revealing their own vulnerabilities. In fact, people come to them because they are respectable, not vulnerable. Almost 100 percent of gurus and popes are men. We praise them for having the answers, for problem solving, not for the way they share their own feelings, weaknesses, and vulnerabilities. **When a guru or pope is vulnerable, we don't praise him, we call it a scandal.** Our love, respect, and income go to these men only if they keep their real feelings private from us.

We *should* praise someone who listens to us, problems solves, and inspires, *and,* if we *also* want men to open up about what upsets them, we must be as quick to praise men who are in touch with their feelings of distress. Currently we praise men who save "the damsel in distress." A marriage between the savior and the damsel in distress is celebrated. But not if the savior is female—there are no Mother Teresas marrying the "sensitive man in distress." A marriage between Mother Teresa and a Homeless Harry would not have led to two and a half billion women glued to their TV sets, as they were when Princess Di married a prince with a castle. We don't celebrate a woman falling in love with a man in distress. We warn her.

Men will express distress when we are as quick to praise women who marry men in distress as we are to praise men who marry "damsels in distress."

KILL THE DRAGON BUT FEAR THE TEAR

Nothing better illustrates the fact that men's weakness is their facade of strength than men's willingness to be fearless before a dragon, but in fear of a tear. The weakness is a male disease I call emotional constipation.[17]

Is emotional constipation unnecessarily graphic? No. Men change when they know the bottom line. And the bottom line is that crying is an excretory process, like going to the bathroom. It removes impurities. It is as dangerous to tell our sons "real men don't cry" as it would be to say "real men don't go to the bathroom." Which is why men who cry are healthier than men who don't.[18] Even children who cry are healthier than those who don't.[19]

This doesn't mean that a man or woman who cries has no problem expressing emotions, or that crying cannot be misused as a form of manipulation, but it does mean that telling boys not to cry is emotionally unhealthy and still representative of our underlying message to boys.

If He Gets in Touch with His Feelings, Will He Avoid a Midlife Crisis? Or Precipitate One?

A man who has been in touch with his feelings all his life will usually avoid a midlife crisis. But a man who has denied his feelings all his life, and then learns to get in touch with them in middle age, will precipitate a midlife crisis. Which is not necessarily a bad thing. If he's precipitating a midlife crisis among people who love him, it can be the first time in his adult life he feels loved for something other than being a wallet. Then he has a chance of directing the movie of his life rather than being the jerk of his life. The alternative to a midlife crisis for a man who has spent his lifetime thus far denying his feelings is an early death. Take your choice.

Being in touch with feelings is very different from expressing feelings. A man who expresses all of his feelings all of his life will *not* avoid a midlife crisis. **A man who *expresses* all of his feelings will be in a crisis all of his life!** He will be in a whole-life crisis. But being *in touch with* feelings gives a man the option of expressing them when appropriate. It is the choice that empowers him— if he makes the right choices.

"When I Say 'Get in Touch with Your Feelings,' Henry Doesn't Quite Know What I Mean"

I was conducting a workshop when Tina told Henry she had been planning to leave him for some time and wanted to tell him at the workshop so he could get support and nurturance. Henry responded, "If that's what's right for you, okay, but it's not gonna be as easy as you think out there."

I asked Henry to get in touch with his feelings. Henry's eyes glazed over. Which is, of course, a feeling state, but not one that spoke to Tina (on any level). Tina's response was, "See? *That's* why I'm leaving him. When I say 'Get in touch with your feelings,' Henry doesn't even know what I mean."

An hour before, Henry had been explaining something to Tina about the stock market. I responded to Tina's impatience by explaining that men need emotional mentors just as women need business mentors. Tina recalled the stock market discussion and softened. Eventually she acknowledged the glazing as a feeling and asked him if he could put words to the glaze, to *help her* by translating his feelings into her language.

If the man you love would like to get in touch with his feelings, but he either doesn't quite know what that means or how to begin (which is just a face-saving way of saying he doesn't quite know what it means), walk him through a check of the six barometers of his feelings.

THE SIX BAROMETERS FOR GETTING IN TOUCH WITH FEELINGS

- Muscle tension
- Breathing patterns
- Shortness of temper
- Drinking, smoking
- Penis
- Dreams

Getting a man in touch with his feelings only creates frustration if he doesn't feel there is a safe environment for expressing them. If he doesn't, then not being in touch with his feelings is an appropriate defense mechanism. Expecting him to express himself without safety is like expecting him to play emotional football without a helmet and with no one on his team.

MUSCLE TENSION

He'll like this one, so start here. (Sorry, the penis one isn't what you think!)

Massage him. Be sure to include his jaw, shoulders, between his eyes, on the side of his eyes, his scalp, and underneath the edges of his shoulder blades. That will tap both of you into his tense areas. Ask him to focus on the most tense area.

Now here is the key. Ask him to pay attention to everything that happens during the day that makes the most tense area more tense (eliminate the ones that are tense from sports activities or physical labor). If he's just received bad news or about to face a difficult decision or tense period, keep asking him to check every hour. Once he catches himself getting tense, that's when he's feeling something.

If he still isn't in touch with what makes him feel tense, massage him, *then start an argument immediately afterward.* Ask him whether the area you just massaged is now more tense. Then, of course, explain what you did. Few men mind when a woman acknowledges she caused the argument—especially when it's a way of loving him. Now massage the same area for him again, and let him feel the decrease in tension.

BREATHING PATTERNS

Notice the difference in his breathing patterns between the times he is tense versus relaxed. Imitate the difference for him. Point out to him when he makes a shift. Help him to see what created the shift.

SHORTNESS OF TEMPER

Usually a short temper is not a sign of one feeling, but an accumulation of feelings. Often an accumulation that is situational depression. It is a golden opportunity to help him unravel what's accumulated. But temper tempts judgment, and if we feel it's being released at us we become both judgmental and defensive, thus losing the golden opportunity.

DRINKING, SMOKING

Help him distinguish between his normal pattern of drinking and smoking, which may accompany relaxing, versus even a small deviation from his pattern. Instead of telling him to stop drinking or smoking, understand that a safe environment for his feelings will reduce his tension and therefore usually reduce drinking and smoking. (Alcoholics Anonymous is valuable in part because it provides a safe environment for expression of feelings. The safer environment, the less he will need to cover up with a bottle or with a cigarette as a pacifier.)

PENIS

A soft penis is usually a penis that *is* working. If his penis is soft when you're making love, don't think of it as impotence, because, assuming no medical problem like diabetes, a soft penis is working exactly as intended. How so?

A penis is like radar. Like radar, it helps us detect what our conscious mind may miss. A soft penis is a signal from a radar station that *is* working to tell us that something is bothering him—he's self-conscious, preoccupied, tired, fearful. (In some way he is uncomfortable.) If he had shut out those feelings, or taken Viagra to cover them up, and his penis became hard as a result, **then his *hardness* would be a sign of his *impotence* because he would have tricked his penis into giving him a false signal.** Whenever a drug "solves" a problem, we need to intensify our look at what nature was telling us by creating the signal—

whether it's in the form of pain when we're cut, or a soft penis when we're under pressure.

The paradox of the penis, then, is that a penis that is soft is usually potent; a penis that is hard can occasionally be impotent. It is potent, though, only if we use its softness as a signal that real feelings aren't being addressed. The penis's softness is signaling that *his real feelings are more important than sex.* (Well, maybe don't mention that last part to him.) It is signaling that he is more than a human doing, he is a human being, exactly because his feelings are not just important, but primary.

The job of a loving couple is to respect the wisdom of the penis.[20]

DREAMS

While the penis is a wiser detector of our feelings than the conscious mind, it nevertheless gives a simple message: feelings off, feelings on. Dreams are as complex as a penis is simple (or, should I say, "straightforward").

Because this isn't a book on dream interpretation—a book that would reveal the extraordinary, rarely tapped brilliance of our unconscious—I will say here only that if you truly want to get your partner and yourself in touch with your feelings and fears, then create a safe environment for sharing your dreams without judgment. No, I take that back. Create a *sacred* environment for sharing without judgment. How?

Perhaps the single biggest fear of using dreams, a fear so great it deprives us of our ability to be nonjudgmental, is the belief our dreams are prognosticators of the future. They are not. Dreams give us a computer printout of our fears, usually in symbols, and most of those fears are meant to be registered, acknowledged, and considered, as any feeling or fear should be, not used as predictors of the future. And not used as instructions for a wiser path. The moment they are treated in either of these ways is the moment we need to repress our dreams rather than express them, because if we express them and our partner moves to the couch (literally or figuratively), we're sure to repress the next one. Ditto for dreams' sexual feelings and desires.

IF MEN EXPRESS THEIR FEELINGS, WHAT WILL THEY BE EXPRESSING—AND AREN'T WOMEN THE BEST ONES TO HELP THEM DO IT?

When a man is upset about his mother dying from cancer, most women will encourage their husbands to cry and use more of the skills of understanding than the average man possesses. In this respect, women provide better emotional support for men than men do for women.

But when a man fails at a job, it's a different story. When a man loses his job, he often loses his wife. And with his wife go the children. And their home. This pattern is worldwide. Before I sat down to write this morning, I saw on CNN the story of a Japanese man who had finally perfected the freezing of sushi. When asked by CNN what motivated him to perfect the process, he said, "My sushi was spoiling, my business was failing, and my wife was threatening to leave. I had to do something. I saved my business, and saved my marriage."[21] Men sense that their support systems are conditional.

Many women do stay with men who are downsized or who earn less money than they do. But men sense women's disappointment just as a woman who gains weight and gathers cellulite might sense her husband's disappointment even if he stays with her. Just as women pick up men's addiction to the sex object, so men pick up women's addiction to the success object.

Men pick up this female support for the successful man by watching what women cheer for. I remember watching the film *An Officer and a Gentleman* when it first appeared. When the officer swept the woman off her feet and proposed marriage, the audience applauded wildly. But the officer had a buddy who looked inside himself during officer training and came to understand that he didn't want to be a pilot, that he marched to a different drummer. Instead of being applauded, he was seen as a failure. His fiancée, who he thought loved him, left him. He was so devastated, he hanged himself.

When the movie ended, Richard Gere, not his character—was the focus of female swooning. The equally good-looking man who was introspective—who did not want to kill—was ignored. By real-life women. Richard Gere's character symbolized a pension; his buddy symbolized introspection. Most men follow the applause. And they see few women applauding *A Dropout and a Gentleman*.

Men who look inside themselves and choose a path to lower income, lower rank, or less status often fear they will be left, not loved; they fear not being honored for their introspection, and thus often struggle with honoring themselves *even if they honor that part of themselves that chose a path with integrity.* Ironically, they find themselves more capable of love but less likely to be loved. So while the traditional male role leads us to respect men, but to not really love men, the new man finds himself more lovable but more likely to be rejected for love. Which is why so many men feel caught between a rock and a hard place, once they learn to feel.

Attraction to the success object is not women's fault; it was what women learned to do to obtain security for their children and themselves. Nor is it men's fault that they fall in love with young and beautiful women—youth created the most years for child-bearing, and beauty represented the best genes. These were each sexes' genetic heritage—a heritage that was functional when we were preoccupied with survival. Now, though, communication and common values are more of a priority. And since adaptation is the key to survival, our challenge now is to begin to develop in our children associations of love with compassionate communication.

Women often ask me with a bit of both curiosity and skepticism what men talk about in these men's groups. Here are some specific questions and topics, but more important is the process. As men listen to each other's stories and discover the relief it creates, they also unconsciously absorb another understanding—the value of listening. When men discover this, their wives and children are enormously relieved, since training to be a man is strong on problem-solving skills and weak on listening skills. Here, though, is a flavor for some of the questions asked and topics discussed that seem to work best when the initial discussions occur in an all-men's group. (A more complete list is in my book *The Liberated Man*.[22])

- *"If I didn't have my children and wife to support, what might I have liked to have done with my life?"* Virtually every man has an artistic part of him, or a love of nature or sports that got repressed as he took on the financial obligations of the family. As men lose this part of themselves, a quiet desperation can set in that leads to drinking, gambling, cynicism, depression, and suicide. Men are usually afraid to explore this part of themselves with their wives because they fear their wife will take it personally. As men explore this side with each other, it takes an enormous burden off their shoulders—they feel understood, and that replaces drinking.

- *Sex Lives.* Many men would give a lot for a week on a Caribbean island with a beautiful young woman. (Especially a weekend that no one finds out about, and that hurts no one—especially not his family.) When he first met the woman who became his wife, he may have fantasized and even experienced weeks like this. But his everyday life with his wife falls far short of that. Men, like women, need same sex groups to help them see that their disappointments are not theirs alone. Eventually, though, the sexes must meet to understand it isn't either sex's alone.

- *Criticism vs. Praise.* Most men learned to improve by accepting criticism and therefore felt that giving criticism would help others improve. However, when a man is critical of his wife, she seems to take it personally. Ultimately, it seemed, her spirit was eroded. Same-sex discussions of issues like this can help men discover in a safe environment how to balance criticism with praise with their children and why women tend to need many compliments for each criticism.

SOME SOLUTIONS

When we advise a man to take a vacation or get counseling, it often feels to him like a contradictory message: "Make more money so you can afford to take a break from making more money" (vacation); or "Make more money so you can afford to question whether you should be money focused" (counseling). One of the first steps toward a solution is to make sure we aren't sending conflicting messages. For a man, the first step is sorting out conflicting messages.

The nontraditional men's group is perhaps the easiest way to begin exhuming a man from his emotional underground. Any man can form a group by contacting just two men who each contact two men who . . . Or by asking for a spiritual leader in his community to help him put out the word. Or by asking his wife or woman friend to inquire among her women friends. But before he starts one, be sure he reads carefully my best thinking on how to avoid the traps to which men's groups are prone (in *The Liberated Man*[23] [excuse the title]). A man who has a poor first experience at being really vulnerable can be discouraged from trying a second time.

Faith-based communities are especially open to starting men's groups. I have personally seen this openness even in the most traditional of faith-based communities, the Baptist Church. When I conducted an all-day workshop for the St. Paul Community Baptist Church in Brooklyn, New York, a congregation of nearly 100 percent African-Americans, most of the congregation began by assuming that the men needed to be more responsible providers. When the men conformed, they were marriage material; when they didn't, they were deadbeats. When we worked on the possibility that many of the African-American women were already good providers and that the men could be married and loved for caring for their children, managing the home, doing remodeling in exchange for rent, taking community-based schooling, and so on, there was not just openness, but applause and reconsideration.

One barrier that the African-American Baptist congregation did confront was the fact that most of the men had been involved in men's ministry which, while providing the support system to help many make a transition from addiction and/or prison time to being functional, nevertheless brought them into contact with government programs that were promising the women more money for not having the father at home than she would receive if the father was at home. No government programs were encouraging men to be caring for their children at home while the mom handled most of the breadwinning. After some discussion, though, most of the congregation agreed that was an option that could benefit not all, but much of the congregation.

If you have children, the most powerful impact you can make is mastering the tools of communicating so your children will unconsciously do the same. When everything else changes, listening skills and the ability to handle criticism will be their rudder.

A woman can get her husband or man friend to express feelings, then, by providing a safe environment. If she thinks men can't adapt, think again. Loving dads who taught literature adapted in a matter of weeks to killing on front lines, feeling their buddies die in their arms, only to be expected to later return to the arms of their wives and children. The reason we don't know men adapt is that they've adapted so well they camouflage their adaptation (*e.g.,* camouflaging the fear of death as "glory"). When men hear they will be loved for being human beings, they will become human beings. Meantime, though, nothing can replace men's taking responsibility: Women can't hear what men don't say.

PART II

In the Home

5

What a Man Doesn't Say When He Hears, "I Work Full-Time and Take Care of the Kids, but You Won't Even Do the Dishes."

From the 1970s through the turn of the century, women worked more and more outside the home and felt that only they were returning home to a "second shift"—not only taking care of the kids, housework, and dinner, but taking psychological responsibility for guiding the children through homework, sibling rivalry, runny noses, and rides to soccer, plus the needs of her husband (and oh, yes, her *own* needs!). If, with all those balls in the air and her husband glued to TV for the all-important-to-him playoffs of whatever, he should "wonder" when dinner will be ready, well, that's the moment she wonders whether she has one more child than she bargained for. And she wonders whether she is being valued or being used.

The very phrase "second shift" became part of our consciousness with the publication of the book *The Second Shift*[1] in 1989. Pictures like the one at the top of the next page from *Time*[2] popularized the already recognized female jug-

The Myth of Male Housework

For women, toil looms from sun to sun

gling act—juggling everything from the baby to the turkey; meanwhile, the male "juggling act," if you will, is a slightly different version: The "turkey" is now in the "lazy" chair, "juggling" the sipping of a drink and the fondling of his remote.

Newsweek's headline claimed, "Woman's Work Is Never Done,"[3] while *People* magazine told working women they had been tricked into double duty: "For Working Women, Having It All May Mean Doing It All."[4] And as for men's con-

They're called men.

tribution? *Time* magazine's headline reduced it to "The Myth of Male House-work" while simultaneously telling women, "For Women, Toil Looms from Sun to Sun."[5] Enter the era of the second shift woman and the shiftless man.

By the mid-'90s, the anger at men had become so palpable that even sedate publications like the *Economist* were characterizing women's vs. men's workload as "A woman's work is never done; a man is drunk from sun to sun."[6] Women themselves were sending each other greeting cards reflecting the fury.

HOW A MYTH IS MADE AND FEMALE FURY IS BREWED

This attitude toward men intensified in the '90s with the media's transformation of another minor publication—a United Nations publication, no less—into a major media event. It was the *Human Development Report 1995.* Remember when Hillary Clinton went to China for the International Women's Conference sponsored by the United Nations? This was the report the U.N. issued just prior to that conference to help publicize it. It created headlines all around the world saying it wasn't just American women who were overworked and underpaid while their husbands were lazy and unappreciative; women everywhere suffered this double standard. These are some typical headlines.[7]

Women's Work Is Never Done
Local Residents Poised to Do Battle at Beijing Conference

By Nora Boustany
Washington Post Staff Writer

The New York Times
U.N. Documents Inequities for Women as World Forum Nears
By BARBARA CROSSETTE
UNITED NATIONS, Aug. 17 —

It's official: Women *do* work harder
U.N. study affirms it,
calls their lot 'unfair'
By DOUG MELLGREN
Associated Press

There was a problem with these headlines. A big problem. The saga I am about to share is to the United Nations like an investigation of first eye contact between Monica Lewinsky and Bill Clinton: The closer you look, the more you uncover.

The "eye contact" started with the U.N.'s "eye contact" with the press—its press release. The U.N. press packet was replete with references to women throughout the world working more than men, including a graph with the title "Women Work More Hours Than Men"[8] (paid and unpaid). However, **the U.N.'s graph and press release excluded every single one of the countries in which the *men* were found to work *more* than the women according to the U.N.'s own study.**[9] The U.N. acknowledged they only sent the actual 230-page study to a few of the major media who themselves ignored the contradiction between the U.N.'s press release about its study and the actual findings of the study.[10]

I would consider the graph deceptive—but not an absolute falsehood—if it had said, "*Countries in which* women work more hours than men." But it was titled as an absolute: "Women Work More Hours Than Men," reinforced by the press packet's no-exception references to women's work as *universally* underpaid and men's as universally overpaid; to women as universally unappreciated, men as universally overappreciated.

It is this competitive approach to women's problems that has been so dangerous in the past thirty years. It was not good enough to ask that women's contributions be appreciated; women's problems came with a blaming of men for causing them; a resentment at men for having it better, and an anger at men for not solving the problem. The collaborative, win-win sex had become the competitive win-lose sex; empowerment feminism had become not just victim feminism, but competitive feminism. Moreover, there was something very wrong with the data.

At its core, the U.N. data saying women work more worldwide was a lie. I confronted the U.N. (politely, of course) with this "conflict" between their press release and their study. I was pleasantly surprised they acknowledged it. I asked if they were conscious of what they had done. The answer? "Yes." Surprised, I asked *why* it was done. They said they felt "they needed to correct people's belief that men worked more."[11]

Think about that. By 1995, we already believed that *women* worked a "second shift," were Superwomen, and were superstressed. But the U.N. was so wedded to the need to reinforce the belief in women as victim it felt justified in falsifying data to prove it.

The distorted data the U.N. did acknowledge, however, was just "the first kiss," if you will.

I became suspicious of the *Human Development Report*—let's just call it the *Report*—when I saw that it had the United States listed as one of the countries in which women worked more hours than men. I knew the most reliable studies showed the opposite. I wanted to find the study they used. But the *Report* didn't list the authors of the individual country studies. The only source listed was a Goldschmidt-Clermont, who allegedly compiled the studies, and this source was available only from the U.N.[12] However, when getting the paper from the U.N. was like getting President Clinton to acknowledge he had more information about Monica, my suspicion intensified. When it was sent I found I needed to pursue even further, for Series K[13]. Together, they then provided the next series of clues.

Series K, the U.N.'s own resource, acknowledged that *women* in the United States "were reported to work *fewer* hours than men—about three hours less per week."[14] (emphasis mine). Could the U.N. *Report* actually be lying about the U.S. study just like the U.N. press release had lied to the press about the laziness of men worldwide? Or was there a reasonable explanation?

Judge for yourself. The U.N. did not report the findings of any study in any country as the authors had reported them. Instead, **the U.N. asked each author to "amend" his or her study with an estimate of *voluntary*, unpaid community work as well as "basket making, weaving, knitting, sewing, etc. for *own consumption*."**[15] The source was listed as a "private communication" either without the name of the person who wrote the communication or without the name of the office from which it derived. For example, the American publication had a university, but no author.

Now here are the problems with the U.N.'s "amendment" solicitation. First, they did not tell the press they had modified all the studies. Second, they asked for modifications that would add female labor, but not male labor. Below I outline fifty areas of contribution to the home that men typically make more than women. None of these fifty were added, and the noninclusion of most of these fifty is already a bias against men in almost all housework studies.

Third, the U.N. asked for work that may legitimately be work in third-world countries, but when knitting and voluntary, unpaid community work is done in the United States and other industrialized nations, it is work by *option,* not by *obligation;* work for *personal* consumption, not family survival. Moreover, in industrialized nations, the time to do this voluntary, unpaid work is a function of luxury, not poverty. Some of it—like knitting for one's own consumption—is considered for American women relaxation as much as work. This type of "work" is an indicator of female well-being in the same way that female charity work comes largely from those with enough income to have the luxury of time to devote to others.

And that *still* wasn't the worst of it.

In the event that the "U.N. Amendment Solicitation System" failed to expand women's contributions enough to create a "finding" of women working more, the U.N. created a system to *ignore* mostly men's contributions. It was done under the neutral guise of a "common format," but it allowed hours to be counted for only two types of traditionally male work—repairs and care of yard—and ten types of traditionally female work: child care, cooking, house cleaning, laundry, shopping, gardening, marketing, errands, mending, and sewing.[17] The "common format" system excluded about 96 percent of the categories I list below as the "Male Housework List." Contributions like shoveling snow, remodeling, coaching, painting, assembling toys. Had any traditionally male contributions other than repairs and yard care been included in other studies, then, the common format system allowed the U.N. to ignore them.

The result? We, the reader, saw only the women-as-victim headlines.

Throughout all of this, I had trouble doubting the U.N. because my image of the U.N. had always been one of an organization creating peace and love, not anger and hate. This impression was first damaged when, ironically, I had addressed some 2,000 women at the U.N.'s 1975 International Woman's Year Conference in Mexico City and, although receiving an extremely positive response personally, I could not help but witness how all the world's problems were blamed on men, patriarchy, and white male capitalistic imperialism.

I saw that even in 1975, feminism already dominated U.N. gender politics, especially Marxist feminism. When a person or two spoke differently, she was swamped with us "feminist missionaries" who tried to "enlighten the sister." As I investigated the 1995 *Report* I realized it was only in that atmosphere that so much could be manipulated without enough protest to make a difference. It also made me aware that feminism today has become the dominant ideology of gender worldwide because it dominates in those countries that dominate—those in which men produce enough money to free women from roles—even as the men are both expected to make that money and be criticized for making it.

What is the impact on our children of this international "Sisterhood Is Victimhood" bonding? The headlines doubtless contribute to millions of women feeling angry at men as they're washing the dishes, which adds to the man bashing (chapter 7), which adds to marital conflict, sometimes tipping the scales of already fragile marriages into divorce, leading to children raised without dads.

After divorce, this downhill slide from "I am woman, I am strong" to "I am woman, I am victim" makes it harder for the woman to find a new lasting relationship, thus leaving the children less likely to have another stable male influence. If the mother does find a father substitute for the children, the anger becomes a thorn in the already much-more-fragile construct called a blended family, thus too often leading to a second divorce and children whose anxiety about stability makes them either so overly anxious for commitment that they "settle," or so distrustful they become commitment phobic.

A man spots this distrust in a woman in little ways that he often just regis-

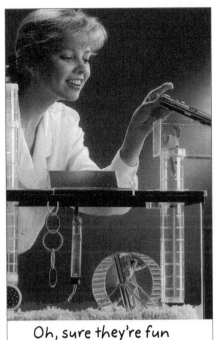

*Enlargement
of upper
male "pet"*

→

*Enlargement
of lower
male "pet"*

→

Oh, sure they're fun
for a while, but you
get tired of cleaning
up after them!

ters unconsciously, maybe by spotting a greeting card she's sending or receiving. For example, if you're a woman, ask yourself if you would sense this distrust in a man who was sending other guys greeting cards with gerbil-size women in a cage, saying "Oh, sure they're fun for a while, but you get tired of paying for them!"?

The U.N. study was built on a foundation of undeserved credibility that had already been established by *The Second Shift,* and a foundation of anger created by *The Second Shift*'s publicity. This publicity had already reinforced such a deep-seated atmosphere of husband bashing that the national media was finding it *de rigueur* to feature successful women like Jane Pauley bashing their husbands (in her case, Garry Trudeau of *Doonesbury* fame) for not being an equal participant in the housework. The stories not only ignored men's reality, but reality itself. For example, here's how my own U.S. senator, Dianne Feinstein of California, was portrayed as Superwoman with a deadbeat hubby by the *New York Times.*

When asked if she does housework, Ms. Feinstein responds, *"Of course,* I think women *always* keep house. It comes with the gender. *Every* career woman with a family does the wash, the laundry, *scrubs floors,* cleans the bathrooms, changes the beds. The man generally does not." (emphases mine) Personalizing the situation to Richard Blum, her third husband, Senator Feinstein complains,

"I haven't taught him to hang up his bath towel yet, but rather than nag I don't bother anymore."[18]

The reality? For starters, Dianne Feinstein has a full-time housekeeper and has had one since her second marriage.[19] Second, Ms. Feinstein lives in Washington; Richard Blum, the "man she had to nag to pick up the towels," lives in San Francisco.[20] (Maybe they had an arrangement: Every night she asks, on the phone, "Honey, did you pick up the towels?" He says, "No." They feel married.)

Third, the New York Times was negligent by not mentioning that Ms. Feinstein's new husband had put $3 million of his own money into his new wife's 1990 gubernatorial primary campaign alone, or that her new husband also raised "hundreds of thousands more from his network of business associates."[21]

Fourth, the New York Times didn't tell us that as a result of his overwhelming financial assistance, Richard Blum's entire business was brought under scrutiny—the same thing that happened to Geraldine Ferraro's husband. In Blum's case the opposition investigating happened to be the state's Attorney General (VanDeKamp).[22] Perhaps Richard Blum should have picked up the towels and Dianne Feinstein could have forfeited his $3 million and earned $3 million of her own money.

In the meantime, according to the biography recommended to me by Feinstein's own Senate staff,[23] it turns out that Ms. Feinstein never took an interest in housework or cooking,[24] "had never run a business or had a real job,"[25] had been economically supported by men, and was the type of mother who, as her daughter (Kathy) recalls, "would always get other mothers to cover for her" rather than do her share in a parent-cooperative nursery school.[26]

The issue, of course, is not Feinstein, but the anger that festers in women when they believe that women who achieve had to do it all. In reality, a survey done by Catalyst, a woman's advocacy group, found that 85 percent of female executives have domestic help, even though more than a third do not have children. And that more than half had time to pursue personal interests such as golf.[27] This type of information makes many fewer headlines, but it is far more constructive to women whose goal is to break "glass ceilings" and have a balanced personal life without guilt about hiring someone. And it's more likely to leave a successful woman with a husband than is lambasting one's husband in the New York Times for not picking up towels while forgetting to mention he picked up the tab.

Female executives do not do it all—any more than do male executives. Yet the atmosphere of male hatred leads even the world's most responsible media to encourage husband-wife conflict in the name of progress for women, without even asking the husband, "In what way do you contribute?" This atmosphere of women good/men bad—competitive feminism—was catalyzed most in the area of housework by Arlie Hochschild's The Second Shift.

THE HOUSEWORK MYTH THAT HOCHSCHILD BUILT

Here is the central finding of *The Second Shift*—the finding that so effectively created the myth of the second shift that the phrase "the second shift" today makes virtually every "informed" reader worldwide think of women overworking and men overshirking. First I'll look at the myth—or the mess—it created, and then I'll do some spring cleaning.

Myth: *Women work an additional month of twenty-four-hour days every year in comparison to men. Overall, women work two shifts; men work one.*

We will look at this more fully as the chapter evolves, but for starters . . .

Fact: The *Journal of Economic Literature* confirmed that the average woman does work almost seventeen hours more per week inside the home, but also reported that the average man works over twenty hours more per week *outside* the home.[28] In addition, the average man commutes two hours more per week than the average woman.[29] Practically speaking, then, **the *average* man works five hours per week more than the average woman.** And this is despite the fact that men's contribution to housework has never been adequately measured (see The Male Housework List below).

Similarly, the University of Michigan's Survey Research Center found men's *total* workload on the average *exceeded* women's by almost three-and-a-half hours per week (57.8 versus 54.4).[30]

When women earn more income than their husbands, husbands do more housework than their wives.[31] (This is, ironically, mentioned in *The Second Shift*, but obviously not reflected in the headlines about *The Second Shift*.)

Even when the wife works full-time and year-round, the husband provides 65 percent of the household income.[32] (For reasons I begin to explain in *The Myth of Male Power*, men earn more than women not for the same work, but very different work, longer hours, *etc.*)

WHAT ABOUT THE WORKING MOTHER'S JUGGLING ACT?

When we think of the second shift, though, we think especially of the juggling act experienced by the working mother. The working mother's juggling act *is* fact. It is only when it is used to imply that the father does not take on equal—or more than equal—burdens, that it degenerates from fact to myth.

Myth: The working mother has two shifts, but her husband has only one.

Fact: The husbands of working mothers are . . . working fathers. **Fathers' total workload exceeds mothers' by four and a half hours per week** (working fathers': 61.4; working mothers': 56.9).[33] Working mothers do more work in the second shift; working fathers, though, do more work in the first shift. Specifically, **fathers work eleven hours more *outside* the home than mothers,**[34*] plus at least two hours extra commuting.[35]

Myth: When it comes to free time, married women have less than married men; mothers have much less than fathers; and mothers with preschool children? Forget it!

Fact: Married women have almost two more hours of leisure time per week than their husbands. Mothers with children five and older have one hour more of free time per week. To my surprise, ***mothers* with preschool children averaged three hours *more* per week of *free time* than dads with preschool children.**[36]

It surprised me most that mothers with preschool children have more free time than dads until I realized that more than a third of these mothers were full-time moms. And I had to update my image of Dad's contribution: **Dad's free time had *decreased* in recent years by ten hours a week; Mom's by four.**[37]

The nature of a dad's work outside the home also gives him less on-the-job freedom. It is harder for a man on a construction site to stop whenever he wants to take a social call than it is for most moms at home. A man working outside the home has a supervisor who is paid to criticize him if he doesn't produce at 100 percent; no one is paid to criticize a woman working in the home if she doesn't produce at 100 percent, and her husband soon learns it doesn't pay for him to criticize her, either! In essence, work outside the home is subject to scrutiny and demands productivity by obligation; work inside the home is subject to less scrutiny and allows for productivity more by option. Mothers' work has, of course, its parallel special difficulties, from diapers and back talk to never being able to "psychologically check out." But Hochschild covered these and "forgot" dads'. And that's, of course, the issue.

When Hochschild and others "forget" this, it sets the stage not only for women shaming men, but for men generating status by shaming themselves and other men. For example, remember my mentioning Jane Pauley publicly shaming

---

*Note these distinctions: full-time working men work ten hours more than women who work *full* time; working fathers work 11 hours more than working mothers (many of whom work part time); the average man works 20 hours more than the average woman outside the home, since many women don't work outside the home at all.

her husband, Garry Trudeau? Well, Trudeau, in turn, shames other men with cartoons like this:

However, were we aware of only men's contributions, then my parody—not Trudeau's—of the above *Doonesbury* cartoon would make as much sense:

Of course, when we acknowledge both sexes' contributions, then either cartoon without the other makes no sense.

How Did Hochschild Reach Her Conclusion that "Women Work an Extra Month of Twenty-Four Hour Days a Year"?[38]

Hochschild used mostly 1960s data in a 1989 book to "prove" that men weren't doing any more housework in 1989 then they were in the '60s! So **headlines were telling the world that men hadn't changed by citing a book that used data that hadn't changed!**—quarter-century-old data. This created so much anger because by 1990 everyone knew women were working more outside the home; when men supposedly weren't working more *inside* the home, that understandably brewed female fury.

Just think about that—if a man claimed *women* in the '90s hadn't changed since the '60s, and based his claim on '60s data, would the press have made his book into headlines or turned him into hash? Instead, the press specifically presented the data as a current study of men's laziness and women's oppression. (*Time* called the studies she cited "recent"[39] and The *New York Times Book Review* praised it as "of *our time*").[40]

The only possible way *The Second Shift* could have been labeled "recent" is if one counted the tiny "study" of fifty two-job couples that Hochschild conducted herself—with almost all her examples coming from only twelve couples.[41]

This little add-on study not only got the book publicized as "recent," it got it publicized as comparing full-time working women with full-time working men. In fact, **Hochschild studied *mostly* part-time working women,** and still other women who fluctuated between working full-time and part-time and not working at all.[42]

Why is this important? The phrase "second shift" implied that *full*-time working women could not expect husbands to share the housework equally even though they shared income-earning equally. In reality, some of these part-time working women's husbands worked sixty hours a week and were portrayed as insensitive for not sharing the housework with a woman who works twenty hours.

To add insult to injury, instead of the man being credited for his forty-or-so *additional* hours of work on the first shift, he is *blamed* for depriving her of her career. It is this damned-if-you-do/damned-if-you-don't approach that has left many men feeling, well, damned if they do and damned if they don't.

Hochschild's biggest mistake, though, was one made by almost every popularized housework study: not adequately measuring men's contribution to work around the home. For example, if Mom drives the children to daycare, it's called housework; if Dad drives the family to Grandma's, well, that doesn't even count.

Look first at Hochschild's list for women vs. men just below, and then compare it with my "Male Housework List." What do you discover?

THE HOCHSCHILD LIST

CHORES TRADITIONALLY DONE BY WOMEN (A LA HOCHSCHILD)
HOUSEWORK

- "picking up"
- vacuuming
- making beds
- cleaning bathrooms
- doing laundry

- routine meal preparation

- cleanup

- grocery shopping

- sewing

- care for house plants

- care for pets

- dealing with the bank

PARENTING/CHILDCARE

- tending a child while sick

- feeding the child

- bathing the child

- driving the child (*e.g.*, to daycare or to doctors)

- educating the child

- daily discipline of the child

- reading to the child

MANAGEMENT OF DOMESTIC LIFE

- remembering domestic chores and events

- planning domestic chores and events

- scheduling domestic chores and events

- making up the grocery list

- paying bills

- sending birthday and holiday cards

- arranging baby-sitting

- preparing birthday parties for the child

CHORES TRADITIONALLY DONE BY *MEN* (A LA HOCHSCHILD)

- putting out the garbage

- car repairs

- lawn

- household repairs[43]

That concludes Hochschild's list. What is left out of the chores traditionally done by men?

THE "MALE HOUSEWORK LIST" (OR "HONEY DO" LIST), *OR* THE SECOND SHIFT, MALE STYLE

Before we compare this to my "Male Housework List" below, I must tell you that my female friends are genuinely dumbfounded when I ask them to come up with even five categories of "male housework." (Don't worry, most men can't either, even if they *do* them!) If you are a woman, check your gut to see whether you are resistant to seeing the fifty categories of what men do. Some women have told me that, on the one hand, they found themselves laughing incredulously that men could ever be that involved in housework, and on the other hand they didn't want to give up their belief in his laziness, that yes, they were hesitant to give up the . . . er . . . victim power. It's nice to have honest women friends.

The more time a woman spends with this list below, the more *she* will feel valued, appreciated, and less angry. Why? **When a woman sees what a man is also doing for her, she feels him valuing her, just as she values him.** She loses that anger, which emanates from feeling, "He feels his time is worth more than mine."

A woman who commits just a few examples to memory will find men shocked at the appreciation and, therefore, more ready to appreciate her. Men depend on appreciation but consider it boyish to ask for the appreciation.

A woman who wants her "honey do" list done will find it gets done when she appreciates. Men learn from infancy to get a woman's approval by doing what she asks. Men have little trouble doing *if* they get the approval.

If the male housework list is going to serve its purpose—of softening female anger and deepening both sexes' compassion—a few caveats are necessary.

First, notice that much of what men do is also done by mothers who are single, so appreciating what men do also helps us appreciate what single moms do.

Second, women do even more than is on Hochschild's list. I have not created a parallel woman's list because *The Superwoman Syndrome* already contains an excellent one.[44] Although my men's list would make it appear men do even more than the Superwoman Syndrome women, comparing lengths is unfair to women because the chores women do are more frequently done on a daily basis, while men's are more on an "as needed" basis ("Honey, the toilet seems backed up").

Now, the big fallacy of housework studies: the word "housework."

The word "housework" does not trigger an image of what men do. It makes us think of contributions made by women *in* the home (cooking, cleaning, *etc.*). Much of what men do is work *around* the home (*e.g.,* car or roof repairs, outdoor painting and planting, coaching, shoveling snow), not *in* the home. This is true all over the world. What follows, then, is not as much a "male *house*work" list as a list of fifty *categories* of *contributions* men make to the family, most never mentioned. All are in addition to earning money. They make up the second shift, male style. No one has ever studied 90 percent of these categories because professors with a tendency to think so specifically of men's contributions are rarely found; and if found, rarely funded.

Few men keep mental lists of what they do, they just do what is on their lists. Overall, men's style is to do, not talk. But *neither* sex is articulate about what they are not trained to do. Remember how, in the '70s, when women were just beginning to apply for management positions? Interviewers asked them if they had any management experience and the women answered, "No." We helped women who were homemakers make their "management" experience conscious and visible, first to themselves and then to the interviewer with answers such as: "Yes. For twenty years, I managed personnel development, life-and-death decisions, inventory, cash flow, cost benefits, ethical nuances, emergencies, and medical decisions for a small, growing company. I then supervised its merger with other small companies. You may have read about the wedding . . . er, merger . . . in the papers!" Now we need to do the same for men in the area of contributions to the home, so they can talk about it and help others appreciate it.

As you're looking over the male housework list, it will be tempting to respond with "yes, buts," like, "Yes, but in *my* house *I* do the repairs," etc. It is my hope, though, that both my list and the *Superwoman Syndrome* list will be used for mutual appreciation, not tit for tats; and used as a take-off point to create your own family's individualized system for distributing responsibilities. Think of this and the *Superwoman Syndrome* list together as a couple's guide to distributing tasks.

WHAT *PERCENTAGE* OF THE TIME DO YOU VS. YOUR PARTNER DO THESE CHORES?

1. **Activities most likely to break an arm, leg, or neck, or to crack a skull:** In your relationship, who climbs tall ladders or checks out the roof? For example, who uses ladders to do house painting (*e.g.*, reaching for a spot we've missed that's too far away on a homemade scaffold on a windy day), or to clean outside windows; or to go into the attic? Who shovels wet snow off a roof to avoid roof damage, resulting in many men slipping off the roof every winter)?

   A man who falls off a roof or ladder is lucky if he breaks only an arm; some men, though, are paralyzed for life, or killed; others find shoveling snow off a roof leads to problems that get them classified in one of the next two categories.

2. **Activities most likely to trigger heart attacks:** Shoveling snow off a driveway or sidewalk; pushing a car that's out of gas off a crowded street into the gas station; playing tag, soccer, or basketball with the kids for a "little too long" while trying to teach the children that a parent can be a playmate too; or carrying a sleepy child from an upstairs bed to the back-seat of a car and back into bed again without waking up the child, only to find Dad's heartbeat getting erratic and pain thrusting through his arm.

3. **Activities most likely to cause lower back problems and hernia operations:** Moving furniture or twisting his back as he juggles a heavy suitcase into the backseat of a two-door car (or behind other suitcases in a trunk); or trying to carry a TV or a computer up a down staircase; or moving the refrigerator or some file cabinets; or moving tables at a church event or picnic.

4. **Assembly:** Mail-order products, toys, bikes, furniture, bookcases, beds; putting up kids' plastic pools, backyard tents.

5. **Barbecuing:** Shopping for barbecue, charcoal, propane; basting, marinating, cooking; cleaning up of grill, tongs, ashes, *etc.*

6. **Bodyguard: at home** (*e.g.*, who usually checks it out in the middle of the night when you and your partner are awakened by a noise that sounds like someone has just broken into your home, and you know they could have a gun?); **in public places** (who plays bodyguard when nightfall turns a beautiful park into a dangerous park or a quaint side street into a

dangerous alley; or when a lonely hiking trail proves to be a rattlesnake haven; or when a ski slope becomes an avalanche?). We've all read stories of a man saving a woman from a burning house or a raging river or a crashed car. Women often save children in these situations—and even lift cars to save children. Although I've asked over a million people (on TV and radio) to send me a story of a woman risking her life to save an *adult* man, so far, no stories. **Every time a woman and man walk together in a public place, he unconsciously serves as an unpaid bodyguard.**[45]

7. **Camping:** It starts with taking psychological responsibility for avoiding disaster (checking weather predictions and safety of the location, buying correct tent and camping gear, taking responsibility for not getting lost, knowing how to use compass, *etc.*), then carrying the primary backpack (often including the stove and a kerosene lamp), erecting the tent, digging drainage trenches, gathering firewood, building the fire, hoisting food away from animals. **The man is often the camping home buyer, home mover, and homemaker.**

8. **Car buying:** Price negotiation, *Consumer Guide/Blue Book*–type research.

9. **Car maintenance and repair:** Checking hoses, belts, tire pressures, vacuuming inside, applying Armor All; comparisons of prices with mechanics, tire changing (see also Emergencies).

10. **Carpentry:** From putting up shelves (in garage, basement, and closets) to repairing loose fence slats, to making bookcases, to building a doghouse.

11. **Christmas:** Putting up lights on house and tree; tree purchase, set-up, dismantling and disposal; retrieving boxes of ornaments from dusty attic or storage area.

12. **"Male cleaning":** Car washing (and waxing); cleaning all painting tools for reuse (brushes, rollers, pans, guides); cleaning out the basement, attic, fireplace and gutters (the darkest, dirtiest, hottest and coldest parts of the house); cleaning filters of air conditioning and heating units; cleaning yard; bathing of dogs; and, if there's a pool or Jacuzzi. . . . (See also: Barbecuing; Diaper Changing, Male Equivalents of; Guns and Weapons; Activities most likely to break. . . .)

13. **Coaching-as-child care:** Baseball (T-Ball, CAP Leagues, Little League), softball (*e.g.,* Bobby Soxers), football (Pop Warner), roller hockey, field hockey, ice hockey, soccer; more informal coaching-as-child care via "playing together" in basketball, or throwing, catching, and hitting a ball;

instructions in individualized sports such as tennis; instructions in self-defense (aikido, boxing, wrestling).

14. **Computer buying:** Researching best hardware and software; comparing prices, new vs. used markets, *etc.*

15. **Confrontations—with neighbors or strangers:** "Go tell the neighbors their dog's barking too loud." Or, you've just gotten into a car accident with a stranger; who approaches the other driver when everyone is emotionally off center?

16. **Dead animal disposal:** DAD quickly comes to mean Dead Animal Disposer when the gerbil dies, the rat's been trapped, when the mouse has been lead into temptation, or when the dog's been run over and the street has blood all over. What's worse for some dads, though, is having to kill the almost-dead animal—when DAD means *Dying* Animal Disposer.

17. **Decks:** Building, sanding, staining, sealing.

18. **Diaper changing, male equivalents of:** Plunging a backed-up toilet; wiping up a child's vomit when carsick on a vacation; cleaning up after dog doo from own dog and neighbors'.

19. **Digging:** Holes and ditches, removing of boulders, tree stumps, *etc.*

20. **Dinner when company's visiting:** Meat carving, wine opening, cocktail making (careful guys, most women still do most everything else when company's visiting).

21. **Disciplining of kids:** "Wait till Daddy comes home."

22. **Dragon-killing—modern version:** Swatting flies, stepping on roaches, squishing spiders—all without a sword (or, for pacifist performers, removing the spider without hurting it!).

23. **Driving:** To and from functions that both sexes go to together, especially when conditions are hazardous (*e.g.,* when caught in rush hour in a strange city; when caught in snow on an icy mountain road; when caught in heavy rain, wind, and fog at night, or when in a foreign country), or when both are exhausted or have had a bit too much to drink; on long trips, especially late at night while the family sleeps; or on a motorcycle (have you ever seen a woman on a motorcycle with a man hanging on?). The automobile and motorcycle are the modern-day white horse. Like the man on the white horse, his role involves more accidents; the man on the white horse, though, never had to worry about a DUI citation!

24. **Emergency prevention:** *In home* (*e.g.,* noticing and repairing frayed wires, plugs, sockets, smoke detectors); *in car* (putting chains on tires; being certain all the cars' fluids [oil, transmission, anti-freeze] are being changed on schedule, tool kit and flares are adequate, flashlight has batteries, *etc.*); *via nature* (battening down windows, putting sand bags in the trunk before a blizzard, making sure trees aren't creating a hazard to house or people should a storm arise), *on the town* (making sure there's cash in the wallet and gas in the car).

25. **When emergencies arise despite prevention:** Sandbagging; changing a tire on a cold night in the rain on a dangerous part of the road in the bad part of town; taking the walk for five gallons of gas when the car runs out; or risking putting the battery cable on the wrong side of the battery.

26. **Post-emergencies:** Roof repair (shingles, holes, leaks, *etc.*); removal of fallen trees and branches; rebuilding and repairing after damage; or arranging for, supervising and helping with rebuilding and repair.

27. **Fences:** Building fences from stone or wood, or installing a wire fence.

28. **Fire building, wood chopping and carting wood** indoors while not getting the carpet dirty.

29. **Garbage:** Real men take out the garbage because, you see, it's in their genes to know how to use the garbage can cover as a shield should anything happen in that journey from the castle to the street. If he takes out the recycled items and the garden waste, it's just because he wants to protect his turf of being the garbage man (excuse me, waste management engineer).

30. **Gas/electric failures:** Resetting clocks and circuit switches; relighting pilot lights; troubleshooting.

31. **Gift-giving as a contribution to maintaining the romance:** We often say men aren't romantic, but we forget that it is men who are more likely to give the flowers she likes; the diamonds with the right 4 Cs (carat size, clarity, cut and color [then he worries about the 5th C—cost]); the earrings with the hypoallergenic studs; the perfume with the scent she prefers; the right-size ring for the correct finger with the right stone and her preferred cut; or to choose a restaurant that fits her definition of romantic, arranging the occasion, taking her there, and paying. Many a man has never had even one of these things done for him by even one woman one time (just as some women have never had a man do their laundry, cook a meal, or even make a cup of tea).

32. **Guns and weapon:** Purchase, cleaning, usage, and safety for protecting family from thieves in city and from animals in rural areas.

33. **Hanging:** Of heavy pictures, wall hangings, clocks, phones (especially when molly bolts, toggle bolts, or drywall or plastic anchors are necessary).

34. **Installation/hook-up:** Of washer, dryer, computer, TV, cables, and antennas.

35. **Life insurance:** Purchasing and choice of carrier.

36. **Risky investment management** (stocks, joint ventures, rental property): The investments that inspire blame when they fail and induce stress even when they succeed.

37. **Opening:** Jars, doors, big boxes, paint cans, windows that are stuck or frozen.

38. **Option generating:** In many couples, the man generates the options, the woman generates the rejections. For example, he asks, "Where would you like to go for dinner?" She answers, "Anywhere." "Chinese?" he offers. "We just had that," she reminds. "Italian?" "Too heavy." "How about that new place—what's its name?" he tries. "I hear that's expensive." When it comes to restaurants and to movies, the man often generates the options and the woman often selects even immediately after she's said, "It makes no difference." Option-generating often involves having one's ideas rejected, which can be emotionally taxing.

39. **Painting:** Inside and outside of the home, and the laying down of masking tape, sheets, and other painting preparation (See also: Male cleaning and Activities most likely to break an arm . . .).

40. **Patio and sidewalk making:** And sealing over cracks, requiring cement mixing, building of frame, making it level, and living with every mistake because it's "laid on concrete."

41. **Planting:** New trees, bushes, larger plants.

42. **Plastering, spackling, grouting, caulking, and mortaring:** And creating the plaster, spackle, grout and mortar mixtures.

43. **Poisons, exposure to:** Use of insecticides to spray for ants and roaches; or to spray trees, flowers, garden vegies.

44. **Programming:** The VCR ("Honey, before we leave, I can't miss the special on male housework; would you program the VCR?"), or the CD player, the telephone speed dial.

45. **Pumping gas, paying for gas, changing oil:** When there's both a man and woman in the car, I notice men pump the gas about 80 percent of the time in Northeast & West Coast urban areas and university towns, and almost 100 percent of the time anywhere else.

46. **Reading the business and financial pages:** To get a feel for business trends that may affect career decisions and information related to investment decisions (which may just look like him "goofing off reading the paper" but is the equivalent of a woman reading recipes in *Better Homes & Gardens* or *Family Circle* [still the best selling magazines to women]). On the other hand, guys, the *sports* pages don't count!

47. **Remodeling:** Taking down walls, putting in windows, finishing garage or basement, and, for better men than I, building entire new rooms.

48. **Repairs:** Toilets, faucets, plumbing, electrical, window screens, sliding glass and screen doors, problems with cabinets, doors, etc.

49. **Sharpening:** Knives, mower blades, pruning shears.

50. **Shopping for:** Paint, hardware, lumber, spackle, lawnmower, tools, much of the "bulk" shopping (Office Depot, Home Depot, Price Club, CostCo, etc.) (See Also: Computer buying; Car buying; Stereo and video buying; and Life insurance, for additional "Male Shopping" categories).

51. **Stereo and video buying:** Hooking up, troubleshooting, repair arranging, and supervising.

52. **Toy and bike care:** Oiling, painting, and fixing kids' bikes, swing sets, jungle gyms, merry-go-rounds, and other outdoor play equipment.

53. **Weather guard:** Guarding a woman against exposure to rain, sleet, and snow by forfeiting his jacket to a woman who is cold even when he is also cold; walking between a woman and a street in which cars and trucks might splash water or slush onto their clothes; scraping ice and snow off a car windshield on a freezing morning; dropping the family off at a restaurant or movie when it's pouring, then parking and walking to the restaurant or theater in the rain (especially if no one has an umbrella); warming up the car before the family gets in it; bringing in the newspaper on a rainy morning; salting the driveway, sidewalk, and stairs when the rain has frozen over, so that if anyone falls, he does. (See Also: "Activities most likely to trigger heart attacks" and "Emergency" categories).

54. **Yard work:** Lawn mowing, fertilizing, weeding, clipping, leaf raking, tree trimming, etc.

So if men do all this, why don't we know about it? In part because instead of complaining, men *offer* to carry the luggage, barbecue, build the shelves, or shop for the stereo. And in part because we perform our roles unconsciously, as with our bodyguard role; it's hard to complain about that of which we're unconscious. Complaining is the shadow side of consciousness. But men were secretly hoping for the lighter side: appreciation and love . . . but someone took the appreciation and love out to the garbage.

Hopefully this list destroys some myths that create anger toward men, and creates instead some of the following understandings.

Myth: *Women's housework is unappreciated.*

Fact: Both sexes' housework is unappreciated, because we all see more of what we do than we see of what our partner does. The fact that virtually every housework study lists most of women's housework even as it neglects about 90 percent of the "Men's Housework List" means men's housework is especially unappreciated.

The frequency with which we hear "women's housework is unappreciated" is actually evidence of its appreciation. Men will feel a lot more appreciated when we're also saying "men's housework is unappreciated."

Myth (Part I): *Women's Housework is Unpaid.*

In the words of the U.N.'s *Report, "Most* of women's work is unpaid." (emphasis mine)"[47]

Fact (Part I): The Men's Housework List makes it apparent that both sexes do housework for which they are unpaid, and both sexes' housework "pays" their partner.

That is, a traditional wife's labor pays her husband because he would either have to pay for it himself or do it himself. Conversely, *his* housework is work for which she would otherwise have to pay or do herself. Most important, the money he earns "pays" for her better home & gardens and family circle, which she generally enjoys (and has more time to enjoy) more than he. Since divorce more often makes their home *her* home, then all his labor often becomes her living space. And should they divorce, community property and divorce settlements are also more likely to make her home his mortgage payments. (The word "mortgage," interestingly, is from the Latin, meaning "death pledge.")

Myth: *Countries' GNPs measure men's work, not women's.*

Fact: Countries' GNPs do not include either sex's contributions to housework.

When the U.N.'s official publication tells us that only women's work is un-paid and that countries' Gross National Products need to be refigured to incor-porate women's unpaid housework, that is a sexist recommendation: If it is to be refigured, it needs to incorporate both sexes' unpaid work. Much of this work, like financial consulting, is worth more per hour in the marketplace than house cleaning; some of it, like someone who will check for a thief in response to your nudge at 3 A.M., while you remain in bed, to see if they're stabbed, is hard to find in the yellow pages. Men can't buy it at any price.

Myth: *"Women's work" requires women to always be "on call."*

Fact: Both sexes are "on call," each in their traditional areas of respon-sibility.

Men also are "on call": for repairs, for moving or lifting furniture, as unpaid bodyguards, as weather guards, as openers of jars, as solvers of emergencies (honey, the roof is leaking!).

Myth: *Women take responsibility, men just help with the housework.*

Fact: It is rare for either sex to truly share psychological responsibility for the type of housework traditionally done by the other sex.

A man may change the diapers in the middle of the night, but a woman is more likely to lose sleep worrying over whether the baby is sick and what should be done. That's an indication she is taking primary psychologically responsibility for the baby—even if he is technically doing more diaper changing. Conversely, if not enough money is coming in, a woman may be helping with the income—she may even be producing more income—but Dad is more likely to lose sleep worrying what he's going to do to pay the doctors' bills, mortgage, and insurance. Rather than quit a job he hates that earns this income, he will "tough it out." Drinking, drugs, or fits of anger are often signs he is feeling psychologically re-sponsible for more than he can cope with, and more than he can express. When he feels he will fulfill this psychological responsibility more via his insurance pol-icy than his life, he is a candidate for suicide.

Myth: *"A man may work from sun to sun, but a woman's work is never done."*

Interestingly, although this is the original myth, when we check the head-lines I've listed above, we can see that women are now portrayed *both* as working from sun to sun *and* doing work that is never done. Our prior acknowledgment of men as working from sun to sun has faded with the sunset and never reappeared.

Fact: By seeing how men are also "on call" twenty-four hours a day, and also share psychological responsibility that haunts them while they're sleeping, we destroy the myth that only a woman's work is never done.

Myth: *Men think marriage entitles them to a domestic slave.*

Articles in women's magazines and guests on Oprah and Sally often complain, "Somehow my husband could do his own laundry when he was single, but he seemed to think the diamond came with the plug to the washing machine."

Fact: Both sexes expect their partner to do chores they used to do themselves before marriage . . . so the real issue is how marriage tempts both sexes into a division of labor.

For example, women take out their own garbage when they live by themselves, but in a relationship, if we see a woman taking out the garbage, that usually means there's no man home, or he forgot. Similarly, women drive under dangerous conditions when they drive alone, but usually men do it when they're a couple. But men don't even think of saying, "My wife could risk an accident driving in fog, ice, or rush hours when she was single, but as soon as I gave her the diamond, she thought it came with rights to a chauffeur."

Some men in dual-earner couples feel her housework has become his and hers, while his remains his. One man put it especially well. "While work in these traditionally women's areas has slopped over into my bailiwick, the reverse is not true. I am still on call 'round the clock when a drain does not work. There's nothing magical about unclogging a toilet; not much upper-body strength is required. But you'd better believe that only I get called on to do it. When all the females in my house talked me into bringing my daughter's class hamster home during Christmas, it was I who waded through the rodent droppings to clean the cage. And I'm the only one in the house who can empty a mousetrap.

"For the record, I am a 6-foot, 200-pound, romping, stomping black male. I can't believe I'm rare. I'm not the perfect husband, and my wife assures me that I'm no treasure."[48]

By looking at the "Male Housework List" *plus* men's extra work time, *plus* men's extra commuting time, *plus* men's greater likelihood to bring more work home and take more hazardous jobs, we understand that the real issue is not the husband expecting wife-as-slave, but both husband and wife expecting a division of labor. To be sure, the sexes divide labor much less than we used to, but constructing this list made me realize the sexes still divide labor much more than we think we do, especially after children arrive.

Overall, as a rule, men's demands are fewer: We hear about wives' "Honey Do" lists for their husbands, but not about husbands' "Honey Do" lists for their wives. Most men's attitude toward a wife who works even *part* time is more laissez-faire: "If she cooks dinner, I love it; if she microwaves a frozen dinner, okay; if she wants to order in pizza or Chinese, fine; if she wants to go out, that's okay, too." If he has something to eat and drink, his loved one in his arms, and a remote in his hand, he's not making "honey do" lists.

Myth: *Single moms do the chores of both sexes.*

Fact: Both sexes, when a single parent, do *some* of the chores of the other sex.

Both sexes often do nontraditional chores when they are single, or a single parent (or when the other sex is unavailable). Interestingly, though, single dads will typically do fast food with their kids. Single women and single moms often get others to do repairs and "male-type" chores. Near my home in San Diego, I occasionally see a truck for a handyman business called "Honey Dos." (In other places it's called "Hire a Husband.") Other single moms persuade fathers, sons, boyfriends, hopeful boyfriends, or neighbors (or neighbors who are hopeful boyfriends!).

Myth: *Men will always do the physical chores because men are so much stronger physically.*

Fact: An Army study found that the average woman civilian volunteer could lift 70 percent of what the average active-duty military man could lift prior to twenty-four weeks of training; after the training, the civilian women averaged 91 percent of what the active-duty military men lifted.[49]

We can increase our daughter's self-sufficiency and decrease the Female Incompetency Defense by telling her it is as much a sign of "being a lady" to help a boy with his luggage as it is a sign of being a gentleman to help a girl with hers. This will help her also build her muscles, rather than having only boys build theirs, which creates the self-fulfilling prophecy that boys are so much stronger that we can just expect them to be girls' luggage carriers, as we would expect of a mule.

Myth: *Women nurture men—they even "mother" them; men don't nurture women.*

Fact: Both sexes nurture each other in different ways. Women's way is called nurturing; men's way is culturally invisible.

One danger of a woman believing that only *she* nurtures her husband is that it makes the woman "feel like his mother," and that feeling desexualizes her.

A man who makes it clear that nurturance is a two-way street will both allow a woman to know how she is being loved and free her from the desexualization that accompanies feeling like a mother. (Finally, an incentive for men to speak up!) For example, the man who digs up a garden to make it easier for a woman to plant a rosebush contributes his form of nurturance even as she contributes hers. The man who drives under dangerous conditions late at night while his wife is sleeping in the passenger seat is nurturing her; when he takes care of killing the mice, spiders, and flies, he nurtures the woman *by freeing her from having to confront the killer in her psyche;* the man who adds a bedroom to the house provides a more beautiful space in which she can care for and nurture herself every night.

If a woman drove, pumped the gas and paid while her husband relaxed in the passenger seat, and if she repaired a flat while he looked on, she might complain, "I feel like his mother." Yet when men do these things for women, they don't complain, "I feel like her father."

The best way to use these lists to replace anger with love in real life is to nurture each other by doing for your partner what your partner normally does for you. I am sad when I hear of a man who has never fixed his wife a cup of tea, or, if she prefers coffee, doesn't know how she likes it. I remember a woman friend of mine getting ready to go out. As she was changing, she spilled something on her skirt. When she returned and saw that I had handwashed her skirt and hung it up to dry, she was so touched that she burst into tears. She had never been nurtured *in that way* before. Similarly, when a woman has bought me flowers or taken me to a nice restaurant for absolutely no reason, I am touched in some unexplainable way. And it increases my respect for her. (Note that I've never known a woman to burst into tears of appreciation when I've picked up a restaurant tab; and I'm appreciative, but not *as* appreciative, if a woman washes a shirt on which I've sprayed some marinara sauce. The point is that **doing for others as they usually do for you is more touching than doing the usual.**)

So I hope using both the list in *The Superwoman Syndrome* and mine together inspires role reversals and appreciation—that they are used in discussions with Part I listening skills, thus creating love, not war.

FOUR MISTAKES HOUSEWORK STUDIES MAKE

The least responsible housework studies will continue to make the headlines and generate anger toward men if we are too ignorant of their flaws to confront the media with them. Here's a guideline to help you understand the journalist's bias the next time you read about men working less.

THE SEXISM OF THE WORD "HOUSEWORK"

We now know that the word "housework" does not trigger men's memory of re-modeling, coaching, driving, or virtually any male contributions, so when we see a Harris poll saying women do more housework we can immediately see the sexism.[50]

The categories must be specific. A vague category like "Cleaning" rarely makes men recall when they cleaned the gutters, fireplace, or paint brushes. Similarly, "Shopping" rarely makes men recall shopping for tools or lumber, for stereos or VCRs, for computers or cars, or even "bulk" item shopping. Examples must list a range of traditional male chores.

Men's housework is also more seasonal and is therefore more easily forgotten in the off-seasons. So when a pollster asks in July how much housework he does, he doesn't think of shoveling snow.

Because men's housework changes from project to project, it is more easily forgotten once the project is completed, regardless of the season.

Add the three biases together, and a man who coached his daughter's soccer team in July and is asked about the housework he does in December doesn't think of coaching—the project is long done, it's another season, and the word housework would never have triggered it anyway. Yet it may have been a turning point in his daughter's life.

THE "TYPICAL DAY" FALLACY

In *The Second Shift,* Hochschild asked women and men "Can you tell me about your typical day?"[51] From this she derived the list of housework we saw above. **The "typical day" question is biased against men because men's chores are not done on a typical day—they are done "as needed."** The man does not repair the toilet on a typical day, he does it "as needed"; ditto for mowing the lawn and virtually every one of the fifty categories on the men's housework list. Which is why 96 percent of men's contributions never made Hochschild's list.

THE DIARY'S BENIGN NEGLECT

Notice that "driving the child to daycare or to doctor" is on Hochschild's list. So the type of driving women are more likely to do is on Hochschild's list. But the type of driving a man is more likely to do—driving the family on the weekend—isn't on Hochschild's list. Would it be on the list of someone who used the diary method to measure contributions to the home?

The diary method is considered the most reliable because it asks the woman and the man to list what he or she does each hour of the day. However, in the driving example, a man's diary entry for Saturday, 6:00 to 7:00 P.M. might be, "Went with the kids to their grandparents'." "Went with the kids" could not be translated by the diary researcher into "father drove," because the researcher has no right to presume the dad drove. Similarly, the dad might also have packed the trunk and pumped gas, and would be unlikely to mention it. So three male contributions become none—even in the diary—because men are unconscious of thinking of them as something worth volunteering.

For these reasons, even diary researchers need to educate themselves as to how men's contributions are camouflaged and to help men bring their unconscious contributions to the conscious level by including consciousness joggers like the Male Housework List.

WOMEN-ONLY INTERVIEWS

The most dangerous of recent trends is concluding how much each sex works by polling only women, as in the recent Women's Sports Foundation study.[52] This is like asking only Republicans *or* Democrats which party works harder for the country.

HUFF, PUFF, AND BLOW THE HOUSEWORK MYTH DOWN

One finding *The Second Shift* popularized was that men do only seventeen minutes of housework per day. Let's look at the facts.

Myth: *Men haven't changed—they still do only seventeen minutes of housework per day[53]—the same as they did in 1965.[54]*

Fact: Even in 1965, men's contribution to housework and child care was an hour and a half per day on weekdays,[55] and three hours a day on his days off.[56] And it's gone way up since then.[57]

The media publicized Hochschild's seventeen-minute per day figure without checking it out. But when Joe Pleck, then at the Wellesley Center for Research on Women went to Hochschild's source,[58] he was surprised to find that this figure was based on two fundamental errors:

- It excluded all the time these employed dads spent on housework during the weekends. The seventeen-minute figure was actually the time spent by employed fathers only on *workdays*.[59]

- Hochschild totally ignored all men's contributions to repairs, paying bills, and other administrative activities. She *excluded* the larger of the study's two categories of housework.[60] Sound a bit like the U.N.?

When I double-checked these figures to be sure it was not Pleck who was wrong, I myself was amazed to find that Hochschild had excluded men's child care.

So what happens when we look at what the mid-'60s man did when weekends and weekdays are averaged together and when categories like repairs and child care are included? **The alleged seventeen-minute man was actually the one-and-a-half-hour-a-day man on his workdays, and the 3-hour-a-day man on his days off.**[61] And the mid-'60s was the era in which almost all married men with children provided 90 to 100 percent of the income for the entire family; when commuting from a suburb into a city took my dad, for example, an additional 3 to 4 hours round-trip, door-to-door every day—a trip so common that all our neighbors' homes in Waldwick, New Jersey (just outside New York) had only one-car garages . . . a car used by the wives while the husbands took some combination of trains, buses, and subways.

Hochschild was disingenuous in a number of other ways. Here are three of the most blatant:

- She never tells her reader that even the study she cites showed that the great majority of women had total workloads that were *less* than men's.[62]

- She tells us that according to a 1965 study, men have more leisure time.[63] Not quite. She tells us only of working mothers—the only group who had less leisure time than their husbands (by four minutes per day). She does not tell us, for example, that the same study found that 1965 housewives with children had 346 more minutes of leisure time per week than their husbands.[64]

- At one point Hochschild acknowledges that the main study she cited was outdated, but says another study showed that men were doing no more housework since 1965.[65] So I looked up that "other study," also by John Robinson. It said the opposite: Women were now doing much less housework, and men much more. In fact, between 1965 and 1985, men increased their housework 147 percent.[66]

Each fact in isolation has little impact. It is the pervasiveness of such women-as-victim findings that leaves us with an impression remembered long after the facts are forgotten. That is what creates the Big Lie.

When I introduce these data manipulations to leading feminists, their response is *not,* "Oh, I didn't realize that—that makes me feel better about men; I'll be sure to double-check what you're saying, and if it's true, to never repeat the false stereotype of men as deadbeats." Rather, the most common response is, "How can you be so naive as to trust what men say about how much men work?" Notice there is not a second's acknowledgment, just a transfer of the focus of male bashing from men as deadbeats to men as liars; but, because the response is so common, I checked that, too. Are men liars?

Myth: *Men exaggerate the amount of work they do. Women work more than they acknowledge.*

Fact: Women report three times as much child care as they themselves record in the more accurate diaries.[67] In contrast, men report only half as much time spent on home repairs and alterations as they actually do.[68]

Women in the workplace are also much more likely to overestimate the hours they work than are men.[69] **Women's average overestimation was approximately six hours per week more than men's average overestimation.**[70] Among women and men who said they worked fifty-five-hour workweeks, women's overestimation was almost double that of men's.[71] (In my forthcoming 25 Ways to Higher Pay, I look at the enormous implications of these findings.)

Okay, guys, before you get on your high horse and accuse women of being the bigger liars, remember that a woman can be watching TV with her daughter and simultaneously have a casserole in the oven, laundry in the dryer, and dishes in the dishwasher for one hour and legitimately claim "one hour child care," "one hour cooking," "one hour laundry," "one hour clean up," or a total of four hours housework in a one hour time slot. Most men find it difficult to simultaneously repair the roof and mow the lawn. The nature of the different responsibilities women and men undertake makes it much easier for a woman to exaggerate the number of hours she worked.

In contrast, men who underestimate their workplace hours are not just being modest. Researchers interviewing men who said they were unemployed would often get interrupted by the man saying he had to leave to work. When the interviewer responded, "I thought you were unemployed" the man affirmed "I *am* unemployed—I just work twenty hours a week." The researchers discovered that men who worked thirty hours or less often categorized themselves as unemployed.[72] For many men, the shame of being underemployed creates the feeling of being unemployed.

Interestingly, both men's and women's tendency to overestimate the workweek has increased over time—but even more so for women.[73] People who work over forty work hours are progressively more inaccurate.[74] Even more fascinating, all three of these trends also hold true in other countries as well, such as Russia.[75]

Myth (Part II): *"Women's work" is unpaid.*

I promised above that I would look at six ways that men pay for the work of married women playing the traditional role.

Fact (Part II): *"Women's work" is paid—in at least six ways.*

1. THE MAN'S PAYCHECK

Item. Hillary Clinton's personal income in 1995 was $0.[76] Yet she lives in a very White House, has bodyguards (men paid to die before she's even hurt), limos, Air Force One, and gets better free food than her husband seems to eat.

A married man's income is not for *him,* it is for the *family.* If he earns three-quarters of the income, he pays three-quarters of the bills. Sometimes more. "His" income becomes *their* home and garden, *their* cars and car insurance, and mostly *her* doctor and therapist bills.[77] Their combined income is about seven times more likely to be spent on *her* personal items (bracelets, rings, earrings, mascara, and more shoes, makeup and designer labels than most men care that women wear) than his.[78]

When a woman cooks and cleans every day for a man, it is only when her husband pays her. We can see from the high number of divorces following a man's continued unemployment, that when a man does not pay a woman, a woman sometimes does not cook and clean for him. And as we have seen, when women earn more income than their husbands, it is the husbands who do more housework than their wives.[79]

2. BY INCREASING HER LIFE EXPECTANCY MANY TIMES FASTER THAN HIS

No payment can be greater than the payment of life. We hear much about how women's labor nurtures men, but little about how men's traditional role led to women's life expectancy going from one year longer than men's in 1920 to seven years longer today.[80] Men's role has increased women's lives by creating cures for almost all contagious diseases, better public sanitation, labor-saving washing machines and dishwashers, the birth control pill, and breech-birth techniques, anesthesia, central heating, computer chips. . . .

3. Giving Her the Freedom To Love

A husband's income often gives his wife the option of being paid to love. That is, only a quarter of married women work full-time during the first five years after a child is born.[81] The remaining three-quarters either do not work at all outside the home or work part-time. His willingness to obligate himself to the workplace gives her the option to be paid to love. As a result, Mom is there when the baby takes her first step: Dad only hears about it second hand. Her pay is even greater when a couple divorces and she gets the children.

The more she is paid to love and nurture, the more her personality becomes more nurturing, and the more he feels pressure to not confront his boss about what he really thinks, to be more tempted to compromise ethics lest he should jeopardize his children's and wife's security and ability to love each other. His personality is also altered. By age forty-five, he may look in the mirror and realize he's become someone he doesn't really like. Often his wife agrees. Only she has been paid to love.

4. Risking His Life To Increase Her Comfort

We saw from the Male Housework List how men often risk their lives so their wives don't have to risk theirs. Most men I know who have back problems have aggravated them by moving furniture, often while a woman he loved directed. When he checks out a roof or paints a house he is often allowing her to be safe while he puts himself at risk. This is men's way of "paying" women for their contribution.

5. The Creation of the Multi-Option Wife

If three-quarters of wives with young children do not work full-time, what about wives who do work full-time? Do they have more options than their husbands? Well, their husband's greater commitment to the workplace leads to the men producing approximately two-thirds of the family income.[82] This is because women choose jobs that are less hazardous, with more flexible hours, shorter commutes, and higher fulfillment. The "return" for women doing more housework is, then, the choice of jobs that pay less because they require fewer sacrifices.

On the other hand, she can choose to pursue a career—to obligate herself to producing enough income to support a family by pursuing jobs that pay more. When I do radio shows, I often ask men and women to call in to tell me whether they would be comfortable having a husband care for the children while a woman provided the income. Many men say "yes"; it is much rarer to get a call from a woman who is okay with that.

"Burn-out" classes are attended almost exclusively by women—often by women whose husband's income is allowing them to take off a year or two "to find meaning." The only time I have seen a wife's income supply this option for a man is after a heart attack and, even then, they were living off a savings produced mostly from his income. This is not because women do not make a crucial contribution. But it is unfair to suggest that women are not compensated for their contribution.

6. Post-Divorce, She Is Protected More than He, Either by His Income or Government Income

Item. A friend of mine earns over $70,000 a year, but lives in a small apartment and feels deprived of his children. Although he would love the children and their home, his ex has both the children and their comfortable three-bedroom home. After child support, alimony, and taxes, he has less than $10,000 to pay for his rent, food, and bills.

If a divorce occurs, he may still continue to pay her even though she does *not* continue to do housework for him. And the woman is more likely than he to have the home while he has the mortgage payments; to have the children while he has child-support payments.

Even the single mother in poverty does not quite have her housework and child care go unpaid. Few people are aware that only one-quarter of *un*married women with children under five work thirty-five hours or more in the workplace.[83] Studies of the combined benefits of Aid to Families with Dependent Children payments, food stamps, Women, Infant and Children payments, Medicaid, housing, utilities, and commodities, allotments find that for a single mother with two children, the pre-tax wage that would be necessary to match the welfare package was between $23,000 and $36,400 in the eleven most-generous states as well as the District of Columbia.[84] Of course, most women accepting aid only receive some of these benefits, and many do not receive what they deserve in child support, but the degree to which men are producing this income via taxes is the degree to which this is another indirect way in which men pay women collectively when they have failed to pay women individually.

SINGLE-MOM SYNDROME

I mentioned above that much of what men do is also done by single mothers. A mother who becomes single without realizing what her husband contributed is on the short route to a place called stress. For example, since a dad who is good at balancing nurturance, rough-housing, and discipline is often not very good at explaining how he does it, Mom sees discipline disintegrate after divorce, assumes the only problem is the divorce, compensates by being easier on the child, and compounds the problem. Thus, with the kids running the show, she is overwhelmed. It is difficult for a divorced woman to say to her ex, "I didn't realize you were contributing so much to the children's lives until you were gone. Would you give me a hand?"

I have seen small events—like a toilet breaking down—trigger outbursts of tears, hurt, and resentment in many of my single mom friends who were in a state of overwhelm. Part of this, of course, is the failure of her dream of "a family forever." But sometimes another portion comes from a feeling; "Damn, *I'm* not supposed to be repairing toilets—*he* is." It occasionally helps, after the tears have been received with empathy, for her to feel what her response would be to her ex saying, "Oh, thanks for dropping the kids by. Would you pick up my dirty underwear before you leave?"

Single mothers who don't have husbands to do the "male housework" often find themselves moving closer to their dads—or never moving away from their dads—or relying on male neighbors, or male friends. Each of these creates separate problems, especially for the woman who is unconscious of men's housework and, therefore, unconscious of the trade-offs and the deals she is making to get that housework done.

Single mothers who keep their dad actively in their lives often resent their dad's judgments and interference. They resent themselves for feeling unable to sever their ties, for being dependent, for "not growing up."

Single moms who rely on male friends for repairs—"he's just a repair friend"—are often unaware that the man really isn't sacrificing his Sunday afternoon in exchange for a Sunday night dinner. The truth is, if he's making that type of sacrifice, it's usually because he's interested in her. I've seen many single moms have men who they claim are "just friends" work on their cars, do repairs, help them move. They think nothing of it. (Which says it all.) When she starts dating someone seriously, the "repair friend" feels hurt and her new boyfriend feels suspicious. And Mom feels caught between a rock and a hard place, so to speak.

The solution? Imagine her new boyfriend spending all Sunday afternoon with a woman who's "just helping me cook, clean and do my laundry. It's nothing." She would dump *him* before she emptied the rest of the garbage! Sometimes these single moms even had sex with these men "in the past"; yet, if her boyfriend had had sex "in the past" with this woman . . . well, he'd be *in* the garbage!

I believe two things are going on when a woman has a "repair friend." First, on some level she knows he is courting her, and thus feels entitled to having a man who is courting her do more for her than she returns. Second, her unwillingness to give as much acknowledgment to the sacrifices involved in "male housework" as in "female housework" makes her less conscious of how she is using him. If she were spending half-days cooking or cleaning for a guy she hoped would show some interest, friends would make her wonder if she were being "used" or if she was a "doormat."

This attitude rests on a deeper foundation. Just as women who are poor turn to the government as a substitute husband (in the form of welfare and AFDC payments), so women without husbands often unconsciously turn to substitute husbands, such as dads, "repair friends," and male neighbors.

If that's the case, where do we go from here?

WHERE DO WE GO FROM HERE?

Turning anger into understanding involves more than changing the biases of housework studies; it involves starting with the media's process of selecting which studies become the headlines.

Bias: The media's tendency to make headlines out of the most anti-male studies without double-checking the facts or the methodology to the degree they would if the study concluded that men work longer.

Change: Because women-as-victim headlines, like "Women's Work Is Never Done," sell better than a headline saying "Men Overworked," the media will have to be confronted directly with their accusations of bias. This may mean careful studies showing patterns of bias, followed by sit-ins and boycotts by readers, and challenges to hire reporters as open to men's issues and male positive studies as to women's issues.

Meantime, circulating responsible studies via the Internet is more viable since a profit is not required. PBS and NPR (National Public Radio) are probably the most vulnerable to challenge because their use of public funding for programs focusing almost exclusively on women's needs (in the area of gender) leaves them in potential violation of FCC fairness regulations and the Fourteenth Amendment's constitutional mandate to provide equal protection under the law for both sexes.

Turning anger into love also involves challenging the biases in the housework studies themselves. Here are the biases and some solutions.

Bias: Sometimes, just the word housework is used to inquire about both sexes' contribution to work around the house, or the examples are mostly of traditional women's housework.

Change: Examples of the work men do around the house need to be even more specifically listed than women's.

Bias: I know of no survey that measures the greater *"quantitative* options" that married women with children are more likely to exercise. For example, married women with children who feel "burned out" often exercise the *option* of cutting back the *number* of hours they work, or they take a job that requires less commuting.

Change: Each survey should measure each sex's quantitative options with a question such as, "Could you take a job working less than thirty-five hours per week without creating a conflict with your spouse?"

Bias: I know of no survey that measures the greater *"qualitative* options" that married women with children are more likely to exercise. For example, married women rarely consider taking a hazardous job like driving a cab, a truck, or being a construction worker; or certain types of tedious, high-pressure positions such as short-order cook; or dirty jobs like being a mechanic; or jobs like pumping gas outdoors in the winter; or being a porter in a hotel; or jobs like coal mining, for example, that combine a number of these problems.

Similarly, women are more likely, when they take a job they believe will be fulfilling but that turns out not to be fulfilling, to declare themselves burned out and desirous of having children, or to quit "for a while." When they return to work, they will often take a more fulfilling job that pays less and that has more satisfying hours.

A survey that fails to factor in a measurement for women's vs. men's qualitative options is a female-biased survey.

Change: Each survey should include a question, to the effect, "On a scale from 1 to 10, to what degree are you working at a job you don't like because its pay and benefits are better than something you like more (*e.g.,* being a teacher, writer, singer, artist)?"

Bias: There are many surveys comparing those women who work the greatest number of hours to their husbands, but none comparing those husbands who work the greatest number of hours to their wives, or even comparing men who do the most housework to their wives.

Change: Study the hardest working men as much as we study the hardest working women.

Bias: Some surveys assume working mothers work equal numbers of hours to working fathers, and they then ask for only the measurements of the hours their spouses spend doing housework. However, since working fathers, for example, work eleven more hours per week outside the home than working mothers,[85] and commute two hours further,[86] this sets up a thirteen-hour per week bias against fathers.

Change: Be certain the number of hours working and the number of hours commuted are both asked for.

These changes will lead to a woman feeling the man she loves values her time and, therefore, values her. It will lead to a man feeling more appreciated and, therefore, being more involved because involvement is now producing intimacy rather than new honey do's without the honey.

Perhaps nothing makes a woman feel less valued, though, than being abused by a man. And perhaps nothing makes a man feel like *less* of a man than hitting a woman. Unfortunately, our current approach to solving the problem is often aggravating it. For all these reasons, there are fewer areas with more potential for deepening love between men and women than understanding what men are keeping secret about violence in the home.

6

...If Your Man Knew You Feared His Potential for Violence

"Dear Abby: Thank you for printing the warning signs of an abusive partner. However, you have unfairly portrayed men as the only abusers. Not so; women can also be abusers.

My brother was married to a physically abusive woman who exhibited all 15 points you mentioned in your column. It wasn't until he joined a support group and realized he wasn't the only man who got beat up by a woman.

After much research, I find that women are just as abusive as men in relationships.

Women are able to get away with abusing men because most men are too embarrassed to report it. With the massive attention now given to domestic violence, it's time the other side of the story is told.

E. V. Liland, Dallas

Dear E. V. Liland: If what you state is true, I would like to see the statistics. Although I have no doubt that many men have been subjected to abuse by their spouses, experts tell me that their numbers are dwarfed by the vast number of women who experience physical abuse at the hands of their husbands or boyfriends.

Abused women are often captives in the abusive relationship, fearing that if they leave, they will be killed. Frequently they have been isolated by their abuser, have no money, credit, or job skills, and feel they'll be unable to support themselves and their children. The same is not true for men."[1]

Even men who share their personal experiences find that, instead of empathy, they get the response Dear Abby gave this man: "Women have it worse." This belief is so strong that over the past quarter century, women's old fantasy of marrying a man-as-protector has been tainted by women's new nightmare of husband-as-batterer. She feels she is being told to *marry the enemy*. Both the Ad Council[2] and the Universal Pictures'[3] ads below reinforce women's Marry-the-Enemy fear.

FORTY-TWO PERCENT OF ALL MURDERED WOMEN ARE KILLED BY THE SAME MAN.

Each day women are beaten to death by their husbands or boyfriends. Just as frightening, each day neighbors just like us make excuses for not getting involved. For information about how you can help stop domestic violence, call 1-800-END-ABUSE.

THERE'S NO EXCUSE for Domestic Violence.

Family Violence Prevention Fund

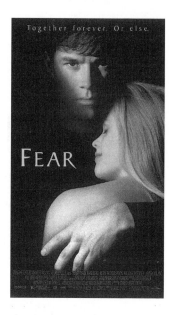

Together forever. Or else.

FEAR

Because men are part of every family, this anger and fear divides families and poisons love. Yet domestic violence is a domestic reality. So why is it that on our wedding day, while almost all of us desire a life of giving and receiving love, some couples end up giving and receiving black eyes and bruises?

I believe that a slide into violence is quickened by the popular assumptions about domestic violence: that it is men who batter women, rarely the other way around; that women hit men only in self-defense; that women can't walk out because they will be found by enraged men who will be even more likely to harm them; that this "male approach" to relationship problem solving emanates from men's feelings of women-as-property and of male power and privilege.

If we believe that it is predominantly men who batter women, it is hard to see why women also need to change: We will continue saying, "Just change the men. *They're* the batterers." United Way, one of the major contributors to funding to prevent domestic violence reinforces this only-the-female-is-victim imagery in brochures such as this, for a program run by a *men's* center, no less:

This assumption prevents us from redoing the male-female dance from a nonblame perspective. The first step is men taking responsibility for sharing their reality. But even as men do, it always surprises me how differently we listen to men's reality.

SAVE THE WHALES, BATTER THE MALES

Item. The *Oprah Winfrey Show.* Four men describe how their wives hit them in the lower back with a pole, cracked them over the head or in the neck with a frying pan. The audience renews its laughter after each story. The men are part of a "PMS Men's Support Group."[5]

Imagine an audience of men laughing as battered women describe how their husbands threatened them with brain or spinal cord injuries by battering them over their heads or in the necks with a frying pan.

Note that all of these battered husbands are still *with* their wives. When a woman stays with a man who batters, we provide shelters to encourage her to *escape.* If she decides not to escape, we say she is a victim of "Battered Woman Syndrome."

When battered women form support groups, we call it a Battered Women's group—her victimization is cited. In the PMS Men's support group, the woman's excuse is cited—the fact that the men were battered is left out. For men, unemployment often precedes battering, but women rarely form a Wives with Unemployed Husbands' Support Group (no mentioning of the battering) to help them understand the *cause* of the battering—the unemployment. The emphasis of the men's group was on understanding, coping, changing the situation and then, if all else failed, getting out; the emphasis of battered women's groups is on getting out first, and second, locking up the problem (the man).

In brief, when women batter, men's first priority is to support the woman and help them change; when men batter, women's first priority is to escape the men and put them in prison. The motto of feminists: "There is never an excuse for hitting a *woman.*" Shouldn't it be, "There is never an excuse for hitting"? None of these distinctions were made by anyone on the show.

An attitude in American culture actually supports the battering of males, as it does the saving of whales. In 100 percent of advertisements in which only one sex is hitting or beating the other, it is the woman who is beating the man.[6] One-hundred percent. Sitcoms routinely portray women hitting men, almost never portray men hitting women. When he fails to leave, it is not called "Battered Man Syndrome"; it is called comedy. In the chapter on man bashing, we will see this pattern in everything from greeting cards sent by women to Disney films watched by children. This makes it hard to listen to a different reality—that of men who are abused.

A DIFFERENT REALITY

Item. Michael, thirty-eight, a construction worker and amateur rugby player, barricaded himself in a spare bedroom at nights to avoid beatings from his diminutive wife. During a three-year marriage he was stabbed, punched, kicked, and pelted with plant pots. Despite his muscular, 15-stone [210 lbs] build, he was frightened to sleep for fear of attack. "Nobody would have believed me if I'd told them the constant bruising was from beatings by my wife. I still have the scars from where she tore at my flesh with her fingernails. The screams from my daughter as she witnessed the abuse will haunt me for the rest of my life."

Item. Paul, thirty-two, a former Royal Marine, said his wife, Claire, an advertising executive, could suddenly become like "a ferocious wild cat." The slightest thing would set her off. "She would pull me to the ground, kick me, and pull large clumps, of hair out of my head. I never fought back because she was a slightly built, petite woman."

Item. A forty-two-year-old British police officer, trained in tackling armed criminals [British police don't carry guns], was twice hospitalized by his 5-foot wife. He didn't report it. When asked why, he explained, "If I was to go up to my mates on the force and tell them my wife was regularly hitting me over the head and body with anything she could get her hands on, they would crease themselves [die laughing]."

All three of these examples are from the *London Times*.[7] It is rare for equally reputable American papers to run a story in which men's feelings and experiences about being battered are reported in their own words in such depth. Notice also that the wives are clearly weaker physically, and the men are not the passive, hen-pecked stereotype of a battered man. And note the men's fear that if they reported this to the authorities, not only would they not be believed, they would be ridiculed ("my mates would crease themselves").

The *London Times* article spoke of the shock experienced by many police officers at the violence meted out by women. As one officer put it, "We have had to review our attitude. Ten years ago it wasn't thought possible that a woman could beat up a man. Now it's a regular occurrence."[8] In reality, husband beating may have occurred just as often ten years ago, but the unwillingness to consider it as a possibility may have blinded officers to the regularity of the occurrence.

American newspapers are just beginning to acknowledge the feelings of some *boys* who are the victims of violence by a girl, but not the feelings of victims who are *men*. For example, fifteen-year-old Bobby Papiere of Houston explains:

> One of my parents' lines that I just hate is, "Like your sister can hit you hard," meaning that if my sister hits me, it's no big deal because she can't hit hard. But sometimes it *is* hard. And my parents don't let me hit her back. So (when they're not around) she'll stand there and hit me—and then she'll say, "I'll tell if *you* hit *me*." I hate that.[9]

Notice that the boy could have told this story to his parents, but didn't. Nowhere is the title *Women Can't Hear What Men Don't Say* more relevant than to boys' and men's silence about domestic violence.

Why the silence? Think of all the ways we teach boys to become men by enduring pain: football, rugby, ice hockey, boxing, boot camp, rodeos, car racing. **Men learn to call pain "glory"; women learn to call the police.**

Why did virtually every culture reward its men for enduring violence? So it would have a cadre of people available to protect it in war. The people considered the most in need of protection were women and children. The sex considered most disposable was men—or males.

The more a man is trained to "be a man," the more he is trained to protect women and children, not hurt women and children. He is trained to volunteer to die before even a stranger is hurt—especially a woman or child. Thus most firefighters are volunteers, and almost all the volunteers are men.

"Try not to hit any females."

THE SATURDAY EVENING POST

Part of the pressure men put on each other to carry out this mandate is ridi-culing a man who complains when he is hurt. We often think that when a man insults another man by calling him a "girl," the insult reflects a contempt for women. No. It reflects a contempt for any man who is unwilling to make himself strong enough to protect someone as precious as a woman. It is an insult to any man unwilling to endure the pain it takes to save a woman's life—including the pain of losing his own life. If you are a woman, imagine someone calling you a "baby" because you cried rather than trying to save your daughter's life at the risk of your own—you would know the term "baby" was meant not to insult babies, but to insult you for being unwilling to protect someone as precious as a baby. The ridicule is pressure to consider ourselves less important than someone even more precious: A baby is more precious than a mother; a mother is more precious than a man.

Those feminists who say that masculinity is about men believing they can batter women display the deepest ignorance possible about men and masculin-ity. **Battering a woman is the male role broken down. A man who batters a woman is like a cross-dresser: he's out of role.** In a Stage I survival-based culture, it is the male role to protect women by taking control of survival needs. Which is why, for example, nineteenth-century British and American law re-quired a husband to go to debtors' prison even if it was his wife who spent them into debt.[10] With responsibility came the ability to enforce. The male role was to his family what the role of the military is to a nation: Both are assigned the role of protector; but the power it takes to protect, when broken down, can be abusive. But the abuse is not the role, it is the role broken down. He was not treating her as property, he was taking responsibility for keeping the property intact for the entire family's protection. If he should fail, he's off to jail. That's why I call it the responsibility to discipline, as opposed to male privilege.

In virtually every culture, then, manhood rests on men learning to protect women, not hurt women.

WHO IS ABUSING WHO?

If we look at only police reports and all-female self-help groups, it appears that men perpetrate about 90 percent of the domestic violence. But when we study male-only self-help groups, we get a different picture: *Only 6 percent of the men involved in domestic violence say they were the perpetrator;* 81 percent said their wives were the perpetrator (13 percent said it was mutual).[11] So who do we believe?: Ninety percent male perpetrators, or 6 percent?

Consider the possibility that the percentages are so different because the people we asked were so different—that everyone might be telling their version of the truth. There was something missing: a nationwide domestic violence study of both sexes.

When the first scientific nationwide sample was conducted in 1975—by Suzanne Steinmetz, Murray Straus, and Richard Gelles[12]—the researchers could hardly believe their results. The sexes appeared to batter each other about equally. Dozens of questions arose ("Don't women batter only in self-defense?"; "Aren't women hurt more?"). Over a hundred researchers during the next quarter century double-checked via their own studies. About half of these researchers were women, and most of the women who were academics were feminists. Most expected to disprove the Steinmetz, Straus, and Gelles findings.

To their credit, despite their assumptions that men were the abusers, *every* domestic violence survey done of both sexes over the next quarter century in the United States, Canada, England, New Zealand, and Australia—more than fifty of which are annotated in the Appendix—found one of two things: **Women and men batter each other about *equally,* or women batter men more. In addition, almost all studies found women were more likely to *initiate* violence and much more likely to inflict the *severe* violence. Women themselves acknowledged they are more likely to be violent and to be the initiators of violence. Finally, women were more likely to engage in severe violence that was not reciprocated.** The larger and better designed the study, the more likely the finding that women were significantly more violent.

Studies also make it clear that the women were 70 percent more likely to use weapons against men than men were to use weapons against women.[13] The weapons women use are more varied and creative than men's, doubtless in compensation for less muscle strength.

Item. "One well-to-do wife I know of turned the tables on her husband. After suffering repeated beatings, she waited until he fell asleep one night, sewed him in the sheets, and broke his bones with a baseball bat."

BARBARA SPENCER-POWELL; Overland Park, KS[14]

The fact that women were more likely to use severe violence does not necessarily mean the men were injured more. I will explain later why we do not yet have valid information about which sex is injured more.

Here are the most basic findings of the most responsible representative nationwide domestic violence study concerning how often wives vs. husbands were victims of *severe* violence.

SEVERE "WIFE-BEATING" VS. SEVERE "HUSBAND-BEATING"*

Wife Victim   1.9%

Husband Victim   4.5%

Explanation: During the year prior to being surveyed, less than 2% of wives and more than 4% of husbands were victims of severe domestic violence. "Severe violence" was measured via Murray Straus's *Conflict Tactics Scale*[15] as: kicking or biting; being hit with an object or a fist; being beaten up; being threatened with a knife or gun; or being stabbed or wounded.

---

*Source: 1992 National Alcohol and Family Violence Survey, a nationwide representative population sample of 1970 persons, conducted by the Institute for Survey Research (Temple University). See Murray Straus and Glenda Kaufman Kantor, in "Change in Spousal Assault Rates from 1975 to 1992: A Comparison of Three National Surveys in the United States," paper presented at the thirteenth World Congress of Sociology, Bielefeld, Germany, July 19, 1994.

If we saw a headline saying, "Severe 'Husband-Beating' Twice as Common as Severe 'Wife-Beating,'" we would think there was a misprint.

Because this chapter's very foundation rests on the counterintuitive findings that women and men batter about equally—or that women batter more—I am including all of the studies, and a summary of their findings, in the Appendix. I do this because it is important for the reader to know that I am not just reporting selected studies "in order to prove a point."

It is also important to know that I contacted the national NOW headquarters and the NOW Legal Defense and Education Fund to ask them if they knew of any two-sex *domestic* violence studies that showed men battered women more. They could not cite a single one. They had relied on *crime* statistics from the *National Crime Victimization Survey*[16] to say that women were battered more.

The *National Crime Victimization Survey* is *not* a survey of domestic violence, but a survey of crime (as the title indicates). That's a big problem. Why? When a man is asked, "Have you ever been hit" or "kicked" and the context is his wife, his answer has his wife in mind; if we ask him if he's ever been hit in the context of a crime, he thinks of whether he's been hit by someone other than his wife. How do we know this? By comparing crime surveys to domestic violence surveys. In all domestic violence surveys the men are much more likely to say they've been victims of violence from their partner.

What creates this difference? We have educated women to think of being punched or kicked by a man as a crime, so a crime survey can get women to report that as a crime; we have not yet educated men to think of being bitten, punched, kicked, or hit with a frying pan as a crime, so a crime survey fails to get men to report these behaviors as a crime. A crime survey cannot hear what men do not say.

Another important consideration leads to men not seeing domestic violence as a crime: the devaluation both sexes place on men's injuries—even when those injuries are equal to their wife's. For example, a U.S. Department of Justice survey finds that Americans consider it 41 percent less severe when a wife stabs her husband *to death* as they do when a husband stabs his wife *to death*.[17]

On the less-severe level, such as when a man or woman hits, bites, or throws something at their partner, *both* sexes consider it more serious if the woman is hurt.[18] When we add this to the male mandate to not "air their dirty laundry in public," we can see why crime surveys do not uncover domestic violence *to* the man, just *by* the man.

The second key to eliciting accurate information from men is "be specific." If we ask a man a vague question, like, "Have you been battered," the answer is likely to be "no" even if he's been repeatedly hit with a frying pan or repeatedly stabbed. But if we ask him specifically, "Have you ever been hit with a frying pan," he'll be more likely to say "yes." (Also, the word "battered" connotes using the fist, which is the male method; it does not imply using an object, the female method. The word "battered," then, holds an implicit bias against men; "domestic violence" is gender neutral.)

When I first became aware of these studies, I mentioned them to a woman friend, Liz, who was the chair of her high school math department.[19] At first, she looked incredulous. But when I asked her to think of what she saw at school, she smiled. "Well, it is true that I do see a lot of the girls hit the guys, but I can think of only one or two cases of guys hitting girls." Then she laughed, "But we sent only the guys to the vice principal's office, so they got all the attention—including, it seems, *my* attention. I guess that's an example of why it was hard for me to believe you at first."

Not one to let a math teacher get away with a subjective observation, I asked if she would keep track of the frequency with which the boys and girls hit each other *the first time*. She agreed, but not one to miss a potential math lesson, she asked one of her classes to "do a survey," to keep track of all the times the boys and girls initiated a slap or punch of a member of the other sex on the playground or in their classes.

When Liz reported the results, she was a tad embarrassed, "Well, it was almost twenty to one when I first started keeping track—mostly girls hitting guys on the arm, occasionally slapping them. But I'm afraid I screwed up the survey. I got so furious at the girls for 'beginning the cycle of violence,' as you put it, that I began to do minilectures in class, and the girls and guys doing the survey started lecturing the people they were observing, and soon there weren't nearly as many girls hitting guys. I contaminated the results!"

I assured Liz that stopping violence was more valuable than surveying violence, but it made me wonder whether Liz's quasi-survey held up in real surveys, once high school and college students started dating. The answer? To some degree. Female high school students are four times as likely as male students to be the *sole abuser* of the other sex (5.7 percent vs. 1.4 percent).[20]

Of course, we have much more information on college students, since academics teach college and their students are captive. The average study showed college women being about 40 percent more likely to be violent than the men. When the questions were very specific, both sexes acknowledged the women hit, kicked, bit, or struck their partner with an object between two and three times as often.

Surveying college women and men, though, may be a bias against men, since it seems that among women and men who have *not* gone to college, women hit men proportionately even more than among those who have gone to college. (Currently, the tendency of less-educated females to hit less-educated males more than vice versa can be observed anecdotally on the *Jerry Springer Show* every weekday. So far, I've never seen a man hit a woman, but about eighty women hit men. That was as much of the show as I could stomach.)

Among all populations, most violence was mutual. But when it was unilateral, it was more likely to have been initiated by the woman. For example, in a study of over 500 university students, women were three times as likely (9 percent vs. 3 percent) to have initiated unilateral violence.[21]

EXACTLY HOW DO HUSBANDS AND WIVES ABUSE EACH OTHER?

Exactly what do husbands and wives do to abuse each other? The most recent scientific national study analyzes violence according to the level of severity by using an updated version of the Conflict Tactics Scale, which has become by far the most acceptable measure in the field. Throughout this chapter, when I refer to severe violence, I am talking about items *four* through *nine* below:

HOW HUSBANDS AND WIVES ABUSE EACH OTHER

TYPES OF VIOLENCE	HUSBAND-TO-WIFE	WIFE-TO-HUSBAND
A. MINOR VIOLENT ACTS		
1. Threw something	4.1%	7.4%
2. Pushed/grabbed/shoved	10.4	10.9
3. Slapped	2.6	3.8
B. SEVERE VIOLENT ACTS		
4. Kicked/bit/hit with fist	1.3	3.4
5. Hit, tried to hit with something	1.6	2.8
6. Beat up	0.8	0.6
7. Choked	0.8	0.6
8 Threatened with knife or gun	0.4	0.7
9. Used knife or gun	0.2	0.1

Number of cases: 1,970

Example: "4.1% of husbands threw something at their wives; 7.4% of wives threw something at their husbands."

Source: *1992 National Alcohol and Family Violence Survey*, based on a nationwide probability sample of 1,970 cases (with a 4X Hispanic over-sample and the data weighted accordingly) conducted by Dr. Glenda Kaufman Kantor of the Family Research Lab (University of New Hampshire). Data printout provided by Dr. Jana L. Jasinski (New Hampshire: Family Research Laboratory, July 8, 1996).

Once we get to couples who are not college students, findings of other large studies are fairly reflective of this one. Many, though, show a much greater propensity for women to engage in severe violence. For example, in a national sample of men and women dating, women were five times more likely to be severely violent.[22] Women were more likely to be more violent in the more-involved relationships, as their emotions got invested.[23]

IF MEN ARE BATTERED MORE, WHY DO THEY REPORT IT LESS?

Item. Men rarely report being battered until their wives have attempted to kill them with a knife or a gun.[24]

Item. The film is *Love at Large,* with Tom Berenger. The TV promo features a woman slugging Tom. The punch knocks him back, but his response is one of gratitude. "[Wow,] that's the first time we've touched."

A man is fearful of reporting being battered to the police because a man being hurt provokes laughter, a problem reinforced in ads and shows such as this:

Why does a promo of a man being hurt show the man laughing, or in Berenger's case, show gratitude, while a promo for a woman being slugged in which a woman was laughing or expressing gratitude to the man for slugging her would provoke outrage? It tickles our funny bone because we love the "weaker" underdog defeating the "stronger" man; because of our anger at men, and in part because of our unconscious understanding of how men reframe abuse and call it love.

And there's the biggie: **Men have learned to associate being abused**

with being loved. For example, becoming the football or ice hockey player some woman will love (and men will respect) requires his enduring physical abuse, name-calling, hazing, or emotional humbling. News magazines such as *Maclean's* help us reinforce our propensity to call men who are physically beaten "heroes," even as we call women who are physically beaten "victims."

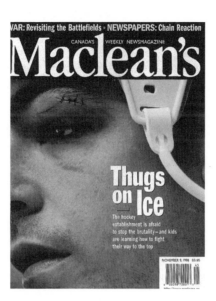

Taking abuse will get him through boot camp so he can become the officer some woman will adore; and it is part of the territory of "death professions" like firefighting or coal mining, where he hopes to earn enough to afford a wife. By the time he is eligible for love, he has been trained to be humbled, hazed, and abused.

THE MALE "LEARNED HELPLESSNESS SYNDROME"

> The weakness of men is their facade of strength;
> the strength of women is their facade of weakness.[25]

Men expect neither life to protect them nor their wife to protect them. But they do expect themselves to protect their wife. So even when men batter in self-defense, they expect to be reported; and even when their wives hit first, men rarely report.

Many men don't report being battered because they believe "private problems must be solved privately." They consider "airing dirty laundry in public" a violation of a relationship's sacredness. Which is also why we don't even report it to our men friends.

Other men don't report abuse because their translation of "when the going gets tough, the tough get going" is "when the going gets tough, the tough don't blame—they do something differently." So even when he's beaten, he still expects himself to be "Timex Tough" (to "take a licking and keep on ticking").

Like women, men feel it's up to them to change. They are amazed when they hear women say the same thing ("I felt it was my fault") and then see the woman call the police. To the man, if you genuinely feel it's your fault, you don't call the police.

A battered man imagines that if he calls the police and says, "Please come over, my wife just hit me," he'll become the precinct's "Wimp of the Night." **A battered man knows there are no shelters for battered men because no one really believes he exists.** Men fear being denounced as an abuser if they beat a woman and laughed at as a wimp if they are beaten by a woman.

Both sexes feel helpless when the love of their life turns into the nightmare of their life. But men, for all these reasons, feel much more helpless about asking for outside help. In brief, women's strength is in knowing when they feel helpless. Men's weakness is not knowing. The fact that we have identified women's "learned helplessness" but not men's is, it turns out, a sign that the women's problem is on its way to being solved, while the men's is as yet unrecognized.

THE ELDERLY MAN'S "LEARNED HELPLESSNESS SYNDROME"

Carlos Mello's wife wouldn't let him sleep. He reported that his wife would grab him by his genitals and "pull, squeeze, and twist them until I could not stand the pain any longer and I would just stay awake."[26] He didn't report to the hospital until she had prevented his sleeping for three days and his genital area was "swollen to the size of a small balloon," according to the report. Although neighbors confirmed they had been hearing loud screams and moans for three days, Mello had been reluctant to discuss the ruckus when neighbors knocked on his door. When he finally did report to the police, his wife denied she had beaten him, dismissing his condition as "he must have fallen out of bed."

Many elderly men who are abused by their wives report their wives' anger at their failure to be useful—as a breadwinner or home repairer. The man has gone from protector to needing protection, and that is a set up for her anger. The man's shame and dependency often prevents him from reporting his wife's abuse.

The unwillingness of abused men to come forward is a classic symptom of "Male Learned Helplessness." The elderly man feels helpless physically, emotionally, and socially: physically, because he is often ten to fifteen years closer to death; emotionally, because male socialization is a retardant to emotional communication; socially, because the network of friends he built up at work is more likely to be spread out among many communities whereas the network of friends his wife built up is more likely to be in her neighborhood and her community. This physical, emotional, and social combination creates the Elderly Man's Learned Helplessness Syndrome.

DO MEN EXPERIENCE A "BATTERED MAN SYNDROME"?

Feminist literature has helped us understand the many reasons a woman may remain in an abusive relationship—from economic fears to low self-esteem to fears of enraging the man and having him track her down and become even more abusive. The usual image is that the woman cannot afford to leave, but low-income wives are more likely than high-income wives to leave abusive situations.[27] This suggests that the man's money may keep a woman but his lack of money does not prevent her from leaving.

Men's fears of leaving can include those, but they are usually quite different. I've already discussed men's fears of asking for help and reporting abuse, and the plight of elderly men's experience of learned helplessness. But three other reasons battered men fear leaving are even more crucial.

A battered man knows that if his wife has been abusing him, she has often been abusing the children; leaving her means leaving his children unprotected from her abuse.

Second, a man who loses his wife often feels his children are his only remaining source of love.

Finally, abused men know that if they leave, their wives will not only get the children, but the home. For many men, "Home, home on the range" is more appealing than "Apartment, apartment on the range."

Many men, then, endure the physical hurt of being beaten rather than endure the emotional torture of feeling they've left their own children unprotected, lost love, and lost their home. When these combine with the helplessness that emerges from the fear of asking for help, they create the "Battered Man Syndrome."

AREN'T WOMEN INJURED MORE THAN MEN?

Dear Editor: Your article [Time] *on domestic violence states that women are unlikely to inflict much damage on men because wives are generally smaller. Yet in my experience as an emergency-room physician, I treated more men than women for such injuries. . . . I have seen men cut with an ax, scalded with hot water, smashed with a fireplace poker, and knocked out by a brick, not to mention suffering the common gunshot wound. One incident involved a woman who walked into the hospital with a broken nose after being punched by her husband during an argument. We set the nasal bones and discharged her. Two hours later, her husband was wheeled in. He was admitted with a fractured spine. As soon as she got home, she had grabbed him by the lapels and thrown him against the kitchen stove.*

VELIMIR SVOREN, MD;
Chatsworth, GA, "Letters," *Time*, Jan. 11, 1988.

Despite the fact that women are more likely to use weapons and severe violence against men, 1.9 percent of the men and 2.3 percent of the women surveyed said they had sought medical treatment for an injury due to partner abuse in 1992.[28] Is this because a frying pan hurts a man less than a fist hurts a woman—because, as a female classmate of Calvin (of *Calvin and Hobbes*) put it, "They can't paddle me! . . . Girls have more delicate heinies"?[29]

Or is there something wrong with the way we are measuring who is injured? To measure which sex is injured more by measuring which sex reports to the doctor more is to make the same mistake we made by assuming women were battered more because they reported domestic violence to the police more. Women are almost twice as likely to go to doctors as are men—men's injuries have to be much more serious before they seek attention.

But that's just the tip of the iceberg. When I do a radio show and ask men who have been severely battered to call in anonymously, it is rare for them to have sought medical attention even for a broken arm. But if they do, they almost always report it as an *athletic* injury ("I was going up for a basket, this guy put his elbow in my eye, I come down on my arm. I end up with a black eye, a broken arm and a "gee, sorry, man'"). No man I ever spoke with said that such an explanation created skepticism. So the second reason that measuring which sex is injured more by looking at the reporting of injuries to doctors is that men's rougher sports gives them a natural excuse to avoid the association of the injury with domestic violence.

Third, doctors are not trained to cross-examine the man to see whether the claim of an athletic injury might be a cover up. If the doctor's a man, he's more likely to bond with the basketball player by asking him if he made the basket. In contrast, doctors are now trained to cross-examine a woman. The U.S. Surgeon General sends out information on spouse abuse only to doctors who deal with women (28,000 obstetricians and gynecologists).[30] It is designed to assist doctors in recognizing the subtle signs of spouse abuse among *women* and to encourage doctors to encourage *women* to report it. This is a result of feminist pressure to educate the medical community. Men's silence has not created much pressure.

It is exactly the feeling that men are stronger—usually true—that gives women permission for hitting them harder and using weapons. This is even true in mothers' attitudes toward their sons vs. their daughters. **Sons are more than twice as likely as daughters to be injured when their mothers hit them.**[31]

How do we learn who actually does experience more injury? First, we need to remember that a "my-injury-is-worse-than-your-injury" approach to family violence does nothing to solve the problem—it just reinforces the one-sided blaming that undermines real solutions, like communication.

If we do want data on who is more hurt, we need to stop asking about *coping* mechanisms—which is what "Who sees a doctor measures?"—and start asking both sexes *specific* questions about the actual damage and healing time of the injuries: "Was your skin broken—did you bleed? Did you suffer any bruises? Any scratches? Black eyes? Broken bones? How long did they take to heal? Was that the time it took with or without treatment?" But again, let's work on solutions rather than on "Who's the biggest victim?" Throughout the book, the only reason that I concern myself with men as victims at all is because the pretense that men are only the perpetrators has led us to ignoring men or blaming men—and that poisons love between the sexes.

WHEN WOMEN BATTER, ISN'T IT IN SELF-DEFENSE?

One of the valid objections to the initial domestic violence surveys was that perhaps women were violent only in self-defense. Interestingly, when Straus and Gelles checked this out, they asked *only women* their opinion as to who had struck the *first* blow. Their findings? Even 53 *percent of the women acknowledged they had struck the first blow.*[32]

Other researchers asked both sexes. And asked not only who struck the first blow, but who did so without retaliation. Here is what they found:

WHO STRUCK THE FIRST BLOW IN YEAR PRIOR TO MARRIAGE?	
Men	13%
Women	26%

**WHO STRUCK THE FIRST BLOW
6 TO 18 MONTHS AFTER MARRIAGE?**

Men	8%
Women	17%

**WHO STRUCK THE FIRST BLOW
18 TO 30 MONTHS AFTER MARRIAGE?**

Men	9%
Women	16%

Explanation: The percentages average both sexes' responses. Both sexes reported both themselves and their partner; both sexes reported their own aggression to be about 10% less than their partner's estimate.

Source: K. Daniel O'Leary, Julian Barling, Ileana Arias, Alan Rosenbaum, Jean Malone, and Andrea Tyree, "Prevalence and Stability of Physical Aggression Between Spouses: A Longitudinal Analysis," *Journal of Consulting and Clinical Psychology,* Vol. 57, No. 2, 1989, p. 263–265.[33]

Many studies now confirm women being more likely to strike the first blow, or to be severely violent without the husband reciprocating.[34] We saw above that this started in high school. I'm unaware of any significant two-sex domestic violence study showing the opposite, nor could NOW headquarters cite any.

Isn't it often claimed that when women *kill* their husbands, it is in self-defense? Yes. However, when Dr. Coramae Richey Mann checked out these claims, she discovered only 10 percent were valid.[35] That is, when women killed their husbands, they usually claimed self-defense, even when their husbands were in wheelchairs. Others explained it was when their husband was asleep. If self-defense is defined as it always has been by the law, as a response to an *immediate* threat to one's life, from which one cannot escape, then neither meets the self-defense standard. But feminists have created a for-women-only defense (the Learned Helplessness Defense, based on the "Battered Woman Syndrome"), allowing a woman who could escape, but was fearful, to kill a sleeping man and then claim in court it was self-defense because he had previously abused her repeatedly and she was afraid to leave. The problem is, the husband is too dead to defend himself. And the court can't hear what men are too dead to say.

In contrast, when men claim self-defense, they are often not even believed by their counselors. For example, when Steve Murray describes the abusive men he counsels, he explains, "They whine and they bitch and they cry and they say,

'She attacked me first.' Pretty soon another guy is saying, 'That's the way it happened to me!'"[36] A second later Murray adds, "When a man resolved a conflict by hitting his wife, there are no longer two sides to the story. No one ever deserves to get hit."

Although Murray says, "No one ever deserves to get hit," he discounts the men the moment they say they were hit. Even when the men claim self-defense ("She attacked me first"), they are discounted as whiners, bitchers, and crybabies. By not believing the men—but believing only their wives—the social worker is able to justify putting the men in groups for perpetrators, their wives in groups for victims. If the women had all claimed the men hit them first, it would be used to reinforce the stereotype that women never hit except in self-defense.

IS THIS FEMALE VIOLENCE
AGAINST MEN A RECENT PHENOMENON?

Is this gap between male and female violence in the home just recent (since laws against wife-battering have just recently become tougher)? It is unlikely, but we can't be positive of the answer, since the first large, nationwide random-sample study was not done until 1975. Here is how the 1975 results compare to 1992.

CHANGES IN *SEVERE* "WIFE-BEATING" VS. SEVERE "HUSBAND-BEATING": 1975 TO 1992

	1975	1985	1992
Wife Victim	3.8%	3.0%	1.9%
Husband Victim	4.6%	4.4%	4.5%

Source: 1975 and 1985 National Family Violence Surveys, based on nationwide probability population samples of 2,143 cases in 1975 and 3,520 cases in 1985, conducted by the Family Research Lab (University of New Hampshire); and the 1992 National Alcohol and Family Violence Survey, based on a national probability sample of 1,970 cases in 1992, conducted by the Institute for Survey Research (Temple University). As cited in Murray Straus and Glenda Kaufman Kantor, "Change in Spouse Assault Rates From 1975 to 1992: A Comparison of Three National Surveys in the United States," paper presented at the thirteenth World Congress of Sociology, Bielefeld, Germany, July 19, 1994.

Fortunately, severe violence against wives decreased 48 percent; against husbands, it decreased 2 percent. However, what the table does not mention is another result of the comparison: Although *overall* violence (including minor violence, like shoving or slapping) against women *decreased,* overall violence against men *increased.*[37]

HAS VIOLENCE AGAINST MEN BEEN CENSORED—
IS THIS WHY WE DON'T KNOW ABOUT IT?

Yes, studies reporting violence against men have been censored. The underlying dynamics of this censorship is the subject of chapter 8 on the Lace Curtain, but when it comes to domestic violence, the censorship is both direct, which is quite a story, and indirect, which is the real story.

Directly, first. Suzanne Steinmetz shared with me that, shortly after she published an article titled "The Battered Husband Syndrome" in 1978,[38] she received a bomb threat at a speech she was giving at the University of Delaware.[39] She received threatening phone calls at home from women who said, "If you don't stop talking about battered men, something's going to happen to your children and it won't be safe for you to go out." It's ironic that women saying that women couldn't be violent were threatening violence.

Although the group of women never harmed Steinmetz physically, they did try to damage her career. Steinmetz recalled that it wasn't until years later that she learned these women had secretly contacted female faculty at the university where she was employed and urged the women to work against her for promotion and tenure.

Richard Gelles, the co-pioneer with Suzanne Steinmetz and Murray Straus of these early studies, reports that Straus was rarely invited to speak at conferences on domestic violence after the three of them published their initial studies. When he was, he was unable to complete his presentation because of yells and shouts from the audience that stopped only when he was driven from the stage.[40] Whereas he used to be nominated frequently for elected office on scientific societies (such as the American Sociological Association), he has not been nominated for *any* office since then.[41]

Now, the more indirect censorship. Richard Gelles wanted to present both feminist and nonfeminist perspectives on domestic violence in a book he was editing. The feminist scholar accepted until she was informed there would be other points of view. Then she told Richard Gelles that she would not only refuse to submit anything, but she would "see to it that no feminist would contribute a chapter."[42]

In Canada, a University of Alberta study found 12 percent of husbands to be victims of violence by their wives and 11 percent of wives to be victims, but only the violence against women was published.[43] Even when Earl Silverman, six years later, was able to get the data from an assistant who had helped prepare the original study, and then wrote it up himself, he was unable to get it published.

Similarly, another major Canadian study of dating couples found 46 percent of women vs. 18 percent of men to be physically violent. You guessed it. The 18 percent male violence was published immediately.[44] Not only was the 46 percent female violence left unpublished, but the authors did not acknowledge in the *Canadian Journal of Sociology* that their study had ever included violence against men.

When a Canadian professor found out, he requested to see the data and was refused.[45] It was only when he exposed the refusal in his next book, combined with another three more years of pressure, that the 46 percent female violence was released and published.[46] By that time (1997), Canadian policy giving government support for abused women but not abused men had been entrenched. As were the bureaucracies; as were the private funding sources like United Way.

By 1999, United Way of Greater Toronto increased their yearly allocation for services to abused women and children by $1 million, to $3.3 million per year. To abused men and children: $0. I asked the research director whether the research to determine need had included abused men and children. The answer? No.[47]

It was the United States, though, that set the precedent for this censorship. In 1979, Louis Harris and Associates conducted a survey of domestic violence commissioned by the Kentucky Commission on Women. However, when the results of the study were published,[48] only the abuse *of* the women was included; abuse *by* the women was censored.[49] (The women themselves acknowledged attacking men who had not attacked them 38 percent of the time.[50] The existence of those data became known and published only when some professors were later able to obtain the original computer tape.[51]

Why would these findings be ignored by academicians whose life passion is seeking the truth? One colleague, R. L. McNeely, who pioneered the analysis of research in domestic violence,[52] told me, "I'll tell you why—as soon as I published results along these lines, I received a letter threatening to stop my funding."

A portion of government funding to a professor usually goes to the university. Funding is often what allows a university to keep a professor hired. If the professor is supporting a family, it creates an ethical dilemma: When does being responsible become irresponsible? And, of course, the instinct to protect the female makes him or her fear that acknowledging male pain means discounting female pain.

ARE THESE STATISTICS FOR REAL?

Headlines like these[53] make it difficult to believe statistics based on equal samplings of both sexes:

50% of women feel cold hand of a batterer

World's Women Speak as One Against Abuse

■ **Strategy:** From Fiji to Israel, Uganda to the U.S., activists raise a new battle cry—treat violence against women as a violation of basic human rights.

By KATHLEEN HENDRIX
TIMES STAFF WRITER

Are these headlines at all true? Yes. It is true that about 50 percent of women are shoved, slapped, or otherwise abused during their lifetime (which is how the article explains the headline), but that is also true *of an even higher percentage of men.* Why do we only know about the women? Because, as the second headline points out, it is the world's women who are "speaking as one" against abuse—the world's men aren't even speaking. The men are the silent battered.

The result? We have solidified our view of men as the perpetrators, making it shocking to view men as equally battered.

One of the biggest barriers to hearing this information is the belief that when women hit, it is in self-defense. So let's check this out emotionally first. Which requires running it past our personal life experience. In my workshops I ask my audiences to ask themselves two questions about each romantic relationship they have had in their life:

- On your right hand, use one finger to represent *each* relationship in which you hit your partner (a nonplayful slap or more) the *first* time—before she or he ever hit you. The number? ___

- On your left hand, use one finger to represent each relationship in which your partner hit you the *first* time. The number? ___

Remember, only one finger per relationship—and only the first time counts. Take a moment to do this. It's crucial to understanding this chapter on the emotional level.

Chances are, if you are a man, you will have a harder time remembering—a man treats a slap as forgettable; a woman does not. Nevertheless, if you've hit or been hit at all, it is likely more women will have hit you *the first time* than vice versa. Now run this by a few friends. The men are likely to recall being hit the first time more than the other way around; the women are likely to recall it being closer to equal, with their hitting the first time slightly more frequently—which basically matches the findings of the fifty surveys I reviewed. (The surveys, after all, came from real people's reports.)

Despite all these findings, early researchers still concluded that we should not be distracted from the current social policy of giving first attention to wives.[54] To rationalize their conclusion, they assumed that women as a group were more locked into marriage and therefore less able to escape abuse. They ignored the data telling us that over 60 percent of divorces are initiated by women—and that when women have children, it goes up to 65 percent.[55] And they ignored findings that **men who are abused also feel locked into marriage because they know their wives are much more likely to retain the children after divorce and they fear the children will be abused.**[56]

WHAT HAPPENS IN OTHER CULTURES?

I reviewed a dozen studies that covered seven non-U.S. countries (Great Britain, New Zealand, Finland, British Honduras, Canada, Puerto Rico, Israel) and a number of subcultures within the United States (Quakers, Mormons, military, Mexican-Americans).

In almost all of these cultures, the women were either equally violent to the men, or more violent than the men (Puerto Rico being the only exception).[57] In addition, the women were much more likely to exercise severe violence. It was not uncommon for the women to be three times as likely to exercise severe violence, although on average it was about twice as often.

One of the best non-U.S. studies was a New Zealand study that followed more than 1,000 children from when they were three until the age of twenty-one. Because the researchers knew these people for eighteen years, the response rate was high, as was the trust level (or at least that's what they tell us!). Their findings? By the age of twenty-one, women had perpetrated minor violence against men in the previous year 36 percent of the time vs. men's 22 percent.[58] However, women had perpetrated severe violence against men 19 percent of the time vs. men's 6 percent—more than three times the rate of severe violence.

I was curious to see if Quakers were, in fact, less violent? The answer? Yes and no. Both husbands and wives reported pushing, shoving, and grabbing at about the 15 percent level, which is slightly higher than it was in the overall American population at the time of the Quaker study (12 percent women; 11 percent men[59]).[60] However, when it came to severe violence, the Quaker women did better than the average American woman (2.5 percent vs. 4.4 percent) and the men were considerably less violent on the severe level than the average American man was (0.8 percent vs. 3 percent).[61] Again, among the Quakers, as in many other groups, severe violence was about three times as frequent for the women as the men.

Among a mostly Mormon sample, the violence levels were similar to the U.S. at large.[62] Among military couples, the men and women both exhibited equal amounts of violence, and more than in the population at large.[63] Among Mexican-Americans, there was no difference between the genders.[64]

The real value of studying both sexes is how many hints it gives us at reducing domestic violence—especially on the severe level. For example, in more traditional cultures, like Puerto Rico and the military, the sexes do not have the tools to know how to stop escalating violence. Whereas among Quakers, with their nontraditional emphasis on peaceful means of conflict resolution, severe violence by women is lower and by men is rare.

It appears, then, that education toward nonviolence helps. Especially men. But if the Quakers are a model, the good news is that they are able to achieve this level of nonviolence by men within the framework of a violent society; the more challenging news is the Quaker education process is not just a few classes, but a way of life. Which is why Part I of this book is really the biggest part of the "solution" to domestic violence.

IS ABUSE THE RESULT OF PATRIARCHY?

Item. Among lesbians who had prior intimate relationships with men, 32 percent had experienced physical aggression from *any male* partner; 45 percent had experienced physical aggression from their *most recent female* partner alone.[65]

Item. When lesbians and heterosexual women (matched for age, race, education, and socioeconomic status) were given identical questionnaires, 9 percent of heterosexual women reported being raped by a man during a dating relationship;

7 percent of lesbians reported being raped by a woman during a dating relationship.[66] Statistically the difference was insignificant.

Lesbian violence shatters the myth that women abuse only when *men* drive them to it. It dispels the myth that male power and male privilege create violence against women. Lesbians do not have much male power and privilege.

Lesbian rape further dispels the myth that rape is also an outgrowth of male power and privilege. We can claim that patriarchy causes lesbians to batter and rape—as some feminists do—but if patriarchy causes all the bad that lesbians do, it must also cause all the good that lesbians do.

IS ABUSE THE RESULT OF POWER—OR POWERLESSNESS?

The domestic violence community often assumes men abuse women due to feelings of male power and privilege. Their treatment programs usually incorporate this assumption.

As it turns out, the evidence supports much different conclusions: that **when *women* abuse, they are sometimes in a position of power, sometimes without power, and sometimes they are experiencing both simultaneously. When men abuse, they are much more likely to be in a position of power*less*ness**—the act of abuse being a momentary act of power designed to compensate for underlying experiences of power*less*ness. Here's the evidence for that paradigm shift, starting with women.

An elderly woman is more than four times as likely to abuse her husband as the other way around.[67] Think about why. If an elderly man is eight years older than his wife, he is an average of fifteen years closer to dying—suffering from arthritis or other ailments. She becomes her own caretaker and his caretaker. He is in about as powerless a place as he can be, and he abuses very little. She is much more powerful in comparison to him and abuses much more. *But* she doubtless *also* feels the powerlessness of being tied to her caretaking responsibilities.

Similarly, two-thirds of mothers with children six years or under hit them three or more times per week.[68] A recent study of *confirmed* child abuse found mothers committed the abuse 58 percent of the time, fathers 16 percent, and both parents 13 percent.[69] We can view this three ways: as mothers exercising their power over their children; as mothers experiencing their powerlessness vis-à-vis their children; or as both. The mother is obviously more powerful, and just as obviously more likely to abuse when the baby is screaming, not smiling: The screaming makes her feel powerless and the feelings of powerlessness tempt physical violence. (Think of how often we hear on the news of a mom putting her infant in a dumpster: The mom has the power to kill, but it is almost always a young single mom with few resources.)

Why are women more likely to abuse men who are powerless while men are more likely to protect women who are powerless? Or, put another way, why, if he feels powerless, is *he* more likely to be abusive *and* she is also more likely to feel abusive? **She perceives him as no longer being able to protect her, so she acts on her instincts to get rid of a man who can't protect her.** (Remember, she survived for millions of years by selecting protectors, which means knowing how to weed out men who can't protect her.) Put another way, female abuse of men who can't perform is instinctive. She feels powerless when he feels powerless.

Among lesbian women, the abused woman was likely to feel that the problem of the batter*er* was *de*pendence, not power.[70]

So among women, feelings of power or powerlessness—or some combination of both—seem in various ways to catalyze abuse.

Among men it seems to be different. In 1997, the American Psychological Association's official journal, the *Journal of Consulting and Clinical Psychology*, found domestic violence by men was more likely to be associated with indicators of power*less*ness than it was when women were violent. The researchers found that physical violence among men was more strongly associated with unemployment, low educational attainment, few social support resources, the use of drugs, personality disorders, and depression[71]—all pretty strong indicators of an underlying experience of powerlessness.

Men's greater physical strength would seem to indicate men's violence toward women involved male power. As I discussed above this is tricky, because men learn to use that strength to protect women and will beat up or even kill a man who uses it against a woman. It is when the power of his masculinity *breaks down* that he is most likely to be violent *toward a woman.*

Many people resist looking at the powerlessness of the batterer because we have been assuming the batterer was a man and we didn't want to blame a woman who was battered. In love, though, both people can feel powerful or both can feel powerless.

The treatment implications are enormous and create much hope. Large numbers of psychologists, social workers, Ys, and battered women's shelters counsel a man who batters a woman to give up his assumptions of male privilege and power. If a woman batters a man, it is by definition in self-defense—he has the power.

This "victim-either-way" rationalization leaves men feeling blamed either way; it increases tensions and, therefore, the battering of spouses and the breakup of marriages. It leaves millions of children raised without the love of their dads. It is, though, good for the lawyers and therapists.

IF MEN HAVE LEARNED "NEVER HIT A WOMAN," THEN WHY DO MEN BATTER AT ALL?

If the beautiful princess chooses the man who is willing to die to protect her, how is it she sometimes winds up being abused by the man who was willing to die for her?

A man writes to Dear Abby that his wife broke his arms and ribs when she threw a heavy chair at him; that she frequently attacked him with her fingernails, drawing blood from his face and neck. But his training to never hit a woman stopped him from retaliating, and he made up lies when he visited emergency rooms. He stayed in the marriage for the child, but when he finally filed for divorce, she accused him of child molestation. Although acquitted, he felt devastated.[72]

The Dear Abby man never hit back. So why do some men violate the male mandate and retaliate—or even initiate? When a man feels the woman he is supposed to protect is threatening him or verbally chopping him apart, he begins to make a mental transfer from protecting her to protecting himself from her. She begins to lose her status as a woman. When the nexus is reached, his protector instinct is compromised. He becomes almost a split personality: protect her; defend self. In turn, when his protector instinct is compromised, her love for him is compromised, and her fear of him becomes irrational—which is her way of protecting herself.

Once this nexus is reached another conflicting message also emerges: "Men don't hit women" conflicts with "She won't respect a man she can push around." Paradoxically, he doesn't have the ability to protect until he has the ability to stand up for himself. And sometimes, the woman may be provoking him to stimulate passion and strength, which she may find preferable to a disconnected blob. In brief, there is often an intricately woven dance going on, which makes one-sided blame so inappropriate.

DON'T HUSBANDS ACTUALLY KILL THEIR WIVES MORE THAN WIVES KILL HUSBANDS, THUS MAKING BATTERING SCARIER TO WOMEN?

We opened the chapter with an Ad Council ad showing how the *visual* image of Marry-the-Enemy is created. But the reason that ad can run without protest is that it manipulates us into believing this is a statistical reality. Here's how . . .

The happy bride is warned: "42 percent of all murdered women are killed by the same man."[73] Look at the ad again and register the *feeling*.

When a woman is looking at a picture of a day that is supposed to be her

FORTY-TWO PERCENT OF ALL MURDERED WOMEN
ARE KILLED BY THE SAME MAN.

Each day women are beaten to death by their husbands or boyfriends. Just as frightening,
each day neighbors just like us make excuses for not getting involved. For information about how
you can help stop domestic violence, call 1-800-END-ABUSE.

THERE'S NO EXCUSE
for Domestic Violence.

Family Violence
Prevention Fund

happiest, that's an *emotional* experience; it does not motivate her to do a statistical analysis of the 42 percent figure. She is manipulated into going with the "feel" of the ad—that her happiest day is almost as likely as not to turn into her death. Most women sense it is a statistical manipulation, but still the "feel" remains and the fear registers. And that is the ad's intent.

The value of stopping to do a statistical look-see is to make the fear appropriate to the reality. When it isn't, it's called paranoia. People who refuse to look at a statistic because they want to remain "heart focused" are subject to having their heart manipulated. In reality, 900 women are murdered each year by the man they married.[74] Out of 54 *million* married women in the United States.[75] That creates a bit of a different feeling. But let's move to the exact statistic: that "42 percent of all *murdered* women are killed by the same man."

The basic trick of the Ad Council's ad is that a high *percentage* of murdered wives are murdered by their husband or ex-husband *exactly because married women are so rarely murdered to begin with.*

But aren't husbands more likely to kill their wives than vice versa? Again, we enter the arena of "who's the biggest victim?" It bothers me to have to document that the sexes kill their spouses about equally, but there are life-and-death consequences that result from feminists persuading the public that it is almost exclusively husbands who kill wives. It leads to financing of only women's shelters and hotlines, without shelters and hotlines for men, thus leaving men with no place to go when they are in danger, so they become powder kegs that can endanger their wives rather than people who can find a supportive retreat temporarily and teach them Part I's relationship language permanently.

The brief answer to this accusation is that no one knows for sure which sex kills the other more. In a second we'll see why it's likely that more wives kill husbands, but until the government is willing to collect data about the three female methods of killing, we can only make an educated guess. I'll explain.

On the surface, the Bureau of Justice reports women are the perpetrators in 41 percent of spousal murders.[76] However, the male method of killing is with a knife or gun, done by himself; it is easily detected and reported. The three female methods of killing are designed to not be detected, to have the man's death appear as an accident, so insurance money can be collected.

The first mostly-female method is poisoning. The second is the wife hiring a professional killer. The third is the wife persuading a boyfriend to do the killing.

These last two methods, *if* discovered, are never listed by the FBI as a woman killing a man. They are listed, rather, as "multiple-offender" killings.[77] We only know that **in multiple-offender killings there are four times as many husbands as victims than wives,** according to the FBI.[78] That is, the 41 percent figure does not include either of these female methods of killing.

How common are multiple-offender, usually contract, killings? We don't know. Perhaps the best hint we have of how many husbands could be killed by contract comes from the FBI, reporting that some *7800 men were killed without the killer being identified* (vs. 1500 women).[79] This number is *almost nine times larger than all of the wives killed by spouses and ex-spouses put together.*[80] However, this "nine times as many" figure is a very inadequate hint since many of these men were doubtless killed by other men, and many are unmarried. It just gives us an understanding that multiple-offender killings must be considered before we can claim that more men murder wives than vice-versa.

Most important, of the hundred or so contract killings about which I have read, only a small percentage were originally recognized as such. The very purpose in hiring a professional, as with poisoning, was to have the husband's death appear as an accident so the wife can collect insurance money.

Roberta Pearce, a teacher's aide, didn't have enough money to hire a real pro. But she knew if she killed her husband and got away with it, she would have $200,000 in life-insurance money and a home of her own. So she offered two of her fifteen-year-old students $50,000 each, sex, and a car if they would do just one thing—kill her husband.[81] Statistically, though, Roberta will not be listed as a wife who killed her husband.

A husband is much more likely to kill in an emotional fit of rage (so much for the rational sex!). Or he kills his wife and children, and then turns the gun to his own head. Next time you read about a husband killing a wife in the newspaper, read a little further in the article and you'll be surprised to see how often he also kills himself. And obviously the killing of himself indicates that money is not his primary motivation. When people commit suicide, it is because they feel there is no one who loves them or needs them.

In brief, a wife's style of killing reflects her motivation, which requires the killing not to be detected; a husband's style of killing reflects his motivation and, well, a husband who kills himself is pretty likely to be caught—a dead husband is a dead giveaway. Even if her killing does get detected, it is much more likely to never be recorded as a spouse killing—but as a multiple-offender killing, or an accident or a heart attack. When a woman is murdered, we are more likely to track down the killer than when a man is murdered.[82]

As a result of the invisibility of the female methods of killing, women who do kill benefit from the stereotype of women as innocent, and are treated very differently by the law: thirteen percent of spousal murder cases with women defendants result in an acquittal vs. 1 percent of murder cases with men defendants. Similarly, the average prison sentence for spousal murder (excluding life sentences and the death penalty) is almost three times longer for men than for women—17.5 years vs. 6.2 years.[83] And, thus far, a woman has never been executed for killing only a man. When we can only see women as innocent, the law becomes equally blind.

Just as there are different male and female styles of killing and the female's has remained invisible, there are also different male and female methods of violence that do not involve killing. The women's style has been so invisible we haven't called it domestic violence.

DOMESTIC VIOLENCE, FEMALE STYLE

"REPUTATION RUINING" VIA FALSE ACCUSATIONS OF ABUSE

Thomas Kiernan, author of *Citizen Murdoch* (as well as twenty-five other books), reported in the *New Jersey Law Journal* his experience attending four different seminars for wives contemplating divorce. He reported that in *all* four cases, a female lawyer conducted the seminar and "recommended, with knowing winks and smirks, the 'advantages' of 'establishing' or 'creating' a 'record' of spousal violence, *whether true or not,* prior to the filing of a divorce complaint."[84]

What upset Kiernan was that a law designed to prevent domestic violence (the Prevention of Domestic Violence Act) was openly being used to falsely accuse men of spouse abuse. But the devastation to a man's reputation and career is the less important consequence. The false accusation allows the woman to obtain the children because the father is a suspected abuser. The false accusation also justifies a woman being able to obtain an emergency restraining order to kick a man out of his home prior to the commencement of divorce proceedings, thereby also increasing her likelihood of obtaining the children because they are "living with the mother now and stability dictates their remaining with the mother."

But this is what most astonished Kiernan: "The number of women attending the seminars who smugly—indeed boastfully—announced that they had already sworn out false or grossly exaggerated domestic-violence complaints against their hapless husbands, and that the device worked! To add amazement to my astonishment, the lawyer-lectures invariably congratulated the self-confessed miscreants."

Unsubstantiated and false accusations of spouse abuse or child abuse ruin a man's reputation even if he is ultimately found to be innocent.

Why are men so damaged by "reputation ruining"? Men's ability to earn leads to their ability to gain love. Destroying earning potential means destroying love potential. Observe how frequently a man will die from a heart attack or cancer—or just commit suicide—shortly after his reputation is ruined. Yet these deaths are recorded as heart attacks, not husband abuse. And not murder.

PROPERTY ABUSE AND CAREER DESTRUCTION

Item. As I walked into the Pannikin—a coffee shop where I occasionally edit my writing—I spotted a friend of mine who looked depressed. It turned out that he and his wife were divorcing; his wife had just destroyed all the architectural plans he was working on.

We have traditionally thought of the body of work that men produce over the course of a lifetime as the psychological equivalent of the children that women produce over the course of a lifetime. Is "husband career damage" via property abuse a female style of abuse, albeit unrecognized and therefore invisible? The only hint we have is that more than *two-thirds* of lesbians who were abused had their property destroyed or damaged.[85] We don't have any data for men. It is interesting that only when women are the victims of property abuse do we care enough to study it. In contrast, when I am watching a film and the woman is ruining a man's career, as in *First Wives' Club,* I am saddened to hear the cheering from among so many in the audience, especially women.

PSYCHOLOGICAL ABUSE

When lesbian abuse is studied, psychological abuse is often considered as important as physical abuse.[86] Studies of heterosexuals, though, have noticeably avoided psychological abuse. Psychological abuse comes up only when the evidence is clear that the sexes physically abuse equally; *then* the first response is, "When women abuse men physically it's because men have abused women psychologically first."

Why have we been so hesitant to study psychological abuse among heterosexuals? Was it because we sensed all along that women are more likely to use psychology to abuse men because verbal communication is women's strength and men's weakness? Were we afraid to explore anything that might make men look less guilty ("the men were also abused") or force women to take responsibility ("the women were also abusers")? If that was not the reason, why is it that psychological abuse is suddenly so important when women (as in the lesbian community) are its victims, or when a woman is the perpetrator of physical abuse?

Now that we know that men are abused at least as much, though, it will be easier to study the entire abuse *system*—male *and* female, psychological *and* physical.

What little we do know about heterosexual psychological abuse seems to indicate that the sexes swear and insult each other about equally, and that women threaten men with violence more. One study is from New Zealand, and the other is unpublished raw data from the University of New Hampshire's Family Research Lab.[87]

A few men have said to me, "And women manipulate us psychologically by crying more." The New Zealand study did verify that women cry more during conflicts, 55 percent vs. 16 percent,[88] but I do not personally feel that all crying can be called manipulative and, therefore, psychological abuse. That is, many men do feel manipulated by a crying woman, but that does not necessarily mean that the woman intended manipulation.

In my own observation of the sexes over three decades, I find women and men psychologically abuse each other in different ways. Men are more likely to disappear at work, disappear into a project in the garage, or disappear into a bottle; to withdraw behind a newspaper or in front of the TV; to become addicted to sports or to gambling. Women are more likely to shop and spend, nag and manipulate, or withdraw from sex or into a romance novel. Contrary to popular opinion, both are about equally likely to have affairs. Both sexes employ forms of power intended to compensate for feelings of powerlessness. Both sexes experience Pyrrhic victories.

"MY PARTNER KNOWS JUST WHICH BUTTONS TO PUSH"

Perhaps the most Pyrrhic victory is "pushing our partner's buttons." Spouse abuse is usually preceded by a pattern of unwanted dialogue that is nevertheless repeated.[89] Think about "unwanted" and "repeated." Meaning both sexes know they are escalating their partner's anger, but continue to do it anyway. Do some people on some level need to verbally batter more than they need to avoid being physically battered?

Yes. Why? Words contain more potential for rejecting us than being hit does. The old saw should be, "Sticks and stones can break my bones, but names *can break my heart.*" For some people, physical battering allows them to express themselves without doing as much damage as they would with words. Which is why the solution is reworking the entire system of communicating criticism. Then we can focus not on abuse and victims, but on ways of using disagreements as opportunities to deepen our compassion and therefore our love.

How Innocent Women Get Hurt When Guilty Women Go Free

Everywhere Cindy Barry of Minnesota turned, she encountered the assumption that her batterer was a man.[90] Even in court, judges continually referred to her batterer as "he." Now she is protesting this assumption. Cindy was abused by her lesbian lover, and the image of women as nonviolent led to Cindy not being taken seriously.

Ironically, a woman is once again discovering that the elimination of men's rights eventually hurts women—those women who have life experiences similar to some men's, such as being battered by a woman. Cindy Barry is having to fight to receive justice because laws were protecting women so completely that Cindy had no protection against these women. Feminism had become a type of female Mafia, protecting women who battered because they were women, but forgetting the rights of women victimized by women, as well as men and children victimized by women.

How Innocent *Children* Get Hurt When Guilty Women Go Free

Item. Laurie Dann was already under investigation by the FBI for extortion. (She was demanding money in return for halting the phone harassment of the family of a doctor she had dated eighteen years previously.) Police in the Chicago area had registered approximately a dozen complaints against her. When she and her husband, Russell, separated, Russell reported to the police "harassment, stabbings, purchasing of guns, and death threats."[91] He then reported that Laurie broke into the house and punctured him in the chest with an ice pick while he was asleep.

When Laurie Dann bought a .357 magnum revolver, Russell informed the police she threatened to kill him with it, but the police did not impound the gun.

They did not even confront Laurie; they confronted only her father. Laurie then took the .357 magnum plus two other handguns and shot six children at an elementary school, leaving eight-year-old Nicholas Corwin to die.[92]

When we fail to believe men who report abuse, we jeopardize children and the community. Is this "the system's" fault, or do our attitudes create the system? Thus even with all the complaints against Laurie, no inhibiting action was taken, and even when Laurie was accused of threatening to kill her husband with a newly purchased .357 magnum, Laurie herself was never approached. The reverse would have led to a national police scandal.

When we think only men are serial killers, we are less likely to look for patterns when a woman is reported, therefore less likely to prioritize catching her, and thus leave all of those we love at risk. When we don't take seriously the men who report women, we unwittingly abuse our children. When we don't take seriously the female who commits a crime, she won't take committing a crime seriously.

DOES THE LAW PROTECT WOMEN MORE THAN MEN?

Item. Evelyn Humphrey was very drunk. She took a gun and killed Albert Hampton, her live-in partner. She claimed he had been abusive the day before. His death prevented him from claiming he wasn't. She claimed "Battered Woman Syndrome." The California Supreme Court gave her an acquittal.[93] Until that time (1996), such a defense could only be used to *reduce* the charges to manslaughter for a woman who killed her spouse or partner. Now it can be used to give an acquittal to a woman—but not a man.

The "Battered Woman Syndrome" legal defense is unconstitutional because there is no "Battered Man Syndrome" legal defense. Allowing a woman to claim she was defenseless when she, in fact, had time to physically escape gives women a permission to kill that is granted to no man under English or American law. In both respects, the "Battered Woman Syndrome" violates the Fourteenth Amendment's guarantee to equal protection of all human beings regardless of sex. The only law more blatantly unconstitutional is male-only draft registration. The "Battered Woman Syndrome" is only one of eight legal defenses I discuss in *The Myth of Male Power*[94] that women can use to kill with impunity that cannot be used by men. Taken together with longer prison sentences for men for the same crime, they give men a clear message: "You are less valued than women. You are second-class citizens."

Is the solution a "Battered Person Syndrome" allowing both sexes to kill abusers? Hardly. The implication? Physical aggression has been used to "resolve marital conflict" at least once in 60 percent of families.[95] But it isn't just spouses who would be able to murder each other. Ninety-three percent of gay men and 88 percent of gay women who were abusers said they had been physically abused as children.[96] Should we allow them to go kill their parents and call it self-defense? That would create a Family Murder Act to replace a Male Murder Act.

CONCLUSION AND SOLUTIONS

If battering is a two-way street, so is its solution. And fortunately, the solution to physical and psychological abuse lies in focusing on prevention—especially the skills to handle personal criticism I discuss in Part I.

ARE LAWS AGAINST PHYSICAL ABUSE HELPFUL?

Legal restriction is *not* the most powerful restraint operating on men. It is the fear of losing the love of the woman. And the self-loathing that emanates from months of slavishly attempting to rebuild trust. One way or another, **the man who physically hits a woman has traded one minute of power for months of powerlessness.**

Crossculturally, laws that punish physical abuse do appear to have an inhibiting effect on physical abuse.[97] But not a big inhibiting effect.[98] In approximately 85 percent of domestic violence assault and homicide cases, police had visited that home address at least once in the two previous years.[99]

Punishment is often society's cop-out from complexity. For example, imprisoning the abusive husband of a pregnant wife is often a cop-out from dealing via pregnancy counseling with the complex anxieties pregnancy creates. Yet, incentives for couples to take part in pregnancy counseling cost less than using taxpayer money to keep a husband in prison. To say nothing of the anxiety a pregnant woman feels when her husband is in jail (as opposed to counseling with jail as a backup).

Both the laws against battering (and the attitude those laws reflect) did doubtless contribute to the 21 percent reduction in severe wife beating. However, the biased application of those laws against male batterers doubtless leads to the less than 4 percent reduction in severe husband beating, as well as to the increase in minor husband beating (but not minor wife beating).

The problem runs deeper with mandatory arrest laws. Once a person is arrested for domestic violence she or he is less likely to be re-arrested than someone to whom the police just give advice,[100] but that doesn't tell us how many people just stay away from calling the police again when the result the last time was a criminal record for life. Also, they tie the hands of the police—turning them into automatons rather than professionals with judgment. It is better to respond to a call for help with a low profile car and police trained in communications work, with the authority to make a range of decisions depending on the situation.

Mandatory arrest laws are usually applied with extreme bias against men. When they aren't, the results are a bit ironic. Feminists pushed for those laws, but when the police arrived, even when the woman had called, it was often so apparent to the police that the woman had been the main abuser that the arrest rates of women for spousal abuse have doubled since implementation of mandatory arrest laws in Los Angeles.[101] Many feminists have thus begun opposing what they previously supported when they thought only men would be arrested.

Given Suzanne Steinmetz's observation that since 60 percent of families have experienced abuse since marriage,[102] strict laws arresting abusers would be like laws allowing the actual arrest of anyone exceeding 55 miles per hour. Most of America would be in prison.

In brief, laws and police intervention can neither be dismissed as irrelevant, be enforced in a sexist manner (and expect not to be eventually found unconstitutional), nor be made so loose as to include virtually everyone. Most important, though, imprisonment is more expensive than empowerment. And imprisonment is less effective than empowerment.

LOVE HIM OR LEAVE HIM; LOVE HER OR LEAVE HER?

Although the culture's attention is focused on helping women leave, we have seen men also fear leaving. They fear that leaving their wife means losing their children; that leaving their wife means leaving their children to be abused (abusive spouses are often abusive parents). It is men who have no shelters to turn to, no hotlines to call, no genetic heritage or socialization to ask for help, no education to request a restraining order; who believe the police will laugh at them; who feel dirty laundry shouldn't be aired in public; who have few men friends, fewer men's support groups, minimal vocabulary for discussing these issues.

One of the most destructive-to-women myths is that women are powerless to leave men—the men will just come after them and kill them. The myth is perpetuated by films like *Sleeping With the Enemy,* in which an abused woman runs away after faking her own death and changing her identity, but her husband nevertheless tracks her down. The message is, "There's no way you can escape an abusive man and remain alive—they're the cleverest, most psychopathic, schizoid terrorists on earth." But is it true?

Some men do come after women, and some women do hire contract killers. There are no guarantees for *either* sex that they will be safe if they leave *or* stay. But almost every time I have read of a spouse "coming after" the party who has left, one or more of these five catalysts to violence-after-leaving has occurred.

THE FIVE CATALYSTS TO VIOLENCE-AFTER-LEAVING:

(1) Deplete the bank account

(2) Leave a vitriolic, rejecting note

(3) Take the kids

(4) Have the spouse arrested

(5) Have a lover and go to her or his house

Obviously, arresting a spouse is sometimes not only necessary but appropriate. But it is a risk factor, to be balanced by the risk factor of not arresting. If the arrest has been manipulated to keep children, the risk of retaliation increases. The purpose of knowing these catalysts is to empower an abused spouse to leave safely. The two rules of thumb are, set firm boundaries and help your partner save face, even as you enforce the boundaries.

For a husband who leaves, there's a sixth catalyst: the larger your life insurance policy, the greater the incentive to have you killed and making it appear as an accident, as discussed above.

The "Battered Woman Syndrome," then, is an insult to women's intelligence. It suggests that only a woman cannot figure out a way of leaving while her spouse is at work, or on a sales trip, or on a fishing weekend; or that only she cannot feign a weekend trip with a woman friend or to her parents. But in the final analysis, there are no guarantees of violence avoidance for either sex. The best we can do is to know that battering decreases as listening increases.

We occasionally read of men banging down the door of their home and hurting the woman and children. But remember, this is almost always when *he* has been *evicted*. Not when *she* has *left*. Were the roles reversed and he-had gotten a restraining order to prevent her from returning home and seeing the children, the chances of her resorting to violence would also increase.

Both sexes harass each other after separation. But women worry more whether his phone calls, for example, indicate physical danger. The three best clues are (1) their personal history of physical violence; (2) how much he feels rejected; and (3) whether or not she has taken the children "behind his back."

If he has no personal history of physical violence, then she protects herself best by negotiating *with* him (not dictating *to* him) a specific contract—of times to talk, of times when he versus she will have the children. Most men who aren't made to feel unilaterally rejected are good about sticking to contracts *if* they know they are firm and *if* the woman is sticking to her end of the deal. A contract allows him to focus on what he will receive rather than on what he has lost.

IF A MAN SLAPS A WOMAN, SHOULD SHE LEAVE HIM?

Since women are more likely to slap men, the question that should be asked is, "If your *partner* slaps you should you leave?" Shelters are only available for women and they see the cases that have escalated, therefore they believe, "A man who slaps you once will slap you twice, will eventually beat you and batter you." They don't see that women are twice as likely to be the first ones to slap a man before and after a marriage—at the rate of 26 percent before a marriage, as we saw above—and that both sexes are *less* likely to hit each other as a relationship matures. Nor do they see why violence decreases when it does—how some couples have used the signal of a slap as a sign that the situation is out of control, that they need help and, *as* they're getting help, set firm boundaries: "If it happens again, I'm out of here."

Walking out doesn't consider the impact on children of one slap leading to the end of life as they knew it.

The power of a slap across the face from someone we love is not in the physical hurt of the slap nearly as much as in the rejection the slap might symbolize. If the slap symbolizes a breakdown in the system that has brought us love, it might hurt more than a broken nose on the football field that was achieved in the process of scoring a touchdown. The issue is not the pain, but the context.

We have allowed to atrophy the ability of our mind to "contextualize pain." Ellen Langer, a Harvard social psychologist, found that once a person has reinterpreted their pain into a more positive context, they are unlikely to return to the original painful context.

The paradigm shift for domestic violence work in the future, then, is to use the slap so that it is eventually contextualized as the start of a better marriage.

INVENTING THE VICTIM: A STAGE II LUXURY

In Stage II marriages, more people can afford to leave partners who physically and psychologically abuse them. They can afford *conditional* love. And this new freedom has spawned whole libraries helping us get in touch with "the victim inside of us" (codependency, addiction, incest, battering, molestation). As the pendulum swings from "endure anything from anyone" to "sue anyone for anything," we have developed a new industry of competition to be the biggest victim. Lawyers and therapists are paid to find victims; when the supply runs short, they create them. We are making a transition from a nation who believed, "When the going gets tough, the tough get going," to a nation who believes, "When the going gets tough, get a tough lawyer."

When it actually pays to be a victim, the pendulum swings from "for better or for worse" marriages to "he slapped me, I'm gone" marriages. Which sometimes means "he slapped me, give me the kids and pay me" marriages.

THE POLITICS OF ABUSE: THE GREAT INEQUALITY

In the arena of relationship arguments, women are about as much the masters as men are on football fields. But *women's misuse of relationship power is legal; men's misuse of physical power is illegal.* The illegality of physical abuse makes men more restrained in the use of their physical power than women are in the use of their relationship power. This might be called "The Great Inequality."

We are now in a bind. We have discovered the need for a two-sex approach to domestic violence, but federal and state governments give tax exemptions to organizations like the United Way, which fund this feminist, blame-the-male approach. It would be naive to think that these interlocking bureaucracies (governments, foundations, and feminism) will change by readers passively absorbing this information. Politicians must know that when it comes to the assumption of men-as-perpetrator, woman-as-victim, their constituencies are in a divided way, not a United Way. Foundations must know their tax-exempt status is being called into question due to their discrimination against men. They must see copies of letters written to Congresspersons and Senators. And be offered solutions.

If we wish to help men and women to help themselves, I believe we will need to do the following:

- Train equal numbers of male and female counselors (worldwide) to take a nonsexist, systems approach to battering—the approach outlined in Part I.

- Establish Family Communication workshops to be available to everyone, without it being associated with domestic violence. A much cheaper investment than prisons.

- Require the police departments to transfer all domestic violence calls to a twenty-four-hour domestic violence hotline funded adequately enough to send out a man and woman to work with an in-crisis couple.

- The police are used only when the man or woman desires the police after the other alternative is offered.

- If the hotline is used more than once, a user fee must be paid by the couple if they do not commit to attend the free Family Communication workshops.

IT IS CHEAPER TO EMPOWER THAN TO IMPRISON

Can mandatory communication workshops be enforced? Yes. If the first-time batterer is given a choice between mandatory arrest or a mandatory communication workshop. It won't take long for workshops to be fuller and prisons to be emptier. Taxpayer money will be sowing seeds of love rather than breeding anger. It is cheaper to empower than it is to imprison.

In conclusion, when domestic violence is seen as a two-way street, it frees us to transfer from a "men must give up their power" model for treatment to a "walk a mile in each other's moccasins" model for treatment. It frees us to focus not on a scapegoat oppressor, but a mutual responsibility dance; not on punishment, but prevention. It frees us not to treat a slap as terminal cancer, but as a signal we need to make our love healthier. We have an opportunity to make a paradigm shift from the world of victimhood—of learned helplessness defenses, battered women's shelters and syndromes, mandatory arrest policies, and restraining orders—to the world of relationship training in elementary school; workshops on "how to hear criticism" and "how to give criticism"—the world of redefining love.

PART III

Outside the Home

7

What Men Would Say When Male Bashing Is Called "Funny," But Female Bashing Is Called "Sexist"

MAN BASHING: TRIVIAL PURSUIT OR A TRUTH WITH CONSEQUENCES?

NOT ALL MEN ARE ANNOYING SOME ARE DEAD [1]

Man bashers focus on the problems *with* men and ignore the problems *of* men. They usually become man bashers by focusing on the problems of women and blaming those problems on men. The combination is misandry.

Misandry—or man hating—is the equivalent of misogyny. If you are unaware of misandry, welcome to the club. Our failure to see it is so complete that even the most careful observer of the human vocabulary, *Webster's Unabridged Dictionary*, is blind to it.[2] One writer calls misandry "the hate that dares us to breathe its name."[3]

Is misandry not acknowledged because it does not exist? A week after you read this chapter, misandry will become apparent in commercials, in films, in everyday conversations. But the bias that is hardest to see is the bias we share. Even allegedly gender-neutral words like "sexist" imply slights only against women.

Man bashing is *not* a problem per se. A person who cannot laugh at her- or himself has a serious problem. But when one group gets singled out far more often than others—whether it be "dumb Poles," "dumb blondes," or "corrupt lawyers"—then a red flag is sent up. And I find man bashing now runs about 9 to 1 over woman bashing. As *Time* magazine puts it, it's as if "masculinity were a bad smell in the room."[4]

The lopsided objectification of a group as the devil always makes us callous to its deaths. Men's life expectancy was one year less than women's in 1920; today, it is seven years less,[5] yet the federal government has only an Office of Research on Women's Health.[6] It's part of what leads us to our blindness toward domestic violence against men and to caring more about saving whales than males.

On a personal level, man bashing hurts women because it undermines the one thing that has most motivated men to work for women and die for women throughout history: appreciation. **I've never seen a greeting card for thanking mentors, or for thanking volunteer firemen.**

THE DOUBLE STANDARD AND ITS CONSEQUENCES

Today, misandry is also in the double standard of our response: **Woman bashing is a lawsuit; man bashing is a Hallmark card.** Public woman bashing is illegal; public man bashing is institutionalized.

Is man bashing less damaging than woman bashing because boys spend a lifetime putting each other down? The two are different. When boys put each other down, there is an unwritten rule that *it goes both ways.* Not true when women put men down. If she implies he's inept, it's a joke; if he implies she's inept, it might be a joke, or it might be a "hostile work environment." If she considers it a joke at the time, but a year later fails to get promoted, yesterday's joke can become tomorrow's lawsuit. And an end to the "joker's" career.

A man whose career ends in shame is often a man whose marriage ends, which often leads to his children calling him visitor (as in "she has the children . . . he has visitation"). When the U.S. Coast Guard's top spokesperson, Captain Ernie Blanchard, told much less offensive jokes than the ones we'll see below, Coast Guard feminists complained. Captain Blanchard apologized. The apologies weren't good enough. He was subjected to a *criminal* probe. He offered to resign to spare his family—on the condition the probe would stop. The Coast Guard refused. Beside himself, he took his grandfather's Smith & Wesson revolver, pointed it to his head, and shot a bullet through his brains.[7]

Why would the Coast Guard refuse to stop a criminal probe for a joke? Once the machinery of a sexual harassment complaint is set into motion, few officers or corporate executives have the guts to stop the machinery for fear they'll become part of the complaint.

This double standard ultimately violates women. Mentors have proven crucial to female success, and women consistently seek male mentors—the higher up, the better. But the higher up the man, the farther he has to fall. Sexual harassment legislation has left potential mentors increasingly feeling there is a thin line between helping a woman advance her career and helping himself hurt his career. Mentoring requires intimacy that includes joking, criticism, and time alone. A joke that seems safe during the intimacy of mentoring can become a lawsuit when the woman being mentored begins to want to create an identity independent of the mentor. Then she often goes through a period of rebellion similar to any adolescent trying to create identity. The jokes and intimacies can come back to haunt him. Once a man sees this happen to someone in the company, or a friend, he thinks twice about being a mentor. Which is why the double standard hurts women.

Misandry's double standard is also in our language.

DOUBLESPEAK

When we make positive references, it is politically correct to include women: chairman becomes chairperson; spokesman becomes spokesperson; yet when the reference is negative, no one cries, "Don't say gunman, say gunperson."

When a wealthy older man marries a younger woman, we say, "He's robbing the cradle." We don't say "She's robbing the bank." When Warren Beatty was single, he was called a "womanizer," as if his women friends were victims; when Madonna was single, she was never called a "manizer." She was called either liberated or promiscuous. The difference? Neither liberated nor promiscuous suggests her men friends were victims. The old double standard of labeling women promiscuous while suggesting men were sowing their wild oats has reversed itself: Women with many partners are now liberated; their male counterparts, womanizers.

Even self-help writers voice only women's complaint that men leave the toilet seat up. No one suggests thanking the man for putting it up so he gets nothing on it. **And no one asks why a woman expects the toilet to always be as it is in women's rooms, and never as half the toilets are in men's rooms: urinals.** Why, when a woman enters the picture, do her rules prevail? When she doesn't prevail, why is *he* criticized—why don't *they* compromise? When self-help writers help only her, are they really just helping themselves?

Unfortunately, the strongest opponents of misogyny are often the greatest misandrists. Feminists rightly ask us to reconsider references to women as "baby," "honey," "doll," and "spinster," but are often the first to call men dead-beats, jerks, perverts, macho, rapists, and womanizers. And should a man protest, he risks being labeled a wimp, whiner, chauvinist, or misogynist. The quotes later in the chapter, from feminists like Gloria Steinem and Andrea Dworkin, novelists like Marilyn French, journalists like former *New York Times* columnist Anna Quindlen, and from former Congresswomen like Barbara Jordan are all examples of misandry from opponents of misogyny.

HAVEN'T MEN ALWAYS DISHED IT OUT?
WHY CAN'T THEY TAKE IT?

When man bashing first appears on someone's radar screen, it is almost always dismissed as a function of the pendulum swinging too far—from woman bashing to man bashing. Not true. Comics like *Dagwood* have portrayed man-as-fool since the 1920s. Prior to the women's movement, shows like *The Three Stooges* made a joke of both verbal and physical man bashing. In *The Honeymooners,* the louder Ralph Kramden said "One of these days, *pow,* right in the kisser," or "To the moon, Alice," the farther *he* would fall. Every *Honeymooners* episode followed this formula—or Ralph's fall from man-as-boastful-jerk to the rediscovery of the greater superiority and wisdom of his wife. Only *he* was wrong; only *he* apologized.

On the other hand, shows like *I Love Lucy* mocked both sexes for the excesses of their sex role. And still others idealized both sexes' role (from the *Father Knows Best* image of masculinity to the "motherhood-and-apple-pie" image of *I Remember Mama*).

In the past, when *either* sex deviated from its role, it was a target of epithets. A woman was cheap, easy, promiscuous, a bitch; a man was a jerk, asshole, bastard, motherfucker, faggot. I am not aware of any time in the past in which men were not also the subject of ridicule. Feminists, though, have specialized in uncovering only the ridicule against women, making the pendulum appear to have been off balance, thus justifying man bashing as returning to balance.

Now the pendulum *is* off to one side. While epithets against women can end a man's career track, epithets against men can begin a career track for writers of cards, comedies, cartoons, and commercials.

ARE MEN *CALLED* JERKS BECAUSE MEN *ARE* JERKS?

A study of thousands of commercials found that if both sexes appeared in the commercial but only one was portrayed as a jerk, *it was the man who was the jerk 100 percent of the time.*[8]

Would men be called jerks less often if they were jerks less often? Yes and no. Men are jerks more often in part because they take risks more often. A woman who doesn't receive a call from a man for a long time after a date often calls her woman friend and they both label him a "jerk." **No one asks why she's expecting *him* to make the call.** He doesn't call her a jerk if she doesn't call *him*.

Suppose he promised to call? That's part of their lopsided expectations—that he will make the promise to do something, not she. Those expected to take most of the risks, make most of the promises, do most of the performing, are most often called a jerk when they fail. When they do it perfectly, they're a hero. **A jerk is a potential hero who messes it up along the way.** Women who repeatedly fall in love with jerks have usually fallen in love with risk-takers rather than take the risks themselves.

Does man bashing make women believe men are getting worse even in areas in which they are improving? Yes. Remember how we saw in the chapter on housework that even though men were doing much more housework, women believed they were doing less?[9] The only thing consistent with that belief was the male-bashing headlines about men and housework.

Obviously, something deeper is going on to generate this anger.

WHY ARE WOMEN SO ANGRY AT MEN?

The anger from women to men that we'll see below can easily make us feel angry toward women. But understanding what creates that anger, and what can be done to change what creates it provides more compassion toward women, and is far more productive to loving each other. Both for ourselves and our children.

Are women angry because they're powerless, and anger is the way the powerless are heard? Yes and no. Never in history has any large single group of people had, on the surface, more options, wealth, education, personal power, privilege, and respect than women in middle- and upper-middle-class industrialized societies today. And never has such a large group been so angry. Why?

Until recently, there was no social permission for divorce. Marriage guaranteed for a lifetime meant economic security guaranteed for a lifetime. Any man who didn't provide that was ostracized, ridiculed, or ignored. Black men, Indian men, homeless men, and gay men have the toughest time among American males. *And they all have something in common: They do not provide an economic security blanket for women.*

Divorce altered the economic relationship between men and women, and, therefore, the psychological relationship between men and women. When divorce was not permitted, men's addiction to sex and the twenty-year-old woman worked for her—the addiction made him agree to support her for a lifetime; the taboo on divorce made him stick to his agreement. When the taboo on divorce weakened and she was forty, his addiction to the twenties worked against her. She felt disposable.

While this was true for all divorced women, the more beautiful the woman was when she was younger, the more she had been treated like a celebrity—what I call a "genetic celebrity." The more she had been a genetic celebrity, the more likely she was to feel anger as age brought feelings of invisibility in the beauty contest of everyday life in which she used to be the winner.

Many divorced women with children feel they are not being treated as a woman, but as a package deal: a woman with children. A woman friend of mine deeply loved a man, but he was supporting his ex and their children and was already working more than he wanted. When he saw my woman friend's guilt about not spending more time with her children, he became afraid marriage would lead to her quitting work as his previous wife had. Thus he would never commit. My woman friend broke up with him and, after that, I noticed she would often make digs at men—digs that never quite disappeared.

Feminism had a powerful effect on helping women become stronger, more independent. But it had almost no impact on the type of man a woman would find suitable if she did marry. In workshops, **when I ask women, "On your wedding day, did you believe the man you married would consistently earn less than you?" almost no woman says "yes."** That is, almost every woman who *marries* still believes her future husband will earn equal to or more than she. If she feels he doesn't "have potential," she might have sex with him, might even live with him, but rarely marries him. Why?

This evolved as part of women's historic and biological obligation to find a good provider and protector, not just for themselves, but for their children. Her search for a successful man was her first step to becoming a responsible mother. But women's biology, like men's, created a barrier to our struggle not to treat each other as objects. Men treated women as sex objects; women treated men as success objects. Feminism confronted men's addiction to women as "sex objects," but no one confronted women's addiction to men as "success objects."

So worldwide, women are still set up with "The Princess Diana Fantasy." President Clinton made clear the problem with the male fantasy, but no one asked Monica to re-examine the problem with the female fantasy. Which is . . . ?

When two-and-a-half-billion people, mostly women, are comparing their own lives to that of the future Princess Diana as they watch the TV broadcast of her marrying the prince, more than a few are likely to find their own lives disappointing. When 25 million American women[10] read an average of twelve romance novels per month,[11] often with *Bridges of Madison County*–type themes of married moms being swept away by roving Clint Eastwoods, again, more than a few are likely to find their own lives disappointing.

Even in the late '60s, the National Longitudinal Survey found that 70 percent of younger women believed they would not be working at age thirty-five, yet when they actually reached age thirty-five, more than 70 percent of them *were* working.[12] *These women's dreams, of being swept away, had been swept away.* This created disappointment and anger.

Then, when women like Diana, who do marry the prince, are themselves disappointed, and that disappointment resonates with her own, and men are not offering their perspective, *marital* problems become interpreted as problems *of* women, *with* men.

Women's greater-than-ever wealth and power fails to predict happiness, then, because it fails to consider disappointed expectations, the hurt and pain of being rejected, and the hopelessness many women feel when they have less beauty power and more children than they did when they were twenty—thus making the princes who were interested in her when she had external beauty be less interested in her now that she has more internal beauty.

The degree to which we help our daughters resist the temptation to feel entitled to a prince is the degree to which they will feel less angry when the prince they marry is half prince and half frog . . . a bit like themselves. When I have seen, in my workshops, women without these expectations, or women who can see the world from men's perspectives without denying their own, I see the anger soften, and openings for love be created.

THE HATRED OF SELF-HATRED

Every group that hates others usually hates itself. As we look at the variety of forms the overt hatred of men takes, it's important to see that at least some of it emanates from self-hatred, even if it is the self-hatred of unrealistic expectations unrealized. This is most apparent in the cruelty toward men in ads for products that unconsciously imply the woman is not perfect: products like Diet Coke and Diet Pepsi, bras, or hair products.

One Diet Coke ad features a woman knocking out three men, then drinking a Diet Coke. No words. End of ad. Another features a woman getting out of her car, dumping a man's belongings in the dirt, stamping on them as he watches, getting back into the car, drinking a Diet Coke, and driving off. Again, no words, end of ad.[13] Diet Pepsi ads, all around the world, also foster this viciously anti-male theme.

Maidenform supports the single woman by assuring her there's a better selection of lingerie than of men.[14] An ad for hair products pictures a man as a slave at auction, sale priced to the point that "you can't even give him away!"[15]

In each case the company is bonding with women by finding a common enemy: men. It is basically gossip between the company and the woman. (The function of gossip is to create an "in-group" bond by creating an "out-group" enemy.)

The anger gets communicated to men in a myriad of forms, but one of the underlying vehicles is "the Sisterhood."

THE SISTERHOOD

One of the things that most scares men is "the Sisterhood." Men see it when they wander into the card shop, look under the "Love and Friendship" section, and see dozens of cards designed for women to send to women, most bashing men, and virtually none saying anything loving about men. They overhear the Sisterhood when they sit in a cafe and listen to groups of only women talk, with each "he said, I said" seeming to betray an intimacy, to use male-female intimacy to create female bonding at the expense of the man. They read it in cartoons.

Sally Forth *By Greg Howard and Craig MacIntosh*

Sally Forth *By Greg Howard and Craig MacIntosh*

I've explained in the chapter on getting men to express feelings why, when men feel that their most vulnerable moments and intimacies are being shared with other women, it feels like "The Worst Infidelity," like it might feel to a girl in high school who finally shared herself sexually only to discover the boy had been

high school who finally shared herself sexually only to discover the boy had been bragging about it the next day in school. Both are experiencing betrayal from someone who they trusted with their most vulnerable form of intimacy.

Female members of Congress formed a sisterhood of "man bashing by fax," faxing to each other man-bashing jokes. Mainstream publications like *Newsweek* felt comfortable reprinting them. Correction. They felt comfortable justifying them, as in "Remember Dumb Blonde jokes? Now, . . . Dumb Men jokes. . . ."[16] Of course, dumb blonde jokes are not the equivalent of dumb men jokes, because only *some* women are blondes, but men includes *all* men. (Dumb blonde jokes are the equivalent of corrupt lawyer jokes—when we hear dumb blonde we think woman; when we hear corrupt lawyer, we think men.)

Here are a few of the jokes that the female congresswomen circulated that were clean enough for *Newsweek* to publish. These jokes are much crueler than the ones that led to feminist complaints about U.S. Coast Guard Captain Blanchard, which led him to commit suicide.[17] They were told at the highest levels of government, yet no feminists protested.

- What's the difference between government bonds and men? *Bonds mature.*

- Why is it a good thing there are female astronauts? *So someone will ask directions if the crew gets lost in space.*

- What's a man's idea of helping with housework? *Lifting his legs so you can vacuum.*

Now, if the men in Congress faxed to each other female-bashing jokes, would *Newsweek* publish them with a reverse rationalization, such as, "Go to any card store and you'll find cards for women to send to women expressing their contempt for men, but no cards for men to express their anger toward women. Now, in the halls of Congress, men are also expressing their feelings. Here's a sample of their responses . . . "? I don't think so.

In the chapter on understanding our loved ones, I explain that "walking a mile in each other's moccasins" is one of the most effective ways of creating empathy—it skips past a lot of intellectualization to create empathy on the emotional level. We do this by reversing roles. Imagine, then, if Congress*men* faxed each other these role reversals of the jokes faxed by the Congresswomen.

- What's the difference between government bonds and women? *Older bonds don't sag.*

- Why is it a good thing there are female astronauts? *Someone complaining will make returning home less traumatic.*

- What's a woman's idea of helping with finances? *Having her credit card debt automatically withdrawn from your account.*

If you can feel the contempt in these, and, on the gut level, you feel they must be worse than the ones about the men, compare them, one for one.

If congressional *men* had circulated these, the *Newsweek* story would not be a justification of the men's sexism but a condemnation of their sexual harassment.

It is not fair to suggest, though, that this attitude has trickled down from Congresswomen to constituency, but rather that the constituency's attitudes have elected the Congresswomen. The evidence for this is most apparent in greeting cards because women in every walk of life are buying and sending each other millions of them. We can't say the women are being manipulated by advertisers—greeting card manufacturers rarely advertise their man-bashing messages. So let's look at the greeting card industry as just one case study of the messengers of misandry, beginning with one message—If I'm Single, It's Because There are No Good Men—and what's behind it.

IF I'M SINGLE, IT'S BECAUSE THERE ARE NO GOOD MEN

A woman who can't find a man can always find a card.

If she's single, she can send her other single women friends greeting cards that read, "Men: The Great Ones are all married, the good ones are all engaged . . . all that are left are some dinkwads, a bunch of geeks, and a couple of slimebuckets."[18] Or "Men are like a box of chocolates . . . Most of them are fruits or nuts, and whatever you pick, you'll regret it later."[19]

Some greeting cards do allow for the possibility of a good man: "What we need is a younger man . . . with older money!!"[20] If men expected women to be young with older money before being eligible, the wedding industry would be out of business. Of course, if *she* were young with older money—then she wouldn't need *his* older money!

If a couple gets a divorce, we can assure the woman it's because he's an old fart. "Congratulations on your divorce!! Now you can say 'Home is where the heart is' . . . instead of 'Home is where the *old fart* is.'"[21] Hopefully, if they get back together, he won't find the card!

Suppose your best friend's fiancée has just broken the engagement? Send her, " . . . Remember—it's better to have loved and lost . . . than to have actually married the bum!"[22]

What, though, if a woman's birthday is reminding her that breaking up may be becoming a lifestyle? She can send, "Happy Birthday! Let's get together and laugh it up about old boyfriends . . . I just love a wienie roast."[23] Of course, the card pictures skewers puncturing wienies. The card manufacturer, Maine Line, which is mainstream, features no breast roasts—for "guys who want to throw a couple of breasts on the grill."

When women create this sisterhood by sending greetings that objectify men as jerks and losers, why do they do it? These are self-assurance cards. They are more assuring than acknowledging, "The Great Ones didn't choose me to marry because I wasn't one of the great ones." It hurts her less to be rejected by an object—a jerk or a loser—than to acknowledge that "a wonderful man rejected me."

Men do the same thing, but in a different way. When a guy fears rejection, he may turn a woman into a sex object ("take a look at that broad"). Why? It hurts less to be rejected by an object than it does to be rejected by a "bright, gorgeous woman who had too much going for her to even look at me." For both sexes, it hurts less to be rejected by an object than by a full human being.

Because the objectification of men as losers, dogs, jerks, and scum is now big business, women have a myriad of choices. The slogan of the greeting card industry should be, "No Good Men, Many Good Cards."

Hallmark, Maine Line, and American Greetings are the Holy Trinity of misandry. But, as a Hallmark spokeswoman said to me, "Our cards are very carefully test-marketed. They are neither ahead of their time nor behind their time. . . . Greeting cards are the most unself-conscious form of expression."[24] I couldn't agree more. And that's the problem. Greeting card companies, like the Pentagon, are just the weapons manufacturers. Their motivation is to profit from women's need to assure themselves that whatever rejection they may have encountered from a man, it is his fault.

How well has this worked? And exactly what have they discovered about women and men with this test marketing and analysis of what sells and who buys?

BAD MARK FOR HALLMARK

When I was young, Hallmark gave words to the love we couldn't express. Today, Hallmark also gives words to the hate we can't express. Fortunately, sales of love cards by Hallmark have increased 550 percent since the '60s.[25] Bought mostly by women.

Hallmark gives words not just to the hate, but also to the hurt women feel toward men. It makes the hate and hurt seem like humor and wit, making it easier to bond in assurance that the problem is not them, but men. As the card on the next page—asking the government to protect women from "the problem"—makes clear.

Ironically, some of these cards are the creations of a division of Hallmark called Ambassador. Ambassador gives us the four stages of a relationship: "One:

26

MAN • ingredients: vanity, self-centeredness, arrogance, insensitivity, thoughtlessness, insincerity. Plus may contain one or more of the following: communication skills of a chimp, obsessive love for his mother; and/or an ego the size of a landfill.

Wouldn't it be great if the FDA put a label on everything?

Boy meets girl. Two: Boy romances girl. Three: Boy begins acting like jerk. Four: Girl runs down boy with steam roller." The picture? A steam roller crushing a man. The punch line? "Don't you love a card with a happy ending?" If Hallmark's Ambassadors have their own steam rollers, just imagine their military.

Hallmark's military is its Shoebox division. It specializes in the man-bashing cards. Here are three of a dozen similar examples of the way the Shoebox division describes men: "If they can make penicillin out of moldy cheese . . . maybe we can make men out of the low-lifes in this town;" "You're better off when the turkey's gone" and "If men are God's gift to women, then God must really love gag gifts."[27]

The Shoebox division calls itself "A Tiny Little Division of Hallmark." They *were* tiny when they started in 1986. But man bashing was so popular by 1998 the Shoebox division was Hallmark's largest selling division. Two hundred fifty million dollars a year cashing in mostly on women's anger toward men. The "tiny little" division grew so quickly that Shoebox is now the most recognizable name in the greeting card industry after Hallmark itself.[28] It is hard to overstate the fame or profit in misandry.

Where can you find these man-hating cards? Try the "Love and Friendship" section. A bit like calling the Pentagon the U.S. Government's "Love and Friend-ship" building. And that symbolizes the problem. When we call anger and objec-tifying "love and friendship" we put sheepskin over the wolf. This is not just denial. Denial is saying we don't have a problem. "Love and friendship" poses as the solution. When the problem is posing as the solution we have a problem.

The problem runs deeper because it is part of a pattern. Calling itself a "Tiny Little Division" when it is the largest selling division is part of a female pattern of denying one's power. When you have great power and are calling it "tiny" and "lit-tle," and great hatred and calling it "love and friendship," there is not just a prob-lem with self, but a danger to others. This *under*stating of personal power is the female portion of the female-male dance.

The male pattern is the *over*stating of their power. Only men would call it power to be the only group required to register for the draft, or to feel obligated to earn money someone else spends while they die sooner. Men are the only group that would endure misandry for thirty years and not have a word for it.

The male and female problem combined creates the irony of the male-female dance—that women's strength is their facade of weakness, and men's weakness is their facade of strength.

Does Shoebox have greeting cards for men to send? Well, sort of . . . A man can send a woman a card of a boy (not a man) saying, "Being humble and apolo-getic does not come easy for me. . . . Unfortunately, being stupid does. Please forgive me."[29] I asked Hallmark if they had an equivalent card for women—with the woman saying it was not easy for her to be humble and apologetic, but easy for her to be stupid. No such card.[30]

There is a conflict between Hallmark's medium and Hallmark's message. The message says it is hard for men to be humble and apologetic. Yet Hallmark has found a market only among men to send cards saying they are stupid (an act of humility), and apologizing. If it were really hard for men to do this, there would be no market. If it were easier for women to do this, Hallmark would have found a market for cards for women to send men saying they are stupid, asking for forgiveness, and acknowledging that humility does not come easily to her.

Hallmark has found what no one else is willing to admit: Men refuse to buy cards putting women down, but are willing to buy cards asking for forgiveness and blaming themselves; women do buy cards putting men down, but are un-willing to buy cards asking for forgiveness and blaming themselves.

Another card company, though, does provide a card for a woman with some remorse to send a man. The card shows a picture of a woman saying, "Thinking of you. . . . Wish you would change."[31]

The second biggest offender among greeting card companies is Maine Line. They have cards in which women send each other resumes, like "I should have been a proctologist . . . I meet so many assholes"[32] and ". . . looking for a man who's your intellectual equal . . . fat chance."[33] Women's security in their one-upswomanship seems to be revealed in a new discovery, which has apparently allowed women to have access to men's brain power *in addition to* their own. How? "When you unzip a man's pants . . . his brains fall out."[34]

And it's Maine Line we have to thank for encouraging violence against men with, "My gynecologist laughed when I told him how bitchy I get during my period . . . so I shot him,"[35] or the birthday card that pictures skewers puncturing wienies ("Let's get together and laugh it up about old boyfriends . . . I just love a wienie roast."[36])

American Greetings' most famous man-bashing card is the one celebrating the serial killers Thelma and Louise, which we'll see later in the context of the celebration of the deaths of men.

Greeting cards, though, are but one example of the messengers of misandry. It is the variety of messages and messengers that give us evidence of the degree to which the hatred toward men has insinuated itself into the fabric of the country.

THE ONLY GOOD MAN IS A DEAD MAN

Item. When Valerie Solanas attempted to kill Andy Warhol, she pointed a gun at his chest and said, "You're not going to control me anymore," then shot him through the chest. Andy lived but was never the same. Ms. Solanas wrote of her plan to kill men in *The SCUM Manifesto*. SCUM stood for Society for Cutting Up Men.

Item. Roseanne Barr of *Roseanne* announces a headline, "Utah Wife Stabs Husband 37 Times." Her commentary: "I admire her *restraint*."[37]

Item. An eight-year-old boy makes a crude remark to an eight-year-old girl. The female principal arranges to have the janitor walk in and place a knife on her desk as she threatens to cut off his penis.[38]

> *Tell him to take gas. I'm serious. You open the oven door like this and you say: "Michael, take gas."*
>
> Aunt advising bride-to-be how to handle husband if the marriage isn't going well by the honeymoon. Scene from the film, *True Love*.

> *For the first time in my life I had crippled a man. . . . It felt absolutely wonderful. . . . I found my spare flashlight and started taking notes on the joys of making men writhe in pain and beg for mercy.*
>
> An article on self-defense for women in *Ithaca Times*, May 26, 1994.

I want to see a man beaten to a bloody pulp with a high-heel shoved in his mouth, like an apple in the mouth of a pig.

ANDREA DWORKIN,
leading feminist speaker on college lecture circuit,
from her book, *Ice and Fire*

Note that the final quote is by Andrea Dworkin, whose hatred toward men is expressed in her novels via certain characters who, as she openly explains, represent her personal perspectives.[39] Gloria Steinem says of Andrea Dworkin, "In every century, there are a handful of writers who help the human race to evolve. Andrea is one of them."[40] Don't we have a name for people who advocate the death of one group so the human race can "better evolve"?

The deeper problem here is that advocates of the death of men are increasingly becoming mainstream. Andrea Dworkin has been given mainstream credibility by repeated reviews and coverage in *The New York Times,* as the next chapter describes. Obviously Roseanne and Gloria Steinem are mainstream. After Valerie Solanas shot Andy Warhol, I was astonished to go to a movie theater, watch a biography of Andy Warhol, and see her be promoted to the level of credible commentator on Andy Warhol's life and art. Cartoons of the type that used to appear in women's magazines (like the cartoon below, of a man killing himself) are now appearing not only in mainstream magazines, but in perhaps the most mainstream magazine appealing to sophisticated, literary intellectuals in the world, *The New Yorker:*[41]

"Well, finally—a man who gets it!"

WHAT MEN WOULD SAY WHEN MALE BASHING IS CALLED "FUNNY," BUT . . .

Perhaps a dozen mainstream films during the late '80s and '90s had one theme in common: Men are insufferable; the only way to change them is to kill them, or at least give them a near-death experience. I am unaware of a single film with the same theme about a woman. When women's lives are threatened by men (women-in-jeopardy films), the film is about trying to save the woman, often with innocent men dying so she isn't hurt, (as we will see in the next chapter). But the theme common to the following films is that men's deaths and near deaths are considered not a source of jeopardy, but a source of self-improvement! Check out the following on video.

In *Switch*, death transforms insensitive men into caring men; in *Ghost*, Patrick Swayze improves with death, as does Albert Brooks in *Defending Your Life*. In *Regarding Henry*, brain damage "kills" the arrogance of an attorney and transforms him into a caring attorney; in *Doctor*, cancer "kills" the arrogant doctor and transforms him into a caring doctor; in *Doc Hollywood*, it takes a car accident and a woman. In *Robin Hood*, it takes the combination of war and his father being hung to jolt Costner's character into "killing" his spoiled nobleman past and saving the poor whose potential had been repressed.

Not all films portraying men being killed portray the killing as literal. In *The First Wives' Club*, women joyfully kill the men financially, or destroy their reputations, or poison a dad's relationship with his children.

If the immoral, uncaring man does not have to experience a loss of life, he has to get a clear message about the incontrovertible loss of someone he loves. In *Liar, Liar*, Jim Carrey's character, the liar/lawyer, had to see that his son would be lost to him forever if he told one more lie.

On a metaphorical level, these films show the man "killing" the career that killed the feeling side of him. On a metaphorical level this is positive. Why? A man makes a transition from a Stage I man, focused only on survival, to a Stage II man who balances survival responsibilities with self-fulfillment by, in a sense, "killing" (metaphorically speaking), the man who must sacrifice his soul to create everyone else's option to discover theirs.

However, something is left out. In none of these films does a woman relieve a man of the role of either financial protector or physical protector. In fact, the man just becomes a different type of protector. The lawyer now saves the people he used to hurt as a lawyer; the doctor becomes a better savior of the patients toward whom he used to be callous; Robin Hood saves the poor rather than exploiting the poor. This looks good in theory; but, until we see a woman *requiring* herself to make sacrifices that free the man to help the poor outside his family, he will be preoccupied with being certain he keeps his own family from becoming poor. Men and women are a team; and their relationship, a dance.

The same applies to the sexual dance. In *Switch,* every few scenes blames the ad executive for taking sexual initiatives toward women in inappropriate ways. But none of the women take responsibility for taking their own initiatives (and risking the rejection that comes with it). Again, there are plenty of films showing women taking sexual initiatives, but almost none showing women acknowledging they have an obligation to share the responsibility for initiating. Treating a woman as liberated because she takes a sexual initiative by option is like treating a man as a chef because he is cooking by option even as his wife is cooking by expectation and being taken for granted.

Whether in work or play, we can't "kill" the Stage I man until both sexes are doing the Stage II dance.

Women's declaration of independence is not a bloodless revolution. In *Thelma & Louise,* the death of men is a byproduct of women's independence. In contrast, when men strike out independently, as in *City Slickers,* they do not kill women either literally or figuratively, but discover how wonderful women are.

The National Organization for Women (NOW) singled out *Thelma & Louise* to celebrate at its twenty-fifth national convention, even featuring T-shirts saying "Thelma and Louise Finishing School."[42] The keynote speakers, Gloria Steinem and early feminist activist Flo Kennedy, dubbed themselves "the Thelma and Louise of the '70s." Had Thelma and Louise been men, they would have been called serial killers.

As a person who served three years on the board of directors of NOW in New York City, I know NOW leadership is not made up of serial killers. But the anger toward men can hardly be overstated, and the nature of that anger is almost perfectly stated in the combination of the films *Thelma & Louise* and *The First Wives' Club* (*The First Wives' Club* had not been released by the time of the twenty-fifth NOW Convention).

Thelma's and Louise's journey is the cinematic version of *Smart Women, Foolish Choices.* Their journey takes them from macho-jerk-husband to leering boss to a man who's afraid of commitment to an obnoxious would-be rapist to a tongue-wagging truck driver to a gentle-appearing stud who liberates Thelma sexually but also steals every penny she has (message: If you "let yourself go" with a man, he'll rob you clean). In brief, what was being praised as the female journey of liberation was a lineup of excuses for women to kill, maim, or wreak havoc on the lives of men.

No one litany of bad men, though, can possibly match all the bad experiences of the women at the NOW convention. *Thelma & Louise* handles this brilliantly. Throughout the movie, we are teased with an Evil Man for All Seasons who did something so terrible to Louise that she can't talk about it. This mystery creates sort of a Rorschach inkblot from which the audience can imagine all the potential evils men could perpetrate that would "force a woman to have to kill men."

This Evil Man for All Seasons represents not just Everyman, but the terror in Everywoman. It is imperative that this image be seen as terrorizing a woman so deeply *she cannot be expected to report her traumas to the police,* creating the rationale for crimes against women to have no statute of limitations. This Man Who Has Terrorized Everywoman allows every woman to violate every man and still come out the victim. This is key to the film, and why it was no coincidence it was chosen as the film to celebrate at the twenty-fifth NOW Convention.

Unfortunately, the male-bashing journey of *Thelma & Louise* contained a warning not heeded by NOW. It took Thelma and Louise over a cliff.

One note here. Some feminists say the fuss over *Thelma & Louise* is ridiculous because men kill all the time. Yes. Men kill men. If they kill women, they are the villains, not heroes. **At men's liberation conferences, men do not cheer men who kill women, men *kill* men who kill women.** And routinely die doing it. In fact, men sacrificing their lives to save women from being killed by men is the theme common to women-in-jeopardy films. But there is more than one way of killing a man.

The First Wives' Club represents a second way of killing men—killing them financially, alienating their children from them, ruining their reputations, destroying their careers.

The First Wives' Club portrays three scorned women and a daughter colluding to "vaporize" their men, to "make them not just suffer, but make them suffer over and over again," to wipe out their businesses and rob their homes, to "destroy them, then declare world peace." It used upper-middle-class white women just as *Waiting to Exhale* used upper-middle-class black women and *Thelma & Louise* used middle-class white women to symbolize the plight of all women whose dream of being swept away was swept away. All of these women felt justified destroying the lives of the men by whom they felt rejected, and destroying a few men in general just to make a broader point.

The scary part of *The First Wives' Club* is its popularity among everyday women: On its opening weekend, one third of all moviegoers in America attended *The First Wives' Club*. Most were women or men brought by women. When men say, "Hell hath no fury like a woman scorned," it's called sexism. But when women cheer at a movie of scorned women ruining men, it is called Hollywood Comedy. And in real life, when Betty Broderick, the La Jolla socialite who felt rejected when her ex-husband married a younger woman, shot and killed both her ex-husband and his younger second wife as they slept in their bed, her crime received the real-life support of feminists, first wives, and the media.[43] That's what's scary.

The problem is, failed marriages hurt both sexes. For each forty-year-old wife turned in for two twenties, there is a forty-year-old husband caught between a sexless marriage and his moral scruples; or a husband desperately seeking understanding for his fears of being disposable if he isn't an adequate success.

For each first wife who loses income, there is a second wife who gains income; for each first husband who loses his home and his children, there is a second wife who struggles with a man who has a depleted bank account and a broken heart, or there is a woman who rejects that man because of his depleted bank account or his broken heart.

For each first wife left with inadequate income, there is a dad driving a cab for seventy hours a week or collecting garbage in the hope that his children can have a better life than he, that his wife can have a home more pleasant than his garbage truck. When such a husband is then criticized for working late, and one day comes home to a note saying his wife has left and taken their children, his life feels meaningless and the women's crisis centers do not invite his call.

For each single mother who is juggling children, a job, and unpaid child support, there is a single dad who has seen his marriage become alimony payments, his home become his ex-wife's home but *his* mortgage payments, their children become child support checks for children who have been psychologically turned against him.

For each woman faced with a deadbeat dad, there is a desperate dad—a dad desperate to love his children, but told that if he comes any closer, she will accuse him of being a child molester or a wife beater.

Instead of seeing both sexes' perspectives, though, even female-positive therapists are often surprised at women's anger toward men. For example, Dan Kiley, the author of *The Peter Pan Syndrome* and *Wendy's Dilemma,* startled himself when, to an audience of several hundred Midwestern women, he was explaining research showing that men who are excessively self-involved are six times more likely to die of coronary heart disease than men who are not, *and four hundred women erupted into applause and cheers.*[44]

In his private practice, Kiley sees how this hatred of men translates into wives' death wishes toward their husbands. One woman secretly wishes her husband's plane would crash during one of his business trips. And "Another, when I noted that her workaholic husband might be heading for a heart attack, simply smiled."[45]

As we have seen, insensitivity to men's deaths is now the law in female-only legislation such as Violence Against Women Acts and male-only draft registration; it is now psychology in battered women's syndromes; it is now government bureaucracy in offices of research only for women's health; it is now a greeting card which, like the one below, reflects an underlying attitude toward men that can at best be described as half entitlement and half benign neglect.

MEN AS *MORALLY* INFERIOR TO WOMEN

I believe that women have a capacity for understanding and compassion which a man structurally does not have, because he cannot have it. He's just incapable of it.

BARBARA JORDAN,
former U.S. Congresswoman,
and Ethics Adviser to former Governor of Texas, Ann Richards

If I were a man, I would strenuously object to the assumption that women have any moral or spiritual superiority as a class. This is . . . female chauvinism. . . .

BETTY FRIEDAN,
author of *The Feminine Mystique,* from her *It Changed My Life.*

I am often asked whether the feminist movement is doing more, or less, man bashing than it used to. The direction can be seen in the contrast between the above two quotes: The founder of the U.S. women's movement, Betty Friedan, warns *against* depicting women as morally superior;[46] a more recent leader advocates *for* the depiction of women as morally superior. And Barbara Jordan was not just a feminist leader, but a Democratic Party keynote speaker at the '92 National Convention.[47] The moral superiority of women is an argument that has many proponents in the academic community, the most prominent of whom is Carol Gilligan of Harvard.

Ironically, the feminists most likely to tout women as biologically more compassionate are the ones least likely to show compassion.

The power of women to take the moral high road is perhaps best stated by novelist Anita Brookner in *Lewis Percy:* "He came, of course, as a suppliant, knowing himself to be deeply in the wrong . . . wrong in the way that men have always felt themselves to be in the light of a woman's accusatory disapproval. . . ."[48]

The best way to take the moral high road is to define morality. Let's see. We have men's area of addiction: women as sex objects. And women's area of addiction: men as success objects. When a woman marries a doctor or a millionaire, we congratulate her. But in men's area of addiction, sex, well, there is no arena in which we have been more judgmental than sex. We are taught that sex is "dirty"—as in dirty jokes, pornography, infidelity, and X-rated; as in letting our children watch a Western in which men kill each other, but would turn the TV off if they were watching a man and woman make love with each other in the nude.

Our sons no sooner get that "sex is dirty" than we announce they're the ones expected to initiate the dirt. As we're doing this, we teach our daughters, "Beware of boys, they're after only one thing." In contrast, we don't tell our sons, "Beware of girls, they just want a free dinner and drinks." Feeding the girl's addiction is not considered immoral—we even give our sons ideas of how to earn money to give the girl what she wants. This is the beginning of our sons internalizing their own moral inferiority, shame, guilt, and feelings that women are better, purer, and more innocent than they.

As a rule, since men want this "shameful" sex more than women, men often feel they are "in the light of a woman's accusatory disapproval." Advertisers then reinforce this mistrust of men. Try on Lady Foot Locker. Two women, laughing in Sisterhood, one saying, "I love men . . . I drink with men . . . I eat lunch with men . . . Occasionally, I even listen to men . . . *but I trust women.*"[49] Unstated message? You can't trust a man. Trust Lady Foot Locker.

Vick's Nyquil portrays a woman suffering. A man is able to help her. He smiles. *He does nothing.* Unstated message? You can't trust a man. Trust Nyquil.

When a film exploits men's moral inferiority, it can reasonably hope for attention well beyond its budget. No film was better at this exploitation than *In the Company of Men,* and although it had a budget that would normally have led to mainstream media neglect, the *New York Times* and other mainstream media brought it to national attention.

In the Company of Men would more appropriately have been called *In the Company of Men Behaving Badly.* Or *Men as Morally Insidious Sociopaths.* Allow me to share my experience, then check out the video to see if yours matches.

As the credits were rolling my stomach was churning. Not a single woman exiting *In the Company of Men* was speaking with even a tinge of warmth toward her male partner. Women in all-female contingents were laying into man-as-bastard in voices easy to hear.

In the lobby, I notice two women who had stopped to read the movie review. I read it with them. As they finish, I gently asked what they thought of the movie. Their bodies shuddered in disgust; they mumbled, "Men." Without embarrassment, they turned their backs and left.

I was shaken. I decided to walk it off. After a light bite, I wandered into a bookstore. There were the two women. My first thought—"Maybe now's a better time"—was canceled by a deeper fear: "Stalker." I left. I felt like a black man at the turn of the century in the deep South approaching the wrong restroom.

The film packs this wallop by portraying two men filled with hatred toward women ("Women . . . they're meat, gristle, hatred—they're all the same"). Each is portrayed as hurt by a woman. They conspire revenge.

So far, it's a touch of *The First Wives' Club,* but in the company of men. But the response is 180-degrees different. *The First Wives' Club* drew approximately half of all the opening weekend female moviegoers in America to cheer the "vaporization" of the husband-as-bastard. In *In the Company of Men,* no one cheers on men to hurt the woman; we all fear a woman being hurt.

In *In the Company of Men,* the target is Christine, the personification of vulnerability: deaf, innocent, beautiful, young, female. Her deafness has made men neglect her romantically, so the men plot to separately but simultaneously court her, send her flowers, confess love, then coldly drop her and laugh as she "reaches for the sleeping pills."

Christine's sweetness courts the audience and . . . uh-oh . . . even the men. We watch even Chad, the ringleader who has thus far come across as an impoverished blend of Iago and Manson, as he softens, weakens, and falls in love. We (the audience) feel Chad becoming a "new person."

Christine returns Chad's love. I can feel my heart attached to their attachment. And then, suddenly, Chad grabs her face, mockingly tells her it's all a game, that he just wanted to hurt her. He haughtily exits the bedroom. The audience realizes that we, like Christine, have been sucked in by Chad's pretenses of love.

Women in the audience have just heard Chad give Christine virtually every loving assurance a man ever gave them. It is the actual feeling of having been sucked in (once again) that emotionally seals their feelings of identity with Christine-as-victim and Chad-as-evil personified (or is it Man personified?).

It is still possible, though, for some social worker somewhere to have the slightest compassion for Chad, remembering it was his woman friend who left him, remembering he had confessed he was hurt. So how does the film erase the trace of sympathy? Chad admits he was lying about his woman friend having left him. Then we meet his woman friend. She is loving, trusting, unsuspecting. She naively feels she knows Chad. She is Everywoman. Meet Everyman.

So what's the point? When a man says he's been hurt, be suspicious. His pleas for compassion are the bait and women are just the fish. Proof? The film waxes on about how men love fishing because it gives them a thrill to exercise their power (by killing the unsuspecting fish who believe in your kindness). Why does a man do this? In the film's words, he does it because he can. Because he has the power. In brief, any woman who listens to a man is like a naive, innocent, trusting fish who will soon be tuna fish on a man's sandwich.

But can't we portray men this way because men do have the money and the power—and because so many of society's problems are caused by men? Let's see now. Didn't Nazis feel that Jews had the money and the power and that so many of society's problems were caused by Jews? No film could portray women, Jews, or African Americans this way and receive a positive review by people as conscious of discrimination as those at *The New York Times*.

MEN AS *COMPLETELY* INFERIOR TO WOMEN

Men have only two faults: Everything they say and everything they do.
POST-ITS™,
by 3M Corporation

When *The Economist* evaluated men, it did so in an article titled "The Trouble with Men." A sample: "The next generation does not need the current crop of men to be carrying around their sperm all the time. A clean, well-run sperm bank, regularly topped off, would be just as good—and would dispense with men's unfortunate social side-effects."[50]

Although "men's unfortunate social side effects" include building the offices, computers, and presses by which *The Economist* is published, and disposing of every employee's bodily and office wastes, neither *The Economist* nor other books claiming an economic evaluation of men, such as Dr. June Stephenson's *Men are Not Cost-Effective,*[51] acknowledge any of that. Rather, the conclusion of poor cost-effectiveness comes from evaluating what is described in its subtitle: *Male Crime in America.* As if men's only side effect was crime, and as if all men were criminals.

Some books are even less subtle. Try *Why I Hate Men,*[52] or *No Good Men.*[53] *No Good Men* was published by Simon & Schuster, one of the world's most successful publishers. When *No Good Men* was successful, the author asked about publishing *No Good Women.* No way. No audience.

The cover of *No Good Men* was clear.

Again, rather than intellectualizing, *feel* the disgust you experience when you witness these equivalent role-reversal book covers I have created as a parody of *No Good Men.*[54]

During periods in our history, the *No Good Blacks* cover would not have created that feeling of disgust. Why does it now? African-Americans refused to sit in the back of our buses. In Nazi Germany, *No Good Jews* would also not have catalyzed the disgust you doubtless just felt. We might think the difference in our reaction has to do with the perception of men as all-powerful, but it was exactly that perception of Jews that led to the passive acceptance of such slurs in Nazi Germany. *Then* we waited for the consequences of that unconsciousness before we created a new consciousness.

"ALL MEN ARE RAPISTS, AND THAT'S ALL THEY ARE"

All men are rapists, and that's all they are.

MARILYN FRENCH,
The Women's Room, in the *New York Times,* December 27, 1987.

Imagine Jay Leno joking that a *rapist* was being *used* by the thirteen-year-old girl he raped. Would he draw stunned silence, laughter, or boos?

In reality, Jay Leno jokes that Kay LeTourneau, then a thirty-nine-year-old female teacher who committed statutory rape on her thirteen-year-old student, was really being used by the boy—to get into R-rated movies.[55] Is this just a joke, or part of an attitude with consequences for the boy? Well, the raped boy was initially required by the courts to pay child support.

There is no man bashing more vicious than expanding the definition of rape so virtually every heterosexual man is a rapist. A *Ms.*-sponsored study—which the mass media widely quoted as saying that 25 percent of all women were raped *by the time they were in college*—used this question to reach the 25 percent figure[56]:

Have you given in to sexual intercourse when you didn't want to because you were overwhelmed by a man's continual arguments and pressure?

Notice that these women did not define themselves as raped, just as *verbally* "overwhelmed." *Ms.* and the media translated this into rape. As for these women, 42 percent said they had sex with these men one or more times after this (the mean was 2.02 times).[57]

In essence, we tell our sons their job is to sell themselves, and then we label them rapists when they sell themselves—if the "buyer" has remorse.

When I conduct role-reversal dates in my workshops and invite the women to initiate, they too begin to "sell" themselves. Why? **The better the initiator sells, the shorter the period of potential rejection.** When they choose a guy who is not attracted to them and persuade him to go further than he really would have preferred, I don't call the women rapists. I try to make it a learning experience for both sexes, not a potential prison term for women who overdo the assignment. The solution, of course, is to socialize both sexes to share the expectation of taking sexual risks. Then we'll do less accusing and more appreciating.

CASTRATION

We live in an era when "First World" feminists protest female circumcision in Africa, while at the same time laughing when Lorena Bobbitt chops off John Wayne Bobbitt's penis and tosses it into an open field.

However, this double standard exists not only among feminists. When I discussed Lorena Bobbitt on the *Maury Povitch* show, the audience (about 80 percent women) sided with the feminist version of, "This sends a message to men." When I reminded the audience that most men who have extramarital affairs have it with a woman, and asked whether they wish to send a message to men that if their wife has an affair it's fine to cut off her clitoris (the female equivalent of a penis), throw it in a field, and wait for the jokes on Leno and Letterman, it put the enthusiasm for Lorena Bobbitt cutlery on pause, but only until the next Bobbitt joke.

The contempt by men for themselves and their sexuality is internalized to such a degree men's own magazines can freely make a joke out of men being castrated. *Penthouse,* of course, objectifies women a lot more than men, but it is by the *admiration* of women's bodies, not the castration of their genitals. And certainly *Cosmopolitan* would never show a woman's breast being chopped off and carted away by a pest control company—they know women would detect the contempt and girlcott *Cosmo:*

190

DAMNED IF HE DOES, DAMNED IF HE DOESN'T

On the TV sitcom *Cheers,* Diane confronts Sam (after their breakup) with being controlled by his new girlfriend. She says, "What happened to the Sam Malone who said, 'We're gonna do what *I* want to do from now on'?" He responds, "We left him in a restaurant with a bowl of fettucine on his face." Diane's response? "That didn't mean I didn't *like* him."

I speak with many Sams who also feel damned if they do, damned if they don't. Some examples:

"A few months ago, my wife blamed me for griping about my work. So I stopped. Last night she said, 'How can you be so compartmentalized?'"

"When I tell a woman at work she looks especially nice in a certain dress, I'm afraid she may interpret that as sexual harassment; so I pretend not to notice. But the other day I overheard one woman say she enjoys working with women because 'they notice little things like my dress—a typical man doesn't.' No matter what I do I feel like I'm being told I'm a 'typical man.'"

THE NEW SEXUAL DOUBLE STANDARD

Item. A woman complains to Ann Landers about her cheating *husband.* She explains that she left him. Ann Landers responds, "How I wish more women would follow your example. Too many wonderful women put up with cheating, lying freeloaders.[59]

Item. A man complains to Ann Landers about his cheating *wife*. He explains that he left her. Ann Landers responds, "You sound like the booby prize at a skunk rassle."[60]

The new sexual double standard is not just in papers, but on every daytime talk show. When I did a show for Oprah on "Men Who Cheat," she was taken aback when I said, "Doing shows mostly on *men* who cheat is sexist, because each man cheats with a woman—for each man who cheats, there's either a married woman who cheats, or a single woman playing co-conspirator."

Someone objected, "Women cheat for different reasons—we need love."

I responded, "Yes, men and women learning to love more effectively will definitely reduce cheating. But your need for love doesn't make your getting it elsewhere less painful for the man. When women tell men sex equals love whereas men tell women sex equals tennis, a woman going elsewhere to get love can be more threatening than a man going elsewhere to play tennis!"

Oprah stopped in her tracks (she was working the audience) and graciously acknowledged, "Yes . . . yes, good point there."

We often hear that men have historically enjoyed the benefits of a sexual double standard. In some ways this is true; in some ways untrue. Most cultures had some version of an unwritten marital deal that might be called a "Marital Triangle": The man must first provide for the economic needs of his wife and children. If he did, but he was not having his sexual needs met, then he could get them met without being ostracized by having a mistress *as long as he also provided for some of the mistress's economic needs*. This "Marital Triangle" allowed for two women to have economic needs met, for a wife to be relieved of sexual expectations, and for one man to have some of his sexual needs met. Often, no one really got their emotional needs met.

This could be thought of as a sexual double standard that benefited mostly him, or as an economic double standard that benefited mostly her: He was expected to provide for his wife's economic needs whether or not she was providing for any of his needs. By seeing only the sexual double standard, we gave men a "bad rap."

Today, though, there *is* a sexual double standard. Men who cheat, as with Bill Clinton, find that cheating ruins their lives and reputations. In contrast, women who cheat are portrayed as unhappy, in need of better communication, more affection, attention, love. Few people ask if Bill Clinton was also unhappy personally, or whether he had a need for more affection, attention, and passion but felt trapped—in the White House, in the marriage, and in a commitment to provide First Ladyhood to a woman who relished the role and had earned it just as he had earned the presidency.

The double standard now being fostered in romance novels is of a married woman having a success object for security, and a sex object on the side and labeling it "romance." This fantasy double standard is portrayed perfectly in one of the most popular romance novels and films marking the end of the millennium: *The Bridges of Madison County.*

I recall walking out of *The Bridges of Madison County* wiping my tears and searching for my Kleenex, feeling not only in awe of Meryl Streep's acting but empathetic for the disappointed dreams of her character, Francesca.

But the light of day—or was it the darkness of night—made me wonder whether I'd crossed that bridge in only one direction. Here was a married woman (Francesca) having an affair and I am calling it a romance. When a married man has an affair, don't we call it infidelity?

As with Francesca's marriage, many men's marriages also continue amid dashed dreams and disappointed hopes. But when the man has an affair, *his* pain is not communicated to the world; in contrast, he is condemned as a womanizer, user, and jerk before millions of women in the courts of *Oprah, Sally, Jenny, Jerry, Montel, Maury, Roseanne, Ricki,* and *Rosie.* These are, if you will, the nine Justices of Women's Supreme Court.

As an author, I got to thinking about publishers—would *Bridges* have been published as a romance if Francesca were Francis? If Francis were from a rural town in Italy and had dreams of coming to America and marrying an American woman who owns lots of land, would he not be seen as a user? Would his story sell as a romance novel to men? *No.* It would sell to no one.

Recall that, in *Bridges,* Francesca refused to join her loving husband and their children for a four-day weekend at the county fair to support their daughter's hope for a prize. And then, only minutes after her husband took the children, Clint Eastwood's character drops by out of nowhere and she has a mad, passionate love affair with him, and then packs her bags with plans to desert her husband and children. If Francesca had been Francis, I would not have walked out of the theater in tears for Francis. If Francesca were Francis, it would not be a romance novel starring Meryl Streep; it would be a Stephen King novel starring Kathy Bates.

I myself was caught up in this double standard. If Francesca had been Francis and Francis had put his family in risk of being ostracized by flagrantly spending hours with this photographer on a busy bridge of Madison County in a rural religious Iowa town, I would not have empathized as I did. And I would have been angry at how his sleeping with a roving photographer who had affairs all over the world would put his wife at risk of an STD.

If we reverse Francesca's role as mother and imagine Francis as a *father* who recorded every detail of the affair in four diaries that his wife could easily have discovered, I would immediately have been judgmental of his insensitivity. And if he had left the diaries in his will for his children to read, altering his children's view of their dad and mom (from his perspective and without the opportunity for dialogue), I would not have left the theater with the impression of him as a devoted father.

The most powerful double standard, though, emerges when we realize that a woman can receive empathy for her affair even when she puts her own children at risk and betrays a loving, faithful husband and devoted father. In the romance novel genre, the unfaithful woman needs no excuse; nor does she need to pay for the equivalent of a mistress; she can betray, be self righteous, and we will cry for her. Never before has a double standard existed to such a degree that we cried for the betrayer.

The double standard deepens when we consider the ostracism of men's fantasies versus the availability of women's. Men's fantasies are hidden from public view and labeled pornography. In contrast, romance novels constitute 40 percent of all paperback book sales in America and are labeled "romance"[61]. Yet the romance novel often involves objectifying one man as a success object and another as a sex object; pornography involves treating women only as sex objects. I call romance novels female pornography because I define pornography as "that which objectifies." In male pornography, women are sex objects; in female pornography, men are at least success objects.

The man is not a success object just because he must have money to obtain love, but also because *the novel ignores the pressures he endures to create that wealth.* This allows her to ignore how she will reduce *his* pressures; it allows only her the freedom to work by option, not by obligation; to work if she wants, at what she wants. This is not partnership, but entitlement.

Do these romance novels help women who have the affairs bring their newly discovered passions and potential back into the marriage? Hardly. In *Bridges,* after Francesca discovers her repressed passion, and her loving husband and children return from the county fair, she kisses them, but not him. She makes not a single attempt in any form to bring into her marriage the part of herself she had discovered in her affair.

Thus the romance novel reinforces the division between marriage and romance. No, it's worse than that. The psychological destruction of her husband is often a central theme of the romance novel—even in those of the respected Danielle Steel. For example, in Steel's *To Love Again,* Isabella "finds herself in love with a man who wants to destroy all she has left of her husband."[62] In Steel's *Crossings,* the heroine's love for a steel magnate destroys her "devotion" to her husband.[63] And, of course, Francesca's love for her husband was never again the same. (And then women's magazines blame men for their fear of commitment.)

Romance novels rarely make heroes of the sensitive man. The novels are called *Sweet Savage Love*,[64] not *He Stopped When I Said No*. Their formula: She attracts, resists; he performs, persists.

This confuses some men: When she says "no" but doesn't mean it, it's a romance novel if he persists. When she says "no" and means it, it's sexual harassment or date rape if he persists. In brief, when he guesses right, it's called courtship; when he guesses wrong, it's called harassment. And if the courtship works, it's called a marriage with her picture in the paper; if the courtship fails, it's called a court *case* with his picture in the paper.

Romance novel readers are not only stay-at-home moms: seventy-one percent have jobs outside the home. After Harlequin Romances discovered this and modified their formula to appeal to the working woman, their net earnings in ten years went from $110,000 to $21 million[65]—an increase of almost 20,000 percent. It transformed Harlequin from a company on the verge of bankruptcy in the early '70s to a company commanding 80 percent of the romance market by the mid-'80s.[66] In the Harlequin romance formula, some man still provides a woman with a source of security, thus giving her options.

This holds true even when the romance novels are romance movies. If, as in *Bridges,* or *The Piano,* the heroine has already gotten her success object, she fantasizes about her sex object; if, as in *Flashdance* or *Pretty Woman,* she has not yet found a success object, she fantasizes about her success object.

In the romance novel, what does she do for him? The fantasy is that her mere existence—her beauty, her soul, her integrity, her spirit—are so superior to his that she does not need to *do* anything for him, she just needs to *be*. He's the human doing; she's the human being. In reality, of course, women *do* a lot for men, but in this fantasy called romance, her presence does enough for him; his presence does not do enough for her—he must also be a wallet.

The film *The Piano* pushes this definition of romance a step further. The husband provides the income for his wife to develop *her soul, her art, or her fantasy profession,* while she has an extramarital affair with a "real man" and soul mate who supports her psychologically and physically. *The Piano* was hailed by critics as a film portraying "a world in which women struggle to find a voice." The heroine, played by Holly Hunter, was portrayed as mute, her "voice" was her piano.

In fact, *The Piano* can be seen as a film in which two men compete in two different ways to hear a woman: her husband providing for her survival needs, a more primal man providing for her more primal needs. Her husband begged to also give affection, love, and sex; she rejected him in all three areas. His wife was expected to do nothing to support him. In addition to being mute, she brought into the marriage a daughter from a past relationship. He, though, took care of the daughter, the cooking, cleaning, provided her with a home, food, and even a cabin of her own. She just rejected him, played a piano, and had an affair. She made no attempt to earn money from her piano. This should have been seen as a woman-bashing movie; instead it was a film women raved about and critics praised as articulating women's needs.

In the world according to *The Piano*, men have all the obligations and women have none. If films like *The Piano* strike such a chord among women, then marriage is a setup for more Princess Dianas being depressed. In the meantime, where are the wives financing husbands to find their piano, their voice? Maybe, today, we live in a world of men who have so little hope of having *their* piano that they find it more realistic to be mute.

The new sexual double standard, of female affairs labeled romance and male affairs labeled impeachment, allows a woman who has an affair to more easily tell the truth because romance creates empathy and excitement, not ostracism and judgment; when a man has an affair he feels more pressure to lie because he will be persecuted, and when he does lie he risks being impeached for perjury, either in the House or in the home.

THE DOUBLE STANDARD AT WORK

Here are four examples that most typify the way men feel subjected to double standards in the workplace that lead to their feeling unfairly bashed.

"Last week I made a decision without consulting my female co-worker. She called me a chauvinist. But this week she made a similar decision without consulting me. I asked why she didn't consult me. She said she was independent, why couldn't I handle an independent woman."

"I was behind deadline and asked my office mate to make me a cup of coffee. She said, 'Typical male.' Yet last Friday she asked me, 'Would you do me a favor and make me some coffee?' How is it her request is a favor and mine is chauvinism?"

"Susan and I were hired at the same time. When I got a promotion first, it was called discrimination. Kristin, though, was hired after both of us and got promoted before either of us. The same women called that equal opportunity."

"I work in a factory. The work is low pay and repetitive. The women often say they're being exploited. When they do, everyone agrees. But once I suggested I was being exploited and was told I should get off my butt and get something better."

WHY CAN'T MEN ASK FOR DIRECTIONS?

You can't miss it. You can't miss the mockery of men not asking for directions. Notice, in the following cartoon, that Dr. Linda is not asking the woman in the passenger seat to appreciate the man for driving, nor is she asking the woman to take responsibility for navigation because he is taking responsibility for driving, but rather, the man is being blamed for what he doesn't do rather than credited for what he does do.

Close to Home   67

Although men are the most frequent navigators of cyberspace, even there they are critiqued for not asking for directions. I found this joke in cyberspace:

Q: Why does it take a million sperm to find one egg?

A: Because men can't ask for directions.

Personally, I agree it is a male flaw to not ask for directions. But not asking for directions is rarely discussed as the shadow side of four male strengths: the socialization of men to be self-reliant, to be problem solvers, to take risks, and to not be afraid of making mistakes—even in front of the woman they love (or anybody, for that matter). In fact, if men had such fragile egos, why wouldn't they take more precautions against looking like a jerk?

We often accuse men of being too goal-oriented. But when men resist asking for directions, aren't they reflecting a willingness to be less focused on the goal ("The party starts at three; we must get there by three.") and more focused on the process ("Let's explore together")?

Women are definitely better about asking for directions, and that's a strength. But like every strength, it also has a shadow side: dependency. We never hear the joke told this way, though, to tease women about giving only lip-service to equality:

Q: Why does it take so many sperm to find one egg?

A: Because the egg is too busy rehearsing its speech on equality to meet the sperm halfway.

Perhaps the real question should be, "In a world of alleged equality, why are we expecting men to take responsibility for *both* the driving and the directions?" When a woman takes on the responsibility of navigating, it's her responsibility to ask for directions.

When I'm a passenger and we're lost, I encourage my partner to stop for directions. But if she doesn't, I find it more productive to pull out a map to help her rather than open my mouth to blame her.

VENUS GOOD, MARS BAD

Venus is the Goddess of Love; Mars, the God of War. If a book had been titled *Men Are from Venus, Women Are from Mars,* feminists would quickly have objected to the misogyny of men being associated with love and women with war. Of course, men do have a history of being warriors, and women nurturers, and these produce different traits that John Gray asks us to understand rather than judge, as we would understand someone from a different culture. And that's one of Gray's many positive contributions. The point here though is that many traits emerge from the sexes' different roles, and had a book been titled *Men Are from Courage, Women Are from Cowardice,* feminists would have objected to those particular traits becoming the title's focus.

Titles like *Men Are from Mars, Women Are from Venus* are not, then, the problem per se—it is that they are part of a culture that does not allow women to be portrayed critically even as titles portraying women as good and men as bad make best-seller lists (*Smart Women, Foolish Choices; Successful Women, Angry Men; No Good Men,* etc.).

Other books with neutral titles are a cover for undercover criticism of men not in the title, but in their content. For example, in *He Says/She Says* he defines a romantic hideaway as Motel 6 and a gourmet meal as "A hot dog with French's mustard . . ."[68] In brief, the neutral *He Says/She Says* is a cover for *She Says He's a Jerk.*

More subtly, titles like *Women Who Love Too Much* suggest women love men more than men are ready to be loved. *Women Who Love Too Much* is a brilliant title because it created the superficial "feel" of women blaming only themselves, when in fact men were being faulted as incapable of loving. Similar titles pandered to the pocketbook of a woman who wanted to appear introspective about her "I love men too much" problem, while in fact blaming men: *Men Who Hate Women and the Women Who Love Them,* as well as *Women Who Love Men Who Kill* and *How to Love a Difficult Man.*

WHEN WOMEN ENTER MEN'S WORLD

Note, in the cartoon below, how "This way, Stupid"[69] is really "Her way, Stupid." It is ironic that, in "male-dominated" corporations, the rules of male-female interactions have been taken over by Human Resources Development (HRD) divisions, in which the feminist version of sensitivity becomes the definition of sensitivity, meekly accepted by men who know they will be less able to support their families by raising money for home if they raise their voice at work.

BENT OFFERINGS By Don Addis

© 1988 Creators Syndicate, Inc.

SENSITIVITY TRAINING

THIS WAY, STUPID

When affirmative action and sexual harassment legislation are added to the "Her Way, Stupid" divisions, many men have come to feel that when women enter a man's world, it quickly becomes a "woman's world."

What happens when a man hints that a woman is less than equally knowledgeable about something in the traditionally male world? Well, remember when Donald Regan, during the Reagan administration, suggested that female legislators were less likely to be knowledgeable about or inclined to discuss military hardware? He was universally condemned. He didn't say women couldn't learn, just that they didn't. Since his condemnation I am unaware of another politician suggesting that women were in any way limited in their knowledge *or interests.*

In contrast . . .

WHEN MEN ENTER WOMEN'S WORLD

We give lip service to wanting men to share the traditional responsibilities of women, but instead of creating affirmative action or affirmation to ease men's transition, we mock them when they try.

A Cascade commercial shows a husband overloading the dishwasher in klutz-like fashion. He thinks he's doing well, but the viewer and his wife know it is only Cascade that rescues him from his stupidity. His wife condescendingly (wink, wink) calls him "perfect." Imagine a Texas Instrument commercial portraying a woman thinking she's doing math well when, in fact, a TI calculator corrects all of her mistakes and her husband condescendingly (wink, wink) calls her "perfect." Universities would soon be boycotting—or would it be "girlcotting"—TI products.

Note in the cartoon below that the man is not acknowledged for shopping, but blamed for getting it wrong.[70] Imagine a wife coming out from under the family car she was repairing and being asked by her husband why on earth she didn't use the right type of oil, and the wife responding, "Because I'm really stupid?"

DRABBLE *by KEVIN FAGAN*

Are men mocked not because they are men, but because they are, well, just plain ignorant? Watch for commercials in which one woman is introducing a product to another woman who is ignorant of it. The less knowledgeable woman is portrayed as turned on by the new product, not as stupid and in need of her fragile ego being saved.

201

DOCTOR MOM, DEADBEAT DAD

Looking for a toothpaste? "Mothers prefer AquaFresh." Looking for a cereal? Kix is "kid-tested, mother approved." "Mother Knows Best" has become institutionalized in commercial slogans.

Mom is portrayed as the responsible parent, as in Pampers' "All the dryness a mother can give."[71] Yet millions of dads change diapers. If Charter Hospitals ran an ad saying, "The best doctor a man can be," we would immediately see the sexism. Instead, while some commercials for cold medicines, as those for Robitussin, portray mothers as "Doctor Mom," other commercials portray Dad as annoyed his sleep is being interrupted by his sick child. Doctor mom, deadbeat dad.

This attitude toward dads is worldwide. A 1998 front page headline in the *Irish Times* read, "Who Needs Fathers When It Comes to Parenting?"[72] The headline did not stop with "Who Needs Fathers?" since everyone demands fathers be wallets, but when it comes to loving and nurturance, well, the article itself portrayed human fathers as worse than monkeys in the zoo. Which might be the case: When someone else is providing room and board, then Dad can spend time with his children.

Fortunately, in the late '90s, commercials and ads portraying dads in a more positive light have become more common. And the greeting card industry does not find a large enough market among women for mocking dad to justify producing many deadbeat dad cards. The viciousness returns not when children are neglected but when the woman is rejected.

MEN AS MORONS

"Hear you're looking for a man who's your intellectual equal. . . . Does the expression 'Fat Chance' mean anything to you?"[73] That's from a greeting card for a woman addicted to the high of being told she's too good for a man. In this case the card manufacturer feeding the addiction is, would you believe, Maine Line.

For a more literal high, the "Liberated" Woman can grow her own dope.[74] Imagine a guy sending his friend a card saying, "Grow your own dope. . . . Plant a woman" or a white university professor who had lost a job to an African-American, and was now sending out cards saying, "Grow your own dope. . . . Plant a black."

If a woman prefers a sugar high, she can send this card about a guy: "I baked some anatomically correct gingerbread men this year—Yeah, I didn't give 'em brains."[75] From your friends at Hallmark.

Not to be outdone, American Greetings chimes in with, "A birthday thought: Everything we need to know, we did learn in kindergarten. . . . Boys are stupid."[76] Then, as if *women* were stupid, the American Greetings cards are labeled on the back: "Feminine Birthday" or "For Women Only."[77]

The men-as-morons message has always been with us; it just gets updated and, recently, more popular. In movies, the *Three Stooges* update of men-as-morons is the *Dumb and Dumber* series. The good news: Today's man is more efficient—it takes only two to be as much of a jerk as three used to be.

A similar way a man can "win" is to acknowledge himself as stupid up front, thus taking himself out of the "equal to us" game; then, the woman, unafraid of competition or rejection, can accept him on those terms. Imagine a cartoon featuring a woman saying, "Al, I'm the new gal . . . as you get to know me, I'll look dumber and dumber."[78]

Dilbert

Imagine an ad agency creating an ad in which a man shouts at a black woman that she has a vacancy sign for a brain? The ad agency would soon have a vacancy sign in its window. Yet, in reality, a TV ad for Ramada Inn shows a woman berating a man who has chosen an inn other than the Ramada: "You wing-tipped weasel . . . You have a vacancy sign for a brain."[79] Instead of the ad agency being told to put up its own vacancy sign, it was asked to make a second version of the ad—the "insult-the-executive" version—in which a female executive berates her male counterpart: "You wing-tipped weasel, what would you know [about hotels]? Your *brain* filed for *bankruptcy.*"[80] When it comes to men, there's Dumb and Dumber.

While situation comedies portray both sexes as stupid, if a movie focuses on the stupidity of one sex as its central theme, it seems that sex is of the *Forrest Gump* or *Billy Madison* variety. There's some good news here too: If a man is unmarried but clearly stupid, he is allowed to be good, even wise, in a limited way. (Remember Peter Sellers in *Being There?*) Why? One reason: These men are not the men women want; therefore women haven't felt rejected by them. These men can be portrayed as wise and single without suggesting a woman is a loser because she isn't with him.

PERFORM IF YOU DON'T, PERFORM MORE IF YOU DO

No sooner had Viagra helped millions of men perform better in one area, than comics were suggesting dozens of other drugs Pfizer must doubtless be working on to overcome men's "impotence" in virtually every area. One of the funniest and best-circulated did a take-off on Viagralike drugs for men overcoming their many forms of impotence.[81] *Directra* would help men ask for directions. *Projectra* would help men finish household repair projects.

Interesting, I've never read an article appreciating men for doing household repairs. Are we in the Era of Criticizing Men for Not Completing What We Don't Acknowledge Them Starting? Perhaps the man could take the *Directra* and read the directions while the woman takes the *Projectra* and does the repairs?

Complimentra increases the output of men's compliments on women's hairstyles. Yes, men could stand some improvement there. Perhaps, though, a *woman* taking a little *Complimentra* would inspire men to finish household repairs without *Projectra!*

Buyagra deepens men's urge to buy women expensive jewelry and gifts. *Buyagra* sounds like a great idea—to be taken on Valentine's Day by the sex least likely to buy the other jewelry and expensive gifts, yes?

Nega-Viagra produces the opposite effect of Viagra, and is said to be helpful to U.S. presidents. Indeed. If President Clinton's penis had not gone up, his place in history would not have gone down. On the other hand, if he had taken *Nega-Viagra,* Monica Lewinsky would not be a celebrity and millionaire.

Nega-Sportagra is said to make men wish to watch less sports and talk with the family more. Good idea. But since women watch more television in every single time slot than men,[82] why are we suggesting a drug to stop only men from watching what they watch? Should the sex that watches the most TV be blaming the sex that watches the least for hiding in front of the TV?

OUR CHILDREN INHERIT THE ANGER

Are our children inheriting this anger? Divorced moms are five times more likely to make negative comments about Dad behind his back than dads are about moms. That's according to the children (54 percent of the children said only their mothers spoke badly of their fathers in front of them; 12 percent said only their fathers spoke badly of their mothers[83]). This poisoning of children's minds toward their dads is camouflaged as humor by women who send each other greeting cards like this one:

84

When our sons look in the mirror and see themselves with their dad's body language, they are learning that half of them is genetically a jerk, or stupid, or a deadbeat. Our daughters are not left unscathed either: They, too, are half their dad's genes. And it's hard to teach our daughter to love if we're also teaching her there's no one worthy of her.

This unconscious abuse of our sons in particular, and more indirectly of our daughters, is evident in our schools.

A Boston teacher reports that, in response to girls wearing T-shirts that said "Girls Rule" and yelling "Boys go to Jupiter to get more stupider; girls go to college to get more knowledge," she made T-shirts for boys saying "Boys Are Good." To her amazement, all ten of the student teachers she was supervising objected only to the pro-boys shirts.[85] The *student* teachers objected. Aren't they our future?

Let's spy on the reading material of some of our future leaders, reading *Scholastic Math* magazine. The column is "Personal Math for the '90s."[86] It's a "He Said, She Said" column, giving him and her an opportunity to describe how they met on the way to math class. He speaks of her brilliance and his hopes for "the start of a beautiful friendship" with "my future girlfriend"; she speaks of his stupidity, his "incredibly lame jokes," and her hopes to be rid of him. Go figure.

The anger in rap music has a reputation for being mostly male to female. It is more accurate to say that the male-to-female anger in rap music draws protests; the female-to-male anger in rap music draws applause. For example, on Valentine's Day, a day that one would expect love between the sexes, an all-female "Black Women in Rap" concert at the Los Angeles Sports Arena featured a lineup of women performers who put down men as "nothin' but dirt" (Yo-Yo). MC Trouble led the men at the concert to chant "*Make* money, money, money, money, money" and had the women chant "*Take* money, money, money, money, money." Another MC—MC Smooth—closed her act by asking, "I want the ladies to look at the man next 'em and say '*Where is the money?*' . . . Peace, I'm outta here." Peace? This is a bit like a peacenik calling his dad a "pig" and then asking for the tuition check. What allows her to take the money? Nikki D gives a hint. She repeatedly exhorts the women in the audience to associate strength with cashing in on their sexual power, telling them, "You're wasting *it*."[87] Isn't taking money for sex called prostitution? One day we're being told women who are prostitutes are exploited; the next day, women who are not prostitutes are being exploited. Both our sons and daughters are being taught to be confused; but only our daughters are being taught to be both entitled and angry.

LET THE MEN TAKE SEXUAL RISKS, REJECT THEM, THEN LAUGH

In the greeting card on the following page,[88] we can see how men's sexual vulnerability stimulates contemptuous laughter not only at the men, but laughter at men's vulnerability to women leading to their deaths. Imagine men sending each

"You're one sick puppy, Nadine"

other greeting cards of their wives crying at a Weight Watchers' Center for the Elderly as they watched their husbands buy diamonds for thin young women.

In a TV commercial for Lifesavers, the woman strings the guy along with the promise of sharing her Lifesavers, only to abandon him mercilessly so she can have the whole roll to herself.[89] This ad hopes to create a bond between Lifesavers and females as together they laugh at the pitiful, rejected man. Interestingly, if this ad were reversed, and the man had mercilessly abandoned a woman who he had strung along, it would also create a bond between Lifesavers and females as together they shared an anger toward the greedy, rejecting man.

Suppose the woman runs out of Lifesavers? She should "Be prepared" with Coty's Nuance perfume, because "Nuance always says Yes, But you can always say No."[90] This way, if he picks up on the "Yes," she can sue for sexual harassment because he ignored her verbal "No." A good lawyer, a good judge, and she'll be able to afford a lifetime of Lifesavers.

The sexual rejection of men is a source of humor in almost every sitcom. For a comedy writer it has the value of being able to generate multiple levels of laughter that increase as the rejection increases. I'll use an example from *Cheers*, since we have both a memory of *Cheers* and an opportunity to check it out again in reruns. When Cliff asks waitress Carla to the mailman's ball, he's so nervous that he reads her his "proposal." Then he agrees to buy her a dress, a VCR, a corsage. Then he assures her she won't even be expected to dance with him. She rejects him and laughs in his face. He cries. She derides him as "obnoxious." The audience laughs at him each time he is rejected. Were a man similarly rejecting a woman, the audience's *anger* at him would increase at each stage of him rejecting her.

MEN AS SEX ADDICTS

"When you unzip a man's pants . . . his brains fall out."[91] Yes, on a greeting card. Someday, I'm sure, on a zipper.

Unfortunately there's too much truth to this one. It's one reason male power is a myth. And it's worth laughing/crying at. Here's a similarly accurate male-bashing joke I've been known to tell myself:

When God created Adam, She explained, "I have some good news and some bad news . . .

"First, the good news: I've given you a penis and a brain.

"Now the bad news: You can use only one at a time."

This is true not only for President Clinton. The more a man is a charismatic leader, the higher his testosterone level . . . thus the more his brain shrinks as his penis expands. This is the "BC" principle. It was true Before Christ; it's true with Bill Clinton; it will certainly be true Beyond Clinton.

Laughing at our foibles is healthy as long as it's an equal opportunity sport. In joke form, the BC equivalent might be, "Scientists have discovered a food that diminishes a woman's sex drive by 90 percent . . . wedding cake."

Or if we use the "God Created" parallel, one candidate is "In the beginning, God created earth and rested. Then God created man and rested. Then God created woman. Since then, neither God nor man has rested."

When President Clinton had his affair with Monica Lewinsky *et al.*, the condemnation of him as a sex addict was universal. And it called to mind a litany of other powerful men who couldn't keep it zipped up. True enough. But not fair enough. For each powerful man who is a sex addict there is a woman addicted to powerful men; for each man willing to spend his life sacrificing his way to power, there is a woman willing to use sexual power to gain access to men without that sacrifice; for each man risking everything for some combination of sex, affection, and love, there is a woman willing to make millions of dollars gossiping about the relationship she made a verbal contract to keep secret.

It is not that Clinton and other men do not have a problem, it is that their problem ruins them even as women's problem profits them; it is that we hold him accountable for his problem, and hold him accountable for her problem. Men's problem is at least in part hormonal and defined by a mostly female standard of fidelity and monogamy that is less natural for men, and especially less natural for the high testosterone men who are the leaders women love. If men could divorce post-menopausal women for not being sexual enough, it would be apparent we were unfairly imposing one sex's standards on another.

Meantime, the anger at men who do not deny their hormones allows for Lorena Bobbitt's castration of her husband to become a joke, and the *Today Show* to applaud scenes in which men's lives are being threatened for being sexually inappropriate.

In the movie *Living Out Loud* (1998), Queen Latifah's character said her cheating husband gave the excuse she wasn't fulfilling his needs, implying it was her fault. Her response? "I picked up a knife and told him it was his fault I was stabbing him." Holly Hunter's character listened with eyes of respect, admiration. "That's great. I wish I would have stabbed my husband."[92]

This clip was chosen by Gene Shalit of the *Today Show* to illustrate his praise of the film—as one in which the term "adult film" was not just a code word for "salacious." When men stab women for cheating, it's called a prison sentence; when women stab men for cheating, it's laughter or art.

MEN AS SEXUALLY INADEQUATE

Do I let a group of power-mongering men with short penises tell me what to do?

CALIFORNIA ASSEMBLY SPEAKER DORIS ALLEN,
on her fellow GOPers' attempts to recall her.

Eeny weeny, teeny weeny shriveled little [short dick man]
words from *Billboard*'s Eleventh best-selling U.S. single
(December 17, 1994), "Short Dick Man,"
sung by Sandra Gillette

If a woman's magazine's audience is married women, sex is usually on the back burner. If the audience is single women, sex is a mixed message: on the one hand men are criticized as sexually addicted; on the other, they are criticized as sexually inadequate (as impotent, premature ejaculators, or minuscule). When the man is portrayed as addicted, women are often taught to exploit this vulnerability, as in "the way to a man's heart is through his penis": give sex, get commitment. If he is viewed as inadequate, he is mocked and ridiculed.

We think of *Playboy* as objectifying women. And it does. But the objectification at least emanates from a *desire for* a woman. Men's magazines do not ridicule women who have just loved them. In contrast, the magazine that sells most to single women worldwide is *Cosmopolitan*. In one issue of *Cosmo*, there were five cartoons putting men down for being sexually inadequate (in a section called "Power Failure," no less!). In each cartoon, the couple has just made love, and the woman ridicules him.[93] For example, in one, the woman ridicules, "Did the earth move? Charlie, the bed hardly moved." In another, a woman mocks a man who asks "How was it?" by answering, "How was it? *What* was it?"

"*H*ow was it?"
What was it?

Of course, men can also be cruel: Gangsta rap is none too kind to women. The difference is we call the man who derides women a gangster, while the woman who derides men is called the *Cosmo* girl. Sadly, the two cartoons mocking men about "impotence" are part of an attitude that not only perpetuates the problem of "impotence," but also creates the opposite of the intimacy women want. Let's look at one example, and then how it hurts women.

*O*h Jerry, not your
soufflé *too!*

The cartoons in *Cosmo* symbolize woman-to-woman talk. The more a man fears a woman will mock him to her women friends if he does not perform, the more he feels performance pressure, the more he experiences "impotence." The ridicule perpetuates the problem.

On a deeper level, ask yourself, "When a man is worried about being 'potent,' what is he worried about?" He is worried about failing to please a woman. Why are we mocking him for that?

Reverse the sexes here. If a woman says she would *love* sex, but isn't lubricated enough, we don't label her "impotent." We label ourselves grateful—for her desire.

What attitude in *Cosmo* would help both cure "impotence" and increase intimacy? Encouraging a man to think of his penis as his radar. That is, when soft, it is his signal that his feelings are "off." **If his penis did not work by being soft, *then* he would be impotent. That is, a soft penis is often a penis that *is* working**—working to inform the man that something is wrong: He's nervous, self-conscious, he doesn't feel he'll be accepted if he doesn't perform, he's moving too quickly. It's time to make love using something other than his penis.

A therapist called me the other day, worried that a number of men who seemed to like her, and who said they loved the fact she loved sex, nevertheless couldn't get hard. She therefore doubted they really wanted a woman who loved sex. I disagreed. "A man might want that a lot, but is afraid you'll be judgmental of him if he doesn't perform."

"If he's not hard, doesn't that mean he's not attracted?"

"No. It may mean the opposite. The more he is attracted, and the more he respects you, the more he may fear losing you if he doesn't perform. If he didn't care, he'd be relaxed because he has nothing to lose."

"So what can I do?"

"Really get into kissing him . . . enjoy the respect for you his softness reflects. Get into enjoying sucking him when his penis is soft as much as you do when it's hard, and let him know that's true for you. When his penis is soft, he's most likely to be relaxed when you're relaxed."

Another example of sexual man bashing is "premature ejaculation," when defined as the man ejaculating before the woman has an orgasm. This is female-defined male sexuality. If she has an orgasm before he does, does *she* suffer from "premature orgasm"?

Men internalize this pressure on themselves to please a woman. These comments mocking men's sexuality were printed in the *Men*'s Forum of the MicroSoft Network in a piece called "58 Things NOT To Say to a Naked Guy"[94]:

- Aww, it's hiding.

- Are you cold?

- Does it come with an air pump?

- Ever hear of Clearasil?

- I didn't know they came that small.

- Look, it fits my Barbie clothes!

- I've smoked joints fatter than that.

Women also put pressure on themselves to please men, but not to the self-ridiculing level of *Cosmo* printing "58 Things Not To Say to a Naked Gal":

- Do your breasts come with an air pump?

- Ever hear of Clearasil?

- I didn't know they came that small.

- Did you get those breasts from your Barbie Doll?

MAN AS MEAT

Cartoons like this illustrate the source of the anger that leads to the bashing and objectification of men: divorce.

BENT OFFERINGS By Don Addis

When this book is published, enough time will have passed for Creators Syndicate, the distributors of the above cartoon, to distribute a reversal (with *men* saying "I lost 200 pounds of ugly fat—I got a divorce"). I challenge them to do just that, and to report the results, which I predict will be: Few papers will print it; and those that do will receive complaints, and so will the Syndicate.

This illustration is the print media version of the TV ad I describe just below it.[96]

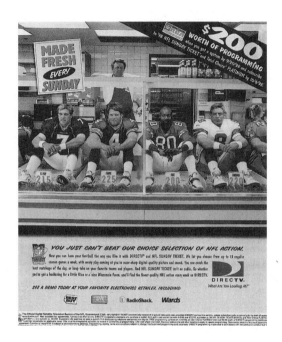

Scene: A supermarket meat counter. The "meat" is John Elway, Brett Favre, Jerry Rice, and Troy Aikman. A female customer has Favre stuffed into a shopping cart. At the counter, the checker fails at scanning Favre's shoe, then requests over the intercom, "Price check on Favre."

Imagine Revlon advertising a perfume by having male customers sniff the "meat" at a meat counter—"meat" like Cindy Crawford, Christie Brinkley, Kathy Ireland, Pamela Anderson Lee, Iman. If a man stuffed Cindy Crawford into a shopping cart and the male checker, after failing to register the scan on her high heel, asked for a "Price check on Crawford," would NOW protest that as sexism, or what? Or would the awareness of the sexism be so obvious that no supermodel would even allow herself to be used that way?

In real life, of course, Cindy Crawford's job requires being looked at and looked over; Favre's job requires him to be knocked down and pushed over. Favre's job is not only more akin to being treated as a piece of meat—he is more likely to be on the bottom of the pile.

MEN AS RATS, CATS, DOGS, PIGS . . .

If you're a woman, imagine going to a male ob/gyn and discovering he had just broken up with his wife. You're about to take down your panties when you notice a greeting card on his desk saying, "Bill conquered his fear of insects . . . by being caught for years in the web of an ugly black widow spider." You inquire. "Oh," he laughs. "Saw that in a card shop and thought it described perfectly my feelings about Mary, so I'm sending it to some of my divorced ob/gyn friends."

How fast would you be out of that office? Would you want a list of his ob/gyn friends that he thought would be receptive? That's the way men feel about women who send each other cards like this.[97]

Yolanda conquered her fear of mice...

...by living for years with a dirty rat.

Of the thousands of TV shows spawned in the '90s, two of the most popular and longest lasting, *Roseanne* and *Home Improvement,* emanated from one theme: man bashing. *Roseanne* sold itself via the male-bashing pilot I describe in the chapter on the Lace Curtain. *Home Improvement,* still top-rated as of 1999, sold itself to ABC in 1991 via a pilot in which all of the best punch lines, according to *People* magazine, came right out of Tim Allen's stand-up routine called "Men Are Pigs."[98] *TV Guide* described Tim Allen's concept of "masculinism" as "a philosophy derived from his mother's belief that 'all men are primitive, grunting Neanderthal pigs.'"[99] Freud would have it that the son kills the father to marry the mother. Maybe Freud had a point.

ABC was so delighted with the ratings for male bashing in *Home Improve-*

ment (which has, to its credit, become more balanced with maturity) that, when it introduced *Grace Under Fire,* it advertised Grace's ex-husband as a "knuckle-dragging, cousin-loving, beer-sucking redneck."[100] For some reason, ABC never invented a description of Grace by her ex.

The photo in the greeting card below exemplifies one of the favorite themes among women about men: how to domesticate the "animal." He's the one who pees on the toilet seat. Maybe every man should have his own fire hydrant (in case he misses the outhouse).

© *Palm Press, Inc. 1995; Berkeley, CA 94709; A1304#-175*

But the usual comparison to animals is more like the greeting card, "Why Cats Are Better than Men." "You can de-claw a cat . . . try to get a guy to clip his toenails."[101] Imagine your dad sending cards to other dads saying cats are better than women because "You can de-claw a cat . . . try to de-claw a woman with a grudge." What would you think of your dad?

Nobody intelligent takes this seriously, right? Well, a colleague of mine writes of his experience sitting in on a meeting of the Gender and Justice Commission of the state of Washington. The guest speaker? Chief Justice of the Washington State Supreme Court, Barbara Durham. Her opening comment: "I just purchased a wonderful book called *101 Reasons Cats are Better than Men.*"[102] She proceeds to strongly recommend the Commission members purchase it. This is the chief justice, talking to the Commission on Gender and Justice!

IF A MAN GETS IN TOUCH WITH HIS FEELINGS,
HERE'S HOW TO KILL HIM

Item. 1998. Los Angeles Judge Joan Comparet-Cassani told Ronald Hawkins not to interrupt her in court. He continued. She ordered the bailiff to zap him for eight seconds with a 50,000 volt electric shock.[103]

Any male judge who gave a talkative woman a 50,000 volt electric shock treatment—as opposed to asking the guard to escort her from the courtroom—would be justly removed from the bench.

When a man speaks up, how should a woman hear him? American Greetings "advises" to call it whining, then suffocate him. Their role models? Thelma and Louise. Remember how Thelma holds a gun to the head of a policeman and suffocates him in a trunk in the 120-degree heat of the New Mexico desert?

American Greetings was so proud of their role models they reproduced the entire card as a full-size ad in fold-out form in magazines like *Newsweek* and *Life*. Yes, life.

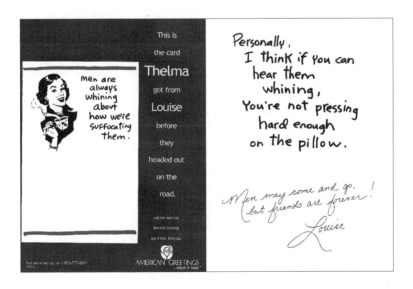

The problem here exists at every level. American Greetings say they sell the card because the card sells. Their tests show that men would not buy a reverse card.[104] So part of the problem is women buyers. Another part is American Greetings. When the price is high enough the prostitute will appear.

The next problem is *Newsweek* and Time-Life, who wouldn't *think* of selling ad space, no matter what the profit, if it made light of suffocating women who whine. They publish it about men exactly because men won't whine.

Suppose a man not only speaks his mind, but changes his mind? Here's the woman-to-woman greeting about a man who changes his mind: "First, he said he liked independent women, so, I played it cool. . . . Then, he said he liked romantic women, so, I played it hot. . . . Then, he said he liked passive women, so, I played it weak. . . . Then, he said he liked strong women, so I crushed his head."[105]

Truth is, both sexes experience mixed messages from the other sex. If men sent these cards, one might say, "First she said she wanted a gentle man, so I became gentle; then she wanted a strong man; then a successful man; then she wanted me home earlier. . . . " Both sexes ideally want it all. The problem comes when a woman wants to crush a man's head for changing his mind while calling it her prerogative to change her own.

All of this reinforces men's underlying fear: "Speaking up" will be considered whining, which will not stimulate women's instinct to listen, but to "murder." A bit scary for an emotionally repressed group whose few emotions are expressed to the very group buying these cards.

CONCLUSION

Man bashing pays. When Hallmark's Shoebox division can orbit from a "tiny little division" to its biggest division and the second most recognizable name in the entire card industry in just a decade (second only to Hallmark itself), we get a sense that man bashing pays. When *Roseanne* and *Home Improvement* can use man-bashing themes to launch two of the most enduring and popular shows of the '90s, we can see that man bashing is a growth industry. When commercials can bond with the female consumer by portraying men as not-to-be-trusted morons, jerks, and fools, then we know that industry is being seduced to make a Faustian deal.

Unfortunately, the people paying the money are mostly female consumers. Consumers who need love, but are paying for hate. I don't believe any woman or man wants to be this way. I do believe we set women up. The Princess Diana, romance novel–type themes are hurting our daughters by giving them expectations that make the probability of disappointment much higher for them than for men. Yes, our sons have their centerfolds. But they are called pornography, dirty, obscene; not romance, love, and coronation balls.

Man bashing, anger, and criticism of men reinforce traditional roles. They place pressure on men to perform to please. To perform more even though men's lifespans vis-à-vis women's went from one year less than women's to seven years less largely from overperforming.[106] (The expression "the good die young" is just another way of saying the overperformers die young.)

SOLUTIONS

Women will bash men who fail to provide until we help our daughters care about men who care rather than about men who provide. The moment she expects more money from him is the moment she will be angry when she doesn't get more money from him.

Underpinning any solution is the replacement of the perpetrator-victim paradigm with understanding that men are not the enemy, that the option of divorce comes with a price of everyone feeling rejected, that men have not changed because the pressures on men have not changed—the pressure to work *full time,* by *obligation,* has not changed; the pressure to risk sexual rejection not by option, but by obligation, has not changed; the obligation to pay, to pick a woman up, to call her in the morning (vs. her option) has not changed. We have expanded women's options and retained men's obligations, then complained men haven't changed. *That* must change.

If we are to revamp the paradigm of our daughters treating themselves as victims and men as perpetrators, how do we begin? As parents, we have an obligation to not protect our daughters from rejection so much that when divorce creates that experience, or a breakup creates it, it is so devastating that she has nowhere to go but to making him the enemy.

How do we protect less, but protect enough? By exposing our daughters to risks of rejection at a time in their life when we can be there to support them through it. For example, by making sure our daughters are not just involved in team sports (which is crucial), but involved in *unsupervised* team sports as well, when protection from rejection is not immediately available from a sensitive adult.

By encouraging our daughters to save up so they can afford to ask a boy out. If the boy for whom she has spent weeks saving money to ask out rejects her, it is at a time in her life when we can hold her, listen to her, and support her to try again with another boy.

Our attitude that sex is dirty and our sons should initiate the dirt is also at the heart of the contempt, anger, and mistrust of men experienced by so many women (and by our sons of themselves in the form of shame and guilt). How do we change that? In part, by resocializing our daughters to be more involved in sharing the risks of rejection. How?

One way is by encouraging our daughters to ask boys out instead of waiting; helping them understand that when we control our life directly that means more rejection, not less. Encouraging her to inform the boy that if she is interested in being physically intimate, she will initiate, rather than to act passive or flirtatious until he initiates. She may not be able to do that, but merely contemplating doing it will send fear through her that will help her feel compassion for the boy's fear. Then she will be more willing, if he initiates before she is ready, to not only say "no" but also tell him she will take the next initiative if she changes her mind.

In brief, we are teaching her how to take responsibility to share the risks of rejection rather than to have him keep taking the risks, call him a wimp when he doesn't do it quickly enough and a date rapist if she said "yes" to him before she said "yes" inside of herself.

How do we introduce these changes into the public consciousness so our children don't feel like social guinea pigs?

Terry Rakolta was upset with the sexual humor of the Bundy family on *Married . . . with Children*. She began a one-woman writing campaign to sponsors such as McDonald's, Kimberly-Clark, Tambrands, and Coca Cola. The result? Coca Cola promised to screen future episodes; and McDonald's, Kimberly-Clark, and Tambrands withdrew their commercial sponsorship.[107]

What distinguished Terry from the average letter writer? Homework. She monitored every program and documented what they said. And persistence. She wrote letters—not one or two, but hundreds, each with more documentation. The media interprets one letter as representing thousands of viewers' thoughts. To survive, it needs to depend on our thoughts. Yes, the media *magnifies* our propensities, but we *create* the media even more than it creates us. The media's concern is profit. Ratings rule. Meaning we rule.

We can take the path, then, of influencing sponsors, or the media. Or we can organize a group. Women in New York advertising organized Advertising Women of New York, and presented "Best and Worst" awards to advertisers.[108] They were surprised at how quickly advertisers, fearful of offending, changed.

I would mislead, though, if I left the impression that protesting misandry will be as easy as protesting misogyny. When Fred Hayward protested man-bashing ads in the *Los Angeles Times,* the *Los Angeles Times* not only mocked the protest, but the protester. ("Come on, Fred, get tough," "Don't feel bad, Fred. Try to take it like a man."[109]) In brief, expect personal attacks. Don't take them personally.

If you need the taste of success to precede rejection, begin with helping father consciousness. The National Easter Seal Society broke ranks with the Doctor Mom/Deadbeat Dad tradition with a beautiful ad of a dad without hands being a loving, caring dad, reminding us that neither breasts nor hands make the parent; love and responsibility do.[110]

No matter where we start, we have the obligation to not leave our sons uncomfortable with themselves the way the depression left some of our dads uncomfortable with money.

What a Man Might Say When He Hears, "It's Men in the News, Men in Government, Men at the Top— Where Are the Women?"

Our hypothesis is that worthy victims will be featured prominently and dramatically, that they will be humanized, and that their victimization will receive the detail and context in story construction that will generate reader interest and sympathetic emotions. In contrast, unworthy victims will merit only slight detail, minimal humanization, and little context that will excite and enrage.

E. S. HERMAN AND N. CHOMSKY,
Manufacturing Consent

INTRODUCTION

Caitlyn left *The Bridges of Madison County* feeling a bit bored with her husband—it had been a long time since a Clint Eastwood had courted and excited her; the following morning she read about a housework study saying men expect their wives to pick up after them. Now she was wandering into the bedroom; her husband's socks were on the floor. She feels, "Who does he think I *am?*"

Caitlyn was experiencing the influence of an attitude toward men generated first by the arts (*Bridges*), and, the next morning, by academia (they did the housework study), the government (they funded it), the media (they reported it), and the helping professions (they were the sources of interpretation used by the media). At times like this, Caitlyn's husband could feel Caitlyn's anger even if she said nothing. He responded by withdrawing. Unwittingly, the love between them was being contaminated by what I will refer to in this chapter as the "Lace Curtain"—the tendency of most major institutions to interpret gender issues from only a feminist perspective or from a combination of feminist and female perspectives.[1]

Is it true, though, that the male point of view is not being represented? In a study of more than 1,200 headlines from seven high-circulation Canadian newspapers, women were referred to as victims of violence thirty-five times for each one reference to men as victims. Not a single article focused on men.[2] Compare this to the reality: Men are three times as likely to be victims of murder, twice as likely to be victims of nondomestic violence, and equally as likely to be victims of domestic violence, but the study found that newspapers virtually ignore the violence against men in each of these areas—no matter who the perpetrator.

More discouraging, when violence against men was reported, it was usually in statistical and raw data form; women's was personalized.[3] That was in Canada. In the United States, neither the government nor academia nor the profession of journalism has financed a comparable study or examined *why* such gaps exist between reality and perception on almost every male-female issue.

One of the most common responses I hear when I introduce some of the findings in this book, or from *The Myth of Male Power,* is an incredulous, "If all this is true, why hasn't the media reported it?" Or "If the news likes what's new, why are they ignoring *new* news?" And, as feminists accurately point out, far more men than women are on the front pages.[4] To many, this implies a bias in favor of men, making it hard to understand why what I discuss goes unseen or unreported—or seen and distorted? Why?

The Paradox of the Visible Invisible Man

How can it be true that men make the front pages more often, but men's underlying issues and internal stories do not? **The process of raising money and climbing leadership's ladders that gets a man on the front page requires a man to repress his fears, not express his fears. So a man's external story is visible; his internal story, invisible.** Whether on the front page or the business pages, we rarely read of a man's sorrow about coming home too late to read his child a bedtime story, or the emotional distance he may be feeling from his wife, or what's worrying him when he can't fall asleep. This is the paradox of the visible invisible man.

If, however, women make the front pages less often, does this mean women's *issues* make the front pages less often? No. One of the major functions of men who make the front pages is to protect women. In general, men make the front pages either when they protect and save us—or threaten our safety. And men are especially concerned about saving and protecting women. So, when the president and Congress unanimously pass male-only draft registration and a Violence Against Women Act, it is mostly *men on the front pages,* even though it is *women being protected.* Ditto for Women, Infant, and Children (WIC) programs, an Office of Research on Women's Health, the Learned Helplessness Defense, sexual harassment legislation, the prosecution of a man for rape or date rape . . . mostly men on the front pages, saving mostly women.

Men are also on the front pages when they violate women's safety, whether on the level of O.J. Simpson or Clarence Thomas. We sometimes forget that those men on the front pages are also portrayed negatively much more often than women.[5]

Let's go beyond the front page. The Life/Style/Women's sections share women's internal stories: her experience of divorce, depression, domestic violence, remarriage, her "juggling act," her battles with harassment and discrimination, even her frustration with the toilet seat being left up. The coverage is legal and emotional. We see statistics and tears.

Conversely, no section shares a man's personal feelings about losing his wife, children, and home after divorce and then being expected to pay for what he doesn't have; we read of him coming home drunk and hitting his wife, but not the disappointed dreams that led him to disappear into a bottle; we read the drama of her depression, but only the fact of his; the dilemmas of her juggling act are not balanced by the dilemmas of his "intensifying act" and "father's catch-22"; we don't read long stories about his fears of remarriage, his experience of depression, his "life of quiet desperation," why he doesn't report domestic violence against him, his thoughts of suicide, or his personal story of what he feels like if he can't tuck enough money away for his children's education after the mortgage, insurance, and orthodontist bills are paid; or what he feels like wanting to make love with his wife but not wanting to be a bother.

We care about men as human doings, not as human beings. We care about him as an individual like I care about the individual parts of my car—I care about its problems only when it's causing me problems. Or I care about prevention only when lack of prevention will cause me problems. Even when a man's problems are affecting his ability to be a protector, we often refer to his problems from the perspective of the problems they create for a woman (he cheated on her; he got drunk and hit her). Which is why the other men who make the front pages are the villains who are causing us problems.

In brief, men's lives count only to the degree they are heroes who perform for us or save us, or villains who disturb our peace. Women's lives count more for their own sake . . . a woman's pain is every talk show.

We so rarely inquire of a man's grief, we forget it exists. When Princess Di had her affair, we asked her about her isolation, her depression, her husband's aloofness; but when Prince Charles had an affair, we accused him of infidelity. As a result, billions of women worldwide identified with Princess Di. Few men had any male fears with which to identify.

For millions of years, this attitude was necessary for survival, but it is now dysfunctional for our dads and sons having a quality life. And it is destroying love between the sexes.

Lack of compassion for men's stories is also dysfunctional to our selection of leadership. Think of the bind Bill Clinton was in as a candidate for president. If he had acknowledged his sexual addiction before he became president, we would have denied him the presidency. We say we want honesty, but reward denial. When we force a man to choose between working on himself and his career, we encourage denial. And we serve neither him nor the country. Nor do we serve women: be they Hillary, Chelsea, Monica, or the millions of women who now trust men even less.

One reason men fear speaking up is that they fear they will be evaluated not by the compassion applied to Princess Di, but by the assumptions applied to Prince Charles. For example, when President Clinton had an affair, we didn't inquire of his emotional isolation or ask compassionately if his and Hillary's political partnerships left him emotionally and sexually starving. Maybe this was not the case, but we didn't ask. Until we treat a man as something other than a replaceable part when we discover him as a human being, he will pose only as a human doing.

Thus far I've been speaking of men who make the front pages. But they are, at best, one tenth of one percent of all men. Meantime, the "invisible" man, the short order cooks, the truck drivers, the garbage collector, or construction worker, the Willy Lomans and Private Ryans of everyday life, have neither their *external* nor *internal* stories told.

Because of our dependency on men as saviors, when men fail, we treat them differently than women who fail. When women commit crimes, we are told of the hardships of their childhood; with men, we are told of the victims of their crime.

Are women prevented from having their external stories told? No. Today women are given scholarships and affirmative action to encourage them full-time into the world of business and politics; men are given neither to encourage them full-time into the world of home and family.

THE LACE CURTAIN

Hearing women's internal stories—without hearing men's—made the world seem unfair to women. **Ironically, because we didn't know men's stories were being left out, the more we heard from women, the more we thought we'd been neglecting women.** Soon it became politically incorrect to interrupt her flow. So women's stories became women's studies, not to be interrupted by men's studies.

Graduates of women's studies courses soon controlled gender-related decisions in almost all large bureaucracies. When an issue about sexual harassment or date rape came up on a college campus, the feminists flooded the committees concerning these decisions, created the agenda, and decided who would be hired as consultants and speakers.

The problem? Women with backgrounds in women's studies were not only *un*educated about men, but often saw men as the problem and women as the solution. They had demonized men. If someone spoke up against them, they weren't just outnumbered, they were labeled sexist. And what we will see in this chapter is how that labeling led to the end of careers in the '80s and '90s as quickly as being labeled Communist ended careers in the 1950s.

The power of feminists to allow only a feminist perspective to be aired (in every field that dealt with gender issues) came to be labeled the "Lace Curtain."

The Iron Curtain shut out opinions considered a threat to Communism. The Lace Curtain shuts out opinions considered a threat to feminism.

In an Iron Curtain country, capitalist bashing was the norm. In a Lace Curtain country, man bashing is the norm. The chapter on man bashing hopefully made clear the *degree* to which man bashing is the norm; this chapter on the Lace Curtain shows us how each institution, from the government to the school

WOMEN CAN'T HEAR WHAT MEN DON'T SAY

system, from the helping professions to the media, produces that outcome, each in its own unique way.

In an Iron Curtain country, being too critical of core Communist tenets could cost you your job. Especially if your job was in the government, media, or education system. In a Lace Curtain country, being too critical of core feminist attitudes (sexual harassment, affirmative action) can cost you your job. Especially if your job is in the government, media, or education system.

The Communist Party achieved this power to censor formally, by revolution and by becoming the one-party system of Soviet politics. Feminism achieved this power informally, by becoming the one-party system of gender politics: creating a new area of study, defining the terms, generating the data, and becoming the only acceptable source of interpretation. This chapter explains how this occurred, and why.

Communists came into power by selling the belief that workers were exploited by capitalists. Feminists came into power by selling the belief that women were exploited by men. Both Communists and feminists defined an enemy and sold themselves as champions of the oppressed.

Once Communism and feminism successfully defined themselves as progressive and morally superior, censoring criticism could be rationalized as progressive and morally necessary.

How do you know if you're part of the Lace Curtain? If you feel more comfortable telling a man-bashing joke than a joke bashing all women. How do you know if you're in an organization that's part of the Lace Curtain? When you tell a man-bashing joke and everyone laughs, then tell a women-bashing joke and no one laughs. In some organizations, the censorship starts sooner . . . we don't even think of telling the woman-bashing joke!

The Lace Curtain is less a "woman thing" than a feminist thing. But feminism has made woman-as-victim so credible we would sooner think of saving whales than saving males. In this respect, almost all of us contribute to the Lace Curtain.

Which institutions create the Lace Curtain? Universities, in all the liberal arts, especially at the top-ranked schools; the school system, especially public high schools; government, especially at the national and United Nations level; the media, especially print media and television; the helping professions, especially social work; advertising, especially on television; book publishing, especially self-help and textbooks; funding institutions, especially those funding health, arts, and university research. Each institution censors and distorts in its own unique way. Each reinforces the other like academics citing each other's research.

If your son or daughter is about to enter a top university in the liberal arts, he or she will be behind the Lace Curtain. You'll notice it next Christmas. It is leaving many of our daughters with a love-hate relationship toward their dads and husbands; when they become mothers of sons, their feelings about men are transmitted to their sons, leaving their sons with mixed feelings about themselves. The Lace Curtain, like the Iron Curtain, ultimately hurts even those it was intended to benefit: leaving many employers fearful of hiring women; making many of our children fearful of marriage.

Is the Lace Curtain a conspiracy? No and yes. "No" by the current meaning of the word (a covert manipulation), but "yes" by the original Latin, meaning "to breathe together" ("*spire*" means to breathe; "*con*" means together). If we think of a conspiracy as people of a similar consciousness, in essence "breathing together," then the Lace Curtain is a conspiracy. For reasons I discuss in the chapter on man bashing, it is a "conspiracy" common to industrialized nations.

HOW I MET THE LACE CURTAIN: MY PERSONAL JOURNEY

As I listen to the stories of authors who have tried to articulate men's issues, I hear one experience of censorship after another. Some I will share, but many authors who are published or still have hopes of being published are afraid to be mentioned—"I'm afraid people will assume the real reason is that my work is inferior"; "I'm afraid it will be seen as sour grapes"; "I'm afraid people will say my book didn't sell well and that's why I'm so angry"; "I'm afraid . . ."

I acknowledge all of these fears myself. But I also know that if I don't practice what I preach—that women can't hear what men don't say—then I have no right to ask other men to take risks I am myself unwilling to take. I know this will leave me vulnerable, and I know some people will never read this book because they will first read some news account of some distorted version of these personal stories that will make them turn off to me before they get started. I can't say, "So be it" because I do care—I write to be read. But every man has exactly these types of fears when he first begins to share his life experience—that his career, his reputation (his readership) will be hurt. And sometimes, when he shares, that is a price he actually pays.

I will ask you to assume that if you have a teenage son, or a husband, that he has these same fears, fears that keep a part of him silent even as another part speaks. If you are able to hear him in the way of Part I above, you will give him your greatest gift. Enough. Here goes.

When I was first elected to the Board of the National Organization for Women (NOW) in New York City, I was twenty-six. I had never written for a national publication. The *New York Times* sought me out, did a major story on me and the men's groups I was running, and asked me to write an op ed piece. I did.

They published it, with hardly a word changed. They asked me to do a second. Again they published it with hardly a word changed. And a third . . .

As long as I was writing from a feminist perspective, the *New York Times* published *everything* I wrote. Once I began questioning the feminist perspective, the *New York Times* published *nothing* I wrote—not a single one of the more than twenty articles I have since submitted to them in the two decades that followed.

Back to the story . . .

The *New York Times* coverage led to the *Today Show.* During my years speaking from the feminist perspective, I was a guest on the *Today Show* three times. Once I began articulating men's perspectives, I was never invited back. I was beginning to notice a pattern.

Phil Donahue had apparently seen me on the *Today Show* and in the *New York Times* and extended an invitation. When we met, we hit it off. He immediately invited his first wife (Marjorie) to meet me and dine together. When he and Marjorie ran into conflicts, he would call me for advice. After each show, he took me to the airport himself. On the seventh show, though, something happened. I began to add men's perspectives. Suddenly, I was not invited back for years.

When *Why Men Are the Way They Are* was published, I was eventually invited for an eighth show. But articulating men's perspectives, even in balance with women's, led to another six-year hiatus. When *The Myth of Male Power* came out, although it was from the male perspective, it was so much up Donahue's line of relationships and politics that three producers were vying to be the one to produce the show. I was scheduled, with a firm date. The producers convinced my agent to book me as an exclusive on *Donahue.* As a result, queries to all other American talk shows were dropped. Then something happened.

The taping kept getting "postponed." Eventually neither I nor my agents, Hilsinger and Mendelson, the most powerful in the book publicity business, could reach them. As I was trying to unravel the stonewalling, a Canadian show called. They were filled with enthusiasm. But suddenly it, too, kept getting "postponed." This producer, though, had previously booked me; I could feel the remorse in his voice; so I pressed him for an explanation.

Finally he caved, "If you promise never to use my name I'll tell you." I promised. Hesitatingly, he started, "We wanted to have a balanced show, so we called a couple of feminists—big names—to be on with you. Instead of just refusing, they said in effect, 'If you have this guy on, don't expect us to bring our next book to you, or supply you with real-life examples to use on your show— we'll do that just for Oprah.' Another one used the moral appeal—something like, 'Feminism is opposed to rape and the battering of women; so, if you have him on, you'd better take responsibility for making women even more vulnerable.' Once the word got out that we were considering you, we got other calls, even one from a guy, sort of repeating the same mantra.

"Warren, most of us saw all this for the attempt at censorship it was, and as for me, I was excited by the controversy, but, well, it just took one of our producers (who's never met you and hasn't read your book) to freak out and, before we knew it, we were all afraid to stir up her indignation." Well, there you have it. Or . . . there *I* had it!

Two things were happening here. Censorship and the *power* to *not* debate. Why did many (not all) leading feminists (e.g., Gloria Steinem, Betty Friedan, Susan Faludi, and Catharine MacKinnon) refuse to debate? For the same reason any one-party system has no interest in debating. When you have the power you have little to gain and a lot to lose by debating. When we speak of power corrupting and absolute power corrupting absolutely, one example is the unwillingness to debate. It is why no dictator suggests a democracy. **The unwillingness to debate is part of the corruption of power.**

How powerful is the media—with its desire for the controversy a debate generates—in comparison to a leading feminist? I got a hint when I did a show with Gloria Steinem in 1986, at a time she viewed me as a 100-percent ally. It was on *Hour Magazine,* a show that was nationally televised at the time. I said, "Never-married women often earn more than never-married men, because . . ." Gloria looked to host Gary Collins as if to signal "Cut!" Gary Collins, who had always treated me with great respect, told me I must have gotten the sexes mixed up, and signaled for the producer to interrupt the taping.

Off air, I explained why I had meant what I said. I could see in Gary's and Gloria's faces that I had "turned the screw." I could feel the segment was being redone merely so they could avoid saying directly that it would never be aired. And yes, it was never aired. My status changed from regular guest to never being invited back. As for Gloria Steinem? Well, she went from being a friend to never returning my calls. Thinking a little humor might break the ice, I sent her a phone from Toys "R" Us with a dime taped to it. Maybe she doesn't like Toys "R" Us.

I had naively believed that leaders as pioneering as I thought Gloria was would be delighted to hear of ways in which women were succeeding. Now I had to face a deeper fear: that some of my feminist colleagues might have an emotional investment in women's victimhood that went so deep as to prevent any discussion that might dilute women's victim status. Since my income came from feminist referrals, and since feminist power was solidifying the Lace Curtain, I felt, well . . . scared.

I was eventually to discover that my fear was well founded. My speaking engagements on college campuses were soon reduced to less than 5 percent—not 50 percent, but 5 percent—of what they were.

It isn't that many women and even individual feminists were not open enough to hearing a different perspective. When I wrote *The Myth of Male Power,* an editor at *Modern Maturity,* the publication with the largest monthly circulation in the United States, read it, loved it, felt it would be perfect for the male readers, and asked me to write two articles for *Modern Maturity.* I did. Both articles were loved, edited, approved, paid in full, and scheduled for publication.

I had just turned fifty, so I was to receive my own copy. I saw it in the mailbox and quickly scanned the front cover to see if they gave it special coverage. No. Then the table of contents. Nothing. I called the editor. She apologized and said they had "changed focus" at the last minute. But something in her voice said "cover-up." I asked the editor to be honest. She was. She explained that one feminist researcher, who admittedly could find nothing wrong with the research, nevertheless protested. Loudly. The management became afraid. The editor felt as awful as I did.

One day, I received a call from *Glamour* magazine. They had done excerpts from *Why Men Are the Way They Are* when other women's magazines had passed. So I was especially happy when both *Glamour* and one of my favorite editors there wanted to co-author a major article with me: "How Does Sex Really Feel to Men?" Here was the deal: I do the research; she does the writing *Glamour*-style. Fine. So I did the research.

I found that many men felt sex was better with *less*-attractive women. In one man's words, "The most attractive women I've been with have been the worst lovers." A few had good experiences with women a little overweight. One explained, "There's kind of a maternal quality that I find very arousing, comforting, very erotic."

The editor loved the material—to her it felt unique and suggested that many different types of women could be loved. But a top Glamour editor marked these very findings with "I'd drop this." Finally, the entire piece was canned. The excuse? "Nothing original." The editor was shocked. She knew the real reason: *Glamour* isn't selling slightly overweight, less-attractive women.

In this case, my findings were compatible with those of virtually every feminist: Put less emphasis on the beautiful, young, quasi-anorexic woman. The censorship came instead from a different portion of the Lace Curtain—a traditional women's magazine, the portion of the Lace Curtain whose investment is not in victim power, but in what I call "genetic celebrity" power:[6] the power of a woman's youth and beauty to garner her attention, "love," dinners, dates, and diamonds due largely to her genes—without her having to earn it.

Traditional women's magazines—the genetic-celebrity-power portion of the Lace Curtain—know that the more a woman has an investment in her genetic celebrity power, the more insecure she is about her youth and beauty. They know a woman's insecurity leads to her buying makeup. Why? **Makeup is what a woman uses to "make up" the gap between the genetic celebrity power she wants to have and the genetic celebrity power she believes she has.** The greater the investment in her beauty, the greater the gap she feels, the deeper her insecurity, and the larger her purchases. Thus my findings—that men found that women who overly focused on beauty and weight were too controlled to be good lovers—were not exactly what *Glamour* wanted to hear. I was discovering that each portion of the Lace Curtain wanted to hear only those men's feelings that they wanted to hear.

Perhaps the most ironic story is still "in process." For more than three years, I have been told I was too *politically incorrect* to be on *Politically Incorrect!* Stuart Pedersen, at the time a paid consultant to the show, finally wrote me, "As if you didn't know, *Politically Incorrect* is clearly censoring you. They're afraid of you."

If my experiences were unique I probably wouldn't have the courage to share them here. For me, part of what I learn from women and feminists is the value of sharing what is "private," helping each of us to determine whether our "personal" experiences are also political ones. Even with that, I may still not have the courage to share these stories had my reception not been so positive for so long when I was writing only from the feminist perspective.

In a moment I'll share some of these other men's perspectives, but first, there are two feminists who refer to themselves as dissident feminists—Camille Paglia and Christina Hoff Sommers—who have also met the Lace Curtain head on. Camille Paglia has not hesitated to speak publicly of being booked on shows and then hearing producers' tales of the feminists calling to persuade them to drop her. Because she receives so many *death threats,* her answering machine announces that she doesn't personally open packages sent to her.

When Christina Hoff Sommers wrote *Who Stole Feminism?* CBS's *Eye to Eye* was doing a special on her. When the show was aired, Connie Chung publicly announced on the show that she was surprised to receive phone calls from so many feminists, *including Gloria Steinem personally,* trying to pressure the producer into not having the show aired. To CBS's credit, and in particular to the credit of reporter Bernard Goldberg, they did not cave.

Men from the United States to England who have tried to express men's perspectives on a broad range of issues have found themselves similarly censored.

A colleague of mine wrote letters to the editor of *The Nation* for years. Nothing published. Finally he signed his name "Stephanie" rather than Steve.[7] Published. American authors Asa Baber and Jack Kammer, both balanced and articulate, and British authors Neil Lyndon and David Thomas, both of whom met with success before they tried to articulate men's perspectives, could not garner among them a single review or article in the *New York Times, Newsweek,* or *Time*.[8] As a result, Neil and David basically forfeited their expertise on men's issues; Asa, a *Playboy* columnist with hundreds of thousands of readers, wrote no more books; and Jack has been unsuccessful in getting his next book published.

The British authors, unpublished in the United States, experienced a different type of Lace Curtain treatment in Britain. Neil Lyndon, author of *No More Sex War,* explains; "The reviews avoided what I said and attacked me personally, saying I must be impotent or angry because I couldn't get a girlfriend. I happened to be involved with a stunningly beautiful woman, but the truth was irrelevant. And then, I was invited to speak at the Cambridge Union [the British pinnacle of intellect and debate]. It was at the time of the threats to Salmon Rushdie's life, about which all intellectuals were outraged. When I finished speaking, the president of the Cambridge Union, a woman, said in no uncertain terms that my book should be burned. Some weeks later, a student told me her history professor said in class that I should be shot. Shot! To me it is too ironic that the same people who are outraged at the censorship of Salmon Rushdie are so quick to censor anything confronting feminism and are blind to their own hypocrisy."

At least Neil did not experience the death threats encountered by Camille Paglia, or the ostracism experienced by Suzanne Steinmetz, Richard Gelles, and Murray Straus when they published their findings showing women batter equally (see the chapter on domestic violence).

HOW THE LACE CURTAIN WORKS: THE EIGHT-STEP PLAN

1. BY THE TRAINING OF FEMINISTS IN WOMEN'S STUDIES' PROGRAMS WHO THEN BECOME THE ONLY EXPERTS ON GENDER IN ALL INSTITUTIONS WORKING ON GENDER QUESTIONS

In the process, the three other major perspectives of the gender dialogue go unrepresented. The perspectives of:

- *nontraditional men* who feel both sexes' traditional role needs changing, and both sexes need equal compassion in making that transition. This group sees itself as temporarily focused on men's issues, but ultimately being part of a gender transition movement. They believe that historically neither sex was a victim, they both had roles necessary to survival. (Although this is the group with which I identify, I do not believe it should be more than one-fourth of the gender discussion.)

- *traditional women*—the 65 percent of women who do not consider themselves feminists (according to a CNN-*Time* poll[9]).

- *traditional men*—the equivalent of the 65 percent of women who do not consider themselves feminists. This includes men who expect themselves to be the sole and primary breadwinners, as well as the more organized Promise Keepers and men agreeing with Rush Limbaugh.

The effect? Almost every aspect of male-female relationships is studied and legislated from the feminist point of view, not the traditional female or male point of view or the perspective of the nontraditional male. Within the feminist point of view, we will see how the victim feminist perspective dominates those of empowerment feminists in the areas that apply to the Lace Curtain.

This bias is not stagnant. It can begin anywhere in the system and spread like the ripple begun by a pebble tossed in a pond. Feminists in the women's bureau of the department of labor may subcontract a study to academic feminists, the results of which are promoted to a feminist media, which does not question the bias, and the resulting hard news and soft news create public support for politicians to create legal changes that in turn fund more feminist academic and government studies.

This gives feminist perspectives so much value the system "buys" more feminists. How?

2. BY AWARDING FEMINISTS WITH HONORS, SCHOLARSHIPS, AND CAREERS

We will see below the 1,700 funding sources for women and the complete lack of comparable sources for men; the way 30,000 women's studies courses support professors who think feminist and teach feminist, while virtually no comparable men's studies courses exist with teachers who think "masculist," if you will; the way the human resource and development divisions of most large corporations allow only a feminist approach to gender, thus creating careers for tens of thousands of additional feminists. Even some of the most prestigious awards, like Pulitzer Prizes and National Book Awards, are given to women with feminist worldviews, like Susan Faludi and Toni Morrison, but never to a man or woman who specializes in men's issues.

With the Lace Curtain's structure and funding intact, its next step is defining the issues and nonissues, the heroes and villains. It does this . . .

3. BY DEFINING TWO-SEX ISSUES FROM ONLY THE WOMAN'S PERSPECTIVE

Thus, we discuss domestic violence against women, not domestic violence against men; we study schools from the perspective of the neglect to our daughters, not our sons; we define health issues as women's health, not the thirty-four neglected areas of men's health outlined below; we define work in the home as housework, remaining blind to the fifty-plus areas of men's contributions; we discuss dating from the girls' perspective of boys coming on too strong, not boys' perspective of fearing being rejected or their feelings about girls not sharing the risks of rejection.

Even if *men* (*e.g.*, legislators) are competing to solve the problem, they are competing to solve a Lace Curtain definition of the problem. The men may be accused of male dominance, but they are actually working *for* women—dominated by women's concerns without even knowing men's exist.

4. BY CREATING VICTIM DATA TO CATALYZE "VICTIM POWER"

Female-as-victim data is publicized, male-as-victim data ignored. We saw in the previous chapters how men-as-equal-victim-of-domestic-violence data has been kept out of the public consciousness for a quarter century. The best way to ignore data is to not ask questions to discover it to begin with. Thus we see below how the Census Bureau asks only women about child support payments. And finally, victim data is also created by falsification, as we saw with the United Nations falsification of housework data.

When the problem is *worse* for American men, as with suicide or circumcision, someone whose thinking is confined by the Lace Curtain finds a country in which it is as bad for women and headlines it as worse for women. Then they portray this as a woman's problem that is caused by men or patriarchy.

The effect? Woman-as-victim catalyzes the protector instinct in all of us, leading us to create advantages for women, from affirmative action and scholarships to special legal defenses. It creates female Victim Power. This tempts feminists to ignore data and perspectives emphatic to men for fear of destroying this female Victim Power.

Does *male* victim data catalyze a parallel male Victim Power? No. It catalyzes the "cringe response." Why? Our fear that a man who needs help cannot protect. Cringe.

5. BY MAKING ILLEGAL THE PROBLEMS GROWING OUT OF THE TRADITIONAL MALE ROLE AND IGNORING THE PROBLEMS GROWING OUT OF THE TRADITIONAL FEMALE ROLE

Men are more likely to have to pay child support, so child support enforcement (via the garnishment of men's wages or putting them in prison) is a major issue; women are more likely to deny a parent access to children, but the enforcement of laws against visitation denial has almost no teeth. Similarly, men are more likely to rape, so we expand the ability to prosecute rape; women are more likely to register false accusations of rape, but we ignore even the data telling us that.

Since women's new role is working outside the home, women's equal right to the workplace is a major issue; men's equal right to the homeplace and to fathering are minor issues. Since men are more likely to supervise women at work, yet are still expected to take the direct sexual initiatives, we call it sexual harassment when that process doesn't work for the woman. But we ignore the problems that grow out of the traditional female role of indirect initiative-taking and female youth-sex-and-beauty power. For example, when Monica Lewinsky used her sexual advantage to gain access to President Clinton thirty-seven times, become a millionaire, and almost ruin the President in the process, should her colleagues be able to sue for unfair access? Should damages be awarded to future interns to compensate for the suspicion with which they will be viewed? We do not attempt to make illegal the problems growing out of the female role.

The effect? Once the man is portrayed as perpetrator, the perpetrator's story is suspect and the media is hesitant to cross-examine the presumed "victim"—it doesn't want to appear to be "blaming the victim," or "not believing the victim." Thus the media drops its investigative mandate.

6. BY NEGLECTING TO DEFINE MEN'S ISSUES

Other men's issues, like the lack of a men's birth control pill, male-only executions, male-only draft registration, men's health, equal pay for equal dating, or *false accusations* of domestic violence or child molestation, especially during custody battles, are not defined in the public consciousness at all.

7. BY LABELING PEOPLE WHO DISAGREE WITH VICTIM FEMINISM AS "SEXIST," AND IF THEY PERSIST, PUTTING THEIR CAREERS AT RISK

While feminist thinking is honored and turned into careers, the reverse is true of nonfeminist thinking. I am often approached by men when speaking to corporations about their fears of being honest about women in the workplace. I recall a man at Bell Atlantic who said, "If I suggested that at seven P.M., the only people left in my department are men—and that's why we get promoted faster—I'd be setting myself up to never be promoted again!"

8. BY MEN'S SILENCE

The reasons for men's silence and the price it exacts are the theme of this book, so no explanation required here except that without it the Lace Curtain would not exist.

Together it has become as hard for men to have their issues heard in industrialized countries as it was for capitalists to have had their issues heard in the Soviet Union between 1917 and the advent of *glasnost.*

The Lace Curtain operates through the government, education, the media, and the helping professions. The government first.

Government and Funding: Manufacturing Woman-as-Victim

Special funding for women only was based on the belief that women were in the minority. In those areas in which that has changed, the belief is an anachronism and, therefore, the funding is sexism.

Lace Curtain Research and the Funding It Finds

Now that men are in the minority in college (45 percent) and boys are doing worse in almost all subjects except math and science in high school, as well as dropping out, committing suicide, and suffering learning disabilities at much higher rates, we would expect special financial aid to be available to boys—perhaps even more than to girls. Not the case.

The *Directory of Financial Aids for Women, 1999–2001* describes "more than 1,700 funding programs . . . set aside specifically for women." This represents **billions** of dollars in female-only financial aid.[10] Much of the funding is directly or indirectly paid for by taxpayers. *There is no equivalent directory for men.* But you probably knew that.

Studies are done when studies are funded. If the area is gender, the funding is feminist.

Although women dominate the humanities, grants to study male-female issues given by the National Endowment for the Humanities are given almost excessively to study only women, and from only a feminist perspective. For example, $27,500 went for "Witchcraft Beliefs and the History of Thought in Ancient Mesopotamia."[11] What is distinctly missing are studies relevant to both sexes knowing how to improve their lives, such as "The Impact of Stepdad vs. Biological Father Involvement in Divorced Families."

The pattern is the same with the National Endowment for the Arts using, for example, $37,500 of our money to fund exhibits titled "A Woman's Life Isn't Worth Much,"[12] but virtually nothing on men's lives.

Other studies are conducted more directly by the government, such as the Census Bureau. Let's look.

Remember the headlines we read telling us how little men pay in child support, based on Census Bureau figures? All these Census Bureau figures are *based on the reports of women.* And only women.

Only recently did the government commission a special survey including men. The men reported paying almost 40 percent more than the women reported receiving (between 80 percent and 93 percent of what the court had ordered), plus more payments in full and on time.[13]

Why haven't we seen any "Men Pay 80 to 93 Percent" headlines? Because **as soon as the men's perspective was discovered to be so different, the Family Support Administration had the study** *discontinued*—**it was not released.**[14] Which is another way of saying "censored." This does not mean, of course, that the men's figures are more accurate than the women's. Only that they deserve to be equally heard.

THE MURDER OF ALL JUSTICE

In the chapter on domestic violence, much of the censorship I discussed emanated from the U.S. Department of Justice. It was the Department of Justice that censored abuse by women from a 1979 poll. Finally some professors discovered the data on the original computer tape.[15] The Bureau of Justice Statistics' "Murder in Families" stressed women-as-victims although its own raw data showed 55.5 percent male and 44.5 percent female victims of family murder.[16] Similarly, it issued a report on Violence Against Women,[17] but none on Violence Against Men—despite the fact that two-thirds of the violence is against men. We saw also how the FBI hides the female method of killing by contract by calling it a multiple-offender killing.[18]

I am unaware of a single government source with a focus on family or gender that does not now have a strong feminist bias. Some are bureaus of feminist bias.

LABOR IN THE WOMEN'S BUREAU

You've probably read that men earn more than women for the same work. Most of us believe it. That statistic evolves from data compiled by the U.S. Department of Labor. But the Department of Labor has only a Women's Bureau, not a Men's Bureau. Thus we are given raw data that tells us women earn 77 cents for each dollar earned by men, but no Men's Bureau looks beyond the surface to show us what's missing.

What's missing? In the research for a forthcoming book (25 *Ways to Higher Pay*), I discovered that men behave differently toward the workplace from women in twenty-five different ways. All these ways lead to men earning more, but for *very different work* (more-hazardous jobs, more technical professions like engineering or brain surgery), *very different behavior at work* (longer hours, working night shifts), and *very different efforts to obtain the work* (working in much less enticing locations [Alaskan oil rigs, coal mines], commuting further, relocating more, working overseas), and so on.

The Women's Bureau gives us breakdowns by all the categories in which men outearn women, but these twenty-five differences that tell us *why* men earn more aren't mentioned; and areas in which women outearn men (entry-level engineers or mechanics) do not become press releases or stories in our local paper. The biases are reinforced by an American school system in which only 58 percent of high school students in 1999 understand even the very basics of supply and demand.[19] So it does not compute to 42 percent of students that when men choose labor that fewer people want to do (because of those twenty-five types of hardships), it means their pay will be higher because of supply and demand, not discrimination. (And higher pay is usually why the men choose that labor.)

Once this Lace Curtain bias (reinforced by a women's bureau without a men's bureau) is in our psyches, it creates the political justification for others: Equal Pay Day is established.[20] Vice President Gore not only says that women are paid less for the *same* work, but that more competent women are deprived of jobs before less competent men. He doesn't mention affirmative action as the legal requirement for the *opposite* to be permitted. Then the Council of Economic Advisers reports women earn only 75 cents to men's dollar.

This confluence of misinformation creates the political atmosphere that allows President Clinton to announce tripling the mechanisms to enforce penalties for discrimination *against women* for the fiscal 2000 budget.[21] A public service campaign will inform women of their rights. Enter a new millennium of lawsuits. For what are the lawsuits a substitute? Women knowing the other twenty-five ways they can receive higher pay. These would make their company need them more rather than fear them more. That's the difference between victim feminism and empowerment feminism.

THE OFFICE OF RESEARCH ON WOMEN'S HEALTH . . . AND THE DEATHS OF OUR SONS, HUSBANDS, AND DADS

There is no misuse of the Lace Curtain that is killing our fathers and their sons more than its misuse in the area of men's and women's health. We all benefit from more research on both sexes' health. So why have we been focusing on women's health during the past three decades to such a degree that we have an Office of Research on Women's Health but none on men's health? Because we were told by government leaders and feminist activists that women's health research received only 10 percent of all health research funding. *We were not told men's research receives only 5 percent of government funding* (the other 85 percent is for nongender-specific research, such as cellular, blood, DNA, etc.).[22]

In certain areas, women's health research was neglected. We were led to believe that is because we didn't care about women. The opposite was true. Men, and especially male prisoners, military men, and African-American men, were the most likely to be the guinea pigs for the testing of new drugs because we cared less if men and prisoners died. That is, we used men for experimental research for the same reason we use rats for experimental research.

Two points are important here: What neglect there was of women came from protecting women too much. **A core theme of this book is the "female protection paradox": that protecting women hurts women.** This is just one example. Second, the neglect was limited to *certain areas* of women's health—overall women's health research has long exceeded men's.[23]

Notice, though, that we are not being told that we needed to pay attention to women's *and* men's health. **The women's health message has, ironically, been a *competitive* one: women neglected, men not. And it has been a *blaming* one: "The male medical community cares more about men."**

The result? Most of the world assumes women just "naturally" live longer than men. They are unaware that in 1920, for example, American men died only one year sooner than women; today, they die seven years sooner.[24] While dozens of studies are being done on the possible damage of silicone breast implants, the causes of men dying seven years sooner are virtually ignored. Nor are most of us aware of how quickly men's health is deteriorating. When I wrote *The Myth of Male Power* in 1993, the gap between male and female suicide was 3.9 to 1; now it is 4.5 to 1 (see table). In Great Britain, there is a recent 339 percent increase in male suicides by hanging alone.[25]

Even as we are increasingly hearing that women die of heart disease as often as men, we are not hearing that when most women die of heart disease, men have been long dead. Here are the *age-adjusted* death rates for the ten leading causes of death.[26]

---

10 LEADING CAUSES OF DEATH

(AGE-ADJUSTED)

	MALE TO FEMALE RATIO
1. Diseases of heart	1.8 to 1
2. Cancerous cysts	1.4 to 1
3. Cerebrovascular diseases	1.2 to 1
4. Obstructive lung disease	1.5 to 1
5. Accidents and adverse effects	2.4 to 1

6. Pneumonia and influenza	1.6 to 1
7. Diabetes Mellitus	1.2 to 1
8. AIDS (HIV)	4.3 to 1
9. Suicide	4.5 to 1
10. Chronic liver disease and cirrhosis	2.4 to 1

Centers for Disease Control and Prevention, National Vital Statistics Report, Vol. 47, No. 9, November 10, 1998, p. 5, Table B

In a sense, our sons, husbands, and dads pay a "10 percent disposability tax" when they are born male. And more important, something can be done about it. Men are less likely than women to have health care coverage, a gap that has widened again recently.[27] And 94 percent of those dying from work-related injuries (on construction sites, or as truckers, roofers, cab drivers) are men,[28] yet the United States has only *one* job safety inspector for every *six* fish and game inspectors.[29]

What is the U.S. government doing about this disposability of almost half its population? It is identifying *women* as the at-risk group in its draft of "Healthy People 2010," the blueprint for legislation and funding for the first decade of the new millennium. It is treating women's *eating disorders* as more important than men's suicides, or men's heart disease, or men's occupational deaths, or men's seven-year-shorter lifespan. More precisely, it is virtually ignoring the causes of men dying. Overall, it specifies thirty-eight health objectives for women, two for men.[30]

The blindness to males at risk hurts our sons. Testicular cancer is one of the most common cancers in men age fifteen to thirty-four. When detected early, there is an 87 percent survival rate.[31] We educate women to examine their breasts, but few parents even know how to teach their fourteen-year-old son to examine his testicles. Girls' suicide rate is decreasing and boys' is increasing. As boys experience the pressures of the male role, their suicide rate increases 25,000 percent.[32] The suicide rate for men over eighty-five is 1,350 percent higher than for women of the same age group.[33]

Each of these groups of men would benefit from media that ran articles educating men, or the establishment of hotlines for men contemplating suicide, along with Public Service Announcements letting men know the symptoms of suicide or testicular cancer. Part of the reason men die sooner is that men go to the doctor less. Which implies we should be educating men more. Instead we educate men less.

What could "Healthy People 2010" be identifying as an agenda for men's health? Here are thirty-four neglected areas, for starters. Notice the leading cause of death among men—heart disease—is not on here because that is not a neglected area (perhaps because it is also the leading cause of death among women?). And notice also how many of these areas we've barely heard of and, therefore, have little emotional investment in doing something about. That's just the point—we can't care about what we don't hear about.

Neglected Areas of Men's Health

1. a men's birth control pill

2. suicide

3. PTSD (post-traumatic stress disorder)

4. circumcision as a possible trauma-producing experience

5. the male midlife crisis

6. dyslexia

7. autism

8. the cause of male violence

9. criminal recidivism

10. street homelessness among veterans (85 percent of street homeless are men; about ⅓ veterans)

11. steroid abuse

12. color blindness

13. testicular cancer

14. prostate cancer

15. BPH—benign prostatic hyperplasia

16. lifespan; why the male-female gap increased from one to seven years; solutions

17. hearing loss over thirty

18. erectile dysfunction: the positive functions and non-drug-related cures

19. nonspecific urethritis

20. epididymitis (a disease of the tubes that transmit sperm)

21. DES sons (diethylstilbestrol, a drug women took in the 1940s and '50s to prevent miscarriages; the problems it created in daughters were attended to, while the sons' problems were neglected)[34]

22. hemophilia

23. ADHD (attention-deficit hyperactivity disorder)—alternatives to Ritalin

24. workplace deaths (93 percent men) and injuries

25. institutions turning backs on HGH (human growth hormone) abuse among male athletes/body builders, the damage of artificial turf

26. concussions, and the cumulative damage from multiple concussions (football)

27. male testosterone reduction between fifty and seventy

28. infertility (40 percent of infertility is male; NIH has increased female infertility research, but has no research for male infertility)

29. depression (women cry, men deny; women check it out, men tough it out; women express, men repress); Rand Corporation finds 70 percent of male depression goes undetected

30. being victim of domestic violence; unwillingness to report battering

31. chlamydia as a creator of heart disease in men between ages of thirty and sixty[35]

32. estrogen transference to men during intercourse[36]

33. Viagra's effect on heart disease, stress, and marital communication

34. LSD (lower sexual desire) Syndrome (seen in more than half of men between twenty-five and fifty)[37]

In some of these areas, such as sexually transmitted diseases, we think of women being more at risk. Yet men are more at risk than women for chlamydia, gonorrhea, and syphilis,[38] and are over four times as likely to die of AIDS. Other areas, such as Viagra and erectile dysfunction, have been in the news a lot lately, but we've only begun to understand the effects of Viagra; and erectile "dysfunction," as I explain in the chapter on helping men express feelings, is often quite functional.

The chance of a man in the United States dying of prostate cancer is now about 20 percent greater than the chance of a woman dying of breast cancer.[39] Yet the government spends almost four times as much money on breast cancer as it does on prostate cancer.[40] This has, at least, improved from the almost 7 to 1 ratio I announced in 1993 in *The Myth of Male Power*. Advocacy for prostate cancer has had an impact.

However, government spending creates only part of the prostate cancer/breast cancer gap. It is impossible to get a figure on the private spending gap, but I estimate it to be approximately 20:1. And this does not include the "special efforts gap," such as the U.S. Post Office printing special 40-cent stamps to raise more than $25 million dollars for breast cancer research.[41] No stamp raises money for prostate cancer research.

How does this impact the life of our dads? Consider one thing: In the 1920s, a new operation for an enlarged prostate replaced the old method. *For sixty years, no one studied the records to determine if the new operation was as beneficial.* When they did, it was found that the new operation resulted in a 45 percent *greater* chance of dying within five years of surgery. When this was discovered, it was discovered by a Canadian researcher—no U.S. taxpayer spent a penny on it.[42] If breast cancer researchers did not have funds to check for sixty years which form of surgery killed more women, the outcry would have been ferocious, and justifiably so.

CAN A LACE CURTAIN GOVERNMENT EXAMINE ITSELF?

The Lace Curtain's power exists even in male-dominated institutions. For example, Dr. Charles McDowell, formerly of the U.S. Air Force's Office of Special Investigations, discovered that 27 percent of Air Force women who claimed they had been raped later admitted making false accusations of rape.[43] The admission usually came when they were asked to take a lie detector test. With these admitted false accusations he was able to develop thirty-five criteria distinguishing false accusations and those known to be genuine. Three independent judges then examined the remainder of the cases. Only if all three reviewers independently concluded the original rape allegations were false did they rank them as "false." *The total of false allegations became 60 percent.* **Rather than publicize the study as an antidote to the Tailhook scandal, the study was buried. Dr. Charles McDowell was ostracized and moved—the Air Force equivalent of being sent to Siberia.**

The states cross-examine their criminal justice systems by forming commissions on gender bias. These commissions invariably find the criminal justice system guilty of discrimination against women. However, these "government" commissions are not really government commissions—they are feminist commissions. That is, the government pays the National Organization for Women and the mostly feminist National Association of Women Judges to choose which issues to research and which to ignore.[44] They are government commissions only in the sense that they are *paid for* by the government—meaning us. Even the key staff members are typically feminist activists.[45]

Here are some of the ways their conclusions are reached. Data: *For the same crime,* women are more likely to go free on probation; men are more likely to get prison sentences. Conclusion: Women are victims of discrimination because women receive longer periods of *probation!*[46] Fallacy: Duh . . .

Data: There are fewer women's prisons than men. Conclusion: Women are the victims of discrimination because this forces relatives to go farther to visit them. Fallacies: Women receiving probation and shorter sentences for the same crime is part of what leads to fewer women's prisons. Second, there is rarely any need for more than one women's prison near a city because so few women are in prison; if more women than men were in prison the commissions would doubtless claim this is a result of women's poverty and downtrodden status—discrimination in the society against women. Third, locating a prison away from a city makes it much easier to create a setting that is more like a country home and set up open grounds for women and children to play. And yes, there is a trade-off—as a result, there are fewer women's prisons near cities and relatives do have to travel farther.

Similarly, the commissions were able to see how women's prisons need to pay attention to problems unique to women, but not problems more common among men, such as guards turning their backs on male-to-male rape; they focus on the overcrowding in women's prisons while barely acknowledging the more intense overcrowding in men's prisons.

When I wrote of these biases on the commissions' part in *The Myth of Male Power,* a Philadelphia TV station decided to do an exposé on my book by showing how much worse the situation was for women. To their credit, they acknowledged that everything I had mentioned was true; off the air, they revealed to me that they had set out to disprove the book.

Sadly, when a Philadelphia TV station investigates, it has little impact on policy. The *New York Times,* with more than enough staff to investigate these conclusions and have an enormous impact on policy, instead reports these conclusions without questioning them.[47]

A feminist government commission on gender bias is the equivalent of a Republican government commission on political party bias. If a political party did this, we'd call it a scandal; when feminists do this, it's called official. It is one more example of the way feminism has become gender politics' one-party system.

While feminists gain credibility from the government's labeling of feminist findings as official, the government itself adds to its credibility by giving grants for the research to be done by feminists in top universities. In turn, feminists who obtain these grants become sources of income for universities, and their publications become sources of promotion for the feminist professors. All of this is happening despite it being against the law, in the same way McCarthyism happened despite the constitutional guarantee for freedom of speech.

Because statistics can be so easily manipulated, it is necessary for them to always emanate from sources in which there are balances of power. Men do not speak up, organize, or publicize, so biases against women are eliminated and biases against men remain. I would object as much if government statistics were written up only by masculist writers who felt women's methods of killings were the only ones worth highlighting.

The government funding gender studies almost exclusively by feminists is like the Department of Agriculture funding tobacco studies almost exclusively by Marlborists. To be a scholar is not to pre-define a perspective. Saying "feminist scholar" is like saying Republican scholar.

EDUCATION OR MS. EDUCATION?: WHERE THE LACE CURTAIN IS WOVEN

Title IX theoretically prevents gender discrimination in education.[48] Yet universities openly discriminate in favor of women even though girls are now both entering and graduating from college at a rate of 55 percent compared to boys' 45 percent.[49] If sexism against *girls* were the issue, African-American girls would not receive 57 percent of all professional degrees awarded to African-Americans.[50]

Despite this, universities have special programs that not only favor female students, but also female staff and faculty. Even in majors like education, in which men are desperately needed, we have Centers for the Education of Women, but no Centers for the Education of Men.

For example, at the University of Michigan, the Michigan Agenda for Women was designed to help only female faculty and staff be promoted and retained and to help only female students get special assistance and scholarships.[51] This Agenda for Women is the umbrella for many men-need-not-apply programs at the University of Michigan. Some examples: the Center for the Education of Women; for the female faculty, the Institute for Research on Women and Gender annually offers forty research awards at $5,000 each (obviously to do research on the various ways in which women are subjected to gender discrimination!); for undergraduate women there is a residential program called WISE (Women in Science and Education); for junior-level female faculty a program called SHARE (Senior Hiring and Recruitment Effort) permits departments to promote thirty-one junior level female faculty to the senior level; and a program on Women of Color in the Academy specializes accordingly.

There are no equivalent special programs for men. At the University of Michigan or anywhere else. Even in fields in which our sons are in the minority, such as all the arts, humanities, social sciences, and languages.

"WE DON'T NEED MEN'S STUDIES . . . HISTORY IS MEN'S STUDIES, RIGHT?"

Women's studies courses are the seeds from which the forest of feminism has grown. They are the Lace Curtain's womb.

Over 30,000 women's studies courses are currently offered at American universities. There are about 700 majors or minors offered on American campuses.[52] If we're looking for predictors for the next millennium, try California: The entire California State University system *requires* women's studies courses as part of their curriculum. Nationwide, between a quarter and a third of the universities now *require* women's studies courses for graduation.

A study of college courses at fifty-five major universities found that every Ivy League school, with the exception of Princeton, "now offers more courses in women's studies than economics, even though economics majors outnumber women's studies majors by roughly 10 to 1."[53]

The University of Pennsylvania offers "The Feminist Critique of Christianity," but none of the fifty-five universities studied offers a "Christian Critique of Feminism."[54] Typically, universities have been critical of religion for believing they had the only answer—for maintaining believers were superior to non-believers. Ironically, feminism has become the religion it is critiquing.

The feminist objection to men's studies sounds convincing: "History is men's studies." Here is why no mother should agree with that. The function of women's studies and men's studies is to question roles so our children have options, not channel our sons and daughters into stereotypical roles without regard for their individuality. Women's studies' original purpose was to do this for women, but history courses do the opposite for men. **Traditional history courses are the history of both sexes' traditional roles—roles without options.**

History is not men's studies because traditional history courses reinforce the traditional male role of performer. It is hard to find a single man in a history book who is *celebrated* for *not* being a performer. (He may have performed as a rebel, but he's in the history book because he was ultimately a successful performer.) In contrast, women's studies courses celebrate women for role deviance (Madame Curie, Susan B. Anthony, Harriet Tubman, Mary Anne Evans [*aka* George Eliot]). As performers, the women were deviating from their traditional role.

History books trap men into stereotyped roles even more than they trap women because when we celebrate and appreciate someone for playing a role, we are really bribing them to keep playing that role. Appreciation keeps the slave a slave.

Men's studies is *currently* needed more than women's studies exactly because men's role has been less-questioned. But even more important, without men's studies, the universities are teaching our children that men have always had options, women haven't, instead of helping them understand that none of our grandparents had options, they had obligations. Our grandma's role was to raise children; our grandpa's role was to raise money (or raise crops). Both had roles, and therefore neither had power.[55]

Women's studies without men's studies means there is no questioning of the process that resocializes, scholarships, and affirmative actions our daughters into enrolling in the traditional fields of both sexes while men remain psychologically closed out of women's traditional fields of liberal arts. Why? Without men's studies, neither our son nor our daughter is taught to question the process of our daughter "marrying up" and, thus, our sons don't question the process of programming themselves to raise money to obtain love. Since they know the most pay comes in engineering, physics, math, medicine, business and law, they will continue to avoid the liberal arts and use the university as a vocational school.

Without men's studies, our daughter ends up with three options (work full time; children full time; some combination of both) while our son ends up with three "slightly different options" (work full-time; work full-time; work full-time). When we have women's studies without men's studies, we create an Era of the Multi-Option Daughter and the No-Option Son. Which is what we have done.

The anger emanating from women's studies has infiltrated all the top universities. For starters, more than 200 universities currently have "speech codes." For example, at the University of Michigan, the phrase "Women just aren't as good as men in this field" is specifically included in the speech code as an example of an offense.[56] Saying "Men just aren't as good as women in this field" is *not* prohibited. Students violating the speech code might be put on probation and even sentenced to mandatory community service. And of course that can be used against them for life (especially if they should run for political office or desire a government or university position). Speech codes prohibit speech which *women* or minorities might consider offensive, but not speech which men might consider offensive.[57]

The students at the University of Michigan are damaged in other ways. Lynne Cheney, chair of the National Endowment for the Humanities, discusses six University of Michigan professors who were charged with sexual harassment for offenses that included "not greeting a student in a friendly enough manner" and "not having read a certain novel."[58] Some of the charges were, of course, more damaging, but the fact that these were even mentioned gives us a sense of the atmosphere. And they send a message to other professors that they are hostage to female students in general and feminists in particular.

Even those who joke, leer, or stare are now subject to campus discipline for "creating a hostile environment." And on college campuses, no less. The founders of the Free Speech Movement must be turning in their graves—or, should we say, turning on their gray hair.

The codes would be less offensive if they were a two-way street, but even that would be undermining the purpose of a university to prepare our children to create dialogue about what offends them, not lawsuits. When speech codes are a one-way street, however, they boomerang against our daughters' preparations for the workplace. By giving women more-than-equal protection under the law, they turn women into a protected class. This overprotection infantilizes our daughters. It also turns them into a privileged class. Because they haven't earned this privilege they learn to feel entitled—a setup for when something goes wrong: blaming and suing rather than looking within and confronting. This undermines our daughters' preparation to be effective employees and fair employers.

These codes are also damaging our daughters' personal lives. Why? The less men express their feelings, the more the male bashing seems justified. They graduate thinking of *their* rights, but not men's. Thus, our daughters graduate with a college education of anger toward men, including a lack of appreciation for their dad. *A woman who does not appreciate her dad does not feel loved.* And that affects her ability to love her husband and raise children. In the process of stifling men's feelings about women, but not women's about men, the codes become divorce training. A setup for children being raised by a single mom who is overwhelmed and angry.

From the perspective of our sons in college, it looks even worse. If your son or daughter told you he'd been kicked out of a course for objecting to its anti-semitism, how would you feel? Well, I was doing a show in Seattle called *Town Meeting*. Also invited was Pete Schaub, a senior at the University of Washington in Seattle. Pete had enrolled in a women's studies course. When he objected that *all* men were not wife beaters, child molesters, and potential rapists, he was classified as sexist. When he persisted with such challenges, *he was asked to withdraw from the class.* Pete was not your political protestor–type, not by a long stretch, but this was too much even for him. He reminded the school that the course description advertised the course as encouraging "vigorous, open inquiry." To him, it felt more like a vigorous inquisition. The associate dean, caught between feminism and free speech, did "the waffle": He *officially* reinstated Pete, but told him it was best to not attend the class![59]

In brief, the speech codes emanating from the atmosphere created by women's studies maketh neither a happy marriage, a good mother, an effective employee, nor a fair employer. (Otherwise, they work great!) Aside from this, such codes are blatantly unconstitutional.

These speech codes do not come out of nowhere. They are justified by a philosophy core to many of the women's studies classes, one of Marxist feminism, in which men in industrialized nations are seen as part of the dominant class, of a capitalist patriarchy, and women are seen as being treated in this system as the subordinate class, as second class citizens, or the property of men. The theory goes that the dominant class under capitalist patriarchy must keep quiet and noncritical in order to have any hope of women making the transition from subordination to equality. In brief, the censorship of men is seen as a prerequisite to equality. Just as censorship of Soviet citizens was seen as a prerequisite to equality. Instead it created a third world nation.

Isn't it true, though, that criticizing women, tasteless humor, and teasing create a hostile environment that inhibits women from learning? In the beginning, yes. But part of an education's purpose is to overcome that response, to use criticism as a growth opportunity, to know how to handle people with different values and senses of humor, which includes knowing how to communicate your perspective as well as to listen to theirs. Which is why the solution is *not* to include man bashing in the speech codes' censorship. **The solution is to use conflict between the sexes to teach both sexes how to listen to each other.** (To practice Part I of this book.)

One positive contribution of early radical feminists was their focus on the value of the process, not just the end product . . . the college degree. A university is a laboratory for learning how to work through our disagreements, not for learning how to put a muzzle on the sex already less likely to complain and stir anger in the sex already most likely to complain.

What is the status of men's studies? In its current form, men's studies is feminist studies. It does focus more on men, but on men as the problem. It is more likely to be taught by a man, but with a few exceptions, it is taught from a feminist perspective. Men's issues, from anything close to the perspective in which I discuss them, is *a portion of* about 3 percent of the courses.[60]

In contrast to the 700 majors and minors in women's studies, there is but one *minor* in men's studies.[61] In it, "feminist theory is the dominant interpretive discourse,"[62] yet a professor assumed that more women were enrolled because men did not want to confront men's problems, but women did.[63]

The goal of men's studies, though, is not men's studies. Nor should the goal of women's studies be women's studies. Both should ultimately be leading to Gender Transition Studies. And both should be integrating the perspectives of more traditional men and women. Either women's or men's studies isolated from the other is the use of taxpayer money to *subsidize mistrust between the sexes.* Gender Transition Studies is the preparation of the sexes to understand each other.

This doesn't mean we can jump right into gender transition studies. If we do, the agenda will be set by women's studies: Domestic violence will assume man-as-oppressor; contributions to the family will measure women's housework and neglect men's work; discussions of dating will not challenge women to risk sexual rejection, just blame men when they do it wrong; men's health will be neglected, the Lace Curtain will go undetected. . . .

The use of public institutions to subsidize sex discrimination is unconstitutional. As of the turn of the millennium, though, no college student has used Title IX to file a suit against his or her university for not having a genuine men's studies department or for not having in its department of gender studies an equal number of courses on men's issues from nonfeminist perspectives.[64]

THE LACE CURTAIN'S UNIVERSITY TARGETS

Aside from the most prestigious universities, the Lace Curtain has been most apparent at previously women-only colleges that are now supposed to be equally open to men; at religious colleges and seminaries; and in the liberal arts. In all three, male attendance has been in dramatic decline.

At women-only colleges such as Mills and Texas Women's University, the slogans were identical: "Better Dead than Co-Ed."[65] The grief on the faces of these women from Mills College is worth a thousand words. These women are now of the age to be teaching boys and raising sons.

Shannon McMacklin, center, and other Mills College students react to announcement that Oakland school will go co-educational in 1991

Mills College Will Begin Admitting Men

*Associated Press—Shannon McMacklin, center, and other Mills College students react to announcement that Oakland school will go co-educational in 1991. "Mills College Will Begin Admitting Men." Photos by Deanne Fitzmaurice/*The Chronicle

In 1980, seminaries were 20 percent female; by the mid-'90s they were 70 percent female.[66] Why? In many seminaries and religious colleges, "male-dominated religions" are seen as hierarchical oppressors of women (rather than seen as involving the sacrifice of a man like Jesus to save mostly female church-goers from their sins). Seminaries have increasingly been influenced by thinkers such as Mary Daly, a religious studies professor whose *Beyond God the Father* had a seminal impact in the 1970s. Daly advocates "the death of God the Father" because he has made "the oppression of women right and fitting."[67]

Positive images that used to refer only to men, like God-as-He, have been changed in books as traditional as the Bible[68]; negative images, like the Devil-as-He, have not been changed. Ironically, since 85 percent of the street homeless are men,[69] this attitude of men as privileged does not prepare many seminarians to deal with their future constituency.

The anger released from women's studies' floodgates has permeated all of the liberal arts. Misandry is most potent in anthropology, literature, foreign languages, and, most ironically, in social work, psychology, and communications.

Some of our sons are growing up in female-only homes and going to schools with mostly female teachers. If they then choose the liberal arts, they are forced into a mantra of "Why can't I be more like a woman?" How does this happen?

Suppose your son or daughter wants to take literature or languages. Prior to the dominance of feminism, she or he would have been exposed to the pros and cons of many potential approaches to literature (*e.g.*, psychoanalytical; post structuralist; reader response critical; new historicist). But in a Modern Language Association (MLA) poll of English professors on 350 campuses, 61 percent said they now approached literature from a feminist perspective.[70]

Thus an atmosphere is created ("If you know on which side your bread is buttered . . ."). Reporters attending the MLA convention for *Newsweek* and *US News & World Report* describe the atmosphere as so anti-male that presentations of Jane Austen, Shakespeare, Emily Dickinson, Emily Bronte, E. L. Doctorow, and most literary giants were quickly converted into condemnations of men, or the white-male-dominated, imperialist, capitalist patriarchy.[71]

If our sons don't adopt the feminist version, they are labeled and ostra-cized—aliens in their chosen profession; if they do adopt it, they are aliens to themselves.

I have felt the impact of this misandry in the liberal arts in my own life. When I began speaking from only a feminist perspective, I was immediately invited to Yale to be as week-long, quasi-resident scholar. (Before I had a Ph.D.) When I began adding men's perspectives, my speaking income at colleges and universities dropped by more than 90 percent.

I responded by agreeing to not just speak alone, but to speak with opposition. But few feminists, now high in credibility on campus, want to put it at risk. Necessity being the parent of invention, I finally found a debate partner: myself. I set up two podiums: "Dr. Warren Farrell, Masculist" and "Dr. Warren Farrell, Feminist." I run back and forth between the two podiums, debating myself, interrupting myself (and otherwise tempting the boundaries of schizophrenia!).

The speaking censorship had its parallel in teaching censorship. Remember how Suzanne Steinmetz, after she published her findings on domestic violence, discovered years later how feminists contacted other feminists at the university at which she taught, to undermine her tenure? I had a parallel, although very different, experience. When I was teaching only from the feminist perspective, it didn't make any difference that my training was in, I was able to teach in five different disciplines within the liberal arts.[72]

Since *Why Men Are the Way They Are* was published, however, I have not been offered a position in a liberal arts discipline at any college or university. Yes, I have taught in the School of *Medicine* at the University of California at San Diego, but not in the liberal arts. Most men who enter the liberal arts cannot afford to make decisions that put their career and family at risk. Ironically, only my savings from the days of speaking from a feminist perspective have allowed me to take those risks.

ELEMENTARY SCHOOLS, HIGH SCHOOLS, AND THE AAUW

> *But in what way has this [ant] society evolved beyond that of humans? It is far ahead in women's liberation. Male ants are totally unimportant. When their biological usefulness is over, they are discarded and not permitted to return to the nest. The entire ant social world is female, including the soldiers, the workers, the farmers, and, of course the queen. Male ants have wings, and they are expected to use them—to get out.*
>
> from *Getting the Facts*, a sixth-grade textbook used in New York state.

For the past decade, no study has had more influence on our belief that schools shortchange only our daughters than the one commissioned and publicized by the American Association of University Women (AAUW) titled "How Schools Shortchange Girls: A Study of Major Findings on Girls and Education."[73]

The report was the catalyst for tens of thousands of schools to pay teachers to be trained to address the way their schools "shortchanged" only girls, especially in four areas: math, science, teacher attention, and self-esteem. Similarly, in response to this research, all-girl schools are forming throughout the United States, even as all-boy schools are being protested.[74] Notice the joy on the faces of these girls attending an all-girl school. Contrast it to the grief and disappointment of the Mills College women forced to attend school with men. It is the imagery of our daughters made happy or sad that makes so many of us desirous of supporting segregated schools—for our daughter's sake.

Classroom Chronicles. High Hopes for All-Girl Schools. Girls' Middle School students Valini Gosini (left) and Makinnon Ross, both 11, found it easy to put their heads together. Bay Area academies stress learning and self-esteem.
By Julie N. Lynem/Chronicle Staff Writer

In Manhattan, most of the seven private girls' schools had ten applications for each $17,000-plus kindergarten opening for the Fall of 1999, and a *public* girls' school that was formed after the AAUW study's publicity took hold, was also deluged with applications.[75]

I applaud teacher training and the encouragement of our daughters to enter math and science. But something happened on the way to the forum. Had the AAUW commissioned a balanced study of studies, they would have found that boys:

- have lower grades (they do worse in reading, writing, social studies, spelling, biology, art, visual arts, music, theater, languages, and every subject except math and science);

- receive fewer honors;

- have lower class ranks;

- are more likely to repeat a grade;

- are more likely to be put in special education;

- are more likely to be diagnosed with learning disabilities (dyslexia);

- are up to four times as likely to commit suicide;

- have a suicide rate that is increasing while girls' is decreasing;

- drop out sooner;

- are much less likely to attend college;

- are much less likely to graduate from college;

- are less likely to take SATs;

- have more attention-deficit disorder problems, including attention-deficit hyperactivity disorders;

- have more discipline problems.

Without incorporating studies of those areas in which boys are the losers in school, it is impossible for the AAUW to fairly conclude that schools shortchange girls. What we do know is that no one is doing worse than African-American boys in urban areas. Yet the public school formed in Harlem after the AAUW study was for girls, not boys.[76]

What did the Lace Curtain of the AAUW and media keep out of the public consciousness? We heard virtually nothing about the first study of arts education by the U.S. Department of Education in twenty years.[77] Why? Perhaps because of the findings. Girls outperformed boys in all the arts (music, visual arts, theater), and in all the modalities of execution—from creating and performing to interpreting. In music performance, girls had an average score of 40 percent; boys, 27 percent. What are we doing about it? First, it helps to *know* about it.

While the AAUW popularized the low self-esteem of girls, we heard little about the Harvard Medical School study asking teenage boys to write a story based on a drawing of an adult man in a shirt and tie sitting at a desk while looking with a neutral expression at a photo of a woman and children. Only 15 percent of the boys envisioned a contented family man. Instead, "the overwhelming majority constructed narratives about lonely husbands working overtime to support their families, divorced men missing their loved ones, and grief-stricken widowers."[78]

The Harvard study found boys from the United States, Canada, Australia, and the United Kingdom doing worse than girls, and concluded it was the boys who are now educationally disadvantaged. Despite these findings, teachers, it discovered, are being required to take gender equity courses that have "become especially vigilant, even obsessive, about making sure that the voices of girls" are heard, even as boys are cast as villains.[79]

For almost two decades the number of women in colleges and universities has exceeded the number of men, even though college-age men outnumber college-age women.[80] But during this period, the U.S. Government started programs on Girl Power to encourage women in schools, but no programs on Boy Power to encourage boys in schools. The Girl Power–type government programs are based on the thinking that girls are the minority—a two-decade–old anachronism.

What our sons lost were the solutions that might have emerged from even a small amount of attention to them. Solutions such as:

- training teachers to understand what boys are missing when they go from mother-only homes to a female teacher in an almost all-female–staffed school (e.g., a male teacher being more likely to see a drug dealer as a potential entrepreneur who needs his energy rechanneled)

- affirmative action programs to recruit and give scholarships to some of the finest young men to become elementary school teachers

- a Dad-in-the-Classroom program to pay companies to allow men to take a week leave of absence to teach, preferably in their own child's class—thus exposing students to a variety of male role models and professional opportunities

One reason the 1990s went without attention to our sons is that no American Association of University Men (AAUM) pointed out the gaps between the AAUW's publicity and the actual data from the very studies they commissioned. For example, that both boys and girls agree that teachers think girls are smarter; both sexes feel that teachers like girls more; both feel teachers would prefer to be around girls more than boys; and both boys and girls feel girls receive more compliments.[81]

Nor did an AAUM explain that all four areas in which the AAUW claimed girls are allegedly shortchanged are contradicted either by their own data or by other research. Let's start with finding that boys do better in math. Boys score only 5 points higher than girls on the nationwide achievement test scores in math (310 to 305).[82] And more girls than boys take high school classes in algebra and geometry.[83] It is in the *choice* of math for a *profession* when girls say, "No thanks—I'd prefer literature" (or foreign languages, art history, or another liberal art). Why that difference in choice?

Boys often choose math for reasons of money, not love. That is, the AAUW did not allow for the possibility that boys choose math or engineering because they know that it will earn them more money than a major in French literature. **As girls were watching Princess Di marry a prince, boys were figuring out that majoring in French literature will leave them short by a castle.** As girls are figuring out whether they want the option of being financially supported when the children are young, boys in college are figuring out how to do the financial supporting if he and his wife should want that option.

Women friends of mine who have chosen math also did it for financial reasons. Liz Brookins's first love was history. When she speaks of history there is a sparkle in her eye. But she had dropped out of college to be married and eventually become a mom to four children. Then she got divorced. When child support did not support the children, she knew she had to return to college. But she also knew a degree in history might leave her unemployed. She didn't have that luxury. So she asked herself a different question: "What degree will leave me best able to support my family?" The answer was math. Math it was.

It is not that Liz was bad at math; it was that it was not even close to her first love. As it turned out, she became very good at math. She became San Diego County's math teacher of the year and now teaches at the University of California in San Diego. *Now* there's a sparkle in Liz's eye when she solves an equation!

And that's the way it is for many men: First, they take care of the family they love; then they try to fall in love with what takes care of the family. When I ask college students what they would prefer to do if they could make equal money doing anything they wish, *both* sexes are more likely to choose music, art, and the liberal arts over math, engineering, or physics.

If schools and society prepare girls to have their *choice* more than boys, is it really the girls who are being shortchanged? Certainly girls have scholarship and admissions advantages over boys in math and science. In brief, **the AAUW left out discrimination against *our sons* as one reason boys may be undertaking math.**

Second, science. Boys outscore girls on science achievement tests by only 8 points (300 to 292). Unpublicized by the AAUW, though, is the fact that boys score 15 points lower than girls in reading and 17 points lower in writing.[84] Nor is it mentioned that a higher percentage of girls take biology and chemistry classes.[85]

Third, teacher attention. The AAUW commissioned a study finding that *both* boys and girls were *much* more likely to feel that girls got called on more than boys and that teachers paid more attention to girls than they did boys.[86] *This research, though, was left out of the AAUW's public relations report.*[87]

Fourth, self-esteem. Recent studies of self-esteem find girls and boys to be between one and three percentage points of each other—in either direction. For example, when both boys and girls are asked, "I feel that I am a person of worth, at least on an equal basis with others," 90 percent of girls either strongly agree or agree; 89 percent of boys either strongly agree or agree.[88]

In 1997, Metropolitan Life examined the way boys and girls were treated and concluded that "contrary to the commonly held view that boys are at an advantage over girls in school, girls appear to have an advantage over boys in terms of their future plans, teachers' expectations, everyday experiences at school, and interactions in the classroom."[89] You did not read about this study in the media. And it had virtually no impact on the schools.

The impact of our belief in women-as-minority? It takes the *New York Times* almost two decades after women are exceeding men in college to acknowledge it in a significant story. When they do, they devote more space to how the gap creates problems for the female students ("There aren't many guys to date") and how it turns into dominant oppressors ("[the guys] have their pick of so many women that they have a tendency to become players").[90] In contrast, articles about men being in the majority at the Citadel, or in the armed services, never mention men as victims because they have few women to date.

When the *New York Times* interviewed students and educators about why the gap exists, they chose answers that justified the gap. For example, "In high school, I always felt women did better and cared more . . ."[91] Or comments that the men just aren't interested, or that women tolerate boredom better, or that men feel that they can make their way in the military or computer work without degrees.

Contrast this with what we give as reasons for why women used to do worse in math and science. We ask ourselves whether the institutions themselves are doing anything to discourage girls. And the answer is always "yes." We don't say that it's because the women care less, or because men tolerate boredom better, or that many women feel they can make money by marrying money and, therefore, don't need degrees. The difference in attitude leads us to offer special opportunities only to girls, and for the government to create Girl Power programs.

To the credit of the *New York Times*, the following week they did devote six sentences to the ways in which boys lose out to girls in schools in many ways, but then immediately justified doing so out of racial concern—that African-American boys are doing worse than any other group.[92]

THE MEDIA

When the media discover a feminist concern, it gets less than five minutes of serious consideration; then comes a five-year attack.
SUSAN FALUDI, *Newsweek*, October 25, 1993

When it comes to gender issues, journalists generally have suspended all their usual skepticism. . . . We accept at face value whatever women's groups say. Why? Because women have sold themselves to us as an oppressed group and any oppressed group gets a free ride in the press. . . . I don't blame feminists for telling us half-truths and sometimes even complete fabrications. I do blame my colleagues in the press for forgetting their skepticism.
BERNARD GOLDBERG, CBS News correspondent

The media contain some of the world's most talented and hard-working people. The media work under deadlines that would be my nightmares. As for ratings, a prime-time TV show must find an audience of 25 million; a book can make a good profit with an audience of 25 thousand, making any concern for "ratings" one-tenth of one percent of the concern of a prime-time TV show.

The most popular stories, the "biggest" stories—Anita Hill, O. J. Simpson, Princess Diana, and Monica—all have one archetypal theme embedded in them: the drama of a male oppressor and a female victim. Following is the media's dilemma.

The popularity of this archetype creates ratings. To question this archetype is to undermine the ratings it is the very purpose of the story to create. And it is asking reporters to introspect when deadlines are demanding something commanding in writing, not a work-in-progress in the mind.

When these "big story" elements surface, newspapers, TV news, talk shows, and even book publishers are all in unison, each with a unique style, but each with a similar message. So the examples in this media section often apply to more than the particular media for which I describe it.

The *New York Times* merits its own section, because, among the media, it has almost Pied Piper status. First, if you read the *New York Times* on any given day, you will be able to predict more of what the rest of the media will be covering the rest of the week than if you attend to any other media source in the world. Second, and not coincidentally, there is no significant media source in which feminism has a greater influence on the content and direction of male-female issues than at the *New York Times*.

Because the media are filled with bright and ambitious people looking for "scoops," we can get a sense of the power of the instinct to protect women and demonize men when it has left virtually untouched for a quarter century the data on domestic violence against men and particularly the thousands of heart-wrenching stories of domestic violence against elderly men, whose real-life stories are in every community. The same can be said for stories of dads fighting to love their children who are told to be wallets first, visitors second; or men who are victims of false accusations, especially during custody battles; or a boy who dies of testicular cancer, or who drops out of school, or a veteran who becomes homeless and dysfunctional.

The instinct to protect women is powerful enough to keep the media from "scoops" like questioning the belief that women are workers and men are shirkers; or the myth of the deadbeat dad. The instinct has directed its focus on the racism of executions and away from the sexism of all-male executions; on sensitivity to dumb blonde jokes more than Bobbitt castration humor; on how Hillary and Princess Diana felt, but not how Bill Clinton or Prince Charles felt; to look at the female tragedies in sex and dating, but not the male's; and on and on and on.

Of the four gender perspectives outlined above (feminists; nontraditional men; traditional men; traditional women), I would estimate that between 90 and 95 percent of the reporters by whom I have been interviewed in the past twenty-five years leaned toward the feminist perspective. About 80 percent of those feminists are women, so **not only is gender politics covered by people from only one gender *political* party, but by people whose gender reinforces their political ideology.** A bit like 90 to 95 percent of the reporters covering the Republican and Democratic political conventions doing it from the point of view of the Republicans—or Democrats.

On top of this political and personal bias, the media relies not only on government and academic circles to feed it information, but on opinion polls.

OPINION POLLS: MEN NEED NOT APPLY

When responsible polling organizations like the *New York Times* supposedly poll both sexes' points of view, they, in fact, poll women at more than a 2-to-1 ratio to men. Why? Here's the *New York Times'* own explanation: "So that there would be enough women interviewed to provide statistically reliable comparisons among various subgroups of women."[93]

What did the *New York Times* just do? They rationalized their discrimination by telling us *how* they discriminate. They avoided the issue of subgroups of men. As if men, well, men need not apply.

The result? The *New York Times* devoted *eleven paragraphs* to the views of black women. *Not one word* on the views of black men.[94] Racist? Yes. Sexist?

Even more so. African-Americans were not undersampled in proportion to the population. Men were.

When Roper conducted a study to discover a women's and men's perspectives on the other, they too oversampled women—this time by a ratio of 3 to 1.[95] Yet, over 90 percent of these women were in favor of marriage. Presumably to men. The headlines, though, told a different story: "Survey Has Message for Men: Shape Up, You Oversexed Pigs"[96] and "Women: More Men Are Pigs."[97]

Message for Men: Shape Up, You Oversexed Pigs

The articles following the headlines not only focus almost exclusively on women's perspectives, but on these types of women's perspectives: "Most men are mean, manipulative, oversexed, self-centered, and lazy" and women are "fed up."[98] Some men silently wonder, "Exactly what am I being married for?"

FIVE WAYS OF IGNORING WHAT MEN DO SAY

What's happening here? Actually, five methods are used to ignore what men *might* say *if* we asked, or what they *do* say when we ask. First, the undersampling of men leads to our having data on men, feelings on women. Second, using only women's perspectives to create the headlines. (Men's perspectives were not turned into headlines such as "Sex Up, You Overweight Pigs.") Third, funding. The poll was sponsored by Virginia Slims. Comparable polls are *not* sponsored by Marlboro. Fourth, attitude. If Marlboro had paid, they would never encourage headlines saying "Message for Women: Shut Up, You Gold-Digging Cows."

Fifth, the press release. When men are polled, the most negative perspectives on men are also conveyed in the press release. When Gallup did a worldwide poll in 1996 to discover the characteristics associated with each sex, the headline in *Gallup's own press release* read "Women Seen as Affectionate; Men as Aggressive."[99] Gallup took the most positive findings about women and most negative findings about men and made those the headline of their press release. Judge for yourself.

The actual findings showed the women were seen as more emotional, talkative, patient, and affectionate. Isn't "affectionate" the best? The men were seen as more courageous, ambitious, and aggressive. Isn't "aggressive" the worst?

The result of these five steps is that when feminist perspectives do not define our view of relationships, women's perspectives do. And it's not just women's perspectives, but the angriest of women's perspectives.

From these sources we receive the news.

NEWS

The covers of new magazines are the only news medium that puts all our focus on *one fixed visual image*. Unlike the front page of a newspaper, there aren't thousands of words and a dozen headlines competing for our attention.

See if you notice a bias common to the four fixed images on the covers of *Time* and *Newsweek* below. [100]

When *Time* apologized for the darkened photo of O. J. Simpson, it acknowledged the appearance of racism. When *Newsweek* was criticized for the beautifying of the mother no one saw the sexism. But nothing is common to all four photos other than the sexism: that is, only a man was doctored to make him look less appealing and therefore less sympathetic; only a woman was doctored to make her look more appealing and therefore more sympathetic. Neither man's photo was doctored to make him look more appealing.

The real-life result of this blindness? Here's a consciousness-raiser. Test yourself. For forty years, the U.S. Public Health Service's Tuskegee Syphilis Study did not tell 399 black men that they had syphilis. (When syphilis is not treated in its early stages, it eats away at bones, the liver, the heart and the brain, and often leads to paralysis, deafness, and blindness.) These 399 black men were denied penicillin and other treatment so the government could experiment with them. It was not until newspapers uncovered the crime that the government stopped the experiment. Years later President Clinton apologized for the racism.[101] What's your take—was Clinton's apology missing something?

President Clinton failed to see the sexism: **Disposing of 399 black men is blatantly racist *and* blatantly sexist.** When we see only the racism we are blind to the African-American man's *double* jeopardy. Had racism been the only issue, African-American women would also have been subjected to the Tuskegee experiment. The sexism is apparent in the fact that not a single African-American woman was. But the deeper sexism is our blindness to it. And the deeper issue is that we haven't been using the lessons we learned from racism to spot de*human*ization.

Our blindness to the way we make women look more sympathetic and men less sympathetic allows the media to also be blind to the way it gives women special advantages even as they highlight women's victimhood.[102] For example, as I write this, *Newsweek* magazine uses the almost naked appearance of Nicole Kidman in a Broadway play to catapult to her to the front cover of *Newsweek*.[103] Rather than see this as an unfair advantage of female beauty power, she is portrayed as a victim fighting for her privacy. Excuse me. Would we portray a man who strips on Broadway as fighting for his *privacy*?! Similarly, instead of saying her career has taken off since her marriage to Tom Cruise, creating for her an advantage not available to any man, she is portrayed as a victim overcoming the *barrier* that her Mrs. Tom Cruise status has been to her becoming a star on her own. Note how the photo incorporates these feelings—of Nicole's anger at being a victim, her need to fight for independence from Tom and for privacy, and her sex appeal.

When we offer our daughters both sex and beauty power *and* the compassion accorded a victim, it just encourages our daughters to use Monica Lewinsky– type power rather than Mother Theresa– or Margaret Thatcher–type power. Why spend a lifetime earning income when you can seduce a man at age twenty-two and earn a lifetime's worth of income from the spin-off of the seduction?

Newspapers create these biases more with words, especially front-page, above-the-fold headlines. **In the 1994 election, when men were the disen-**

franchised voters, they were condemned as "Angry White Men." In the 1996 election, when women were the disenfranchised voters, they were acknowledged as "Worried Women" or "Concerned Women."[104]

The impact of labeling a woman concerned and a man angry? When a woman is worried or concerned, it catalyzes a man's desire to be a problem solver, a savior, her ally. When a man is seen as angry, it stimulates a woman's fear, her desire to protect herself *against* him, to become his enemy. Men want to listen to a worried woman; no one wants to listen to an angry man. Notice that the men were not labeled angry before they spoke (with their vote), but as soon as they did they were labeled so we could ignore them and return to our focus on worried and concerned women.

This is what makes men afraid of speaking up: men feel no one can hear what men *do* say.

The labeling bias also reveals itself in the double standard of our treatment of domestic violence. When domestic violence occurs against men, it is often as a joke. Here is a headline from the *St. Louis Post-Dispatch*.[105]

When a colleague confronted the editor, she responded, "It was supposed to be an upbeat story."[106] Excuse me. Have you ever seen an "upbeat story" about domestic violence against women? Editor, bite your lip.

Couple's Makeup Kiss Gets A Bit Nippy For Husband

KINGSPORT, Tenn. (AP) — Helen Carson told her husband she wanted to kiss and make up after they had a fight. Apparently she wasn't that forgiving — she bit off the end of his tongue.

MEN DIE; WOMEN VICTIM

It is the last Valentine's Day of the second millennium. *Newsweek* celebrates it by telling women that men's deaths means women are victims, this time of yet "Another Biological Clock."[107]

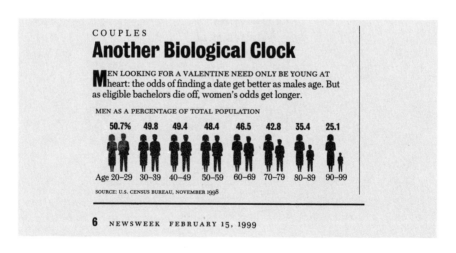

COUPLES

Another Biological Clock

MEN LOOKING FOR A VALENTINE NEED ONLY BE YOUNG AT heart: the odds of finding a date get better as males age. But as eligible bachelors die off, women's odds get longer.

MEN AS A PERCENTAGE OF TOTAL POPULATION

| 50.7% | 49.8 | 49.4 | 48.4 | 46.5 | 42.8 | 35.4 | 25.1 |

| Age 20–29 | 30–39 | 40–49 | 50–59 | 60–69 | 70–79 | 80–89 | 90–99 |

SOURCE: U.S. CENSUS BUREAU, NOVEMBER 1998

6 NEWSWEEK FEBRUARY 15, 1999

More precisely, there are three messages in this *Newsweek* snippet: Men die, women victims; women live, women victims; men die, men benefit. Check it out.

If that's love, let's check out war. *Forty million* Soviet men were killed between 1914 and 1945. Some families lost every man in the family: dad, son, brother, uncle. Yet a headline in *Parade,* the largest-selling weekly magazine in the world, reads "Short End of the Stick" with the article explaining Soviet *women* are getting the short end of the stick because they are stuck with factory and street-cleaner positions.[108]

In Bosnia, the civil war has wiped out men so disproportionately that only 30 percent of the Bosnian population are men. Do headlines tell us, "War leaves Bosnia with 30 percent Men"? No. *Parade*'s headline reads, "Women Look to Gain Power in Bosnia."[109] The focus on the sacrifice made by men as a gender was not only ignored, but Bosnia has specifically been used as an example of the type of war in which both sexes are killed equally. When there's a story about a man being killed, the focus is not on the sacrifice of men, but of their role. We discover the sacrifice of men as a gender only when it is needed to help us understand the new burdens on women. For example, here is the page-one headline from the *Los Angeles Times*[110]:

Los Angeles Times

THURSDAY, MAY 16, 1996
COPYRIGHT 1996 / THE TIMES MIRROR COMPANY, CCVI / 312 PAGES

COLUMN ONE

Women of Bosnia Try to Rebuild

■ The war has robbed many communities of their husbands, fathers and sons. In this patriarchal society, those left behind must learn to handle money, deal with authorities and survive bitter loneliness.

By TRACY WILKINSON
TIMES STAFF WRITER

Watch how carefully, and doubtless unconsciously, men's deaths are treated as women's victimization.

Men have died, but the headline tells of only the female effort ("Women of Bosnia Try to Rebuild"). The loss of men is explained only to tell us the burden on the women "left behind." The focus is on *the communities* that are robbed ("The war has robbed many communities . . ."), not "Husbands, fathers, and sons robbed of lives."

Now observe how women's new *burdens* are seen as men's previous *privi-*

leges. (Male privilege is implied by phrases like "In this patriarchal society . . .") However, it is only as we read down into the story that we discover: ". . . the women must haul kindling, draw water, and till the fields."[111] But wait . . . why was tilling the fields and hauling kindling left out of the headline? Because tilling fields and hauling kindling would have allowed us to laugh at the use of the word "patriarchal" to describe the men.

Now return to the secondary headline. Note that *the very three words that shift the emphasis to women—"those left behind"—also shifts the emphasis to victim language:* "left behind," " must learn to handle," "must learn to deal," and "must survive bitter loneliness."

There is something about women's role that is also never mentioned. Can you figure it out? Women not sacrificing their lives in war is never discussed as female privilege, as matriarchy.

Is it possible we are still ignoring men's deaths exactly so we can prepare men to die in war to protect women? Almost as if to answer, three issues of *Time* and *Newsweek* arrived at my home, in *deus ex machina* fashion, as I was writing this in 1999. There were two issues devoted to women; one to men. The two issues devoted to women were both devoted to women *living.* The one issue devoted to men honored men for *dying.* Note, in the *Newsweek* covers, how the photos are of a man and woman at the prime of life, but the photos and text combined emphasize women living *after* the prime of life, and men dying *in* the prime of life. ("The Truth About Women's Bodies"[112] and "Health for Life: What Every Woman Needs to Know"[113] versus "From WWI to Vietnam: The Grunts and the Great Men."[114])

Isn't it good we honor men for dying? Let's put it this way: If we honored women for dying while we produced special issues on men's health and none on women's, would we ask whether that was good? Or would we intuitively see that the appreciation of women for dying is appreciation that keeps the slave a slave?

FEMALE VICTIMHOOD IS DEPENDENT ON KEEPING MEN'S DEATHS INVISIBLE

If female victimhood is dependent on keeping men's deaths invisible, it follows it is also dependent on keeping invisible the contributions men make. Again, most of this not conscious. But neither is it coincidence. Have you *ever* seen an article on the *responsibilities* of third world *men*? (Or men of any world!)

In the housework chapter, we saw the dynamic that kept men's fifty areas of contributions to the home invisible. Similarly, one of the fastest growing segments of the population at the turn of the century is the single dad, but we are still keeping invisible his contributions. And in the workforce we have ignored the longer hours, more hazardous jobs, more technical fields, and other contributions made by men that lead to higher pay.[115]

The incentive to keep men's contributions invisible? Victim power is a prerequisite to everything from affirmative action to Women, Infants, and Children Programs.

The price we pay? Perhaps, if we studied the single dads we might help single moms? And, oh yes, might this help the children? And perhaps, if women know the twenty-five behaviors that create higher pay for men rather than tossing off men's higher pay as discrimination, they would empower themselves?

Dependency on victim power is part of women's search for security, but, ironically, the very process is leading to women losing security. Why? Many business owners have shared with me their fear of lawsuits by women, and their awareness that down-sizing and outsourcing women reduces their fear. *Thus, many women, in search of security, are losing security.*

Notice that in most of these cases there are five parts of the Lace Curtain working together: funding sources that finance only feminists as gender scholars (such as Arlie Hochschild, the author of *The Second Shift*); top universities like UC Berkeley hiring feminist scholars, thus giving credibility to research with a built-in female-as-victim bias; the press making insignificant studies into headlines when it contains woman-as-victim while ignoring studies that defy that stereotype; men not speaking up; too few of us questioning.

NEWSPAPER PUBLISHING

We saw in the Canadian study of newspapers discussed above how violence against women was portrayed disproportionately to men's and was personalized even as men's was at best a cold statistic.

Here's why this bias hurts *women*: When only women's suffering is personalized, it motivates us to rescue the woman and assume the cause must be the man. So in problems like domestic violence we blame the man and ignore the male-female dance that leads to both sexes battering each other equally.[116]

This hurts women because, when the man feels he is the assumed cause, he becomes resistant to counseling. **He then experiences the counseling as identical to his wife—unable to hear him.** To him, the counseling is now part of the problem. No, it's worse than that. Hope disappears and cynicism appears. And it doesn't stop there. He feels both his wife and the system are ganging up on him. Now it's him against the world, and that's the set up for mass killings followed by a suicide, which is, and will remain, the male style until men become no more or less worthy as victims than women.

To illustrate the Lace Curtain in newspapers, I will look at the *New York Times,* but parallel analyses can be made of most papers. The experience of Jack Kammer's *Good Will Toward Men,*[117] consisting of many independent women explaining why they support feminism's empowering of women but not its demonizing of men, illustrates the ubiquity of the bias. When *Good Will Toward Men* was published, *it did not receive a single review* in any mainstream newspaper in the United States. Only the *San Francisco Chronicle* came close. It assigned a review to Armin Brott. Brott liked the book. But Brott explains, when he submitted it to the *Chronicle* book review editor at the time, she acknowledged to him that she had *not* read the book, but felt she knew enough of its thesis to tell Armin, "I don't want a review like this . . . I don't like this book." She killed the review.

When I mentioned this to a friend, he exclaimed, "That's censorship! What the *Chronicle* did is censorship! Doesn't that make you furious?"

I responded, "No. Overt censorship scares me less than covert censorship—what scares me is the hundred big city newspapers that didn't even assign it to be reviewed even as they were reviewing dozens of feminist books. And what scares me is that almost every book on men's issues is neglected by almost every paper."

The only *single* newspaper whose censorship scares me is the *New York Times,* because it is the Pied Piper of not just print journalism, but the visual media as well. I double-checked this with Bernard Goldberg, a reporter with CBS news for twenty-seven years. He estimated that **more than 90 percent of *television* news stories are picked up from one source: the *New York Times.***[118] And, as will become apparent, when it comes to issues of gender, no source with even close to comparable influence is more anti-male. Take a look.

THE *NEW YORK TIMES*: UNHEALTHY TIMES

It's June 1998—Men's Health Month. The *New York Times* features a special section on *women's* health. Coincidence? On Men's Health Month 1997 they did the same thing.[119] Yet no Men's Health section appeared in *any* month of 1997 or 1998. In fact, prior to 1999, no section on Men's Health has ever appeared. Oh, yes, the *day* the 1998 section on Women's Health appears is *Father's* Day.

Here is the *New York Times* headline for a story about Father's Day, in this Women's Health section.[120]

10   WH   THE NEW YORK TIMES, SUNDAY, JUNE 21, 1998

                                                W O M E N ' S   H E A L T H

Men. Are Women Better Off With Them, or Without Them?

By NATALIE ANGIER

10 WH The New York Times, *Sunday, June 21, 1998 Women's Health*
Men. Are Women Better Off With Them, or Without Them? By Natalie Angier

The story is written by Natalie Angier. See if you can find the anger:

"Today is Father's Day . . . we women are supposed to . . . make them feel like princes while letting them act like turnips.

"The section you are reading is about women's health. And so what better place to address the question: Are they worth it? Do we live better with men or without them . . . ? The answer, like marriage itself, is a glorious mess."[121]

Let's see, now. The woman's question on Father's Day is "Do we [women] live better?" Isn't that like your dad saying to your mom, "It's Mother's Day . . . what better day to ask 'Are you worth it? Am I better off with you or without you?'"

Angier's anger is not Angier's alone. The section's first page teases "Men have Viagra. Women have outdated, inadequate data on questions of desire and arousal."[122]

Would we honor Mother's Day with articles saying "Women have the birth control pill, an Office of Research on Women's Health, a seven-year longer lifespan. Men have outdated condoms, hazardous jobs, and male-only draft registration"?

The *New York Times* finally did a men's health section of sorts in 1999.[123] Unlike the large women's health sections, the men's was brief. (Excluding ads, a total of about seven pages of print and usable illustrations such as graphs.) There was nothing in depth on thirty-three of the thirty-four neglected areas of men's health—the list of which I had sent the *New York Times*. Instead, articles focused on men's *tailoring*, cosmetic surgery, men's gyms, and "Confessions of a Former 'Jake,'" as in a men's columnist for *Glamour*.

While a few of the articles contained useful information, the tone was the opposite of the women's health section: Instead of criticizing and blaming women, as the women's health section did to men, *the men's health section criticized and blamed men.* Men are told they die sooner because they self-destruct:

"Why Men Don't Last: Self-Destruction as a Way of Life."[124] Could it also have to do with the absence of compassion?

While the women's health section told women they were victims, the men's told men they have lots of advantages ("Men have lots of health advantages"[125]) and all the luck ("When it Comes to Food, Guys Have All the Luck"[126]).

The attitude begins on page one, above the fold. Bored, beleaguered, or can't-be-bothered men (with the exception of the African-American man, the only type of man portrayed with occasional empathy by the *Times*) reluctantly waiting to see a doctor. The subhead lectures men: "As Patients, Men Are Impatient, or Uneasy, or Both. They Need To Get a Grip, Like women."[127]

*Men's Health Y D1 Wednesday, February 17, 1999 The New York Times
Don't Take Your Medicine Like a Man. As Patients, Men are Impatient,
or Uneasy, or Both. They Need to Get a Grip, Like Women.*

How does the *New York Times* cover health on an everyday level, say a front page news story? The headline reads "New Cancer Cases Decreasing . . . But Minorities and Women Are Still Particularly at Risk."[128]

The headline should have ended, ". . . But Minorities and *Men* Are Still Particularly at Risk." Why? **According to the *New York Times'* own graphs, these special risks applied to men, not women.** The graphs showed men have lung cancer at almost *twice* the rate of women. Similarly, the colon/rectum graphs show men's rates were more than 50 percent higher than women's. And in the only other breakdown, men's prostate cancer rates were higher than women's breast cancer rates for every year since 1991.

Check out the headline and illustration again. Notice anything else? The

front page illustration features only a woman. Men die, women victim. Men's risks are increased by our blindness to them.

MEN ARE FROM CAVES, WOMEN ARE FROM VENUS

When research uncovers women having a biological superiority, the *New York Times* publicizes it, praises it, and uses it as a springboard for attacking men. Many of these pieces are written by Natalie Angier, the *New York Times'* expert on female biology, male biology, female health, and male health. One article begins "Women may not find this surprising, but one of the most persistent and frustrating problems in evolutionary biology is the male. Specifically, why doesn't he just go away?" I spotted this article reprinted, as "Report Finds Males Weak Link in the Evolution of Species."[129] No alternative perspective is offered within the article. Nor are alternative perspectives—praising research on men being biologically superior—printed elsewhere in the *Times*, at any time. Wasn't there another group that believed this about Jews?

What happens when research discovers unflattering tendencies about women? The *New York Times* shoots it down. In an article by Angier titled "Men, Women, Sex, and Darwin" and featured on the front cover of the *New York Times Magazine*,[130] every biological observation about women that might be construed as negative is reduced to an explanation of how men have manipulated the society to make women turn out that way. Example: When research finds that *wealthy* women worldwide marry up or don't marry at all, she blames men for preventing women from making as much and claims women will *never* make as much (italics hers). By missing the point that the wealthy woman has already made *more* than 99 percent of men she is able to dismiss wealthy women marrying for money or not marrying at all as men's fault.

From the perspective of the *New York Times,* even watching the Super Bowl actually causes men to return to this cave past and smash their wives. When feminists reported that violence against women increased after the Super Bowl, reporters like the *New York Times'* Robert Lipsyte branded the Super Bowl the "Abuse Bowl."[131] More precisely, he states that "If Super Bowl tradition holds, more women than usual will be battered today in their homes by the men in their lives. It seems an *inevitable* part of the post-game show. A big football game on television *invariably* becomes the Abuse Bowl for men conditioned by the sports culture to act out their rage on someone smaller" (emphases mine).

"Facts" stated as "inevitable" and "invariable" call for statistical evidence. While Lipstyle claimed to have statistical evidence, he didn't present a shred of it, but stopped instead at anecdotes. He even ignores the admonition of a shelter worker who tells him, "The Super Bowl doesn't cause abuse."

As it turns out, the shelter worker was right. When Christina Hoff Sommers checked it out, she discovered the feminist circulated "research" was false.[132] I explain why in the endnote, but the point here is that no editor of the *New York Times* would have published as fact that man bashing "invariably" and "inevitably" causes violence against men without the support of statistical evidence.

The contempt for men is palpable in the *New York Times.* The *New York Times* does not hesitate to translate that contempt into the disposal of dads.

MOTHERHOOD, VICTIMHOOD, CHILDHOOD?

Look at the *small* print on the magazine cover on the facing page. It tells us this special Sunday *New York Times Magazine* issue is supposed to be on the *joy* and guilt of modern motherhood, but every *large* print word on the cover is about motherhood as victimhood—about "Mothers Can't Win."[133]

Note that there is no father in the picture. Yet this is not a special issue on single mothers. Why no dad? *Is it that a picture of Dad would diminish the impact of mother-as-victim?* Think about it. A picture of Dad would create the possibility of a mom *and* dad as victims . . . two victims would cancel out "*Mothers* Can't Win."

In contrast, there is no comparable *New York Times Magazine* section called "Fathers Can't Win." With a headline reading, "The Catch-22's of Fatherhood: How the Obligation To Work Full-time Leads Dads To Loving Their Family by Being Away from the Family They Love." Read that hypothetical dad "headline" again. It's a whole article in one sentence. (It also tells you why I don't write headlines!)

There's another story missing from the *New York Times Magazine.* It's a story not about deadbeat dads, but the 15 percent of single parents who are dads.

About how these dads "do it all," loving their children in their own style. No victims here. No story either.

And yet another missing story, about how every fathers' rights group wants the right for fathers to be more involved with their children, not less involved. Or a story about these fathers' struggle to take the burden off mothers. Or about their struggle to love. And be loved.

In a world in which love is needed even more than money, why don't we read about these dads? Because these dads are encountering fierce resistance from feminists. Why? Weren't feminists the pioneers of asking men to share women's traditional role? Yes. They *were*. But when that meant mothers not receiving money from dads for child support, the politics shifted quickly. It was exactly this issue—the greater concern of my feminist friends that dads give money to moms than love to children—that led to my deviance from what feminism was becoming.

The *New York Times,* in what it neglects, is neglecting children. The *Times* has a choice. Motherhood as victimhood. Or parenthood and childhood.

THE MAN BEHIND THE *TIMES*

What's going on at the *New York Times?* Are feminists reponsible? Not quite. An organization is the primary responsibility of the person at the top. And the person at the top is a man. The man behind the *Times,* if you will, is Arthur Sulzberger, Jr., the publisher. (The reader will smile at the irony of my representing the Board of NOW in New York City to "educate" his dad on biases against women in the *New York Times* in the early '70s.)

We gain some insight into Sulzberger Jr. and therefore the *Times'* inner workings from Nan Robertson, the feminist author of *The Girls in the Balcony: Women, Men and the* New York Times.[134] She explains that Sulzberger Jr. "considers himself a feminist . . . is an ardent fan of the writer Marilyn French," and keeps in his desk a typed page of excerpts by French.[136] Marilyn French is the author of *The War Against Women,* in which she concurs with women who believe "men are well on their way to exterminating women from the world,"[136] and also the author of *The Women's Room,* in which French states that "All men are rapists and that's all they are."[137]

When a paper is run by someone who is a fan of people who believe men are just rapists who are conducting a *War Against Women,* people will be hired who believe the enemy must be defeated, the means justifies the end. Thus Marilyn French's books are given multiple reviews and special interviews and the *New York Times* Censorship List becomes almost as clearly defined as the *New York Times* Best Seller List.

THE *NEW YORK TIMES* CENSORSHIP LIST

The *New York Times* Book Review, a section that depends on objectivity, has instead an "attitude" toward men that is perhaps best reflected in this Book Review headline:[138]

The New York Times
Book Review
Don't Expect Too Much of Men

March 11, 1990

This "attitude" is reflected in man-haters like Marilyn French and Andrea Dworkin having *every book* they write reviewed while books written by men who articulate the issues of adult men with compassion and criticize the feminist perspective have *none* of those books reviewed.

I'll document this in a second, but first the significance of this breach of the core journalistic ethic of fairness and balance. **When the *New York Times* Book Review ignores a book it sends a message: "You are not one of the**

players." Other media take the cue. When it systematically ignores books on a topic with one point of view and gives double reviews to books with the opposite perspective, the violation is not just one of journalistic ethics, but of the responsibility of power.

Now to the documentation. A review of the *New York Times Index* from 1971 through 1998 reveals that Marilyn French, the woman loved by publisher Sulzberger, and her book, *The Women's Room*—the one that states, "All men are rapists and that's all they are"—was misandrist enough to be given not one, but two reviews by the *New York Times*. The first review was by another feminist who is a *New York Times* favorite, Ann Tyler.[139] To make sure no opinion leader missed the book, it was given a second review within two weeks, and this time by one of the *New York Times'* most respected reviewers, Christopher Lehmann-Haupt.[140]

The corollary of the *New York Times'* message, "You are not one of the players," when it ignores a book is that when the *New York Times* does review you, especially positively, and especially twice, and particularly by its favorite and more respected reviewers, it *makes you* one of the players. Soon other things start a-happening. In Marilyn French's case, *The Women's Room* was made into a motion picture.

To this day the *New York Times* has not dropped its promotion of French, giving multiple reviews to three more of her books, including *The War Against Women*. When *The War Against Women* is given to feminist reviewer Isabelle de Courtivron, French is made to sound like a major thinker rather than a sexist man-hater.[141]

In a similar manner, Andrea Dworkin, whose hatred toward men is expressed in her novels via certain characters who, as she openly explains, represent her personal perspectives,[142] also has each of her five books between 1981 and 1991 reviewed. I will look a bit more closely at her later, but the relevant issue here is that her career was also jump-started by the *New York Times* assigning her book, *Pornography,* to a feminist (Ellen Willis) to review.[143]

In both cases, when a feminist can virtually lock in a book review by the *New York Times,* she or he can guarantee a publisher no matter how man-hating the book. When in addition, the *Times* sets the author up with an ideological ally as a reviewer, the book is virtually guaranteed mainstream credibility. Then the *New York Times* is no longer reviewing a book, it is making an author. It is not covering news, it is creating news.

In contrast are books written by men who articulate the issues of adult men with compassion and criticize the feminist perspective. I promised documentation for the *New York Times* reviewing *none* of those books. Specifically, books fitting that category have been written by Asa Baber, Sanford Braver, Phil Cook, Richard Driscoll, Herb Goldberg, Jack Kammer, Andrew Kimbrell, Aaron Kipnis, Jeffrey Leving, Neil Lyndon, David Thomas, and myself. None have been reviewed.

It is also *rare* for authors of books on gender from any of the two *traditional* gender perspectives to be reviewed as well, but exceptional circumstances do allow an occasional review of those books.

Perhaps, though, there are legitimate reasons for this? Let's check it out.

First possibility: These are authors who are not worth reviewing. That can't be said: Andrew Kimbrell wrote *The Human Body Shop* in 1993.[144] Nothing to do with feminism. The *New York Times* gave it a rave review. Two years later he wrote *The Masculine Mystique,*[145] critical of the distortions of academic feminism. The *New York Times* ignored it. Herb Goldberg wrote the first book critical of feminism by a name who questions traditional roles, *The Hazards of Being Male.* The *New York Times* ignored it. He later wrote *The New Male,* which was *not* critical of feminism. The *New York Times* reviewed it.

When I wrote *The Liberated Man,*[146] I had never published a book. But it was written *from a feminist perspective.* The *New York Times* reviewed it *twice.* Both times in the best place in the world: the Sunday Book Review. My next two books were more male positive and questioned feminism. The *New York Times* ignored them both.

Is it possible the *New York Times* just ignores books on gender issues? No. They reviewed, I would estimate, between nine hundred and a thousand pro-feminist books between the mid-'70s and 1999.

Is it possible they just ignore books on men's issues? Not quite. When Michael Kimmel, an ardent pro-feminist, wrote his pro-feminist *attack* on men's issues, the *New York Times* reviewed it. That is, they reviewed a book attacking what they had themselves refused to cover: books positive about adult men's issues that were critical of any portion of feminism. And of course they reviewed those particular books by Herb Goldberg and me on men's issues when we were not critical of feminism.

The *New York Times* does do an occasional review of two other types of books on males: books on boys, and books on male spirituality. Why? Boys' vulnerabilities trigger women's protective instinct. Boys have not rejected women, men have. Boys do not threaten the feminist political or legal agenda.

Similarly, male spiritual issues also do not threaten core feminist doctrine on political issues, so if one becomes a best-seller, like Robert Bly's *Iron John,* the *New York Times* can review it. And as for authors like Rush Limbaugh, from the political right, they are far enough away from the *New York Times* Book Review readers' thinking they can occasionally be reviewed (usually panned) without feminists being threatened. Second, they deal only tangentially with gender issues.

And finally, the *New York Times* does review books critical of feminism *if* they are written *by women.* But . . . they then assign feminists to tear them apart. When Christina Hoff Sommers wrote *Who Stole Feminism,* the *New York Times* assigned the review to Nina Auerbach (a feminist). A bit like asking Phyllis Schlafly to review Gloria Steinem's next book. The exception here is Katie Roiphe's book critical of feminism. But then again, her mother wrote for the *New York Times*.

What the *New York Times* Book Review censors, then, is books written by men who criticize the feminist perspective and articulate adult men's issues with compassion.

In the sense that books critical of feminism go through a markedly different screening process prior to being reviewed, the *New York Times* can be said to censor all feminist-critical books.

We have also begun to see that the editors at the *New York Times* employ their feminism to violate the second biggest ethic (after censorship) in book review journalism—neutrality: to select book reviewers knowledgeable enough to understand a book's goal and the importance of that goal, and neutral enough to impart to the reader how well the goal is achieved. Instead, books on gender are most frequently given "Sisterhood Reviews."

For example, a Gloria Steinem book is reviewed by Deidre English, a socialist feminist and former editor of the socialist feminist *Mother Jones* magazine.[147] When Mary Daly, the radical feminist religious studies professor I discuss above[148] wrote a more recent book, *Outercourse,* it was reviewed by another radical feminist religious studies professor. Similarly, Carol Gilligan is reviewed by feminist colleague Carolyn Heilbrun; Carolyn Heilbrun is reviewed by UCLA feminist Barbara Packer. So Packer is able to agree with Heilbrun that no sane person could want the female role. When a book has a feminist orientation, the *New York Times* quickly drops the journalistic standard of a neutral reviewer and often searches out a compatible colleague.

In many cases of feminist authors, it finds more than a compatible colleague. It finds a good friend. And this is a practice that has been going on since the early '70s. I can remember dining with an early feminist who was telling me about her new book and her best friend. I was a bit surprised to see in the following Sunday's the *New York Times* Book Review her best friend's review of her book.

THE *NEW YORK TIMES:* MAN-HATERS MADE HERE

Some of my best friends are men. It is simply that I think women are superior to men.

ANNA QUINDLEN,
Columnist, the *New York Times*, 1977–1994, in the column titled,
"Why Can't a Man Be More Like a Woman?"

Theoretically, any columnist for the *New York Times* that wrote, "Some of my best friends are blacks. It is simply that I think whites are superior to blacks," would be fired. I say theoretically, because, practically speaking, the column would never clear the supervising editor's desk; it would never be printed. If it were, the editor would also be fired.

The *New York Times* does not exactly make man-haters. It just makes them famous. And credible. It is the single most responsible source for integrating man-haters like Marilyn French, Catharine MacKinnon, Andrea Dworkin, and Barbara Ehrenreich into the mainstream of feminist respectability.

The *New York Times Magazine* introduced Catharine MacKinnon on their front cover, with her head photographed in such a way as to be surrounded by light, creating a subtle appearance of a halo.[149] The article portrayed her thinking as being pioneering, at the cutting edge of the feminist legal community. What is her thinking?

MacKinnon claims that women are forced to say "yes" to sex *in order to survive*[150] and, therefore, sex—even after a "yes"—is often rape. I had heard MacKinnon quoted as taking this a step further, saying *all sexual intercourse is rape:* the man penetrates the woman, and therefore invades her. But since I'm more often misquoted than not, I just assumed it was a misquote. I had an opportunity to check out my assumption when I did a special with MacKinnon and Peter Jennings on rape on ABC's *Evening News.* During the panel she did not say that. So, off the air, I asked her if her perspective was correctly represented by the belief that "all sexual intercourse is rape." She not only confirmed, but reiterated it voluntarily and emphatically.

Back to the *New York Times.* Right after MacKinnon appeared on the *New York Times Magazine's* cover, NBC selected her as the only consistent outside comoderator (with Tom Brokaw) of the Clarence Thomas–Anita Hill hearings. The way much of the press interpreted the hearings was colored at least in part by MacKinnon's perspectives on male-female sexuality.

We met Andrea Dworkin in the chapter on man bashing—the woman who admits to purposely using certain fictional characters to represent her perspective. Although a woman, she claims to understand the male consciousness enough to tell her readers that "sex and murder are fused in the male consciousness, so that one without the imminent possibility of the other is unthinkable and impossible."[151]

Dworkin's comments, if made about any other group in a business, the government, or an academic setting, would be a career ender. For the *New York Times,* they are career makers. Needless to say, the *New York Times* reviews Dworkin and helps make her famous. Fortunately, one reviewer at least made Dworkin's perspectives clear: "Ms. Dworkin advocates nothing short of killing men."[152]

For the *New York Times'* staff, with its sensitivity to anti-Semitism, to make credible a woman equating heterosexual sex with murder; to sponsor for more than one-and-a-half decades a weekly columnist writing, "I think women are superior to men" (Quindlen); to celebrate as cutting-edge legal opinions of all heterosexual sex as rape (MacKinnon); to applaud and review a woman who says all men are rapists (French) suggest an inability to extrapolate from anti-Semitism's deeper lessons.

MEN'S VS. WOMEN'S INTERNAL STORIES: THE ANATOMY OF THE FRONT PAGE

When I took a break from writing this morning, I sneaked out to my driveway in my bathrobe and mussed up hair and ran back in with the *New York Times* (which I still love!). I woke up my woman friend, gave it to her, and, while I was making breakfast, she pointed to this page-one headline with the comment, "Remember last night . . ."

"Yes . . ."

"No, I mean when you mentioned how the newspapers tell the internal stories of unknown women more than unknown men? Look at the *New York Times* front page."[153]

The Lace Curtain's impact on the *New York Times* is so pervasive, it is apparent almost daily. A story of woman-as-victim, usually accompanied by a poignant picture of a woman victim, is almost *de rigeur* for Sunday's front page, perhaps the most influential single page of newsprint published weekly anywhere in the world. But whether during the week or on Sunday, there are patterns to the biases. Compare the above front page with the one on the following page, also January of 1999.[154]

The New York Times

SUNDAY, JANUARY 24, 1999

Women's Suicides Reveal
Rural China's Bitter Roots

Nation Starts to Confront World's Highest Rate

By ELISABETH ROSENTHAL

Both front pages headline women's tragedies. In both, women's tragedies are personalized (so much so, that in the first story, about Kendra, I felt considerable sadness and anger at the tragedy of a lovely woman's life being randomly robbed in her twenties). In both, men are highlighted as the cause of the female victimization.

In both, the type of tragedies experienced by the women are, in fact, much more common to men (men are murdered three times more frequently than women; men now commit suicide in the United States four and a half times more frequently than women). China is the only country in the world that has more females committing suicide than males.[155] Why aren't we seeing front page *New York Times* headlines about each of the countries in which men commit suicide more and why the men are doing it—men's internal stories? Why are we not seeing stories about why men over eighty-five commit suicide 1,350 percent more frequently than women over eighty-five?[156]

But let's go beyond the surface—to why the China story does not justify the woman-as-victim headline. In China, suicide is a two-sex problem. For every quarter million Chinese, only five fewer men commit suicide than women.[157] Nothing in the article helps us understand men's reasons for suicide. Yet female suicide is blamed on male patriarchy and female isolation. But when one sex is isolated, isn't the other? When a spouse dies, men—the widowers—are ten times more likely than widows to commit suicide.[158] Perhaps that has something to do with isolation?

All this is part of a principal central to the Lace Curtain: When the problem is worse for American men, find a country in which it is as bad for women and headline it as worse for women. Then portray this woman's problem as caused by men or patriarchy. The result? The American reader now knows how to detect suicide's warnings for a woman living in rural China, but not for our teenage son or aging dad.

Do men who commit suicide make the front page of the *New York Times*? *If* they are famous, yes. If they are "just a man," no. Women make it for being women.

And unknown women make it for being victims in almost every conceivable manner. Here are three examples on just *one front page* of the Sunday *New York Times,* March 7, 1999. (There is not a single story focused on a man as a victim of any type.) Top of the page is a picture of a woman near Algiers mourning.[159] Her grandchildren were killed in the war. We don't see stories of the personal misery her grandchildren are enduring in war—that might have included the misery of men.

Directly underneath is the story of a female health worker allergic to latex gloves. Turns out that 10 percent of health workers have such allergies,[160] but the only story personalized on the front page is that of a female health worker.

Still on the same front page is the story of a woman who sued her coach for sexual harassment.

When women are benefiting from women's sports going from 300,000 student athletes in 1972 with the passage of Title IX, to 3 million student athletes currently,[161] what makes the front page is the picture and personal story of a female victim.

The very next day, March 8, front page again . . .

Wait, there is something underneath this Medicaid mom article: "Police Abuses Start to Get Attention in China."[162] It turns out that four men are victims. But as male victims they are not worthy of a headline. Or a picture. What makes the headline is the image of a man-as-abuser: Chinese police (read: men). Even when only men are the victims, the New York Times finds a way of headlining the men who are the perpetrators.

The problem? This is reinforcing the message to our daughters that the path to attention and empathy is victimhood. This disempowers women. And it tells our sons their path to attention is saving women. Which leaves our daughters feeling entitled, and angry when men don't deliver.

ABOUT THE GOOD TIMES

I had hopes for the New York Times when it began to do a weekly "About Men" column. And some of its columns did hit home. But overall the column focused on self-effacing, personal anecdotes that consistently stopped short of touching on underlying men's issues such as why our teenage sons' suicide rate is increasing (and what we can learn from the decrease in our daughters' rate). I flew from San Diego to New York to meet with the editor and discuss incorporating these underlying issues into the "About Men" column. I could feel, even as I was getting through to him, that he felt the column had a formula, and his hands were tied. The column was ultimately reduced to twice per month (alternating with a column called "Hers") and was then replaced.

All this said, about one or two articles per year appear somewhere in the New York Times with at least an attempt at looking at men's issues. One was, "A Few Good Men? Don't Look in the Movies."[163] And don't look in the New York Times.

THE LACE CURTAIN IN MAGAZINE PUBLISHING

Switch with me to the largest circulating weekly magazine in the United States, Parade. Perhaps Parade's most visible weekly feature is a column by Marilyn vos Savant, whose claim to fame is having the "highest IQ on record."

She is asked, "Are women really better at 'being good people' than men are?"[164] Her answer: "Yes." She gives two pieces of "evidence." First, more men are in prison. If more women were in prison, might Ms. Savant be suggesting that it is because women are the most disadvantaged? Would she say African-Americans are worse people because higher percentages are in prison?

Second, she says, men caused the wars. If we had required only women to be drafted, then blamed women for causing the wars, wouldn't someone call that "blaming the victim"? We have already seen Parade's headlines turning men's deaths in war into female victimhood. Is there a pattern here?

Behind this Lace Curtain, a few exceptions have been found. Time ran two cover stories with male-positive themes: one on a father searching for his kid-napped children[165]; the other on man bashing.[166] *Forbes* did a feature on men committing suicide and why they do it.[167] Some of the worst examples of the Lace Curtain, though, are in the women's and even men's magazines.

Go to any news stand any month. The titles of the articles in women's and men's magazines are basically the same as they were when I reported my first analysis (1986) of women's and men's magazines in *Why Men Are the Way They Are*.[168] In fact, *Cosmopolitan* has a book filled with titles and how long it should be before they are recycled.

Women's magazines promise the world and deliver male dependency; men's magazines promise little and deliver female avoidance. Men's and women's magazines work together: His keeps the man "out to lunch," which keeps the woman wanting him to buy lunch; hers keeps the woman complaining and misunder-standing, which keeps the man searching for a woman who isn't just faking un-derstanding. Here's how.

OPEN A WOMAN'S MAGAZINE, FIND A MIXED MESSAGE

Are women's magazines still teaching women how to seduce their boss in one ar-ticle and sue for sexual harassment in another? Yes. Metaphorically and literally. Let's start with literally. The title is "How to Seduce Your Boss."[169] Working women are given the working plan.

- Step one: ask boss to explain some aspect of the job . . . and "Sit close while he does so . . . don't be afraid to show him that you're physically interested."

- Step two: "Start involving him in your personal life . . . ask him advice on private matters. . . ." By this time,

- Step three is either the indirect method, that is, he asks her out or, if all else fails, the direct method, such as she invites him to a "small cocktail party at your apartment." Then, when he wants to go to bed, use

- Step four: "*Act innocent and defenseless and girlish* (although quite adamant that he's not going to take you to bed). And, believe me, you'll have him hooked." (Emphasis mine.) Of course, once she says an adamant no, next time she's free to say yes. Which leads to

- Step five: "Every two hours or so during your first night together, wake him up and tease him into giving you more."

- Step six is after his wife finds out: "There is no onus on you to feel guilty about his wife . . . These days, there is so much more at stake in human relationships than unquestioning loyalty."

This article appeared about the same time a woman named Monica was an intern—"innocent and defenseless and girlish"—who had nevertheless been fired from her internship for doing too much hanging around at every presidential appearance to which she could gain access.

The articles in women's magazines are enormously male dependent. But they almost always leave a woman with as much misunderstanding as understanding. As a result, the women are left with failed relationships, buy another woman's magazine with another new title offering new hope, find reality dashing that hope, which leads to depression and anger. Meantime, the men in her life are deprived of what I call men's primary need: understanding, without which there is no intimacy.

OPEN A MEN'S MAGAZINE, FIND A FEMINIST

Most of the men's magazines are no better. They are less about female dependency than female avoidance. They focus on "the five male crutches": business, politics, sports, equipment, and women in a sexual sense. As a result, *women feel less than misunderstood. They feel they don't matter enough for him to even make an attempt at understanding.* Men, and men's magazines, keep men pleasing women by buying women things rather than psychologically connecting with women.

There is, though, a new twist. When magazines with mostly male subscribers, such as *Money* and *Fortune,* do focus on relationship or gender issues, it is surprising how often they too are from a feminist perspective. Susan Forward, author of *Men Who Hate Women and the Women Who Love Them,* was chosen to write a piece for *Money* called "Next Oprah: Men Who Waste Money and the Women Who Love Them."[170] The focus is money-reckless men and their female victims . . . without a single reference to money-reckless women.

The men's magazines are now sometimes run by women. Even *Playboy* is run by a woman, and its "Forum" section is run by a feminist.[171] *Playboy* funds feminist causes much more than men's causes. And *Penthouse?* Let's take a look.

A sixty-four-year-old male teacher explains to a female *Penthouse* advice columnist (Xaviera Hollander—of *The Happy Hooker* fame) that he had a stroke after thirty-four years of teaching, which led to money problems, and to sexual problems with his wife[172]:

> . . . Although she lets me have intercourse with her twice a week, she does it with scorn. . . . My wife tells me that breasts are for nursing babies, not husbands, and now I can't even enjoy seeing them because she hardly ever goes naked in front of me. . . . I can't touch her. If I do, she spins around and twists away from me. . . .

Now, here is how the *Penthouse* columnist's response to the man began:

> If any American wife could go before a court and have the judge declare her
> husband to be an incompetent nincompoop, what a wonderful place the
> world would be—and what a victory for women's lib. Luckily for you, the law
> is not really prepared to accept a wife's unsupported opinion concerning her
> husband's imbecility, because I suspect if this were the case, *all* the hus-
> bands would be safely tucked away in sanitariums and we women would be
> running the country. (emphasis mine)

There are good men's magazines, like *Men's Health*; and an exceptional
columnist on men's issues, Asa Baber in *Playboy*. The good news of men's magazines is no false hope and no self-righteousness; the bad news is no consciousness.

MODERN MATURITY OR MODERN MISANDRY?

You're too old for women's and men's magazines? Then the word is not "old," it's
"mature." *Modern Maturity* is the largest-selling monthly magazine in the United
States. After it censored my article (see above), I couldn't help but keep an eye
out for whether it ran other articles that discussed the positive aspects of men
and masculinity. One, titled "He Said, She Said" and written by a husband and
wife, held out hope. Until I saw the formula.

He puts himself down, and she puts him down. Well, that explains their
marital harmony! Here's how she explains him (all her words): "as a scratching,
swearing, uncaring, grunting, insensitive member of a sex that is lower on the
evolutionary scale than herself and her sex." Then, in a moment of compassion,
she condescends: "I realize you are not entirely responsible for your limited ability to perceive the more elevating aspects of existence. There are two ways to
look at life: the female way, a way of warmth and beauty; and the male way, a way
of bashed heads and broken bones. You, unfortunately, are limited by your sex.
You're male."[173]

The man she is writing about, her husband, is not Mike Tyson, but Alfred
Martinez, a *columnist* for the *Los Angeles Times*. She writes, "He grunts when
words are just too much trouble." He makes his living grunting? *Her* only bio description is "running the Martinez household." Translation: This living he makes
"grunting" pays not only his bills, but hers. Talk about biting the hand that feeds
you. Maybe I should try this grunting. Don't worry, Alfred . . . you'll die sooner.

There is a gap here between the medium and the message. The sex or
warmth and beauty is ripping him to shreds; the sex of uncaring insensitivity ar-
gues his point with enough caring and sensitivity to never once criticize her.

Had she taken a more troubled man—like Mike Tyson—and declared him to be a member of a *race* that is lower on the evolutionary scale than her Caucasian self, could *Modern Maturity* publish it and claim to be either modern or mature?

THE FIVE STAGES OF LACE CURTAIN CENSORSHIP IN BOOK PUBLISHING

1. CENSORSHIP BY CONSTITUENCY

Why do books like *No Good Men* get published, but not *No Good Women, No Good Blacks,* or *No Good Jews?* And why do titles like *Men Who Hate Women and the Women Who Love Them* become big best-sellers while titles like *Men Who Love Women and the Women Who Hate Them* can't even get published? The spate of "women good/men bad" books (under the guise of "self-improvement") inspired one author to do a take-off on the genre: *Men Who Hate Themselves and the Women Who Agree with Them.*

Had this occurred because approximately 90 percent of relationship book readers are women and—as Jesse Owens put it—"You don't get nowhere by giving people the lowdown on themselves"? Yes. Why do women need this self-assurance? Both sexes need it when rejected. When rejected, a self-assurance book is to a woman what a bar is to a man—each disappears into a safe place of assurance. Why do women attack men? Because it is men who have rejected them. When you expected that man to save you, well, that's a long hard drop.

It's not that men who are rejected don't want to attack the woman, it's that it creates more of a conflict for a man. It conflicts with his male credo: Heroes protect women; villains and sissies attack women. And that's in his genes. So men have to be really down and out before they could read a Men Good/Women Bad book. However, when women reject men, men also have their not-so-pretty defenses (gambling, porn, midlife crises, drinking). It's just that when men reject women, women's more likely defenses include reading.

The self-assurance book's job is to assure a woman she is better off without him, that she is better than he, that she lost him because *she* is capable of love, *he* is not. Thus, the three most ingenious titles: *Women Who Love Too Much,* the above-mentioned *Men Who Hate Women and the Women Who Love Them* and *Everything Men Know About Women*—the blank book that gets that knowing look. From there, they specialize.

If he is afraid to commit, it must be because he can't love (*Men Who Can't Love*), is immature (*Peter Pan Syndrome*), is psychologically disturbed (*Casanova Complex*), or is a scared wimp (*Cold Feet*).

If he wasn't afraid to commit, but the commitment didn't last, she can be assured it is his fault—he was either Foolish Choice A or Foolish Choice B (*Smart Women, Foolish Choices; The Field Guide to North American Males,* a Peter Pan,

Casanova, or some type of "man who can't love") or a woman hater (*Men Who Hate Women and the Women Who Love Them*). Meantime, she is smart, mature, and filled with love.

Worst of all, if he committed to another woman, a younger woman, a woman with a type of power she *used* to have, he will ideally be seen as having a psychological problem with a name (*Jennifer Syndrome*). The inevitable conclusion: For "self improvement," a woman must undo her addiction to loving these jerks too much. And if she fails? Read *Why It's Always the Man's Fault.*

Suppose, though, she is married to a faithful, dependable man, but she's feeling the stale air of his dependability and yearns for fresh air? She can run to the *Bridges of Madison County*; then, once addicted (when the stale air of the affair requires more fresh air), to any of a hundred thousand romance novels. What to do if he's the one to have an affair? Well, er . . . impeach him.

The newest layer of men-are-evil, women-are-victims books to make it big are Christian romance novels. Frank Peretti, the "king" of the genre, spins tales of men serial killers in books like *The Oath*.[174] In secular romances, these male serial killers are usually balanced by an idealized male hero. In the Christian romance, man-as-hero is replaced by God-as-hero, and the best men are vulnerable heroes unless they submit to the Lord.

The good news is that the Christian romance encourages women to select men who can ask for help. The bad news is, the man is still expected to save her, but God is thanked when he does. In brief, the unadulterated set on the Christian novel's bus of virtue is reserved for God.

2. CENSORSHIP BY EDITOR AND WRITER

Most of this "I'm okay, he's not" bias is generated by the power of a female constituency, but there is also the Lace Curtain in publishing, which starts with the background of relationship book writers and editors.

Virtually no relationship book editor has the two experiences common to millions of everyday American men: job experience in a hazardous job, engineering, corporate sales, or career military with little choice of leaving because of responsibilities to be the primary breadwinner for both a spouse and children. A few relationships book writers have this experience, but they are more likely to have psychological and academic backgrounds with career-oriented wives. Writers who are exceptions find it difficult to find editors who are exceptions. (If one editor is an exception, it is almost impossible for him to persuade his colleagues, in part because relationship books are bought by about 90 percent women—and so we come full circle!)

Here's how this works, based on my three decades among relationship book editors and other authors. Both the author of relationship books and the relationship book editor are usually graduates from top colleges, and liberal arts majors. I documented above how these majors are taught largely by professors with a feminist orientation. The person who chooses liberal arts enters it knowing she or he is making a monetary sacrifice vs. going for an engineering degree or an MBA. It therefore selects for a more feminine-sensitive and feminist-sensitive personality than that of the teamster or engineer. The men editor and writer is more likely to have his wife's help with income (or have no one to support) than does the average American man; the female editor is more likely to have a man help with the children, or have no children.

That's the basics with the heterosexual male relationship book writers and editors. Among male editors, though, many are gay. The gay man, while subject to many biases himself, does not have the same pressure to take jobs that are high enough paying to give a wife the options to be full time or part time with the children. That's the key differentiation between the heterosexual family man and the gay family man. It makes it as difficult for the gay male editor to identify with the heterosexual male life experience as it does for the heterosexual editor to identify with the books on the gay experience. This doesn't mean it cannot be done, but our life experiences are our most powerful single reference point.

Approximately three quarters of relationship book editors, though, are women.[175] Almost all are feminists. A colleague of mine reported to me that his editor on a book about relationships (due to be published in 2000) made him take out *all* references to females who cheat on their husbands. No, it was worse than that. *The names were changed so that real-life women who had cheated became men who cheated!* He was forced to choose: the woman-as-victim point of view or not be published.

The nature of these backgrounds leaves most relationship book editors and writers believing what she or he reads in the news about the "new woman" being out there initiating sex, paying for dinners, marrying aspiring househusbands, and doing all those liberated things. Bottom line? When this combines with the purchasing power of the female book buyer, few books on the male perspective make it through this Lace Curtain.

3. CENSORSHIP BY ACQUISITION

In a totalitarian society, the government censors. In a capitalist society, our purchases "censor." More precisely, we don't produce what the masses won't buy. Books that are sensitive to female and feminist concerns are much more likely to be acquired by publishers than are books representing men's perspectives exactly because women buy this type of book, and women are 85 percent–90 percent of relationship book buyers. It is not true just that women can't hear what men don't say, but also true that no one sells what men don't buy.

When both writers and editors are also tuned in to females and feminism, then the three most important filters determining which books should be acquired—the consumer, the writer and the editor—are all of "one political party," if you will. Thus Simon & Schuster acquires *No Good Men* but does not acquire *No Good Women* because they know *No Good Men* will sell, and because it doesn't offend the editor's sensibilities as *No Good Women* would.

4. CENSORSHIP DURING THE WRITING

The book you are reading has itself endured a Lace-Curtain censorship experience, stage one. It was originally under contract with Simon & Schuster with a wonderful feminist editor named Marilyn Abraham, also a vice president. Marilyn had been my editor for *The Myth of Male Power.* As her questioning and double-checking my data left her satisfied she became my spokesperson at S&S. Unfortunately, Marilyn retired after editing some chapters for this book and my next one (*Father and Child Reunion*). At the time, all the chapters were to be part of this book. They were soon turned over to another feminist editor, and that's when the fun started.

The new editor, let's call her Frances, has since left the company (I don't believe it had to do with the experience I am about to share except, perhaps, to the degree that it was representative). To be fair to Frances, when she got to my chapters on fathers' issues, she had just become a first-time mother. I was bringing to bear some cross-cultural data that showed that children living only with dads fared better than children living only with moms. I made it clear that this did not imply men made better parents, but only that the type of man motivated enough to be a father today seemed more effective than the average mom. Nevertheless, Frances had a visceral reaction to these chapters.

Of course, Frances could not say "censored" directly. She said it indirectly by requiring I eliminate that material that described children of divorce and focus instead on the intact family. Of course, in an intact family it is impossible to separate out the influence of the dad from the mom, preventing me from articulating my core theme. I explained. She insisted. I submitted the manuscript essentially as it was when Marilyn had approved it. She rejected it, along with two chapters that now appear in this book (on domestic violence and housework).

When I received the rejection letter my brain gave way to a stomach that had lost its bearing. I suddenly deepened my empathy for the men from whom I receive calls reporting false accusations. I called other editors at Simon & Schuster who I had heard respected my work. They were empathetic but were fearful of becoming political. I suddenly felt isolated and lonely—me against the world's biggest publisher. I felt like David, with a broken slingshot, encountering Goliath.

The isolation abated a bit when I took my own advice and reached out to my support system. Certainly I was tempted to sue for censorship, but pretty quickly I submitted my material to other publishers and was fortunate enough to obtain an editor I thus far love. I sit here with letters in front of me from other men who have been less fortunate. Some will publish with small publishers. Others, even brilliant writers like Fred Hayward, have clear voices yet to be heard. I hope this book will bring them some satisfaction our voices can be heard, but I know it will also bring them grief their voice was not the one heard, that they could have expressed this better than I.

5. CENSORSHIP AFTER PUBLICATION

From the *New York Times* Book Review to talk shows, from feature pages to CNN news, the male-positive book encounters media land mines (or, on the air waves I suppose it's air mines) at every turn except radio. But the most important resistance it encounters returns us to the beginning of the cycle: the female constituency.

Nothing defeats censorship more than good sales. But I make that statement with caution derived of some strange experiences. For example, when *The Myth of Male Power* became a number one bestseller in Australia and an substantial first printing quickly sold out, Random House of Australia refused to do a second printing. When Andrew Kimbrell's first printing of *The Masculine Mystique* sold out quite quickly, Random House of the United States refused to do a second printing, or publish it in paperback—despite sending Andrew the money for the paperback.[176] Censorship? Coincidence? Conscious? Unconscious? Some things we'll never know.

THE LACE CURTAIN IN FILM

HI AND LOIS

Perhaps the art that best reflects life is film. In the chapter on man bashing I review the way films bashing men reflect our culture. But 1998 did at least see two films that were masterpieces in their empathetic representation of the male experience: *Saving Private Ryan* and *Life is Beautiful.* I review them on my website, but suffice it to say here that part of their significance is that they were both commercial and critical successes, representing, therefore, holes in the Lace Curtain.

Unfortunately, these films were more the exception than the rule among recent films. *Titanic* is the rule. No reality-based film had a greater opportunity to allow the world a clearer look at men's willingness to sacrifice their lives for women and children than *Titanic,* on which men died more than women at a rate of more than 9 to 1.[177]

While we know *Titanic* had a fictionalized story line, it developed a reputation for being meticulously researched with many characters based on reality. In some ways that was true. But one of the most fascinating stories behind the movie is the story revealed by what is and is not fiction. **When we uncover how we fictionalize reality, we discover ourselves.** And we also discover the *methods* used by the Lace Curtain to fictionalize reality. (Which is what distinguishes this analysis from the previous chapter's look at man bashing in films.) So welcome aboard.

***Titanic* Fiction:** A woman saves a man at the repeated risk of her life.

***Titanic* Fact:** There is no record of a woman risking her life to save an adult man, no less repeatedly.

***Titanic* Fiction:** Men in charge decided to lock third class (steerage) passengers below the decks.

***Titanic* Fact:** Public Record Office documents in London show that this never happened—in fact, a higher percentage of men from second class died than from third class (92 percent vs. 88 percent) and 55 percent of the third class women lived, which would not have been possible had they been locked below.[178]

***Titanic* Fiction:** Being poor made one even more disposable than being a man.

***Titanic* Fact:** Being a man and being poor both increased disposability, but being a man increased it significantly more than being poor. First class men were 22 times more likely to die (66 percent vs. 3 percent) than first class women.[179] The richest men were significantly more likely to die than the poorest women.

Theoretically, there were three classes on the *Titanic.* Practically, though, men were more likely to die than the citizens of the first, second, or third class. In reality, the men were the invisible fourth class citizens. Here is the breakdown by class and sex.[180]

TITANIC AND THE INVISIBLE FOURTH CLASS

CLASS	% OF MEN DYING	% OF WOMEN DYING
1st	66%	3%
2nd	92%	16%
3rd	88%	45%

Finally, the multiple scenes of men as cowards ("Men first! Leave the women and children behind"[181]) negates the reality, especially regarding First Officer William Murdoch, who was portrayed in the film as taking a bribe, shooting a third-class passenger, and then killing himself. In real life, "Murdoch behaved heroically, sacrificing his life after laboring frantically to save others."[182] Twentieth Century Fox did apologize for their distortion, but all the scenes of his corruption and cowardice remain.[183]

In brief, **the mandate of masculinity, to be more disposable than a third-class citizen, was diluted** by three methods, all fiction: (1) Showing a woman also willing to die to save a man; (2) Turning a heroic man (William Murdoch) into a coward and killer; and (3) Sensationalizing class disposability (via the lockout scene and the portrayal of Murdoch killing a third-class passenger while accepting a bribe from a rich man). When disposability is falsely made a characteristic of both sexes and class disposability is played up, it leaves us downplaying the true disposability of masculinity—only 8 percent of the second-class men saving themselves while saving 84 percent of their wives and 100 percent of their children.

WHAT DO "GUY FILMS" AND "CHICK FILMS" HAVE IN COMMON?

Many trees have given their lives to tell us how "guy films" and "chick flicks" differ. But what they have in common is just as telling. The formula for fiction-based films that I document in *The Myth of Male Power* still prevails: **Any woman in jeopardy who is portrayed as positive and feminine in a fiction film for more than three scenes does not die.**

Ironically, although many men might die saving her, only she is viewed as in jeopardy. Often she doesn't shed blood, even if the men around her are dying. Even in an era of supposed equality **the Lace Curtain in all of us makes the woman in jeopardy bullet proof.** Remember, though, she must be seen for at least three scenes, otherwise we have not had a chance to become attached to her—that is, she had not developed in our minds as a woman; and the film must be fiction—in real life, women do get hurt, we just don't want to make it part of our fantasy life.

BELOW-THE-BELT FILMS, AN ITSY BITSY TEENY WEENIE DIVISION OF LACE CURTAIN STUDIOS

In *The War of the Roses,* it's about two hours into the divorce wars when Michael Douglas's character, still believing his future ex-wife may be his friend, is lulled into believing she wants to have, er, . . . the pleasure of his penis. It is only when she takes a bite out of it that he "gets it." Quite a metaphor for what may sidetrack a man here or there from seeing a woman's anger.

The anger at men not investing their sexuality in marriage is an international theme. We could see it as early as 1976 in the Japanese-French film *In the Realm of the Senses.* A prostitute strangles her lover, then slices off his penis, Lorena Bobbitt–style (perhaps Lorena's inspiration?), then spends some four days deliriously wandering the streets of Tokyo "resplendent with happiness" (neither a typo nor a pun).[184] The man can't say he wasn't warned. The prostitute's name is Sada.

In many movies, the gross castration of men seems more for its entertainment value. *Caligula* features a man's penis being chopped off and fed to a pack of dogs; in *The World According to Garp,* a car accident results in Garp's penis being unwittingly bitten off by Ms. Hurt (another foreboding name?). Yes, it's a metaphor for Garp's life, but isn't illustrating it like that a bit, well, below-the-belt? Yet no one protests this treatment of men's genitals; in fact, Disney promotes it.

Disney films normally take care to avoid sex, and certainly violence against women, yet often make trailers out of violence against men's and boys' sexual organs—as in kicking a boy in the groin, or having a puck hit a boy in the testicles (*The Mighty Ducks*). In *The Three Musketeers,* for example, a woman threatens a man's penis with a knife ("I'm going to change your religion").[185] These are frequently the scenes selected for the trailers for Disney films, thus seen repeatedly even if the movie is seen only once. And since the average child watches 25,000 hours of TV before his or her eighteenth birthday, this can have some impact![186]

I don't think we would feel comfortable sending our daughters to Disney movies in which the trailer showed a scene of a man threatening to cut off a woman's clitoris with a knife. Our attitude is part of what creates the Lace Curtain.

TV's Lace Curtain

> *The network that most endears itself to the lady of the house has the best chance of survival.*

Newsweek

WHAT A MAN MIGHT SAY WHEN HE HEARS, "IT'S MEN IN THE NEWS, . . .

Item. *Dead Husbands.* The description in *TV Guide:* "A rollicking 1998 cable comedy about wives who try to dispose of their insignificant others."[187] The "insignificant others" are their husbands. When John Ritter's character decides to give up writing, his wife and her women's group try to have him shot, stabbed, strangled, and poisoned. That's what makes it so funny. (And that's what keeps me writing!)

An analysis of the Boston TV schedule on a random day found that 80 percent of the programming addressed women's problems and interests, and that a high percentage of it was blatantly man bashing.[188] Women in jeopardy TV fits all these requirements.

"WOMEN IN JEP"

In one year, half of the 250 made-for-TV movies depicted women as victims.[189] Although three-quarters of real-life murders are of men, there is no "men in jep" TV (with women competing to earn a man's love by saving his life at the risk of her own). In real life, women are as likely to batter men as men are to batter women, but a man being battered by a woman is to your TV what a four leaf clover is to your backyard.

Note in the TV ad below that she's kicking *him* out.[190] Yet *she's* seen as the victim. How? He's labeled a bum. Thus his victimization—being thrown out—is seen as deserved; she is subliminally viewed as finally getting the self-esteem to do what she should have done long ago. Imagine, though, a "Throw the Leech Out Week!" with his heel kicking her in the rear, and her clothes flying out the

door. In reverse, the ad would be evidence of the reason women can't file for divorce—they'd be kicked and beaten. The ability of the networks to have *only* a "Throw the Bum Out Week!" reflects a more deep-seated prejudice that men encounter when divorced—she's the victim, he's the bum.

All of this creates a culture in which men feel self-hatred. Yet the ratings generated by women-in-jeopardy TV (what the industry calls "women in jep") create few reasons for the usually male executives to look within.

Some shows, like *20/20,* and occasionally *Dateline,* although dominated by feminist concerns when it comes to male-female issues, nevertheless do some excellent pieces representing men's or male-positive perspectives. Overall, though, here's what happens when the story of a man in jeopardy attempts to be told.

Michael Durant spent eleven days in captivity in Somalia after the Army helicopter of which he was the pilot was shot down. Eighteen U.S. soldiers were killed. Michael wanted a movie to remember the soldiers who died. He got a contract when he agreed to have it told from *his wife's point of view.*[191]

Darin Detwiler tells how his sixteen-month-old-son, Riley, was killed by E. coli poisoning from improperly cooked hamburger from a Jack-in-the-Box. After national attention, talking to President Clinton, and meeting with TV producers, he and his wife agreed to a made-for-TV movie to "put a human face" on the problem.

One problem. He was told the "story would have a better chance of being used if my wife were portrayed as a single mother—thereby qualifying it for the 'woman overcoming the odds' category."[192] Son dies, only Mom is victim; to portray Mom as victim, dispose of Dad. Sound familiar? Recall the front cover of the *New York Times Magazine,* portraying the mom as victim by disposing of the dad?

After all this, feminists often cite women-in-jeopardy TV as examples of discrimination against women. Think about that. If men were in jeopardy and women were the evil perpetrators, would not that be cited as discrimination against women?[193] In the deeper sense, though, feminists are correct. Women in jeopardy begets women in jeopardy. If only the feminists would practice what they preach.

In the '80s and '90s, TV programming came to be defined as "progressive" when it showed how women are victims (raped, molested) and how men are victimizers, but "progressive" programming rarely pointed out how men saved women. In our everyday lives we might see six firefighters saving women, but no TV special called "Men as Saviors" points out that all six were men—that firemen who save women's lives are far more ubiquitous than men who jeopardize women's lives. Similarly, it is defined as progressive to listen to a feminist on PBS critique "male legislators" for making war, but, when democracies triumph over

Hitler or the Cold War ends, never crediting "male legislators" for making democracy. To acknowledge the full truth is no longer considered progressive, but regressive.

Once we understand the Lace Curtain, most murder mysteries become more formula than mystery. Take ABC's *Murder One*.[194] When a man is on trial for a crime against a woman, who's guilty? Now, was that a mystery? If that crime is a sex crime, who's guilty? If his lawyer is a man, and the woman's lawyer is a woman, why watch?

So why do we watch? For the same reason we watched Princess Diana walk down the aisle even though we knew the outcome would be a wedding. In our deepest psyche, we need reinforcement of the dichotomy between man-as-savior and man-as-enemy. Any man who is not a savior is a potential enemy. We need that reinforcement more than we need a mystery

THE "SISTERHOOD OF THE TUBE"

The old, predominantly male producer was bottom-line focused—how to attract the most commercial dollars. He cared about one thing: ratings—female or male. Who he pleased was a subset of who it was profitable to please. In contrast, "the Sisterhood of the Tube," as they called themselves, had a feminist mission. Alternatively known as the "Class of '72"[195] (the year the Equal Employment Opportunity Act first gave women an affirmative action advantage), they solidified the feminization of network television during the '80s and '90s.

The Sisterhood agenda took root in the late '80s, included shows with virtually all-female casts, such as *Designing Women* (women in business), *The Golden Girls* (women in retirement), *China Beach* (women in war), *HeartBeat* (women in medicine), *Nightingales* (women in nursing school), *A Different World* (women in college), *Studio 5B* (women in television).[196] It included prime-time soap operas (*e.g., Dynasty, Falcon Crest*) and female-centered shows such as *A Fine Romance, Day by Day, Room 227, Murder She Wrote, Kate & Allie,* and *Who's the Boss?*

Empowerment feminist themes ran through some of these shows, like *Who's the Boss?* And the soaps did not whitewash the female shadow side. But most had more of the *Designing Women* flavor, in which every show is some version of man as exploiter of women—either supposedly professional men like therapists or professors who harass those they're paid to help, thus violating their trust, or the deadbeat dad or a "wannabe" rapist. Like the *Honeymooners*, the man is always, in the end, wrong, sees the error of his ways, and increases his love for the more virtuous woman.

The Sisterhood of the Tube could succeed because of the sisterhood of their audience. Women watch more television in every time slot of every day of the week,[197] and buy more household items and personal items so it isn't surprising that, as *Newsweek* puts it, "The network that most endears itself to the lady of the house has the best chance of survival."[198] The networks increasingly attracted females, pushing males out and into the smaller audience cable channels.

Lace Curtain funding, though, is also infiltrating the cable channels. Disney and Hearst own Lifetime Cable. *Forbes* reports Lifetime is ranked "Number one in delivering the critical category of women to advertisers."[199] That is, they're outdoing even the networks' devotion to women.

The next millennium will combine another cable network for women's programming with the Internet's capability to zero in more precisely on what each individual woman desires. This breath of female air will be called Oxygen Media. Brought to you by Oprah Winfrey, Marcy Carsey (the coproducer of *Roseanne*) and Geraldine Laybourne.[200]

The New York Times

3 Women in TV to Create a Cable Channel for Women (Surprise!)

By BILL CARTER

November 24, 1998

PRIME-TIME JERKS AND THE SISTERHOOD WHO SOWS THEIR SEEDS

The prime-time jerk was certainly not invented by the "Sisterhood of the Tube"—*The Honeymooners'* Ralph Kramden and Ed Norton were jerks in almost every segment, their wives compassionate and wise. Archie Bunker was an egotistical bigot, his wife compassionate and wise. The "contribution" of the Sisterhood was *not the invention* of male-as-jerk, *but the integration* of male-as-jerk into virtually every prime-time sitcom in which there was a male presence.

The Sisterhood brought about the transition from the option of male-as-jerk to the obligation of male-as-jerk. It is not that women are exempt from jerk status in sitcoms. It is that men are portrayed as jerks (*e.g.*, after back-and-forth insults, revealed to be the *real* fool), by my rough count, at a ratio of about 6 to 1 vis-à-vis women. When the women do make a mistake, it's more likely to be the subject of a one-liner or, at most, a segment. With the men, it's one-liners, segments, and the whole episode. Jerk is his character.

The sitcoms are important because the same characters are with us each week . . . they work their way into our bloodstream. For women, we speak of the importance of role models; for men we give them jerks. Of course, putting down men is seen as funny, because men are seen as having the power, as being strong enough to take it. In their graves.

WHAT A MAN MIGHT SAY WHEN HE HEARS, "IT'S MEN IN THE NEWS, . . .

The male-as-jerk is so integral to a sitcom that *The Wall Street Journal* explained that *Roseanne* was sold to the networks on the strength of a pilot episode in which Roseanne picks up a chocolate doughnut, methodically tears it apart, and says, "A guy is like this doughnut. First, you gotta get rid of all the stuff his mom did to him" (she flicks off the nuts), "then you gotta get rid of all that macho crap that they pick up from the beer commercials" (she tears off another piece), "and then there's my personal favorite, the male ego." She pops the last piece into her mouth and gnashes ferociously on the "male ego."[201]

When *Roseanne* entered the sitcom scene, it was not only given prime time, but, in industry terms, "hammocked" between the two top-rated ABC sitcoms at the time.[202] Half a decade later, TV's equivalent of a century, Roseanne was being touted as TV's Domestic Goddess, which is a bit like touting Archie Bunker as TV's Sensitive New-Age Man. Roseanne's bio tells us a lot: born in a Jewish family, moved to Salt Lake City, spent time in a mental hospital, married postal worker, hates men, becomes star.[203]

Tom Werner, of the Carsey-Werner Production Company that made *Roseanne*, sums it up: "Men are slime."[204] We can look forward to more *Roseanne*s. The Carsey of Carsey-Werner is the Marcy Carsey of the new Oxygen Media, focusing on women's programming, available in your home in the year 2000.

TV'S LACE CURTAIN IN DAYTIME TALK SHOWS

A talk show cannot break a relationship book, but it can certainly make one. However, a favorite talk show theme is man-as-oppressor, woman-as-victim. Sally, Ricki, Jenny, Jerry, Maury, Montel, and Oprah vie for a heavily female following with a ratio of about seven female producers for each male producer. Show titles such as "Impossible Men" (but less often "Impossible Women"), "Getting Husbands to Clean Up Their Act,"[205] "Deceived by the Man I Loved," "He Left Me When I Needed Him Most," and "Daddy Was a Monster"[206] tend to be a bit man bashing.

All this leaves the book on the male perspective with less exposure, making it harder to justify a reasonable advance. And without a reasonable advance, a book gets few initial purchases by the book chains, is almost never put up front on display, and is advertised minimally. All of this creates a self-fulfilling prophecy of few sales, thus justifying the editorial board saying they can't afford to publish a book written from a man's perspective.

TV NEWS

When Prince Charles confessed he'd had an affair, it was hyped by the media as *Charles's betrayal* of Di. When CNN reported that Princess Di had a secret affair

"Was it something I said, something Oprah said, something Phil said, or something Geraldo said?"

GLASBERGEN

with James Hewitt, they headlined it as Princess *Di's* *"journey of courage."*[207] When we encourage either sex to see their affairs as part of a journey of courage caused by their partner, we are making divorce into a virtue. That will leave yet another generation of children destabilized. Their rebellion will be a yearning for rules, regulations, and structure in a futile attempt to heal the wounds of elusive love.

Most of us pride ourselves on being fair. So how do we come to look at a marriage in such an unfair way and not even know we are doing it? One way is by being presented with an attitude about male-female relationships when we think we are watching the news, even watching politics.

For example, when *CNN and Company* aired "The New Face of Feminism"—inspired by a *Time* magazine cover story on feminism—it invited four feminists to analyze it.[208] Sound reasonable? Yes, until we understand what's being discussed. For starters, it is pay inequity between women and men—that is, *male-female* issues. By presenting only the feminist perspective—that women earn 76 cents to the dollar for the same work—and invite no one to say that it's for very different work, they leave many women feeling that it's a journey of courage to expect a fair shake from all-powerful men.

That is, **CNN was theoretically analyzing only feminism, but in reality it was also analyzing the relationship between women and men, but from only a feminist perspective.** And that creates misunderstandings, anger, and divorce.

Once we see the relationship issues behind the theoretically political issues and ask why men's perspectives aren't being aired, many shows look different. I mentioned this to a friend over dinner. I could feel his skepticism. But a few days later I got a call.

"I see what you mean. Last night I'm watching *Dateline* and I see Jane

Pauley doing two evenings worth of interviews with Anita Hill. And then I thought, what about Clarence Thomas? There was no interview with him, and no mention they had invited him. Then I saw she did no cross-examination whatsoever. She seemed to lose all her journalistic skills. And then, on *Dateline*, I heard a report about research saying, 'Men can't understand what goes on except in a linear fashion.' And they didn't offer a counterperspective to that either."

Once the feminist perspective that men have the power goes unquestioned for long enough, put-downs of men can be integrated into the news and called humor without a call for equal time. Thus CNN Headline News devoted five minutes of worldwide coverage to *How to Make Your Man Behave in 21 Days or Less Using the Secrets of Professional Dog Trainers.*[209]

When feminism defines gender and relationships and all four gender perspectives are not invited to the table, divorce follows. When all four parties are at the table, the FCC can be satisfied the media is facilitating communication.

When all four parties are not at the table, we begin to not only use a double standard in hiring the sexes, but also a double standard in firing the sexes.

HOW WE HIRE, WHO WE FIRE

When Jimmy (the Greek) Synder suggested that black football players may have certain genetic advantages, he was fired.[210] When Andy Rooney of *60 Minutes* *denied* making comments that a gay advocacy magazine claimed he made about gays and blacks, he was, despite the lack of proof, suspended for three months without pay.[211] When Al Campanis, who had spent his life working for minorities in baseball, made some tasteless remarks, he was labeled a racist and virtually destroyed.[212] They were men.

But when Katie Couric told Senator Tom Harkin, "The one benefit of cloning is that we'll no longer need men (just kidding),"[213] everyone just laughed. Imagine Bryant Gumbel, an African-American former host of the *Today Show,* telling Ehud Barak, "The one benefit of cloning is that we'll no longer need Jews (just kidding)." Would NBC have fired him?

Frankly, I do not favor firing Jimmy the Greek or Katie. Not for that incident, at least. But just months later, when Katie was interviewing a bride who had been deserted at the altar, she asked, "Have you considered castration as an option?"[214] Had Matt Lauer asked the jilted groom, "Have you considered the option of cutting off her breasts?" NBC would be considering the option of cutting off his contract.

These Couricisms—or sexisms—though, are only the tip of Katie's iceberg. I watch the *Today Show* most mornings. When Katie co-hosted with Bryant Gumbel, her anger toward him was palpable. I saw her hit Bryant Gumbel on air more than a dozen times. Some of the hits were playful, but others were hard and

appeared motivated by disgust. They often took Bryant by surprise. The consequences? NBC got rid of *Bryant*, transferring him away from one of the most
prestigious spots on TV. He, Bryant, was called the chauvinist.

It doesn't take a Sensitive New Age Guy to wonder what would have happened if Bryant had been consistently hitting Katie over the course of two or more
years—even if *all* the hits were playful. Would feminists have been saying, "Well,
she deserves it, maybe it will teach her not to make sexist comments about elim-
inating all men and castrating a groom"? I don't think so. It is not conceivable
that feminists would call *Katie* the chauvinist if *Bryant* had been hitting Katie.

But . . . Bryant got the boot from one of the most prestigious positions in TV
to a much less prestigious position. (He was eventually picked up by CBS for a
return to anchoring in 1999, indicating it was not his desire to leave the world of
morning anchoring.) Bryant said nothing, and held up no placards lamenting
"Katie, Katie, Unfair Lady." If Katie had been repeatedly hit, then let go by NBC
without ever protesting, feminists would have called this "learned helplessness."
One problem. Feminists see it only when it happens to a woman and, since feminism is the only interpreter of relationships, we do not see learned helplessness
when it happens to a man.

The real issue here is not Bryant—I don't consider Bryant to be either battered or helpless. The issue is the double standard. And even the double standard would be trivial if it didn't reflect an attitude at the *Today* show that could
have life or death consequences. As in the *Today* show's coverage of women's vs.
men's health. . . .

I asked the *Today* show to give me a printout of their segments related to
women's and men's health coverage, but they refused.[215] Certainly NBC has no
legitimate reason to keep a printout of their segments secret, but it forced me to
fall back on my own less-than-perfect tabulations (between wake-up and writing,
pre- and post-shower, on varied sized Post-its at different stages of dress!). All
women's health concerns were at about an 11 to 1 ratio over all men's health concerns between 1996 and '98. Breast cancer coverage alone exceeded *all* men's
health areas *combined,* including the thirty-four neglected areas I list above. And,
from what I could tell, the men's health segments were shorter.

The trivialization of men's health is also reflected in NBC's humor. Jay Leno
joked, when Bob Dole was running for president, that the vice presidency would
be especially important—should Bob Dole win, the vice president would be only
"a prostate away from the presidency." If Elizabeth Dole had breast cancer, would
he joke that if she becomes president, the vice presidency will be important because he or she would be only "a breast away from the presidency"?

On a lighter note, watch how these attitudes are reflected in smaller ways
when the *Today Show* goes to the outside audience. In the front row are about

five women for each man. We can find the men in the back rows. When men do get up front, they usually have a special reason for being there (*e.g.*, a clown costume, a marriage proposal, anniversary, carrying a baby). It's humorous and petty until I recall blacks in the south in the '50s—in the back of the bus. Blacks were in the back unless they had a special reason for being up front—like Jackie Robinson or Arthur Ashe.

How responsive is NBC to looking at these issues? The author of a study of *The Cosby Show,* one of the *least* sexist, nevertheless documented the sexist depiction of men 142 times in twenty-two episodes, or 3.4 per minute.[216] When he sent the study to Warren Littlefield, in charge of NBC programming, he received no response.

Maybe NBC's slogan, "Now more than ever," really means just that: "NOW (the National Organization for Women) more than ever."

RADIO

Radio, especially drive time, pulls in the commute-to-work male audience who let hazing, confronting, and affronting roll off their wheels. Which gives talk show hosts fewer constraints than people in any of the other media. Thus radio has a Rush from the Right, a Larry from the Left, a Schlessinger from "no sex before marriage-ville," and a Stern from "Sex in my studio, vil-u?" They all made it first on radio even if they later also made it on TV.

Radio's flexibility allows hosts like Howard Stern the latitude to drag his guests out from behind the Lace Curtain. Once he made it to radio, he could transfer his style to TV. I once watched him relentlessly cross-examine a gorgeous model who had dated Dodi al-Fayed (of Harrod's fortune and Princess Di fame). Howard pointed her to the cliffs of honesty, then click-and-dragged her to its precipice. . . .[217]

"Why," he hammered, "do models like you go from one multimillionaire to another rather than to loving, supportive men who can accompany you on your shoots?"—or something like that. When she fudged one way, Howard pushed the other, always on point: Why do women who have the options choose men with money and then wonder why they can't find men who love?

Questions like this, from behind the Lace Curtain, if you will, are rarely asked at all on television, in the newspapers, in women's studies, in the liberal arts, in government studies, in Gallop opinion polls. The first time I saw it broached on quasi-prime time was by David Letterman, just a couple of days after Howard's handiwork.[218] David asked the superstar *Sports Illustrated* swimsuit model who she was engaged to and she said it was to the son of Rupert Murdoch. He joke-asked, "Why do beautiful women always marry money, what about some gentle, caring cashier in a supermarket, eh?" On TV though, when the model laughed off David with some "Oh, he has a great personality, too" comment, David dropped it. Howard had permission to relentlessly pursue until the model revealed more of herself than she had in her photos.

This male audience latitude also allowed radio talk show psychologist Dr. Laura (55 percent of her audience is men) more freedom to open herself up to men's stories. Dr. Laura could write books like *Ten Stupid Things Women Do to Mess Up Their Lives* and speak sympathetically about women, and then ask for letters from men for a parallel book, *Ten Stupid Things Men Do to Mess Up Their Lives,* and say "When I read what men wrote, I sat there sobbing. I had a lot of prejudices and notions about men–give them a beer and they're happy. . . . Writing this book changed that."[219] When she completed the book, she could air some of her new views without them being filtered through the constraints of political correctness or even objective journalism. When she was shocked to find many women so unwilling to hear men's feelings—defining sensitivity only as men hearing their feelings—she was able to say that.

Radio is often considered the last bastion of conservatism in the media—of the Angry White Man. It is more accurate to say, though, that in today's climate, radio is the only medium that selects for "the emperor has no clothes" talk show personalities. Our willingness to dismiss the medium with the *widest* range as if it had the narrowest range (angry white men), is really a comment on our need to dismiss anything that makes us question Lace Curtain political correctness.

Two radio networks are, though, quite limited in their range when it comes to gender issues: Christian radio and National Public Radio. Christian radio believes God intended men to be breadwinners, so gender transition is viewed with caution at best. However, Christian radio is male-positive and feminist-negative, so men's health, the powerlessness many men experience, and feminist distortions of men are received with open heart.

National Public Radio is another story. I will take the risk of sharing a personal example. When *The Myth of Male Power* was released, National Public Radio invited me to do *Talk of the Nation*. My publicist at Simon & Schuster told me I'd be on the full hour by myself. My publicist was happy, but I was overjoyed—I had just done an hour on the NPR station in the DC area, with Diane Rehm, and hundreds of listeners flooded my DC-area evening presentation wanting more. Besides, this was the first time since my feminist-only days that I had been invited by NPR to present nationally. I began preparing myself.

A few days before the show, my publicist and I were talking. I told her of my enthusiasm, but I felt a discomfort in her silence. NPR had just informed her they wanted to cut me back to the second half hour only and have two feminists do the first half hour (Ellie Smeal, a former president of NOW, and a colleague). I knew the issue wasn't fairness, since NPR had had hundreds of hour-long feminist-only shows, so I knew NPR had been "gotten to." I felt sad, but I consoled myself with the format: I'll listen when they talk; they'll listen when I talk. I like listening. I like talking. At least everyone has a chance to be heard.

The show was scheduled while I was on the San Francisco leg of my book tour, so I was on the phone. I double-checked with the NPR producer the format: half-hour each, no interruption. She confirmed. Fifteen minutes till air time. I settled into my meditation preparation. As Ellie and host Ray Suarez began the feminist half, I poured some 16-herb Mu tea from one of those Nissan stainless steel thermoses. As I heard Ellie speak, memories flooded in—memories of leading the "Men for the ERA" portion of NOW's march on Washington when Ellie was president. They wound down. I wound up. Poured some Starbucks.

Ray Suarez introduced my background with NOW and asked me how *The Myth of Male Power* departs. I began by sharing the positive contributions of NOW, of feminism opening up options my mother never had. Then I added a first item of departure. Immediately, Ellie and her colleague jumped in. I was taken aback, but said nothing. Soon it became apparent I could say nothing! Okay, I held off until commercial break so no one needed to be embarrassed. What, this is NPR . . . no commercial break!

So, on air, *live,* I reiterated our agreement to alternate listening. I assumed that would settle it. Wrong. Ray's response was, "Who is going to *respond* to what you are saying?" I began to say, "One million of the most informed listeners in America," but suddenly Ray interrupted, declaring a need for a break. I'm relieved. Perhaps Ray was never fully informed, maybe he felt caught between a rock and a hard place. Some seconds pass, then Ray got on the phone with me off the air.

"We're just going to continue with the women."

"Can you check with your producer about our agreement?"

"I never make agreements like that. I've got to get back to the show now. . . ."

Shocked, I called the producer even as the show was continuing. She was just as shocked, affirmed our agreement, and affirmed that she had the authority to make the agreement—that was all she could tell me. I called Simon & Schuster. They were dismayed and empathetic, but "I don't know what we can do." I realized they had a relationship to keep.

A month or so later I called the NPR producer again. "We've never had more complaints about anything we've done than about Ray disconnecting you. It's over a month later and we're still averaging five calls a day."

I volunteered that I was open to working out something, but I could feel that she had already gotten into trouble and couldn't afford to jeopardize her job. I let it go. NPR never called back. I had met the Lace Curtain.

THE INTERNET: AOL OR AWOL?

Other than radio, are there outlets for men's feelings? The Internet originally held out hope. In the beginning, it was dominated by men. At first there was not much discussion of men and women. Then men discovered the environment was safe for discussing relationships. And men began speaking up. Especially the non-techie men on America Online, which has more American subscribers than the next fifteen largest Internet service providers combined.[220] They created forums such as the "Men's Equal Rights" folder, "Moving Toward Equity," and the Men's Center. But two not-so funny things happened on the way to their forum.

First, censorship. The keyword "women" gives one access to virtually every conceivable female interest. At first, the keyword "men" also gave access to a more limited range of men's interests. Then these forums got hot, especially the "Men's Equal Rights" folder. Active dialogue. Men expressing themselves. The result? All three forums either disappeared or were closed down without notice. AOL subscriber friends informed me they encountered responses like "This Group Is Not Valid," and "No longer connected to Internet news groups."[221] Nothing seemed to work and certainly not the keyword "men."

As you can imagine, AOL got mail. Male mail. And to their credit, they responded. Folders like "Moving Toward Equity" had been replaced. But . . . these **men's interests could be found only if, would you believe, the men would look under the prefix "Feminist Views."** They must post in Talk*Women* folders and abide by "the AOL Women's Forum Rules of the Road," posted on the "TalkWomen main screen."[222]

Is this *chutzpah,* or what? Imagine telling women they could express their feelings only by searching for "Masculist Views" in TalkMen folders and by following Men's Rules of the Road? Right. Not exactly the way we get the emotionally constipated sex to open up. It's led to AOL being labeled AWOL, or American Women on Line.[223]

Is it fair to declare that if this censorship happened to any other group on the Internet that it would have made the front page? Yes. Evidence? When the *New York Times* discovered America Online had suspended the heated debate between two opposing discussion groups on Ireland, the suspension made a three-column headline on the front page of the Sunday *Times.*[224] And AOL's censorship of men? Ignored.

Oh yes, *two* things happened. As men were encountering roadblocks to expression, women's pathways to expression were proliferating on the formerly male-dominated Internet. Almost every directory page offers special subdirectories tailored to women's interests that solicit her expression. And hate-men pages not only avoid censorship, but thrive. Here's one run by Kashka, affectionately titled (by her) the "All Men Must Die" page. Notice the dead man behind the "All Men Must Die" logo.

Kashka started the "All Men Must Die" page after she and her boyfriend broke up (remember the common denominator of the "hate men" greeting cards?). She begins with the Kashka Deathlist, "to put an end to the annoying problem that's been troubling our planet for too long. We all know men suck. Now what are we going to do about it? The Kashka Deathlist hopes to include each and every man on this planet, but . . . first priority to those men who have made my life even more annoying than the rest. You know who you are, and you are going to **DIE**" (emphasis Kashka's).[225] This web page exceeds 100,000 hits per year. If the term "hit man" was sexist before. . . .

It is the combination of censorship for men discussing equality with freedom for women compiling death lists that leads many men to feel that their feelings are consigned to the backseat.

We would assume, though, that there is one place in which men's feeling would not be consigned to the backseat—on the therapist's chair. Would we assume correctly?

HELPING PROFESSIONS

A controlled study of social workers judged female clients to be significantly more intelligent than male clients, to be more mature emotionally, and therefore capable of benefiting from less directive, or more permissive treatment, than male clients.[226] The study concluded there was discrimination against men. I felt that might be a rush to judgment: "Maybe it's because the female clients *are* more mature . . ." Then I read further: *The descriptions of the clients were identical—except Mr. T was changed to Mrs. T., or vice versa.*

With the clients' interchangeability in mind, here's the most powerful social worker bias: The social workers *liked* the clients labeled "females" better.[227]

Does this bias hold with psychologists, who have more training than social workers? Let's see.

One group of therapists was asked to watch a videotape of a simulated counseling session in which the "client" with problems said he was an engineer whose wife stayed home to care for the children. Another group of therapists was asked to watch the same "client" with the same problems, but who this time said he was a househusband whose wife was an engineer.[228]

Not a single therapist questioned the domestic arrangement of the client who pretended to have a traditional arrangement. Almost all the therapists did question the "client" who pretended to be a househusband with questions like, "What messages do you have from your childhood about what a man is?" Typical solutions were, "You probably need to renegotiate the contract that you've got at home." The therapists rated the man who pretended to be a househusband as much more severely depressed even though in both tapes the client insisted he was very happy with his work arrangement, his wife, and his family.

In actual practice, a *Washington Post* article describes the experience of Dean and his then-girlfriend, who went to see a therapist to discuss, among other things, her violence toward him. "During one session, Dean told the therapist about an occasion when he had fallen asleep on the couch while watching television. About two A.M., he was awakened by his girlfriend's pounding on the front door. When Dean opened the door, she clobbered him over the head with a glass seltzer bottle. Hearing of this incident, the therapist looked at Dean and said: 'Do you often fall asleep in front of the TV?'"[229]

That's the foundation upon which the Lace Curtain in the helping professions is built. Increasingly, it is difficult to get funding for such objective and controlled studies on gender bias, because, as we have seen, if the area is gender, the funding is feminist. This underlying bias, though, is just the starting point.

Feminist therapy is increasingly powerful in the professions of social work and psychology. Clinical psychologists study feminist therapy for their licensing exam.[230] Graduate training programs in clinical psychology offer it as a specialty track. University-run student health clinics hire feminist therapists to counsel undergraduates.

Feminist therapy is now built into the law. It can be used as a legal defense in court, allowing a woman who murders her husband to use a Learned Helplessness Defense but not allowing a man who murders his wife to do the same.

(Which is a pretty blatant violation of the Fourteenth Amendment's guarantee of equal protection.) And feminist therapy is now used to allow a woman to continue having sex with a man for weeks and still claim she was raped. She can apply posttraumatic stress syndrome to date rape as the excuse for *continuing the sex* and not reporting the "rape."

Feminist therapists have convinced the legal system that a woman would be afraid to report a rape if she thought her past would be brought out in the trial. So rape shield laws allow her past not to be relevant even if she has made a pattern of false accusations. They allow only her name to be kept secret, so only his reputation is ruined even if he is innocent. The rape shield law forgets that the purpose of a trial is to protect the innocent and determine who is guilty, not protect a woman even if the man is found innocent. To protect one sex more than the other before the trial is a violation of due process because it assumes a greater probability of guilt before the trial. Feminist therapy has been strong enough for the violation of due process to be virtually ignored.

It is, though, the everyday practice of feminist therapy that is hurting especially the poor and uneducated women it desires to help. When couples are involved in domestic violence, California law requires treatment programs in which the sexes are portrayed as the races, with men oppressing women as whites oppress blacks.[231] In many county programs, such as Santa Clara County in California, men are lectured by ex-battered women who become untrained counselors, but no one is counseled by ex-battered men.[232]

These, though, are the lesser crimes. The real crime is that *couples therapy is rejected because, by asking the woman to also look at her role, it is seen as "blaming the victim."* Conversely, a man who denies he abused his wife is assumed to be "in denial." If he says they both hit each other, he is rationalizing. He cannot graduate that program until he acknowledges what he may not have done.

I said this especially hurts poor and uneducated *women.* How? Women are the most financially dependent, and when a program like this promises to help the man, it gives her a false sense of security, a reason to stay. When it fails, as one-sided blame to a two-sided problem always does, she is there for the next round of violence.

While feminist therapy holds as a core tenet that there is "never an excuse for violence against women," when women commit violence there is almost always an excuse. Even when Khoua Her killed her six *children,* the headline in the *Minneapolis Star-Tribune* read, "Why Do Mothers Kill Their Children?" featuring a psychologist explaining that mothers who kill feel totally abandoned.[233]

Feminist therapy in social work becomes a self-fulfilling prophecy because as its biases dominate the social work community it has led to men increasingly avoiding social work as a profession, or entering only if they've had a feminist studies background in college. The few exceptions have felt the pressure to adapt or exit.

Ironically, even the poor pay of social workers reinforces the unconscious feminist bias against the poor. I was on a plane trip a few months ago. The mid-twenties man sitting next to me noticed me working on this book, which turned out to be the end of my working on this book! He explained he was a social worker. And a feminist. And a Marxist.

I asked him why he was flying on this capitalist-created jet. When he said it was for a job interview with a major corporation, I asked him if he didn't feel that a bit ironic, being a capitalist Marxist. He explained, "I'm lonely. I'd like to marry, and this job, if I get it, will allow me to triple my pay and afford a family."

Now watch. His corporate job and traditional breadwinner role will challenge his Marxist feminist ideology. But by the time all that happens, he will no longer be a social worker! The poor pay of the social worker forces out of it the type of man who would support a family on that pay, who could understand the average primary breadwinner man.

This feminist therapy bias against men, the family, and the poor is especially devastating because it is the poor and less-educated families it is the mandate of social workers to serve.

The term feminist therapist, like feminist scholar, is an oxymoron.

For a bias against one sex to be built into a profession whose ethic is helping both sexes is *unethical*.

To use that bias to prevent introspection in a profession whose practice is introspection is *malpractice*.

To use public funds to pay for malpractice is *corruption*.

CONCLUSIONS AND SOLUTIONS

The political genius of the women's movement is feminism's six unspoken rules: define the issues; define an oppressor; sell feminism as the champion of the oppressed; always open options for women; never close options for women; when something is wrong, never hold women responsible. The effect? The groups of women who benefit will grow, and their aggregate political power will outweigh that of any group directly impacted by any one measure.

The strategy worked because it was driven by working parts: from at-home discussions and guerrilla theater to federal legislation and the *New York Times* infiltration. It worked because although many women didn't have time, many women did and could articulate their resentment. And it worked because men's egos were so wrapped up in competing to be a recognized savior that we couldn't see that while we were saving women in the short run, we were hurting women in the long run because we weren't making a transition *with* women. Therefore, we were really hurting everyone.

As feminism made a transition from ridiculed "bra burners" to the one-party system of gender politics, it lost its checks and balances, and the Lace Curtain was woven. The speech codes are an example of how the feminist movement has evolved—originally objecting to protective legislation because it discriminated against women to now creating protective legislation that allows only women to discriminate against men. The speech codes not only deny men free speech and equal protection under the law, but by suspending and sentencing a man who violates the code, it violates men's civil rights to pursue education. It is an example of women's liberation evolving into feminist totalitarianism. As such, feminism was no different from any other one-party system—or any *person* without boundaries.

No solution will address more underlying problems than a willingness to confront our instinct to protect women more than men. But that's long term. In the short run, the media, academia, the government and the helping professions need to hold up Lace Curtain biases against their founding principles of fairness and objectivity. And the taxpayer must demand an investigation of the misuse of its money to undermine the government's own mandate to protect both sexes equally, the FCC's own mandate for all sides to be represented by the media, and the mission of its public universities to foster freedom of speech and inquiry.

Finally, corporations must ask whether Lace Curtain biases are making them fearful of hiring women and fearful of mentoring women. They must be more active in confronting the government with the understanding that the free market system has its own built-in punishment to people willing to pay more money for less competent help. Any company that really paid a man one dollar for a job a woman could do for 76 cents would lose out to any company that hired only women. Capitalism's built-in punishment for short-term discrimination is loss of profit; for long-term discrimination: bankruptcy.

When a company can't hire and can't fire freely, it becomes afraid to hire at all—so it outsources, or merges and "downsizes." Thus forced stability begets instability; the protection of women is undermined by the protection of women. Which is the paradox of protection.

Opening the Lace Curtain and closing down feminism as the one-party system of gender politics frees women to hear what men at least could say if the media, academia, and government were not frustrating the already silent sex. It would bring the four major gender perspectives into communication with each other. It would provide the groundwork for discussions about redistributing housework, child care, and work outside the home within each family; and create more two-sex inclusive solutions to domestic violence, date rape, and sexual harassment. It would open up new areas of exploration, from the thirty-four neglected areas of men's health to men's experiences of date rejection and workplace entitlement. It would facilitate new science, as in men's birth control, and new studies, as in studies of stepfathering.

Opening the Lace Curtain also frees women to speak more honestly to other women. For example, Amy Gage, a business consultant, shared how female business reporters, constantly on deadline, quietly call men because the men are less likely to change their answers after the interview, are less "prickly and sensitive," want less control, are more willing to speak their mind without official clearance, are less likely to want a colleague to sit in on interviews, and are more willing to talk about profits or revenue.[234] In brief, the men are more willing to take risks and be held accountable. To me, this type of honest communication woman-to-woman can occur only when neither sex fears being labeled "anti-woman."

Realistically speaking, *can* the Lace Curtain be opened? First, the less realistic, the more necessary. Second, yes, it's more realistic now than ever before, because we have finally invented "men's telephone": the Internet. But even a letter will do. A colleague of mine wrote to *America's Funniest Home Videos* about the damage to boys' psyches when being hit in the genitals is so often considered so funny.[235] Those videos didn't appear the next season. Coincidence? Maybe; maybe not.

What can you, the reader, do? Live shows allow the most freedom from censorship. When you're listening to a live talk show, like Larry King, or PBS's *Washington Journal,* NPR's *Talk of the Nation,* or some MSNBC or CNN shows, and you hear a Lace Curtain–based misunderstanding about men, call in. The first time, just speak from your heart, from your experience; the second time, add some data to create a new understanding of the larger picture—move the heart *and* shift the paradigm (just an inch or two). If you're shaking in you boots, give a "stage name" until you feel secure.

If you've got a bit more ambition and a talent for organizing, organize a protest. Protest the *New York Times* or your local paper, or AOL. Create a web page about the Lace Curtain, reproduce portions of this chapter on the web page, and organize a response. E-mail the section to every reporter who falls prey to the Lace Curtain, with a copy to her or his boss, and the boss's boss. Start a chat room about the Lace Curtain.

If demonstrations are more your style, protest outside a major paper or your local TV station. Ask the other media to cover it. On a twenty-foot poster, list all the media that refuse. Organize the protest with a telephone tree. Solicit the cooperation of one of the organizations on the Resource List at the end of this book.

Make an effort to organize men. There's a lot of good women out there just waiting for a good man to have that perfect blend of enough sensitivity to be in touch with his feelings and enough courage to take some initiative.

No matter what profession you're in, there's an organization within that profession promoting women's interests and, chances are, no organization promoting men's interests. Until there is neither there needs to be both. So form one. If you're an elementary school teacher, for example, create the Male Association of Teachers in Elementary Schools (MATES), and help us understand about our sons and our schools.

In brief, we must all take responsibility to bring all four gender parties to the table of gender issues—traditional men, traditional women, nontraditional men, feminists—to replace the Lace Curtain with open dialogue on how we can allow maximum freedom for both sexes without losing sight of our commitments to our partners and children.

Well, this chapter has been exhausting to write. I could tell it was taking its toll this morning. I read in the *Los Angeles Times* about students using the Internet to pay for others to do their homework assignments on topics like "morality in *Medea*" and the only thing I could see was "morality in the media"!

In Conclusion...

A conclusion is often used to inspire. I love inspiration and like inspiring. The usual method of inspiring, though, is to skip realities that could be roadblocks to inspiration. But to me, when I know I have dealt with reality, I feel my hope rests on more solid ground. Inspiration without reality often results in disillusion that becomes cynicism and withdrawal. And that's exactly what has happened with many men.

I will use the conclusion, then, to look at the nature of the metaphorical elephant that emerges when we piece together all the chapters that are its parts. I will give that elephant direction. We will see the greatest opportunity the sexes have ever had to love each other, a clearer view of what is preventing that love from happening, and why those of us who care about that love being available for our children—if not ourselves—must get off our duffs and act.

The first piece is relationship language.

RELATIONSHIP LANGUAGE

If my reader takes away only one thing from Part I, it is that both sexes have in common our desire to be understood. To achieve that goal, nothing is more important than the four "relationship language" skills: experiencing empathy ("walking a mile in each other's moccasins"); communicating empathy; giving criticism so it can be easily heard; hearing criticism so it can be easily given. Of these, our vulnerability to personal criticism is what needs the most work—it is the Achilles' heel by which our love for each other is most frequently wounded.

The good news about the first four chapters is that relationship language, like computer language, can be learned. And it facilitates a type of love our parents couldn't have dreamed of. Which doesn't mean this love will be better than that of our parents. Why not? When technology made it affordable to live without a partner, marriage was no longer a guarantee of being a team for life. We lost the love that grew out of the certainty of being a team forever, "for better or worse."

Relationship language has the potential for stabilizing what technology destabilized. Without it, our yearning for stability will be so great that we will look to others to create it for us: We will beg for stabilizing rules and lists of rights and wrongs from the law, the church, family, and even universities. With relationship language, stability will be a natural byproduct of feeling emotionally safe and supported in a relationship. **Once relationship language is mastered, the church and family can be used as an *additional support* system, not as a substitute legislative system.**

Notice, though, that I said relationship language has the *potential* for stabilizing. No human or technological change occurs without trade-offs. If we create change without being prepared for the trade-offs, we raise expectations, breed disappointment, and thus destabilize.

A downside of relationship language as a pathway to understanding is that it requires practice—like computer language, it is forgettable if not practiced frequently. And when we do practice it frequently, another trade-off pops up: We expect our partner to do the same. That is, we up our ante. *And* we can easily become self-righteous. These grow out of our belief that we have changed more than our partner.

The solution? It starts with remembering that because growth is painful and we can feel only our own pain, not our partner's, then only our growth is apparent. This requires pro-actively soliciting our partner's efforts and growth. And verbalizing our appreciation. The price of not doing that is that a new set of problems—rising expectations and self-righteousness—will replace the old.

While both sexes are fearful of expressing their deepest feelings and risking the rejection and fights that even one criticism often engenders, we have been most blind as to why this fear is embedded in men. Because our survival historically depended on men protecting women even at the expense of their own lives, any feeling of male weakness makes us cringe, and any criticism of a woman makes him look like a bully to others and feel like a bully to himself. Once society has mastered Stage I survival skills, men expressing feelings and criticizing lovingly—before they are out of control—is in the interest of every family, church, and business.

When a society *first* enters the Stage II world of balancing survival with self-fulfillment, it will overemphasize self-fulfillment and provide options *only for women*. That is happening today in most of Europe, in the United States, Canada, Australia, and New Zealand, and in most industrialized urban areas in the rest of the world. However, **when a society begins to care about men's feelings and self-fulfillment, without neglecting women's, it is the key indicator of a society becoming a mature Stage II society.** This will be the work of the entire twenty-first century.

Why so long?

THE NEXT EVOLUTIONARY SHIFT: THE EXPECTATION
OF EQUAL PROTECTION

Getting men to express feelings requires more than a paradigm shift; it requires an evolutionary shift. A shift in how we view the sexes' historic and genetic role of men protecting women.

Historically, when a woman complained, she discovered who was interested in rescuing her. It was a way of finding a savior—not just for herself, but also for her children. Complaining is part of what was functional for a woman and her family. When a man complained, women ran away. Complaining was dysfunctional for men. The man on the white horse, a prince, Christ, Superman, the football hero, the brain surgeon, and the Mafia don were not found in therapy, *Analyze This*–style. "Real men" did not attend "burnout" classes. The next evolutionary challenge of men is the *ability* to complain without shame (within reason!); the next evolutionary challenge of women is challenging each other to complain less, supporting each other to do more, educating each other that men are the allies of people whose slogan is "just do it."

Women's complaints began to be aimed at men big time when they perceived men's promise to them—of marriage as economic security for a lifetime— to be broken. That began with the divorces of the '60s. Divorces meant women's dreams of being "swept away" were swept away. Women were swept into the workplace without equal experience and swept back into the meat market of men at the age of forty, only to find men more addicted to two twenties than to one forty. Men became jerks. Anger was building. The prince on the white horse turned from savior to devil.

There was little anger at men for earning more than women in the workplace until men stopped providing that income to their families. Then the rage at men earning more was so deep that no man dared respond, "It's for longer hours, more experience, more-hazardous jobs."

Feminism did not plant the seeds of anger. The seeds of both sexes' anger were planted in the soil of each generation's soul as both sexes in every generation repressed self-gratification and made whatever sacrifice it took to make their children's life better than their own (sometimes without appreciation). But for generations this was called love, and, when interpreted this way, it created not only survival, but much gratification and considerable community.

Feminism, however, did not interpret women's sacrifices-as-love as women's role in a world in which *both* sexes had learned to love by making sacrifices so their children could have what they did not. Feminism held that women's loving nature made women vulnerable to exploitation by men in a way that was not true in reverse. What made women, who had always been men's partners, vulnerable to this interpretation?

FEMINISM AS SUBSTITUTE MAN

When divorces left women vulnerable, without their male protector, feminism became some women's substitute man. Feminism guided women-in-transition.

Collectively, feminism became women's labor union, if you will. By making women feel the cause of their anger was unique to them and not a byproduct of both sexes' transition, it developed victim power—as does any union for its members. And, as any labor union does, it defined an enemy. Feminism's was not management, but man. Thus empowerment feminism became victim feminism became competitive feminism. Divorce had undone the marital team, making women vulnerable to the suggestion of an enemy.

In the '60s and '70s, when religion represented the restrictions from which many women were trying to set themselves free, feminism became the new savior of secular women, divorced women, lesbian women, and many single women. It became these women's new God the Mother. It nurtured women's self-esteem but also promoted women's anger by telling her that only she had been socialized to focus on others, and that was a conspiracy of the patriarchy, or God the Father. It created itself as God and man as Devil.

In brief, feminism became some women's substitute man, many women's union, and many secular women's religion. As women's union, men in the workplace became the "bossman" who was portrayed as neither heeding women nor needing women; as women's religion, men at home became "father the patriarch." In combination, men became the devil whose design it was to seduce women into dependency on their protection. Like male Sirens.

Once men were defined as the enemy, and every aspect of sex roles was examined from only the female point of view, myths about men were easy to develop. The greatest of these myths was that male power was designed to serve only men rather than also protect women and families. Each myth in this book grows out of that one in combination with the trashing of women's dream of being protected by that power. The result is the most dangerous forcefield of anger ever aimed at either sex, one which will leave, if not caught soon, even more generations of our children alienated from their dads.

This force field of anger was magnified by two of the three faces of feminism, the faces that promoted "victim power" . . .

THE POLITICS OF "VICTIM POWER"

The three faces of feminism—empowerment feminism, victim feminism, and competitive feminism—have, politically, come in the same package. As feminism matures, I witness, on the one hand, millions of women developing sides of themselves they never would have discovered thirty years ago; of being assertive rather than passive-aggressive, of leading independent rather than dependent lives. And this gives me great joy—for women, for feminism, and for the little piece I contributed to that change. On the other hand, I feel sad that empowerment feminism has never uncoupled from the victim feminism and competitive feminism that have created men as the devil.

Ironically, this unwillingness of empowerment feminism to stand alone has been part of feminism's political genius. **The political genius of the women's movement is "feminism's unspoken holy trinity": Always open options for women; never close options for women; when something is wrong in the society, never hold women responsible.** Why is this so ingenious? Women who benefit will have more interest in advocacy than the people who do not benefit will have in protesting.

Men are confused because "I am woman; I am strong" does not compute with "I am woman; I am victim." When a man sees a female victim, his reflex is to save her; but no one playing the male role is supposed to be saved. Women were claiming they could play the male role and were still supposed to be saved.

From women's perspective, there was no contradiction—women were taking on new responsibilities and had to be strong, and these new responsibilities were often thrust upon them—which made them feel like a victim. And it went deeper than that.

Women felt even more victimized because, in the past, most of women's responsibilities came with little accountability. In the past, lack of permission for divorce kept the woman from being "fired" from her role. If a child stole something, we did not fire the mother for failing in her role. In contrast, if a man coached a team that failed, he would *expect* to get fired. Women had the *option* of setting high standards *for themselves,* and most did; men had the *obligation* of living up to standards *set by others.*

Feminism reinforced this traditional heritage of women not having anything but their own standards of accountability. A woman was not to be held accountable for how she used child support money. If a woman at work wore a miniskirt and a low-cut blouse and the wrong man responded, feminists suggested he should be held accountable for sexual harassment, but she should not be held accountable for sexual solicitation. When a man who hits a woman says, "It was self-defense. She hit me first," the feminist response was, "There is never an excuse for violence against women." When a woman hits a man, the response is, "What did *he* do to provoke her?" Women were taking on more responsibility, but not more accountability.

Although men's intellect told them that no one who failed to be held accountable could truly be an equal, men's savior instinct could not refuse the cry of a woman asking for help. So they passed laws protecting women against unwanted sexual overtures; preventing pay discrimination against women, *creating* pay discrimination against men (Affirmative Action); protecting only women against stranger violence (the Federal Violence Against Women Act; rape crisis centers; date rape laws, rape shield laws) and domestic violence (learned helplessness defenses, battered women's shelters); to make certain that mothers were protected to be mothers (Women, Infants, and Children programs; increased enforcement of child support to moms), but not that dads were protected to be dads (no presupposition of joint custody; no "visitation" enforcement). Unlike men, when women feel, women speak. And when women speak for protection, men make the laws. And so do women.

The few men who could get in touch with their feelings had no political party for an outlet. Men's concerns do not fall on a continuum between conservatism and liberalism, but in a triangular relationship. Both conservatives and liberals are protective of women and thus reinforce the traditional male-female sex roles, but they use different rationalizations for that protectiveness. The conservative expects women to receive special protection via social custom. The liberal expects women to receive special protection via government programs. The conservative assumes most women want the traditional female roles, and the traditional female role requires men to protect women. The liberal assumes men's old roles were power and privilege designed to serve men rather than be men's way of protecting women, so the liberal feels women need protection to compensate for the male power structure. Both conservative and liberal therefore conclude that men should protect women, and no one should protect men.

Are conservatives and liberals in favor of sexual equality? Not really. Special protection with real equality is oxymoronic. In the short run, special protection goes to the privileged. But too often it becomes a double-edged sword. The man who got the Mafia to protect him soon found himself the prisoner of the Mafia's protection. The woman who depends on man-as-protector will find herself male-dependent; when she substitutes the government for a man, she soon become government-dependent (even tempted to "marry" government subsidies instead of men). This is why protecting women creates sexual equality no more than welfare payments created class equality.

Is there a legitimate role for protecting women? Yes, there's a need to protect

women during transition *just as there's a need to protect men in transition.* But **317**
protection-in-transition always requires weaning—or phasing out. **We have
been protecting women as a part of women's rights, not as part of gender transition.**

How Do We Help Our Children Make the Transition to Love?

How can we use *Women Can't Hear What Men Don't Say* to help our daughters
and sons drop the perpetrator-victim paradigm and more effectively love each
other? Kim's parents found one way . . .

Kim's parents saw that Kim was bright and ambitious. When Kim returned
from parties excited about the popular boys who took an interest in her, Kim's
parents would listen, of course, but then also ask for who *else* was there and what
Kim's conversations with those boys were like. They were encouraging her to *notice* the quieter men, to pro-actively seek out a man who was loving and caring,
able to support *her* career. They told her directly this may come in the package of
a man who would always earn less than she. Kim found such a man, and rather
than feel she had disappointed her parents or herself, she was able to take pleasure in her husband being devoted to her, her career, and the children while she
put more energy into her career than would otherwise have been possible.

That was the outcome. But as any parent knows, the process of getting there
was more complex. The man Kim married was Kurt. But Kurt was quieter and
would never have asked Kim, who was more outgoing, on a date. Kim was afraid
to call Kurt because the last few boys she had called, well, for one reason or another, it hadn't turned out that well. One rejected her, one thought she must be
really interested and tried to take advantage, another was boring. And Kim feared
she might be getting a bit of a reputation just for taking initiatives.

Kim's parents let her see how her goal, of being a success, was most likely to
be achieved by learning how to control her life and take risks. The mostly men
she would be competing with were going to be taking risks by *expectation,* not
choice—that if she wanted to be equally prepared she needed to *expect* herself
to ask, and keep asking. She needed to not just risk failure, but experience failure: that the experience of failure was a prerequisite to success. And there was
no better time to experience failure than when she had the support system of her
family there for her. (What Kim didn't understand is that this was as difficult for
her parents to say as it was for her to hear!)

Kim's dad let Kim know how scared he was to ask out girls when he was in
high school. He explained that she could have what most girls have—"veto
power"—by saying yes or no to guys who choose her, or have "original choice

power" by choosing exactly the boy she wanted. Asking out, rather than waiting to be asked, was preparation for controlling her own life. Both in the world of work and in the world of love.

Kim's brightness allowed her to understand all this intellectually, but she was attractive enough to be asked out, and emotionally she liked being sought after a lot more than fearing rejection. And what really got to Kim was being expected to pay for guys she had asked out. Which meant she had to work longer hours at jobs she liked less. As she said, only half-jokingly, "You'd think if I risk the rejection, at least the guy could pay!" Her dad understood the sentiment.

Kim had a lot of second thoughts about what her parents were asking her to consider, but by her senior year she was voted "most likely to succeed" and had a reputation for being her own person and having a compassion for boys shared by no other girl. She had a reputation, all right, but it was one of respect, exactly because of the courage it took to achieve.

Kim's parents also had a lot of second thoughts. The area that was the most difficult was sex. If they encouraged Kim to ask a guy out, were they indirectly encouraging her to initiate sex? They had attended my workshops a few times and intellectually agreed with me that our attitude that sex is dirty and our sons should initiate the dirt is at the heart of the mistrust of men experienced by so many women, but it was another thing to even discuss with Kim the importance of sharing risks of rejection. They agreed that telling only boys to "initiate the dirt" left boys with shame and guilt and girls with innocence, but when it came to sex, they were fearful of diluting Kim's innocence. What they did do, though, was have these discussions openly with Kim. Kim's friends soon wanted "in" on these discussions.

What Kim's parents paid a lot of attention to was exposing Kim to the option of sharing roles without forcing it down her throat. They didn't want to make her into "their experiment"—into a social guinea pig. They seemed to come the closest to achieving with Kim when they worked on sharing roles themselves—modeling, not lecturing.

For most parents, modeling usually means our children seeing Dad do more of the three C's: cooking, cleaning, and child caring. And usually means our children seeing Mom do more of the three P's: performing, paying, and pursuing.

If you have younger children, and you think these messages are getting through to them, double-check by asking them to draw some pictures: "Draw a picture of the house being cleaned," or "Draw a picture of dinner being paid for," or "Draw a picture of the dishwasher being loaded and one of us kissing the person loading the washer." Watch who they put in which role.

Double-check by observing the questions we ask our children during their years of dating. Are we saying "Why don't you call her?" to your son more than "Why don't you call him?" to your daughter? Before they leave on the date, are we more likely to give our daughter a curfew than our son? Are we giving her more warnings about a boy manipulating her into sex with false promises of marriage than we are giving him about a girl manipulating him into marriage with false promises about being on birth control?

If you're a single man and are secure enough, let a woman know on the first date that you'd like to be deciding together what to do on a second date, and, just as you both share in the decision, you'd like it if both of you shared the expenses.

If you're a woman, and you like the idea of a man who cooks, cleans, and cares, ask yourself this question: Is the man I'm sitting with more likely to find it easier to provide me with the four Cs it takes to buy a fine diamond (cut, clarity, cost, and carat size) or the three Cs it takes to care, cook, and clean?

The solution for men? Being secure enough to feel worthy of a woman's company without feeling he has to pay for her more than she pays for him. (Whether in the form of dates, dinners, drinks, diamonds, or a dull, demanding job.) Being vulnerable enough to let a woman know these feelings. Being brave enough to "weed out" the women who cannot hear his feelings due to her need for a "success object" (a man who provides an economic security blanket from which she has more options to raise the children than he). These are masculinity's new rites of passage.

On a societal level, the issue to me is not what the sexes choose to do, but that they have equal opportunity to make all choices. I favor a generation or two of affirmative action incentives for *both* sexes, but only in those areas where gender socialization has effectively discouraged a sex. Today this means helping women in areas like construction, welding, mining, trucking; helping men be at home with the children, do elementary school teaching, nursing, improving reading, verbal, and emotional skills.

Prescriptions, though, are different than predictions. Were I to venture my top ten predictions about the sexes for the next century, in David Letterman order of priority, here are some possibilities.

WARREN'S TOP TEN PREDICTIONS ABOUT WOMEN AND MEN FOR THE TWENTY-FIRST CENTURY

10. *Domestic Violence*—Domestic violence will slowly emerge as a two-sex issue. As the male-perpetrator assumption is questioned, the addition of shelters and hotlines for men will lead to treatment programs placing greater emphasis on prevention via communication skills. Men will gradually feel more welcome into the social work profession again.

9. *Marriages of Executive Women and Multi-Option Men*—Men will more frequently seek the option of caring for the children and working out of

the home, and making proportionately less money than wives who have away-from-home careers. Simultaneously, being the primary breadwinner will become a strategy for top-executive women to attain the support they need to break through the "glass ceiling." These marriages will be about average in stability, but breakups will often be high profile and establish legal precedents as to whether laws designed to protect women will also protect these men. Most of the breakups will be catalyzed by women having affairs with men they meet through work, and men complaining about being taken for granted.

8. *Female Team Sports*—Female team sports will grow in popularity so that the average person will recognize the names of the heroines of female *team* sports (not just the heroines of *individual* sports like tennis, ice skating, gymnastics, swimming). Girls will play more unsupervised, unprotected team sports before and after school, sandlot style. Girls' soccer, basketball, and volleyball will make the first breakthroughs. Girls' participation in team sports will have a positive impact on girls' happiness in life, success at work and marital happiness.

7. *The Lace Curtain*—Of the four major components of the Lace Curtain (media, academia, government, and helping professions), the media will lead the way in balancing their news coverage with attention to the personal stories of men and men's issues. The government and helping professions will follow suit, with universities dragging behind. It will take more than a decade for men's studies programs to focus on the real feelings of most men rather than feminist perspectives on the problems men cause. Lawsuits will initiate some of these changes in all four areas.

6. *Discrimination Against Women and Its Irony*—Companies' fear of sexual harassment lawsuits, sex discrimination accusations, and demands for flexible hours, child care, and maternity leave will lead to underground discrimination against women as in-house employees, especially in low- and mid-level positions. Fear of sexual harassment lawsuits will make the mentorship of women by executive men less common. Women will be hired more as independent contractors, and on a project basis. Ironically, this discrimination against women will ultimately benefit many women, who will develop new ways of looking at financial security (many clients rather than one employer), and more self-starting and risk-taking skills. Many will feel more in common with many men.

5. *Discrimination Against Men*—Lawsuits will allege discrimination in hiring men as elementary school teachers, nurses, flight attendants, cocktail

servers, secretaries, and receptionists. Male affirmative action will become a political issue. The pay-equity debate will reemerge, but this time with both sexes alleging discrimination. Guidelines to determine discrimination will become more complex. (This will be the subject of my book 25 *Ways to Higher Pay.*)

4. *Protecting Women*—The legal system will confront the constitutionality of male-only draft registration, the Violence Against Women Act, the "learned helplessness" defense, the rape shield law, Women, Infant, and Children Programs, Offices of Women's Health, and other laws that protect women more than men.

3. *Relationship Language and our Children*—Grammar schools will make the four "relationship language" skills (experiencing empathy; communicating empathy; giving criticism so it can be easily heard; hearing criticism so it can be easily given) part of required curriculum. Some schools will give these as much priority as computer language and teach these at the same age children learn reading. Many schools will be stimulated to provide these programs after mass shootings by teenage boys who feel rejected and unable to gain attention constructively and therefore do it destructively, often followed by suicide. When relationship language curriculum stems this tide best it will be when the curriculum also integrates male-sensitive outreach programs, and as fathers become more involved with their sons, providing a balance of nurturance and discipline.

2. *A Men's Birth Control Pill*—A men's birth control pill will alter men's lives and male-female relationships almost as much as the female pill did for women: It will reduce commitment borne of women becoming pregnant without the man's agreement, and therefore reduce men's fear of commitment and increase men's trust in women; it will lead to many fewer premarital pregnancies; there will be fewer abortions; it will lead to men taking more responsibility for children; it will be used by poor men more than people believe. A men's birth control pill will sell better than Viagra.

1. *Fathers*—Fathers' issues will be to the early twenty-first century what women's issues were to the late twentieth century. Fathers will have greater success obtaining joint and primary custody. Denial of "visitation" will be treated more seriously. More men will ask for paternity tests. Single dads will increasingly work out of their home and will continue to be less likely than women to receive child support, either from the mother or the government, even when he has sole custody of the children. Single dads will become between 25 and 30 percent of single parents by 2015.

For the first time in history, the sexes have an opportunity to redefine love, to create not a woman's movement blaming men, or a men's movement blaming women, but a gender transition movement.

In the past, we have been challenged by a paradox: Political movements have been led mostly by unhealthy people, but few healthy changes have occurred without political movements.

In the future, we are challenged with the possibility of a movement producing healthy changes being led by mostly healthy people. This will happen only if men do their homework, study their internal worlds, have the courage to take their perspectives to the external world, and invite women to join them. Men can't say what men don't know, and women can't hear what men don't say.

APPENDIX

DOMESTIC VIOLENCE STUDIES OF *BOTH* SEXES

1. John Archer and Natasha Ray, "Dating Violence in the United Kingdom: a Preliminary Study," *Aggressive Behavior,* Vol. 15, 1989, pp. 337–43. Dating couples (college students) report that 48% of male partners and 65% of female partners committed at least one violent act in their current relationship (using Conflict Tactics Scale, as described in chapter 6).

2. Ileana Arias and Patti Johnson, "Evaluations of Physical Aggression Among Intimate Dyads," *Journal of Interpersonal Violence,* Vol. 4, September 1989, pp. 298–307. Ten percent of female college students and 15% of male students were physically aggressive in a current relationship; 19% of female students and 18% of male students were physically aggressive in a past relationship (using Conflict Tactics Scale).

3. Ileana Arias, Mary Samos, and K. Daniel O'Leary, "Prevalence and Correlates of Physical Aggression During Courtship," *Journal of Interpersonal Violence,* Vol. 2, March 1987, pp. 82–90. Ten percent of female and 10% of male students used severe physical aggression against current dating partner; 19% of female and 10% of male students used severe physical aggression against past dating partners (using Conflict Tactics Scale).

4. M. L. Bernard and J. L. Bernard, "Violent Intimacy: The Family as a Model for Love Relationships," *Family Relations,* Vol. 32, 1983, pp. 283–86. Four hundred sixty-one college students revealed that more females than males were abusive in dating relationships (21% vs. 15%).

5. R. E. Billingham and A. R. Sack, "Courtship Violence and the Interactive Status of the Relationship," *Journal of Adolescent Research,* Vol. 1, 1986, pp. 315–25. A survey of 526 university students revealed similar rates of violence between men and women, but women were three times more likely (9% vs. 3%) to have initiated violence when their partner did not.

6. Roger Bland and Helene Orn, "Family Violence and Psychiatric Disorder," *Canadian Journal of Psychiatry*, Vol. 31, March 1986, pp. 129–37. Random sample of 1,200 Canadians found that 14.6% of men and 22.6% of women hit or threw things at their spouse or partner.

7. Judy Rollins Bohannon, David A. Dosser Jr., and S. Eugene Lindley, "Using Couple Data to Determine Domestic Violence Rates: An Attempt to Replicate Previous Work," *Violence and Victims,* Vol.. 10, 1995, pp. 133–41. Eleven percent of wives and 7% of husbands in military couples were physically aggressive, as reported by the wives.

8. Jamaica Bookwala, Irene H. Frieze, Christine Smith, and Kathryn Ryan, "Predictors of Dating Violence: A Multivariate Analysis," *Violence and Victims,* Vol. 7, 1992, pp. 297–311. Twenty-two percent of women and 17% of men admitted being violent while their partner was not violent, in their current relationship.

9. Merlin B. Brinkerhoff and Eugene Lupri, "Interspousal Violence," *Canadian Journal of Sociology,* Vol. 13, 1988, pp. 407–34. A random sample of 562 couples in Calgary, Alberta, revealed severe violence rates of 10.7% wife-to-husband, and 4.8% husband-to-wife. Overall violence rates were 13.2% wife-to-husband and 10.3% husband-to-wife.

10. Lisa Brush, "Violent Acts and Injurious Outcomes in Married Couples: Methodological Issues in the *National Survey of Families and Households,*" *Gender and Society,* Vol. 4, March 1990, pp. 56–67.[1] A feminist found both sexes agree that 2.8% of women were victims of men; 3.8% of men were victims of women.[2] The survey contained over 13,000 respondents.

11. Judith Brutz and Bron B. Ingoldsby, "Conflict Resolution in Quaker Families," *Journal of Marriage and the Family,* Vol. 46, 1984, pp. 21–26. Quaker females acknowledged inflicting severe violence three times as frequently as Quaker males did (2.5% vs. 0.8%).

12. P. J. Burke, Jan E. Stets, and Maureen A. Pirog-Good, "Gender Identity, Self-Esteem, and Physical and Sexual Abuse in Dating Relationships," *Social Psychology Quarterly,* Vol. 51, 1988, pp. 272–85. A sample of 505 college students reported that in a one-year period, 14% of the men and 18% of the women inflicted physical abuse on their partners, while 10% of the men and 14% of the women received physical abuse from their partners.

13. Michelle Carrado, Malcolm George, Elizabeth Loxam, L. Jones, and Dale Templar, "Aggression in British Heterosexual Relationships: A Descriptive Analysis," *Aggressive Behavior,* Vol. 22, 1996, pp. 401–15. Eleven percent of men and 5% of women were victimized in their current relationships. A representative sample of 1,978 men and women in Great Britain was surveyed.

14. Michele Cascardi, Jennifer Langhinrichen, and Dina Vivian, "Marital Aggression: Impact, Injury and Health Correlates for Husbands and Wives," *Archives of Internal Medicine,* Vol. 152, June 1992, pp. 1178–84. According to the *wives,* 33% of husbands and 36% of wives were severely aggressive toward their spouse.

15. Marie B. Caulfield and David S. Riggs, "The Assessment of Dating Aggression: Empirical Evaluation of the Conflict Tactics Scale," *Journal of Interpersonal Violence*, Vol. 7, December 1992, pp. 549–58. In a sample of 667 college students, more women than men beat up their partner (2.3% vs. 1.9%), threw something at their partner (14.6% vs. 6.9%) and kicked, bit, or hit their partner with a fist (13.0% vs. 3.1%).

16. James E. Deal and Karen Smith Wampler, "Dating Violence: the Primacy of Previous Experience," *Journal of Social and Personal Relationships*, Vol. 3, 1986, pp. 457–71. Of 410 students at two southern universities, 6% of females and 4% of males were aggressors; 15% of males and 5% of females were victims in a current or most recent relationship.

17. Alfred DeMaris, "The Efficacy of a Spouse Abuse Model in Accounting for Courtship Violence," *Journal of Family Issues*, Vol. 8, September 1987, pp. 291–305. Of 484 students from four southeastern universities, 31.1% of females and 23.5% of males inflicted violence on their partners in the previous year (using the Conflict Tactics Scale).

18. Diane R. Follingstad, Shannon Wright, Shirley Lloyd, and Jeri A. Sebastian, "Sex Differences in Motivations and Effects in Dating Violence," *Family Relations*, Vol. 40, 1991, pp. 51–57. In a sample of 495 college students, 20% of females and 12% of males admitted using physical force in a relationship.

19. June Henton, Rodney Cate, James Koval, Sally Lloyd, and Scott Christopher, "Romance and Violence in Dating Relationships," *Journal of Family Issues*, Vol. 4, September 1983, pp. 467–82. Female high school students were more likely than male students to be the sole abuser of the other sex (5.7% vs. 1.4%). Sample size: 644.

20. Ernest N. Jouriles and K. Daniel O'Leary, "Interspousal Reliability of Reports of Marital Violence," *Journal of Consulting and Clinical Psychology*, Vol. 53, 1987, pp. 419–21. Husbands and wives agreed that rates of marital violence between them were approximately equal in clinic and community samples of married couples.

21. Leslie W. Kennedy and Donald G. Dutton, "The Incidence of Wife Assault in Canada," *Canadian Journal of Behavioral Science*, Vol. 21, 1989, pp. 40–54; and Earl Silverman, "A Proposal to Prevent Spouse Abuse Through Crisis Intervention for Male Partners," unpublished manuscript, Calgary Men's Cultural and Family Crisis Center (1996). The Kennedy/Dutton study collected data on violence by husbands and wives, but only the violence by husbands was published in the article, despite the fact that rates of overall violence by wives (12.4% vs. 11.2%) and severe violence by wives (4.7% vs. 2.3%) were higher. The Silverman article contains the data on violence by wives.

22. Katherine E. Lane and Patricia A. Gwartney-Gibbs, "Violence in the Context of Dating and Sex," *Journal of Family Issues*, Vol. 6, March 1985, pp. 45–59. More men than women said they had been beaten up (6.7% vs. 4.4%), but almost no women (0.5%) acknowledged doing the beating! The men were slightly more

likely to acknowledge beating up a woman (5.0%) than the woman was to feel that she had been beaten up (4.4%).

23. Mary Riege Laner and Jeanine Thompson, "Abuse and Aggression in Courting Couples." *Deviant Behavior,* Vol. 3, 1982, pp. 229–44. In "more involved" dating relationships, higher percentages of women slapped, scratched, and grabbed (23% vs. 11%), punched or kicked (5.5% vs. 4%), and hit with a hard object (0.5% vs. 0%).

24. Lynn Magdol, Terrie E. Moffitt, Avshalom Caspi, Denise L. Newman, Jeffrey Fagan, and Phil A. Silva, "Gender Differences in Partner Violence in a Birth Cohort of 21-Year-Olds: Bridging the Gap Between Clinical and Epidemiological Approaches," *Journal of Consulting and Clinical Psychology,* Vol. 65, No. 1, 1997, pp. 68–78. A survey of partner violence among 861 twenty-one-year-olds in New Zealand revealed that women had significantly higher rates of perpetration of minor violence (35.8% vs. 21.8%), severe violence (18.6% vs. 5.7%) and overall violence (37.2% vs. 21.8%) than men.

25. Jean Malone, Andrea Tyree, and K. Daniel O'Leary, "Generalization and Containment: Different Effects of Past Aggression for Wives and Husbands," *Journal of Marriage and the Family,* Vol. 51, 1989, pp. 687–97. A sample of 328 couples were measured just prior to marriage, then at six months and eighteen months after marriage. At each point, women were more likely to slap, kick/bite/hit, or hit their spouse with an object. There were no significant sex differences for the other aggressive acts measured.

26. Linda L. Marshall and Patricia Rose, "Premarital Violence: The Impact of Family of Origin Violence, Stress, and Reciprocity," *Violence and Victims,* Vol. 5, 1990, pp. 51–64. Four hundred fifty-four college students reveal that a higher percentage of women than men committed violent acts in eight out of ten categories of the Conflict Tactics Scale.

27. Linda L. Marshall and Patricia Rose, "Gender, Stress, and Violence in the Adult Relationships of a Sample of College Students," *Journal of Social and Personal Relationships,* Vol. 4, 1987, pp. 299–316. Among 93 single college students not in a current relationship, women expressed a higher percentage of actual violence than the men (46% vs. 39%) in previous relationships. Among 185 single college students in a relationship, a higher percentage of women than men (59% vs. 45%) expressed actual violence the previous year, and men had a higher rate among 30 married college students (73% vs. 53%).

28. Avonne Mason and Virginia Blankenship, "Power and Affiliation Motivation, Stress, and Abuse in Intimate Relationships," *Journal of Personality and Social Psychology,* Vol. 52, 1987, pp. 203–10. A sample of college undergraduates revealed that there were no sex differences in physical abuse or use of reasoning in conflict situations, but women inflicted significantly higher psychological abuse on their partners than did men.

29. Kathleen McKinney, "Measures of Verbal, Physical and Sexual Dating Violence by Gender," *Free Inquiry In Creative Sociology,* Vol. 14, 1986, pp. 55–60. Seven-

teen percent of women and 22% of men committed courtship violence that was self-defined; 26% of women and 21% of men committed courtship violence as defined by the researchers.

30. William H. Meredith, Douglas A. Abbott, and Scot L. Adams, "Family Violence: Its Relation to Marital and Parental Satisfaction and Family Strengths," *Journal of Family Violence,* Vol. 1, 1986, pp. 299–305. A sample of Nebraskans found 6% of male Nebraskans and 5% of female Nebraskans reported using severe violence at least once in the previous year.

31. Barbara J. Morse, "Beyond the Conflict Tactics Scale: Assessing Gender Differences in Partner Violence," *Violence and Victims,* Vol. 10, 1995, pp. 251–72. A national longitudinal study of young adults revealed that in 1992 women were more likely than men to commit any violence (27.9% vs. 20.2%) and severe violence (13.8% vs. 5.7%) against their partner the previous year.

32. Linda Nisonoff and Irving Bitman, "Spouse Abuse: Incidence and Relationship to Selected Demographic Variables," *Victimology,* Vol. 4, 1979, pp. 131–40. Random sample, finding 19% of husbands hit by wife; 13% of wives hit by husband; equal frequency and severity.[3]

33. Nona K. O'Keefe, Karen Brockopp, and Esther Chew, "Teen Dating Violence," *Social Work,* Vol. 31, 1986, p. 465. Two hundred fifty-six high school students reveal that more girls than boys were perpetrators of abuse (11.9% to 7.4%).

34. K. Daniel O'Leary, Julian Barling, Ileana Arias, Alan Rosenbaum, Jean Malone, and Andrea Tyree, "Prevalence and Stability of Physical Aggression Between Spouses: A Longitudinal Analysis," *Journal of Consulting and Clinical Psychology,* Vol. 57, No. 2, 1989, pp. 263–68. See tables in chapter 7.

35. David S. Riggs, K. Daniel O'Leary, and F. Curtis Breslin, "Multiple Correlates of Physical Aggression in Dating Couples," *Journal of Interpersonal Violence,* Vol. 5, March 1990, pp. 61–73. Thirty-nine percent of women and 23% of men report engaging in physical aggression against their current or most recent partner.

36. Boyd C. Rollins and Yaw Oheneba-Sakyi, "Physical Violence in Utah Households," *Journals of Family Violence,* Vol. 5, 1990, pp. 301–9. Random sample; finding severe physical violence by 5.3% of wives and 3.4% of husbands.

37. Linda P. Rouse, Richard Breen, and Marilyn Howell, "Abuse In Intimate Relationships: A Comparison of Married and Dating College Students," *Journal of Interpersonal Violence,* Vol. 3, 1988, pp. 414–29. More males than females reported being pushed or grabbed (25.0% vs. 14.6%), slapped or punched (18.8% vs. 9.8%), and struck with an object (8.3% vs. 1.2%) by their partner during their marriage.

38. R. J. H. Russell and B. Hulson, "Physical and Psychological Abuse of Heterosexual Partners," *Personality and Individual Differences,* Vol. 13, 1992, pp. 457–73. A pilot study of fifty-three couples in Great Britain showed overall violence rates of 25.0% and severe violence rates of 5.8% for the men; the women had an overall violence rate of 25.0% and a severe violence rate of 11.3%.

39. Carol K. Siegelman, Carol J. Berry, and Katharine A. Wiles, "Violence in College Students' Dating Relationships," *Journal of Applied Social Psychology,* Vol. 5, 1984, pp. 530–48. Using the Conflict Tactics Scale, 18.4% of women vs. 9.0% of men kicked, hit, and bit their partner; 18.6% of women and 11.8% of men hit their partner with something; 2.7% of men vs. 1.3% of women beat up their partner. Sample size: 504.

40. Reena Sommer, *Male and Female Perpetrated Partner Abuse: Testing a Diathesis-Stress Model.* Unpublished Ph.D. Dissertation, University of Manitoba, 1994. The Winnipeg [Canada] Health and Drinking Survey, with a random sample of 1,257 respondents, reports overall spousal abuse rates of 39.1% by women, and 26.3% by men. Women had higher rates of minor violence (38.0% vs. 25.9%) and severe violence (16.2% vs. 7.6%).

41. Susan B. Sorenson and Cynthia A. Telles, "Self-Reports of Spousal Violence in a Mexican-American and Non-Hispanic White Population," *Violence and Victims,* Vol. 6, 1991, pp. 3–15. Probability sample: authors report that "[non-Hispanic white] Women reported higher rates than men of hitting or throwing things at a spouse or partner. Women . . . were more likely to have struck first and to have struck first more than once." Gender did not predict spousal violence among the Mexican-Americans.

42. Suzanne K. Steinmetz, *The Cycle of Violence: Assertive, Aggressive, and Abusive Family Interaction* (New York: Praeger, 1977). She found that 19% of husbands and 18% of wives threw things; 10% of husbands and 10% of wives hit their spouse with their hands; and 5% of husbands and 5% of wives hit their spouse with something hard.[4]

43. Suzanne K. Steinmetz, "A Cross-Cultural Comparison of Marital Abuse," *Journal of Sociology and Social Welfare,* Vol. 8, 1981, pp. 404–14. In five of six countries (Finland, British Honduras, United States, Canada, Israel) she found that "the percentage of husbands who used violence was similar to the percentage of violent wives." Puerto Rico was the exception, with husbands more violent.

44. Jan E. Stets and Maureen A. Pirog-Good, "Patterns of Physical and Sexual Abuse for Men and Women in Dating Relationships: A Descriptive Analysis," *Journal of Family Violence,* Vol. 4, 1989, pp. 63–76. More males than females were slapped or had something thrown at them; more females than males were beaten up, hit, kicked, pushed, or shoved, in at least one relationship.

45. Jan E. Stets and Debra A. Henderson, "Contextual Factors Surrounding a Conflict Resolution While Dating: Results from a National Study," *Family Relations,* Vol. 40, January 1991, pp. 20–36. A national representative sample of 277 single dating men and women between the ages of eighteen and thirty found women engaged in higher rates of minor physical violence (38.4% vs. 21.9%) and severe physical violence (19.2% vs. 3.4%) than the men.

46. Murray A. Straus, Richard J. Gelles, and Suzanne K. Steinmetz, *Behind Closed Doors: Violence in the American Family* (New York: Anchor Press/Doubleday, 1980). This was the original nationwide random sample that sparked the contro-

versy after finding that 3.8% of husbands beat their wives; 4.6% of wives beat their husbands.

47. Murray A. Straus and Richard J. Gelles, "Societal Change and Change in Family Violence from 1975 to 1985 as Revealed by Two National Surveys," *Journal of Marriage and the Family*, Vol. 18, 1986, pp. 465–79. The 1985 survey was a national probability sample of 6,002 households; 12.1% of women vs. 11.3% of men were violent overall, while 4.4% of women vs. 3.0% of men used severe violence (using Conflict Tactics Scale).

48. Murray A. Straus and Glenda Kaufman Kantor, "Change in Spouse Assault Rates from 1975 to 1992: A Comparison of Three National Surveys in the United States," unpublished manuscript, July 1994. The most recent of the three surveys cited in the title had a national probability sample of 1,970 people and revealed minor assault rates of 9.5% by wives and 9.3% by husbands; severe assaults were perpetrated by 4.5% of the wives and 1.9% of the husbands.

49. Murray A. Straus, Sherry L. Hamby, Sue Boney-McCoy, and David B. Sugarman, "The Revised Conflict Tactics Scales (CTS2): Development and Preliminary Psychometric Data," *Journal of Family Issues*, Vol. 17, May 1996, pp. 283–316. Preliminary research using the revised Conflict Tactics Scale with 317 college students in dating, cohabiting, or marital relationships yielded 47% of men and 35% of women inflicting physical assault on their partners, and 49% of men and 31% of women receiving physical assault from their partner.

50. Maximiliane E. Szinovacz, "Using Couple Data as a Methodological Tool: The Case of Marital Violence," *Journal of Marriage and the Family*, Vol. 45, 1983, pp. 633–44.[5] Thirty percent of wives and 26% of husbands were physically aggressive with their spouses in a one-year period.

51. Edward H. Thompson, "The Maleness of Violence in Dating Relationships: An Appraisal of Stereotypes," *Sex Roles*, Vol. 24, 1991, pp. 261–78. Of 336 college students questioned, more women than men had used physical aggression (29.6% vs. 27.5%) and severe aggression (10.7% vs. 7.2%) against a dating partner in the previous two years (using the Conflict Tactics Scale).

52. Waiping Alice Lo and Michael J. Sporakowski, "The Continuation of Violent Dating Relationships Among College Students," *Journal of College Student Development*, Vol. 30, September 1989, pp. 432–39. The authors state that "more often women (women 35.3%, men 20.3%) claimed themselves as abusers."

53. Jacquelyn W. White and Mary P. Koss, "Courtship Violence: Incidence in a National Sample of Higher Education Students," *Violence and Victims*, Vol. 6, 1991, pp. 247–56. Feminists conducted a national survey of 6,159 college students and found 37% of men and 35% of women inflicted physical aggression; 39% of men and 32% of women were victims.

***See also Martin S. Fiebert, "References Examining Assaults by Women on Their Spouses/Partners," *Sexuality & Culture* (New Brunswick, NJ: Transaction Publishers, 1998), Vol. 1, pp. 273–86. Or www.csulb.edu/~mfiebert/assaults.htm.

BIBLIOGRAPHY

August, Eugene R. *The New Men's Studies* (Englewood, CO: Libraries Unlimited, 1993).

Baber, Asa. *Naked at Gender Gap* (New York: Carol Publishing Group, 1992).

Berkowitz, Robert. *What Men Won't Tell You But Women Need to Know* (New York: Morrow, 1990).

Bloom, Allan. *The Closing of the American Mind* (New York: Simon & Schuster, 1988).

Bloomfield, Harold. *Making Peace with Your Parents* (New York: Random House, 1983).

Bly, Robert. *Iron John* (New York: Addison-Wesley, 1990).

Branden, Nathaniel. *Taking Responsibility* (New York: Simon & Schuster, 1996).

Braver, Sanford L. *Divorced Dads* (New York: Tarcher/Putnam, 1998).

Brott, Armin A. *The New Father* (New York: Abbeville Publishing Group, 1997).

DeAngelis, Barbara. *Are You the One for Me?* (New York: Delcorte, 1992).

Dineen, Tana. *Manufacturing Victims* (Montreal: Robert Davies Publishing, 1996).

Dowling, Colette. *Cinderella Complex* (New York: Pocket Books, 1981).

Driscoll, Richard. *The Stronger Sex* (Rocklin, CA: Prima Publishing, 1998).

Farrell, Warren. *The Liberated Man* (New York: Random House, 1974; New York: Berkley Books, revised 1993).

Farrell, Warren. *The Myth of Male Power* (New York: Simon & Schuster, 1993; New York: Berkley Books, 1994, trade paperback).

Farrell, Warren. *Why Men Are the Way They Are* (New York: McGraw-Hill, 1986; New York: Berkley Books, 1988).

Fekete, John. *Moral Panic* (Montreal: Robert Davies Publishing, 1994).

Fillion, Kate. *Lip Service* (New York: HarperCollins Publishers, Inc., 1996).

Friday, Nancy. *The Power of Beauty* (New York: HarperCollins Publishers, Inc., 1996).

Friedan, Betty. *The Second Stage* (New York: Summit Books, 1981).

Gelles, Richard J. and Murray A. Straus. *Intimate Violence* (New York: Simon & Schuster, 1988).

Gilder, George. *Men and Marriage* (Gretna, LA: Pelican, 1987).

Goldberg, Herb. *The Hazards of Being Male* (New York: Nash Publishing Corp., 1976; New York: Signet, 1977).

Gurian, Michael. *The Wonder of Boys* (New York: Tarcher/Putnam, 1996).

Halpern, Howard. *Finally Getting It Right* (New York: Bantam, 1994).

Jeffers, Susan. *Opening Our Hearts to Men* (New York: Ballantine Books, 1989).

Jesser, Clinton J. *Fierce & Tender Men* (Westport, CT: Praeger Publishers, 1996).

Kammer, Jack. *Good Will Toward Men* (New York: St. Martin's Press, 1994).

Keen, Sam. *Fire in the Belly* (New York: Bantam, 1991).

Kiley, Dan. *Living Together, Feeling Alone* (New York: Prentice Hall, 1989).

Kimbrell, Andrew. *The Masculine Mystique* (New York: Ballantine Books, 1995).

Kipnis, Aaron R. *Knights Without Armor* (Los Angeles: Tarcher, 1991).

Kirsta, Alix. *Deadlier Than the Male* (London: HarperCollins Publishers, 1994).

LaFramboise, Donna. *The Princess at the Window* (New York: Penguin Books, 1996).

Lynch, Frederick R. *The Diversity Machine* (New York: Free Press, 1997).

Lyndon, Neil. *No More Sex War: The Failures of Feminism* (London: Sinclair-Stevenson, 1992).

Money, John. *Gay, Straight, and in Between* (New York: Oxford University Press, 1988).

Paglia, Camille. *Vamps and Tramps* (New York: Vintage Books, 1994).

Parke, Ross D. and Armin A. Brott. *Throwaway Dads* (Boston: Houghton Mifflin Co., 1999).

Pearson, Patricia. *When She Was Bad* (New York: Viking, 1997).

Philpot, Carol L., Gary R. Brooks, Don-David Lusterman, and Roberta L. Nutt. *Bridging Separate Gender Worlds* (Washington, DC: American Psychological Association, 1997).

Pleck, Joseph H. *The Myth of Masculinity* (Cambridge, MA: The MIT Press, 1981).

Robbins, Anthony. *The Giant Within* (New York: Simon & Schuster, 1992).

Roiphe, Katie. *The Morning After* (New York: Little, Brown & Company, 1993).

Rosenberg, Marshall. *Nonviolent Communication* (Sherman, TX: CNVC, 1998).

Schenk, Roy U. *The Other Side of the Coin* (Madison, WI: Bioenergetics Press, 1982).

Sexton, Patricia C. *The Feminized Male* (New York: Random House, 1969).

Sherven, Judith and James Sniechowski. *The New Intimacy* (Deerfield Beach, FL: Health Communications, Inc., 1997).

Simon, Rita J., Ed. *Neither Victim Nor Enemy* (Lanham, MD: University Press of America/ Women's Freedom Network, 1995).

Sommers, Christina Hoff. *Who Stole Feminism?* (New York: Simon & Schuster, 1994).

Steele, Betty. *The Feminist Takeover* (Gaithersburg, Md.: Human Life International, 1990).

Tannen, Deborah. *You Just Don't Understand* (New York: Ballantine Books, 1991 trade paperback).

Thomas, David. *Not Guilty* (London: Weidenfeld & Nicolson, 1993).

Thompson, Keith, Ed. *To Be a Man* (Los Angeles: Tarcher, 1991).

Tiger, Lionel. *The Pursuit of Pleasure* (New York: Little, Brown, 1992).

Wetcher, Ken, Art Barker, and Rex McCaughtry. *Save the Males* (Washington, DC: PIA, 1991).

Youngs, Bettie B. *Gifts of the Heart* (Deerfield Beach, FL: Health Communications, Inc., 1996).

AUDIOTAPES

Farrell, Warren. *The Myth of Male Power.* Check www.warrenfarrell.com

Farrell, Warren. *Understanding Each Other.* Check www.warrenfarrell.com

Farrell, Warren. *Why Men Are the Way They Are,* abridged. Check www.warrenfarrell.com

Farrell, Warren. *Why Men Are the Way They Are,* unabridged (Costa Mesa, CA: Books-on-Tape, 1988).

Farrell, Warren. *Women Can't Hear What Men Don't Say* (New York: Audio Renaissance, 1999).

RESOURCES

Men's Rights
www.mensrights.org

MenWeb & *Men's Voices Magazine*
www.vix.com/menmag

National Center for Fathering
www.fathers.com

The National Center for Men
www.teleport.com/~ncmen/index.htm

National Coalition of Free Men
www.ncfm.org

National Congress for Fathers & Children
com.primenet.com/ncfc

National Organization for Men (NOM)
www.tnom.com

The National Men's Resource Center
(*Menstuff*)
www.menstuff.org

(NOCIRC) Circumcision Information
www.nocirc.org

Non Custodial Parent's Resource Center
(NCPRC)
www.bayou.com/~ncprc

United Fathers of America
www.ufa.org

Wingspan
www.honeycreekpublishing.com/resources/
index.html

MEN'S ORGANIZATIONS WITHOUT WEB PAGES

Fathers at Home Support Group
PO Box 27161
Seattle, WA 98125

Joint Custody Association
(310) 475-5352

Men's Resource center/Lakeland C.C.
jshelley@lakeland.cc.oh.us

National Black Men's Health Network
(404) 524-7237

Society Against False Accusations of Rape
(SAFAR)
3405 Deer Park Dr SE
Salem, OR 97301-9385

Victims of Child Abuse Laws (VOCAL)
(206) 878-5135

Worldwide Christian Divorced Fathers
(WCDF)
(800) MY–DADDY

NOTES

1. Warren Farrell, *The Liberated Man* (New York: Random House and Bantam, 1975: New York: Berkley, revised 1993).
2. Warren Farrell, *Why Men Are the Way They Are* (New York: Berkley, 1988).
3. National Center for Health Statistics, 1996; based on estimated number of suicides calculated using 1993 U.S. population figures and suicide rates, as cited by Peter Brimelow, "Save the Males?" *Forbes,* December 2, 1996, pp. 46–47.
4. Interview of Dr. Laura Schlessinger in September of 1997 by Barbara Hoover of the *Detroit News* in "'Dr. Laura' Examines Why Men Do Such 'Stupid' Things To Their Lives."
5. George McCasland, discussing calls during the early '90s.
6. Term coined by Nicholas Davidson, author of *The Failure of Feminism* (Buffalo, NY: Prometheus, 1988).

PART I: THE SECRET TO BEING LOVED
1. UNDERSTANDING THE MOST IMPORTANT THING TO UNDERSTAND ABOUT MEN . . .

1. John Gray, *Men Are from Mars/Women Are from Venus* (New York: HarperCollins, 1992).
2. The root of the word "hero" is *"ser-ow."* In Greek, the connotation was "protector." The Latin root word for "protector" is *"servare."* From the same root-word family comes the word *"servire,"* meaning "slave," from which we get our word "serve." See Julius Pokorny, *Indogermanisches Etymologisches Worterbuch* (Bern: Francke, 1959); or, for slightly easier reading, *The American Heritage Dictionary of the English Language* (New York: American Heritage Publishing Co., Inc. & Houghton Mifflin Co., 1969), p. 1538.

2. GIVING CRITICISM

1. John M. Gottman, James Coan, Sybil Carrere, and Catherine Swanson, "Predicting Marital Happiness and Stability from Newlywed Interactions," *Journal of Marriage and the Family,* Vol. 60, February 1998, pp. 16–17.
2. Ibid., p. 13.
3. Harriet Lerner, *The Dance of Anger* (New York: Perennial Library, 1985), p. 5.
4. John M. Gottman, "Why Marriages Fail," *Family Therapy Networker,* May/June 1994, pp. 40–48.
5. John M. Gottman and R. Levenson, "Assessing the Role of Emotion in Marriage," *Behavioral Assessment,* Vol. 8, 1986, pp. 31–48; and John M. Gottman, "How Marriages Change," *Family Social Interaction: Content and Methodological Issues in the Study of Aggression and Depression* (Hillsdale, NY: Erlbaum, 1990), G. Patterson, ed., pp. 75–101.
6. A. Christensen and C. Heavey, "Gender and Social Structure in the Demand/Withdraw Pattern of Marital Conflict," *Journal of Personality and Social Psychology,* Vol. 59, No. 1, 1990, pp. 73–81.
7. M. Komarovsky, *Blue Collar Marriage* (New York: Random House, 1962); L. Rubin, *Worlds of Pain: Life in the Working Class Family* (New York: Basic Books, 1976). Cited in Richard Driscoll, Ph. D., *The Stronger Sex* (Rocklin, CA: Prima Publishing, 1998), p. 8.
8. M. Komarovsky, *Dilemmas of Masculinity* (New York: Norton, 1976); L. Rubin, *Intimate Strangers: Men and Women Together* (New York: Harper and Row, 1983); H. Kelly, J. Cunningham, J. Grisham, L. Lefebvre, C. Sink, and G. Yablon, "Sex Differences in Comments Made During Conflict Within Close Heterosexual Pairs," *Sex Roles,* Vol. 4, 1978, pp. 473–79. Cited in Driscoll, ibid.

2. Giving Criticism (cont'd)

9. G. Margolin and B. Wampold, "Sequential Analysis of Conflict and Accord in Distressed and Nondistressed Marital Partners," *Journal of Consulting and Clinical Psychology*, Vol. 49, 1981, pp. 554–67; C. Notarius and J. Johnson, "Emotional Expression in Husbands and Wives," *Journal of Marriage and the Family*, Vol. 44, 1982, pp. 483–89; H. Raush, L. Barry, W. Hertel, and M. Swain, *Communication, Conflict, and Marriage* (San Francisco: Jossey-Bass, 1974); C. Schaap, *Communication and Adjustment in Marriage* (Lisse, the Netherlands: Swets and Zeitlinger, 1982). Cited in Driscoll, ibid.

10. Driscoll, op. cit., p. 6.

11. John M. Gottman and R. Levenson, "The Social Psychophysiology of Marriage," *Perspectives on Marital Interaction* (Clevedon, Avon, England: Multilingual Matters, 1988), P. Noller and M. Fitzpatrick, eds., pp. 182–202; D. Baucom, *et al.*, "Gender Differences and Sex Role Identity in Marriage," *The Psychology of Marriage: Basic Issues and Applications* (NY: Guilford, 1990), F. Fincham and T. Bradbury, eds. Cited in Driscoll, ibid., p. 7.

12. Acknowledgment to Ron Henry for thought about the battle of the sexes.

13. John Condrey and Sandra Condrey, "Sex Differences: A Study in the Eye of the Beholder," *Child Development*, Vol. 47, 1976, pp. 812–19.

14. Alan Rozanski, MD, "Mental Stress and the Induction of Silent Ischemia in Patients with Coronary Artery Disease," *New England Journal of Medicine*, Vol. 318, No. 16, April 21, 1988, pp. 1005–12.

15. Gottman, *et al.*, "Predicting Marital Happiness . . . ," p. 17.

16. See my *Why Men Are the Way They Are* (New York: Berkley, 1988), pp. 342–43.

17. Survey conducted by Mark Clements Research of 720 teenage girls, 6% of whom had been pregnant. Sample representative of U.S. Census data geographically, and according to household income and size. Research commissioned by, and reported in, *Parade*, February 2, 1997, pp. 4–5.

18. For a full chapter explaining the differences between Stage I and Stage II societies, see my *The Myth of Male Power* (New York: Simon & Schuster, 1993; New York: Berkley, paper, 1994), chapter 2. If you wish to understand your parents, or children, this is the best chapter I've written on that issue.

3. Hearing Criticism

1. Warren Farrell, *Why Men Are the Way They Are* (New York: Berkeley, 1988), chapter 5: "What Makes a Man Successful at Work that Makes Him Unsuccessful at Home? Or Why Can't Men Listen?"

4. Expressing Feelings

1. If you're explaining this to someone else, just use the acronym "B•WISE" to remember them.

2. Sixty-four percent of working women left the workforce for six months or longer to take care of the family; 1.5% of men did. U.S. Department of Commerce, Bureau of the Census, *Current Population Reports* (Washington, DC: USGPO, 1984), Ser. P-23, No. 136, see p. 6, Table A, and p. 7, Table B.

3. U.S. Bureau of the Census, *Current Population Reports* (Washington, DC: USGPO, 1987), "Male-Female Differences in Work Experience, Occupation, and Earnings: 1984," Ser. P-70, No. 10, p. 13, Table 1: "Workers with One or More Work Interruptions Lasting Six Months or Longer, by Reason for Interruption." This is the latest data available as of 1998. (Often, data like this, which show women's work performance to be less than equal to men's in a given way, is discontinued "for budgetary reasons." Of course, a budget is just a priority list, and the pattern of studies with findings like this being discontinued may indicate an unconscious, or even conscious, priority.)

4. Douglas A. Smith and G. Roger Jarjoura, "Social Structure and Criminal Victimization," *Journal of Research in Crime and Delinquency*, Vol. 25, No. 1, February 1988, pp. 27–52. This study is especially significant not only because it controlled the poverty factor in this way, but because it analyzed data from 11,000 individuals in different urban areas.

5. Bryce Christensen, "American's Academic Dilemma: The Family and the Schools," *The Family in America*, Vol. 2, No. 6, June 1988.

6. Alison Clarke-Stewart and Craig Hayward, "Advantages of Father Custody and Contact for the Psychological Well-Being of School-Age Children," *Journal of Applied Developmental Psychology*, Vol. 17, No. 2, April–June 1996. The study *controlled the income of the dad and mom*, and compared the child in the dad's custody with the child in the mom's custody.

7. U.S. Bureau of the Census, *Current Population Reports*, Ser. P-70, op. cit.

8. The ten-hour difference comes from a combination of two sources: U.S. Bureau of Labor Statistics' findings that full-time working men average 45 hours per week, while full-time working women average 41; and the best diary research published in the U.S. Bureau of Labor Statistics' *Monthly Labor Review*, which shows that full-time working women overestimate the number of

4. EXPRESSING FEELINGS (CONT'D)

hours they work by seven hours a week, while men overestimate by one. The four-hour and six-hour differences are the source of the ten hours.

See U.S. Department of Labor, Bureau of Labor Statistics, unpublished data for 1996 from the *Current Populations Survey*, Table 25B, "Persons at Work by Actual Hours of Work at All Jobs During the References Week, Age, Sex, Race, and Hispanic Origin, Annual Average 1996." The men worked an average of 44.9 hours per week; the women, 41.0. Data provided by Mr. Howard Hayghe, Economist, Bureau of Labor Statistics, Office of Employment and Unemployment Statistics.

See also John P. Robinson and Ann Bostrom, "The Overestimated Workweek? What Time Diary Measures Suggest," *Monthly Labor Review*, Vol. 117, No. 8, August 1994, p. 19, Chart 1, "Values of the Difference Between Estimated and Diary Work Hours for Men and Women, 1985 Data (in Hours Per Week)." Among workers estimating 42 hours per week, men's overestimate was one hour; women's was seven hours. The *Monthly Labor Review* is a publication of the Bureau of Labor Statistics.

9. See Warren Farrell, *The Myth of Male Power* (New York: Simon & Schuster, 1993; New York: Berkeley, 1994), Part III: Government as Substitute Husband.

10. Richard H. Ropers, "The Rise of the New Urban Homeless," *Public Affairs Report* (Berkeley: University of California/Berkeley, Institute of Governmental Studies, 1985), October–December 1985, Vol. 26, Nos. 5 and 6, p. 4, Table 1 "Comparisons of Homeless Samples from Select Cities."

11. Department of Education, National Center for Education Statistics, Washington, DC. Their latest information available as of April 14, 1999, for school year 1995–96, shows that 642,338 women and 522,454 men received bachelor's degrees. That's a 23% difference. Put another way, women receive 55% of the degrees; men, 45%. The center projects the percentage of men will be 43% by 2003.

12. *Encyclopedia of Associations,* 1995, a guide to more than 22,000 national and international organizations, including business, governmental, military, educational, fraternal, hereditary, patriotic, sports, professional, etc. The ratio from the encyclopedia is 21:1. There were 1,908 women's organizations, and 89 men's organizations. I reduced the ratio to 20:1 because I based my ratio on a hand count from the name and key work index, which included organizations with either "woman," "women," "man," or "men" in the title. This missed sororities and fraternities with Greek names, and adult organizations with the names like Kiwanis and Elks, which are more likely to be men's organizations (although most are now integrated).

13. The Supreme Court has developed the "Compensatory Purpose Doctrine" in cases such as *Kahn v. Shevin* (1974). It is discussed in journals such as the *Harvard Civil Rights–Civil Liberties Law Review*, Vol. 21, pp. 171–225.

14. Jack C. Smith, James A. Mercy, and Judith M. Conn, "Marital Status and the Risk of Suicide," *American Journal of Public Health*, Vol. 78, No. 1, January 1988, p. 79, Figure 3.

15. Warren Farrell, *Why Men Are the Way They Are* (New York: Berkley, 1988), chapter 5: What Makes a Man Successful at Work that Makes Him Unsuccessful at Home? Or Why Can't Men Listen?, pp. 139–49.

16. Warren Farrell, *The Liberated Man* (New York: Random House and Bantam, 1975; New York: Berkley, revised 1993), see Part III on forming and running men's groups and joint groups with women.

17. Ibid.

18. Dr. Margaret Crepeau, a Marquette University behaviorist, studied 150 participants of matched backgrounds and discovered that those who cried were healthy while those who didn't suffered from problems like colitis and ulcers.

19. Dr. William Frey, a biochemist at St. Paul-Ramsey Medical Center, found that children born with a genetic disorder that prevents them from crying (*familical dysautonomia*) respond to even mild anxiety with an increase in blood pressure, perspiration, salivation, and red blotches.

20. Herb Goldberg, *The Hazards of Being Male* (New York: Nash Publishing, 1976), chapter 3: The Wisdom of the Penis, pp. 33–52.

21. *CNN Headline News*, July 14, 1998.

22. Farrell, *The Liberated Man*, op. cit., chapters 13–15, especially chapter 15.

23. Ibid., chapters 13–15.

PART II: IN THE HOME
5. HOUSEWORK

1. Arlie Hochschild, *The Second Shift* (New York: Avon Books, 1990).

2. John Skow, "The Myth of Male Housework," *Time*, August 7, 1989, p. 62.

3. Jim Miller, "Women's Work Is Never Done," *Newsweek,* July 31, 1989, p. 65.

4. D. Waggoner, "For Working Women, Having It All May Mean Doing It All," *People*, September 4, 1989, p. 51.

5. Skow, op. cit.

6. "The Trouble with Men," *The Economist*, September 28, 1996, p. 19.

557

7. Nora Boustany, "Women's Work Is Never Done," *Washington Post*, August 24, 1995; Barbara Crossette, "U.N. Documents Inequities for Women as World Forum Nears," *The New York Times*, August 18, 1995; and Doug Mellgren, Associated Press, "It's Official: Women Do Work Harder," *San Diego Union-Tribune*, August 18, 1995.

8. The press report graph is from the United Nations Development Programme, *Human Development Report 1995* (New York: Oxford University Press, 1995), p. 88, Figure 4.1 "Women Work More Hours Than Men."

9. Ibid. For the full list of countries (including those in which men were found to work more than the women), see p. 91, Table 4.1 "Burden of Work by Gender, Selected Developing Countries"; and p. 94, Table 4.3 "Burden of Work by Gender, Selected Industrial Countries."

10. Telephone interview on February 22, 1996, with Alexandra Bodanza, U.N. Division of Public Affairs.

11. Telephone interview on February 23, 1996, with Terry McKinley, U.N. Development Programme, Human Development Report Office.

12. Luisella Goldschmidt-Clermont and Elizabetta Pagnossin-Aligisakis, "Measure of Unrecorded Economic Activities in Fourteen Countries," U.N. Human Development Report Office Occasional Papers, a background paper for the *Human Development Report 1995,* op. cit.

13. United Nations Development Programme, Human Development Report Office, "The World's Women 1995—Trends and Statistics," *Social Statistics and Indicators* (New York: United Nations Publications, 1995), Series K, No. 12.

14. Ibid., pp. 105–6, 132. Table 8 on p. 132, shows that men in the United States in 1986 worked 59.5 hours to women's 56.4 hours. Study of Americans' Use of Time, 1986 (Survey Research Centre, University of Maryland) as cited in the United Nations. The study is by John Robinson.

15. Goldschmidt-Clermont, op. cit., p. 1.

16. Ibid., pp. 53–56. Another example of a citation: "*Statistics Norway*. 1994. Private Communication."

17. United Nations Development Programme, Human Development Report Office, "The World's Women 1995," op. cit. p. 104–5.

18. This paragraph is from Marian Burros, "Even Women at Top Still Have Floors to Do," *New York Times,* May 31, 1993, p. 11L.

19. Jerry Roberts, *Dianne Feinstein—Never Let Them See You Cry* (New York: HarperCollins, 1994), pp. 62 & 119, and telephone interview conducted May 6, 1996 by Alexa Deere with Colleen Haggerty, public relations/press assistant, Feinstein Senate Staff, Washington, D.C.

20. Telephone interview conducted April 19, 1996, by Alexa Deere with Colleen Haggerty, ibid.

21. Roberts, op. cit., p. 251, and Jordan Bonfante, "Charm is Only Half Her Story," *Time,* June 18, 1990, p. 24.

22. Roberts, ibid.

23. Telephone interview conducted February 20, 1996, by Alexa Deere with Ann Eagan, Senator Feinstein Community Liaison, San Francisco office. The biography recommended by her office is Roberts, ibid.

24. Roberts, ibid., p. 46.

25. Ibid., p. 87.

26. Ibid., p. 48.

27. Stuart Silverstein, "Differing Views of the Executive Glass Ceiling," *Los Angeles Times,* February 28, 1996, D1 and D13.

28. F. Thomas Juster and Frank P. Stafford, "The Allocation of Time: Empirical Findings, Behavioral Models, and Problems of Measurement," *Journal of Economic Literature,* Vol. 29, No. 2, June 1991, p. 477, Table 3 "Changes in Time Allocation in Five Societies, 1965–1980s."

29. John Robinson, "Americans on the Road," *American Demographics,* September 1989, p. 10. Men commute four hours per week to women's two hours per week. Of course, working mothers with young children are likely to commute even less, and fathers, because of their income-producing responsibilities, to commute even more.

30. Juster, "The Allocation of Time," op. cit.

31. Hochschild, op. cit., p. 284.

32. U.S. Bureau of the Census, Housing and Household Economics Division, Industry, Occupation, and Statistical Information Branch, Table FINC-08, "Earnings of Wife by Earnings of Husband in 1997." This is the latest data (as of April 8, 1999) for earnings of husbands and wives working full-time, year-round:

Total Household Income:	$66,205
Husband's Income:	$43,070
Wife's Income:	$23,135

Percentage of household income provided by full-time working husband: 65.1%

33. F. Thomas Juster, "A Note on Recent Changes in Time Use," in F. Thomas Juster and Frank P. Stafford, eds., *Time, Goods, and Well-Being* (Ann Arbor Institute for Social Research, University

5. HOUSEWORK (CONT'D)

of Michigan, 1985), p. 317, Table 12.1 "Hours Per Week in Activities by Age and Sex, 1975–1981 Samples of Rural and Urban Households," 1981 data for ages 25–44.

34. U.S. Bureau of Labor Statistics, Current Population Survey supplement file, March 1996, Table 2 "Hours Usually or Actually Worked per Week by Working Mothers and Fathers in Husband-Wife Families with Own Children Under 18 in Household, by Age of Children." With children under 18, working fathers averaged 45.4 hours per week; working mothers, 34.6. Some statistics in this table are estimates, but the 45.4 vs. 34.6 statistic is the average *actual* hours worked in March 1996. Special unpublished computer run requested by author. Computer run supplied by Bob McIntire.

35. Robinson, "Americans on the Road," op. cit.

36. This paragraph is from John P. Robinson, "Up Close and Personal," *American Demographics*, Vol. 11, No. 11, November 1989, p. 10. Men: 72.9 hours of leisure time; women: 74.7. Included in leisure time was time to eat, sleep, groom, take care of personal medical care, and other personal care, as well as the travel related to these activities.

37. John Robinson, "Time's Up," *American Demographics*, July 1989, Vol. VII, No. 7, p. 35.

38. Hochschild, op. cit., p. 3.

39. Skow, op. cit.

40. Hochschild, op. cit., back cover.

41. Ibid., p. 280. In addition, forty-five others were interviewed, consisting of babysitters, traditional couples, and single people, thereby making them irrelevant for publicity as to two-career couples sharing contributions to the home.

42. Ibid., pp. 63, 64, 80, 90, 99, 111, 115, 116, 134, 143, 151, 161, 166, 180.

43. Ibid., p. 282.

44. Marjorie Hansen Shaevitz, *The Superwoman Syndrome* (New York: Warner Books, Inc., 1984), Appendix B.

45. Credit to Fred Hayward of Men's Rights, Inc. in Sacramento for this thought.

46. CNA is a registered service mark and trade name of CNA Financial Corporation. Reprinted with permission.

47. United Nations Development Programme, *Human Development Report 1995*, op. cit., p. 88.

48. Sue Shellenbarger, "Work and Family," *The Wall Street Journal*, March 13, 1996.

49. Study was conducted by the Army Research Institute of Environmental Medicine from May to November of 1995. Cited in Robin Estrin (Associated Press), "With Training, Women Can Carry Heavy Load in Military," *The Indianapolis Star*, January 30, 1996, p. A3.

50. "The Harris Poll 1995 #68," Louis Harris & Associates, Inc., 111 Fifth Avenue, New York, NY. The survey asked, "We would like to know approximately how many hours a week you spend at your job or occupation, and that includes keeping house or going to school as well as working for pay or profit. How many hours would you estimate you spend at work, housekeeping or studies, including any travel time to and from the job or school?" Study available from David Sheaves, Institute for Research in Social Science, University of North Carolina, Chapel Hill.

51. Hochschild, op. cit., p. 281.

52. Don Sabo and Marjorie Snyder, *Miller Lite Report on Sports & Fitness in the Lives of Working Women*, March 9, 1993. The study is done by the Women's Sports Foundation, Eisenhower Park, East Meadow, NY 11554.

53. Hochschild, op. cit., p. 3.

54. Ibid., p. 278.

55. Joseph Pleck, "Are 'Family-Supportive' Employer Policies Relevant to Men?" in *Men, Work, & Family* (Newbury Park, CA: Sage Publications, 1993), Jane C. Hood, ed., p. 220. Pleck found this by examining the source Hochschild cites, which is John Robinson's 1965 research as adapted in *The Use of Time: Daily Activities of Urban and Suburban Populations in Twelve Countries* (The Hague: Mouton, 1972), Alexander Szalai, ed., Tables 3-2.2 through 3-2.4, pp. 642–47. In Pleck's words (and Hood, footnote #1, p. 234), "Although Hochschild (1989, p. 279, note 2) cites Szalai (1972, p. 668) as the source for the 17-minute estimate and a corresponding figure of 3-hours per day for working women, these numbers are actually taken from p. 642, and concern the subgroups of men and women who are employed and have children. My calculation is based on data reported on pp. 642, 644, and 646 for employed married men with children."

56. *The Use of Time*, ibid.

57. Pleck, "Are 'Family-Supportive' Employer Policies Relevant to Men?" op. cit. pp. 219–20.

58. *The Use of Time*, op. cit. Pleck is now at the University of Illinois.

59. The source was derived from research by John Robinson, reported in Pleck, "Are 'Family-Supportive' Employer Policies Relevant to Men?" op. cit., p. 220. Pleck found this by examining *The Use of Time*, op. cit., Table 3-2.2, p. 642.

60. Ibid. Pleck found this by examining *The Use of Time*, op. cit., pp. 642–645.

61. Ibid., *The Use of Time*, Tables 3-2.2–3-2.4, pp. 642–47.

62. Ibid. Tables 3-2.1 to 3-2.4, pp. 640–47.

63. Hochschild, op. cit., p. 4.

64. *The Use of Time*, op. cit., Table 3-2.9, pp. 656–57.

65. Hochschild says Robinson found that "men weren't doing more housework" between 1965 and 1975. See Hochschild, op. cit., p. 278.

66. Robinson found that between 1965 and 1975, married men had a 51% increase in their total housework (from 4.5 to 6.8 hours per week). See John Robinson, "Who's Doing the Housework?" *American Demographics,* December 1988, p. 31.
67. Juster, "The Allocation of Time," op. cit., p. 484.
68. Martha S. Hill and F. Thomas Juster, "Constraints and Complementaries in Time Use," in Juster and Stafford 1985, pp. 429–70, as cited in Juster, ibid., Table 3 "Changes in Time Allocation in Five Societies, 1965–1980s."
69. John P. Robinson and Ann Bostrom, "The Overestimated Workweek? What Time Diary Measures Suggest," *Monthly Labor Review,* Vol. 117, No. 8, August 1994, p. 17.
70. Ibid. p. 19, Chart 1 "Values of the Difference Between Estimated and Diary Work Hours for Men and Women, 1985 Data (in hours per week)."
71. Ibid. The men actually worked 43 hours per week; the women, 33 hours per week. (The men exaggerated by 12 hours, the women by 22 hours.)
72. Ibid., p. 18 and telephone interview April 26, 1996, by Warren Farrell and Alexa Deere with John Robinson, director, Americans' Use of Time Project, 1849 Spruce Street, Berkeley, CA 94709.
73. Robinson, ibid., p. 17.
74. Robinson, ibid., p. 16.
75. The *Bulletin of Labor Statistics,* January 1994. Pages XI–XVII list Australia, Canada, Denmark, Finland, France, Norway, Great Britain, and the Netherlands. In an interview December 19, 1996 with John Robinson, he said this was also true in Russia.
76. *Working Woman,* February 1996.
77. U.S. National Center for Health Statistics, *Advance Data,* No. 295, December 17, 1997, Health and Nutrition Table No. 195. "Visits to Office Based Physicians: 1996." Women averaged 59.2% of all visits to men's 40.8%, or 47% more office visits.
78. This is a rough measurement of floor space devoted to female personal items vs. male personal items that I do in shopping malls of U.S., Canadian, Australian, and British cities and suburbs (before or after speaking engagements). I have done this from 1985–98 as opportunity permits (Alberta, Cleveland, Kansas City, London, Los Angeles, Melbourne, New York, Orlando, Phoenix, San Diego, Seattle, Sydney, Vancouver). I look at floor space on the assumption that if women's or men's departments were not creating profit per square foot, they would be forced to give way to general departments or those of the other sex. In addition, I found that the more-valuable floor space (*e.g.,* perfume counters immediately as we enter a department store) was devoted to women's items. The survey is informal, by eye only, and subject to much improvement.
79. Hochschild, op. cit., p. 284.
80. R. N. Anderson, K. D. Kochanek, S. L. Murphy, "Advance Report of Final Mortality Statistics, 1995," *Monthly Vital Statistics Report* (Hyattsville, MD: National Center for Health Statistics, 1997), Vol. 45, No. 11, Suppl. 2, p. 19.
81. U.S. Department of Labor, Bureau of Labor Statistics, unpublished data from the *Current Population Survey,* March 1990. Interview with Howard Hayghe, February 20, 1996. The exact breakdowns are:

PERCENTAGE OF MOTHERS WORKING FULL-TIME, YEAR-ROUND,
WITH CHILDREN IN SPECIFIED AGE CATEGORY

Age of Children	Married Mothers	Unmarried
1–5	26.3	25.8
Under 18	33.4	38.6

82. U.S. Bureau of the Census, FINC-08, op. cit.
83. *Current Population Survey,* March 1990, op. cit.
84. Michael Tanner, Stephen Moore, and David Hartman, "The Work vs. Welfare Trade-Off: An Analysis of the Total Level of Welfare Benefits by State," *Policy Analysis,* No. 240, September 19, 1995, p. 21, Table 9, "Pre-Tax Wages Required to Earn the Equivalent to the Value of the Welfare Package, 1995." This is the total annual value in 1995 of state and federal welfare packages for a single mother and two children, counting tax-free cash and noncash benefits.
85. U.S. Bureau of Labor Statistics, *Current Population Survey,* supplement file, March 1996, op. cit.
86. Robinson, "Americans on the Road," op. cit.

6. Domestic Violence

1. Abigail VanBuren, "Dear Abby," syndicated column, *San Diego Union-Tribune,* Tuesday, May 28, 1996.
2. Sponsored by Ad Council and Family Violence Prevention Fund, as seen in *Time.* August 5, 1996.
3. Imagine Entertainment poster for *Fear,* which opened April 10, 1996.

6. DOMESTIC VIOLENCE (CONT'D)

4. Brochure titled "A Slap in the Face is No Solution," distributed by AMEND (Abusive Men Exploring New Directions), an agency of the United Way and a member of the Colorado Domestic Violence Coalition.
5. *Oprah Winfrey Show,* June 26, 1991.
6. Fred Hayward, Director of Men's Rights, Inc., *Media Watch Annual Survey, 1991.*
7. Ian Burrell and Lisa Brinkworth, "Police Alarm over Battered Husbands," *Sunday Times* [London], April 24, 1994, pp. 1 and 6.
8. Ibid., p. 1. Quote from Inspector Stephen Bloomfield of Kilburn, northwest London.
9. "Sisters *Can* Hit Hard," from the Teen page of *Parade,* September 27, 1998.
10. In nineteenth-century England and America, a man was imprisoned for his wife's crime. *Calvin Bradley v. the State,* 156, Mississippi, 1824. See R. J. Walker, *Reports of Case Adjudged in the Supreme Court of Mississippi* (St. Paul: West Publishing, 1910), p. 73, section 157.
11. Eric Anderson, Jimmy Boyd, and Tom Prihoda, "Fifty-One City Study of Issues Concerning Divorcing Fathers in Self-Help Groups," conducted by the Texas Children's Rights Coalition (Austin, TX), September 10, 1990.
12. Murray A. Straus, Richard J. Gelles, and Suzanne K. Steinmetz, *Behind Closed Doors: Violence in the American Family* (New York: Anchor Press/Doubleday, 1980). This was the original nationwide random sample that sparked the controversy after finding that 3.8% of husbands beat their wives; 4.6% of wives beat their husbands.
13. U.S. Department of Justice, Bureau of Justice Statistics, "Violence by Intimates," March 1998, NCJ-167237, from the BJS website: www.ojp.usodj.gov/bjs/. Twenty-nine percent of male victims vs. 17% of female victims reported that the offender had used a weapon.
14. "Letters" section, *Time,* January 11, 1988, p. 12.
15. Murray A. Straus, "Measuring Intrafamily Conflict and Violence: The Conflict Tactics (CT) Scales," *Journal of Marriage and the Family,* Vol. 41, pp. 75–88.
16. U.S. Department of Justice, Bureau of Justice Statistics, *Criminal Victimization in the United States, 1993* (Washington, DC: U.S. Department of Justice, Bureau of Justice Statistics, 1995), p. 10.
17. U.S. Department of Justice, Federal Bureau of Investigation, Bureau of Justice Statistics, *National Survey of Crime Severity* (Washington, DC: U.S. Government Printing Office, 1985), #NCJ-96017; conducted by Marvin E. Wolfgang, Robert M. Figlio, Paul E. Tracy, and Simon I. Singer from the Center for Studies in Criminology and Criminal Law, the Wharton School, University of Pennsylvania.
18. Ileana Arias and Patti Johnson, "Evaluations of Physical Aggression Among Intimate Dyads," *Journal of Interpersonal Violence,* Vol. 4, September 1989, p. 303.
19. Liz Brookins, Chairperson, Math Department, El Camino High School, Oceanside, CA; currently on leave, teaching at the University of California, San Diego.
20. June Henton, Rodney Cate, James Koval, Sally Lloyd, and Scott Christopher, "Romance and Violence in Dating Relationships," *Journal of Family Issues,* Vol. 4, September 1983, pp. 467–82. Sample size: 644. The smaller survey was by Nona K. O'Keefe, Karen Brockopp, and Esther Chew, "Teen Dating Violence," *Social Work,* Vol. 31, 1986, p. 465. Two hundred fifty-six high school students reveal that more girls than boys were perpetrators of abuse (11.9% to 7.4%).
21. R. E. Billingham and A. R. Sack, "Courtship Violence and the Interactive Status of the Relationship," *Journal of Adolescent Research,* Vol. 1, 1986, pp. 315–25.
22. Jan E. Stets and Debra A. Henderson, "Contextual Factors Surrounding a Conflict Resolution While Dating: Results from a National Study," *Family Relations,* Vol. 40, January 1991, pp. 29–36.
23. Mary Riege Laner and Jeanine Thompson, "Abuse and Aggression in Courting Couples," *Deviant Behavior.* Vol. 3, 1982, pp. 229–44. In "more-involved" dating relationships, higher percentages of women slapped, scratched, and grabbed (23% vs. 11%); punched or kicked (5.5% vs. 4%); and hit with a hard object (0.5% vs. 0%) than in the less-involved relationships.
24. M. McLeod, "Women Against Men: An Examination of Domestic Violence Based on an Analysis of Official Data and National Victimization Data," *Justice Quarterly,* Volume 1, 1984, pp. 171–93. As cited in R. L. McNeely and Gloria Robinson-Simpson, "The Truth About Domestic Violence: A Falsely Framed Issue," *Social Work,* November/December 1987, pp. 485–90.
25. Lawrence Diggs, "Sexual Abuse of Men by Women," *Transitions,* November/December 1990, p. 10.
26. Associated Press, "Elderly Man Says Wife Beat Him for Three Days," *Dayton Daily News,* March 9, 1984, p. 32.
27. Suzanne Steinmetz, "Women and Violence," *American Journal of Psychotherapy,* Vol. 34, No. 3, 1980, pp. 334–50.
28. Barbara J. Morse, "Beyond the Conflict Tactics Scale: Assessing Gender Differences in Partner Violence," *Violence and Victims,* Vol. 10, No. 4, 1995, pp. 251–72. Of the 13.5% of men who were injured, 14.3% of them sought medical attention (0.135 x 0.143 ≈ 0.019 or 1.9%). Similarly, of the 20.1% of women who were injured, 11.8% of them sought medical attention (0.201 x 0.118 ≈ 0.023 or 2.3%). Acknowledgement to Cathy Young.
29. Bill Waterson, *Calvin and Hobbes,* June 5, 1986.

30. The packet was sent by U.S. Surgeon General Dr. C. Everett Koop to the American College of Obstetricians and Gynecologists, January 1989. See "U.S. To Help Doctors Spot Spouse Abuse," Chicago Sun-Times Wires, *Chicago Sun-Times,* January 4, 1989.

31. Steinmetz, "Women and Violence," op. cit., p. 339. As cited in McNeely, "The Truth About Domestic Violence," op. cit.

32. Murray A. Straus and Richard J. Gelles, *Physical Violence in American Families: Risk Factors and Adaptations to Violence in 8,145 Families* (New Brunswick, NJ: Transaction Press, 1990). As cited in Murray A. Straus, "Assaults on Wives by Husbands: Implications for Primary Prevention of Marital Violence," Family Research Laboratory, University of New Hampshire, November 1989.

33. Study was of 272 couples, recruited for a study of "marriage and the family"—without preselection for their interest in domestic violence.

34. See for examples: Susan B. Sorenson and Cynthia A. Telles, "Self-Reports of Spousal Violence in a Mexican-American and Non-Hispanic White Population," *Violence and Victims,* Vol. 6, 1991, pp. 3–15; Henton, et. al., "Romance and Violence in Dating Relationships," op. cit.; and Boyd C. Rollins and Yaw Oheneba-Sakyi, "Physical Violence in Utah Households," *Journal of Family Violence,* Vol. 5, 1990, pp. 301–09.

35. Coramae Richey Mann, "Getting Even? Women Who Kill in Domestic Encounters," *Justice Quarterly* (Academy of Criminal Justice Sciences: 1988), Vol. 5, No. 1, March 1988, pp. 33–51.

36. I. P. Weston, "Battered Women Walk Legal, Lethal Tightropes," *Santa Barbara News-Press,* May 13, 1991, p. A1.

37. 1975 and 1985 National Family Violence Surveys, based on nationwide random population samples of 2,143 cases in 1975 and 3,520 cases in 1985, conducted by the Family Research Lab (University of New Hampshire), as cited in Murray Straus and Richard Gelles, "Societal Change and Change in Family Violence from 1975 to 1985 as Revealed by Two National Surveys," *Journal of Marriage and the Family,* Vol. 48, 1986, p. 470, Table 2.

38. Suzanne Steinmetz, "The Battered Husband Syndrome," *Victimology,* Vol. 2, 1977/78, pp. 499–509.

39. Interview with Suzanne Steinmetz, September 11, 1997.

40. Richard J. Gelles, "Research and Advocacy: Can One Wear Two Hats?" *Family Process,* Vol. 33, March 1994, p. 94. Confirmed in phone interview with Murray Straus, March 31, 1999.

41. Murray Straus, Phone interview, March 31, 1999.

42. Richard J. Gelles, "Research and Advocacy," op. cit. Gelles's co-editor was Donileen Loseke.

43. Leslie W. Kennedy and Donald G. Dutton, "The Incidence of Wife Assault in Alberta," *Canadian Journal of Behavioral Science,* Vol. 21, 1989, pp. 40–54. The research was conducted in 1987 by the University of Alberta's Population Research Laboratory. In an interview with Earl Silverman on September 2, 1997, he explained he received the censored research six years later from Bob Adebayo, who had assisted Kennedy and Dutton in the preparation of their original data. Even after Silverman received the data, he could not get it published. See Earl Silverman, "A Proposal to Prevent Spouse Abuse Through Crisis Intervention for Male Partners," unpublished manuscript, May 1996, p. 10.

44. Walter DeKeseredy and Katharine Kelly. "The Incidence and Prevalence of Woman Abuse in Canadian University and College Dating Relationships," *Canadian Journal of Sociology,* Vol. 18, 1993, pp. 137–59.

45. John Fekete, *Morale Panic: Biopolitics Rising* (Montreal: Robert Davies Publishing, 1994), pp. 79–80.

46. Walter S. DeKeseredy, Daniel G. Saunders, Martin D. Schwartz, and Shahlid Alvi, "The Meanings and Motives for Women's Use of Violence in Canadian College Dating Relationships: Results from a National Survey," *Sociological Spectrum,* Vol. 17, 1997, pp. 199–222.

47. Diane Hill, Director of Policy and Research for the United Way of Greater Toronto, E-mail of February 22, 1999.

48. Mark Schulman, "A Survey of Spousal Violence Against Women in Kentucky" (Washington, DC: U.S. Government Printing Office, July 1979), Study No. 792701, conducted for Kentucky Commission on Women and sponsored by the U.S. Department of Justice, Law Enforcement Assistance Administration.

49. See discussion in Murray A. Straus, "Physical Assaults by Wives: A Major Social Problem," *Current Controversies on Family Violence,* Richard Gelles and Donileen Loseke, eds. (Newbury Park, CA: Sage, 1993), pp. 72–73.

50. Ibid.

51. Tape obtained by Carlton A. Hornung, B. Claire McCullough, and Taichi Sugimoto, "Status Relationships in Marriage: Risk Factors in Spouse Abuse," *Journal of Marriage and the Family,* Vol. 43, August 1981, pp. 675–92.

52. McNeely, "The Truth About Domestic Violence," op. cit.

53. Linda Castrone, "50% of Women Feel Cold Hand of a Batterer," *Rocky Mountain News,* February 5, 1990, and Kathleen Hendrix, "World's Women Speak as One Against Abuse," *Los Angeles Times,* May 27, 1991, p. E1.

54. Straus, *Behind Closed Doors,* op. cit., pp. 43–44.

6. DOMESTIC VIOLENCE (CONT'D)

55. Wives initiate 61% of *all* divorce cases. When the couple has children, women initiate 65% of divorces. See "Monthly Vital Statistics Report: Advance Report of Final Divorce Statistics, 1987," National Center for Health Statistics, Vol. 38, No. 12, Supplement 2, May 15, 1990, p. 5.
56. Steinmetz, "The Battered Husband Syndrome," op. cit.
57. Suzanne K. Steinmetz, "A Cross-Cultural Comparison of Marital Abuse," *Journal of Sociology and Social Welfare*, Vol. 8, No. 2, July 1981, pp. 404–14. The sample from Puerto Rico was very small (82), as were the samples from Finland (44), Canada (52), and the United States (94).
58. Lynn Magdol, Terrie E. Moffitt, Avshalom Caspi, Denise L. Newman, Jeffrey Fagan, and Phil A. Silva, "Gender Differences in Partner Violence in a Birth Cohort of 21-Year-Olds: Bridging the Gap Between Clinical and Epidemiological Approaches," *Journal of Consulting and Clinical Psychology*, Vol. 65. No. 1, 1997, pp. 68–78.
59. Murray A. Straus, "Societal Change and Change in Family Violence from 1975 to 1985 as Revealed by Two National Surveys," op. cit. pp. 465–79. I am citing the 1985 survey for comparability to the Quaker survey published in 1984.
60. Judith Brutz and Bron B. Ingoldsby, "Conflict Resolution in Quaker Families," *Journal of Marriage and the Family*, Vol. 46, 1984, pp. 21–26.
61. Straus, "Societal Change and Change in Family Violence from 1975 to 1985 as Revealed by Two National Surveys," op. cit. to Brutz, ibid. I am citing the 1985 Straus survey for comparability to the Quaker survey published in 1984.
62. Rollins, "Physical Violence in Utah Households," op. cit.
63. Judy Rollins Bohannon, David A. Dosser Jr., and S. Eugene Lindley, "Using Couple Data to Determine Domestic Violence Rates: An Attempt to Replicate Previous Work," *Violence and Victims*, Vol. 10, 1995, pp. 133–41.
64. Sorenson, "Self-Reports of Spousal Violence in a Mexican-American and Non-Hispanic White Population," op. cit.
65. Gwat-Yong Lie, Rebecca Schilit, Judy Bush, Marilyn Montagne, and Lynn Reyes, "Lesbians in Currently Aggressive Relationships: How Frequently Do They Report Aggressive Past Relationships?" *Violence and Victims*, Vol. 6, 1991, pp. 125–26.
66. Pamela A. Brand and Aline H. Kidd, "Frequency of Physical Aggression in Heterosexual and Female Homosexual Dyads," *Psychological Reports*, Vol. 59, 1986, p. 1311.
67. Karl Pillemer and David Finkelhor, "The Prevalence of Elder Abuse: A Random Sample Survey," *The Gerontologist*, Vol. 28, 1988, pp. 51–57. The physical abuse rate of husbands by their wives is 26 per 1000; of wives by their husbands, 6 per 1000.
68. The National Longitudinal Study of Youth, Appendix C in Murray A. Straus, *Beating the Devil Out of Them: Corporal Punishment in American Families* (New York: Lexington Books, 1994), p. 25.
69. Joan Ditson and Sharon Shay, "Use of a Home-Based Microcomputer to Analyze Community Data from Reported Cases of Child Abuse and Neglect," *Child Abuse and Neglect*, Volume 8, Issue 4, 1984, pp. 503–9.
70. Claire M. Renzetti, "Violence in Lesbian Relationships: A Preliminary Analysis of Causal Factors," *Journal of Interpersonal Violence*, Vol. 3, No. 4, December 1988, pp. 318–99, Table 2, "Relationship Characteristics: Relative Dependency versus Autonomy Indices."
71. Magdol, *et al.*, "Gender Differences in Partner Violence in a Birth Cohort of 21-Year-Olds," op. cit.
72. Abigail VanBuren, "Dear Abby—Reflections from an Abused Husband," syndicated column, *Los Angeles Times*, March 8, 1989, Part V, p. 3.
73. *Time*, August 5, 1996. It is an Ad Council public service ad.
74. U.S. Department of Justice, Bureau of Justice Statistics, *Special Report—Violence Against Women: Estimates from the Redesigned Survey* (Washington, DC: U.S. Department of Justice, Bureau of Justice Statistics, 1995), p. 4. According to the FBI's *Uniform Crime Reports, 1992*, 900 women were killed by their spouses or ex-spouses (18% of 5,000 women).
75. *Information Please Almanac 1995* (New York: Houghton Mifflin Company, 1994), p. 838.
76. U.S. Department of Justice, Bureau of Justice Statistics, *Special Report: Murder in Families* (Washington, DC: U.S. Department of Justice, Bureau of Justice Statistics, 1994), p. 3. This survey is much better than the FBI's *Uniform Crime Reports* as an indicator of the percentage of wives and husbands who kill their spouse, since the FBI data has such a high percentage of the killers not identified (31% of the female victims' killers; 41% of the male victims' killers).
77. U.S. Department of Justice, Federal Bureau of Investigation, *Crime in the United States* (Washington, DC: USGPO, 1990), p. 11, table titled "Victim Offender Relationship by Race and Sex." The notes adjoining the tables state that Multiple-Offender killings are not broken down into gender categories. Only "Single Victim & Single Offender" crimes are broken down into gender categories.
78. The closest the government comes to reporting contract killing is the creation of a "multiple-offender" category (e.g., wife plus contract killer), which is what registers more than four times as many husbands as victims than wives as victims. See James A. Mercy, Ph.D., and Linda E. Saltzman, Ph.D., "Fatal Violence Among Spouses in the United States, 1976–85," *American Journal of Public Health*, Vol. 79, No. 5, May 1989, p. 596, Table 1—see Multiple Offender category. Based on 16,595 spouse homicides reported to the FBI from 1976 through 1985.

This contract-killing-as-the-female-method perspective is also confirmed by Louis Mizell, **6.** the world's foremost expert on contract killings, in an interview on July 18, 1996.

79. U.S. Department of Justice, Bureau of Justice Statistics, *Special Report—Violence Against Women,* op. cit.

80. Ibid., *Special Report—Violence Against Women,* op. cit. shows 900 wives killed by spouses or ex-spouses and 7,824 unidentified male victims, or 8.7 times as many unidentified male victims.

81. Eric Bailey, "Teen Sentenced for Helping Kill Wayne Pearce" *Los Angeles Times,* May 25, 1989; and Rocky Rushing, "Pearce Admits Having Sex with High Schooler," *North County Blade-Citizen* (Oceanside/San Diego, CA), March 2, 1990, p. A-1.

82. U.S. Department of Justice, Bureau of Justice Statistics, *Special Report—Violence Against Women,* op. cit. According to the FBI's *Uniform Crime Reports, 1992,* 41% of the killers of men were not identified, vs. 31% of the killers of women.

83. This paragraph is from the U.S. Department of Justice, Bureau of Justice Statistics, *Selected Finding: Violence Between Intimates* (Washington, DC: U.S. Department of Justice, Bureau of Justice Statistics, 1994), p. 6.

84. Thomas Kiernan in the "Voice of the Bar," the letter-to-the-editor section of the *New Jersey Law Journal,* April 21, 1988, p. 6. Kiernan said, "These events were advertised under such titles as 'Women's Strategies for Divorce' and 'Women: Know Your Rights in Divorce.'"

85. Renzetti, "Violence in Lesbian Relationships," op. cit., p. 391, Table 1.

86. Ibid.

87. The New Zealand study by Magdol, *et. al.,* "Gender Differences in Partner Violence in a Birth Cohort of 21-Year-Olds," op. cit., found that women were more likely to insult or swear: 67% vs. 53%. The New Hampshire study, from the 1992 National Alcohol and Family Violence Survey and based on a nationwide probability sample of 1,970 cases (with a 4X Hispanic oversample and the data weighed accordingly) was conducted by Dr. Glenda Kaufman Kantor of the Family Research Lab (University of New Hampshire). Raw data printout provided by Dr. Jana L. Jasinski (New Hampshire: Family Research Laboratory, July 8, 1996). It found 11% of the women threatened to hit or throw something at the man; 8% of the men threatened to hit or throw something at the women; 46% of the women insulted or swore at the men; 45% of the men insulted or swore at the women.

88. Ibid., the 1992 National Alcohol and Family Violence Survey.

89. Linda M. Harris, Ph.D. and Ali R. Sadeghi, "Realizing: How Facts Are Created in Human Interaction," *Journal of Social and Personal Relationships,* Vol. 4, 1987, pp. 481–95. She found this true not only of spouse abuse, but of sibling abuse and abuse between generations.

90. Julio Ojeda-Zapata, staff writer, *Saint Paul (MN) Pioneer Press,* October 21, 1990, p. 1B.

91. Todd Sloane, "Laurie Dann: Anatomy of a Killer," *Winnetka (IL) Talk,* May 26, 1988, p. D2.

92. *Chicago Tribune,* May 21, 1988, Section 1.

93. Maura Dolan, "Court Ruling Aids Women Who Kill Batterers," *Los Angeles Times,* August 30, 1996, pp. A1 and A26.

94. Warren Farrell, *The Myth of Male Power* (New York: Simon & Schuster, 1993; New York: Berkley, paper, 1994).

95. Suzanne K. Steinmetz, *The Cycle of Violence: Assertive, Aggressive, and Abusive Family Interaction* (New York: Praeger Publishers, 1977), p. 86. This was based on a random sample of families in Delaware. The percentage is so high doubtless in part because families were asked to keep a record of their conflicts and therefore did not just have to rely on memory—in which, perhaps, only the more severe conflicts are recalled.

96. The study's author is Ned Farley of the Seattle Counseling Service for Sexual Minorities. The study consisted of 114 lesbian abusers and 165 gay batterers. Cited in Ojeda-Zapata, op. cit.

97. Suzanne K. Steinmetz, "Battered Husbands: A Historical and Cross-Cultural Study" as reprinted in Francis Baumli, Ph.D., *Men Freeing Men* (New Jersey: New Atlantis Press, 1985), pp. 203–13.

98. Only 19% of those arrested under a mandatory arrest policy were re-arrested, whereas 37% of those to whom advice was given by police officers were re-arrested. Sherman and Berk, "The Specific Deterrent Effects," *American Sociological Review,* Vol. 49, No. 2, 1984, pp. 261–72.

99. G. M. Wilt, J. D. Bannon, R. K. Breedlove, D. M. Sandker, J. W. Kennish, R. K. Sawtell, S. Michaelson, and P. B. Fox, *Domestic Violence and the Police: Studies in Detroit and Kansas City* (Washington, D.C.: Police Foundation, 1977).

100. Sherman and Berk, "The Specific Deterrent Effects," op. cit.

101. John Johnson, "A New Side to Domestic Violence," *Los Angeles Times,* April 27, 1996.

102. Ibid.; and Steinmetz, *The Cycle of Violence,* op. cit.

PART III: OUTSIDE THE HOME
7. MAN BASHING

1. ©1997 Ephemera, Inc.: 541-535-4195; style 5560, in case you want to buy one.

2. *Webster's Unabridged Dictionary,* Second Edition (New York: Simon & Schuster, 1979). As of April 23, 1999, Merriman-Webster on-line had no definition of misandry.

7. Man Bashing (cont'd)

3. John Waters, "A Hate That Dares Us To Breathe Its Name," Opinion section, *Irish Times,* November 25, 1997. My favorite definition is in Patrick Arnold, *Wildmen, Warriors and Kings* (Crossword, 1992). Arnold says, "Misandry is the hatred of men. 1: the attribution of negative qualities to the entire male gender. 2: the claim that masculinity is the source of human vices such as domination, violence, oppression, and racism. 3: a sexist assumption that (a) male genes, hormones, and physiology or (b) male cultural conditioning produces war, rape, and physical abuse. 4: the assignment of blame solely to men for humanity's historic evils without including women's responsibility or giving men credit for civilization's achievements. 5: the assumption that any male person is probably dominating, oppressive, violent, sexually abusive, and spiritually immature."
4. Lance Morrow, "Are Men Really That Bad," *Time,* February 14, 1994.
5. R. N. Anderson, K. D. Kochanek, and S. L. Murphy, "Advance Report of Final Mortality Statistics, 1995," *Monthly Vital Statistics Report* (Hyattsville, MD: National Center for Health Statistics, 1997), Vol. 45, No. 11, Suppl. 2, p. 19.
6. The Office of Research on Women's Health is part of the Department of Health and Human Services' National Institutes of Health in Bethesda, Maryland.
7. Mark Thompson, "A Political Suicide," *Time,* May 13, 1996, p. 44.
8. After two years of analyzing thousands of print and video ads, Fred Hayward, director of Men's Rights, Inc., found that in every instance of a male-female relationship, if one was portrayed as incompetent, it was always the man. Men were also the objects of rejection, anger, and violence in the ads "100 percent of the time," he adds.
9. "Poll of Women Says Men Getting Nastier," *Herald-Star* (Steubenville, OH), April 26, 1990. Article cites poll by Roper Organization. In 1970, when women were asked if they felt men were neglecting the home, only 39% of women agreed; in 1990, it was up to 53%.
10. Interview on February 18, 1985, with John Markert, independent researcher and author of "Romancing the Reader: A Demographic Profile," *Romantic Times,* No. 18, September 1984 (based on his doctoral dissertation). Markert is the source for 25 million women reading romance novels. The "12 per month figure" comes from the calculation based on this plus the *Forbes* data in the next note.
11. Dana Wechsler Linden and Matt Rees, "I'm Hungry. But Not for Food," *Forbes,* July 6, 1992, pp. 70–75. *Forbes* reports that the average romance novel buyer spent $1,200 in 1991. The average romance cost about $5 in paperback in 1991, about $18 in hardcover. About three-quarters are bought in paperback, leading to the purchase of approximately 145 books a year, or 12 books per month.
12. June Ellenoff O'Neill, "The Shrinking Pay Gap," *The Wall Street Journal,* October 7, 1994. Ms. O'Neill is a professor of economics at Baruch College in New York.
13. The ads appeared in 1995. Thanks to the National Center for Men (NYC).
14. This ad spotted in *Glamour,* April 1990.
15. Ad for Dep hair styling products ("DEPreciate") in *People,* December 14, 1987.
16. This paragraph is from "Just Deserts," Periscope section, *Newsweek,* August 10, 1992, p. 4.
17. *Time,* May 13, 1996.
18. "Askew to You" by Recycled Paper Products, Inc., Chicago, IL.
19. In Your Face Cards (801-272-5357) by Recycled Paper Greetings, Inc., Chicago, IL.
20. Terrific T's; Langley, WA.
21. Penelope by Oatmeal Studios, Rochester, VT 05767.
22. From the Couch by Maine Line Company, Rockport, ME 04856.
23. Tastefully Yours by Maine Line Company, Rockport, ME 04856.
24. Interview November 11, 1998, Rachel Bolton, Hallmark media relations manager.
25. Ibid.
26. Shoebox Greetings/Hallmark Cards, Inc.
27. Quotes in this paragraph are from Shoebox Greetings/Hallmark Cards, Inc.
28. This paragraph is from Bolton interview, op. cit.
29. Shoebox Greetings, op. cit.
30. Bolton interview, op. cit.
31. Fresh Air from Paper Moon Graphics, Inc., Los Angeles, CA 90034.
32. Honestly Speaking from The Maine Line Company, Rockport, ME 04856.
33. Special Delivery from The Maine Line Company, Rockport, ME 04856.
34. Tastefully Yours, op. cit.
35. This is Not Art . . . Arnold J. Pigbutt III from The Maine Line Company, Rockport, ME 04856.
36. Tastefully Yours, op. cit.
37. Bernard R. Goldberg, "Father Knows Zip," *Men's Health,* Winter 1989, p. 94.
38. Associated Press, November 8, 1998. The story was reported on November 7, 1998 by *The Baltimore Sun.* The principal was about to retire, but was given an early leave of absence.
39. Wendy Steiner, "Declaring War on Men," *New York Times* Book Review, September 15, 1991, p. 11, in a review of Andrea Dworkin's *Mercy: A Novel About Rape* (New York: Four Walls Eight Windows, 1991).
40. This was from an ad in the *New York Times* Book Review, September, 1991, p. 11, endorsing Andrea Dworkin's book *Mercy: A Novel About Rape* (New York: Four Walls Eight Windows, 1991).

41. *The New Yorker*, July 6, 1992, p. 39.
42. Diane Mason, "Like Thelma, NOW's Ready to Kick Some," *San Jose Mercury News*, July 10, 1991, p. 9B.
43. Jeannette De Wyze, "Three Bullets and Nine Years Later: Betty Broderick Talks About Her Life in Prison," *San Diego Reader*, November 5, 1998, pp. 40–55.
44. Dan Kiley, *Living Together, Feeling Alone: Healing Your Hidden Loneliness* (Pawcett Book Group, 1991), pp. 5–6 of the hardcover version.
45. Ibid., p. 6 of the hardcover version.
46. Betty Friedan, *It Changed My Life* (New York: Random House, 1976), p. 244.
47. Elisabeth Hickey, "Honor Thy Father," *Washington Times*, June 18, 1992, E2. Also, AP, "Men's Rights Groups Want Jordan to Resign," *Houston Post*, February 4, 1992, p. A10.
48. Philip Lopate, "Can Innocence Go Unpunished?" *New York Times* Book Review, March 11, 1990. Review of Anita Brookner's *Lewis Percy* (New York: Pantheon Books, 1990).
49. The bold is Lady Foot Locker's. Copyright Lady Foot Locker, 1992.
50. This paragraph is from "The Trouble with Men," *The Economist*, September 28, 1996, p. 19.
51. *Mother Jones*, November/December 1991, p. 14. Ad for June Stephenson, Ph.D., *Men Are Not Cost-Effective: Male Crime in America* (Napa, CA: Diemer, Smith Publishing Co., Inc., 1991).
52. *Why I Hate Men* (Bayside, NY: Once Upon A Planet, Inc.; 1981). This is a Greeting Book, ISBN 0-88009-001-4. Once Upon A Planet, Inc. is at Box 220, Bayside, NY 11361.
53. Genevieve Richardson, *No Good Men: Things Men Do That Make Women Crazy* (New York: Simon & Schuster, 1983).
54. Author's role reversals.
55. NBC, *Tonight Show*, May 28, 1998.
56. The study is by Mary Koss, Christine A. Gidycz, and Nadine Wisniewski, "The Scope of Rape: Incidence and Prevalence of Sexual Aggression and Victimization in a National Sample of Higher Education Students," *Journal of Consulting and Clinical Psychology*. Vol. 55, No. 2, 1987, pp. 162–70 and Table 3. Among its publicity outlets were the *New York Times*, April 21, 1987, and Peter Jennings's ABC special "Rape Forum," following the documentary *Men, Sex, & Rape*, May 5, 1992.
57. See Robin Warshaw, *I Never Called It Rape: The Ms. Report on Recognizing, Fighting, and Surviving Date and Acquaintance Rape* (New York: Harper & Row, 1988), p. 63. This book is based on Mary Koss's survey.
58. Tom Cheney, "Axwell Pest Control," as seen in *Penthouse*, April 1989, p. 64.
59. Ann Landers, *Leader-Telegram* (WI), May 5, 1998, p. 3C.
60. Ann Landers, *Los Angeles Times*, June 12, 1988.
61. *Romantic Times*, estimate from their New York office, February 12, 1985. This estimate is also the agreed-upon figure of the publishing industry in New York.
62. Danielle Steel, *To Love Again* (New York: Dell Books, 1987 paperback).
63. Danielle Steel, *Crossings* (New York: Dell Books, 1987 paperback).
64. Rosemary Rogers, *Sweet Savage Love* (New York: Avon, 1990 reissue).
65. Lawrence Heisley. president, Harlequin Enterprises, as quoted in *Los Angeles Times*, September 26, 1984, p. 5.
66. John Markert, independent researcher and author of "Romancing the Reader: A Demographic Profile," *Romantic Times*, No. 18, September 1984 (based on his doctoral dissertation).
67. John McPherson, *Close to Home*, 6/27/97, Universal Press Syndicate.
68. Marine Winston-Macauley and Cindy Garner, *He Says/She Says* (Kansas City: Andrews and McMeel, a Universal Press Syndicate Company, 1995).
69. Don Addis, *Bent Offerings*, August 4, 1988, Creators Syndicate, Inc.
70. Kevin Fagan, *Drabble*, September 12, 1998, United Features Syndicate, Inc.
71. Sent by Fred Hayward, director of Men's Rights, Inc., Sacramento, CA.
72. Kathryn Holmquist, "Single Mothers Rule OK," *Irish Times*, February 2, 1998, Features section.
73. "Special Delivery," op. cit.
74. Recycled Paper Greetings; FAL-216847.
75. Shoebox Greetings, Hallmark Cards, Inc.; 165ZX 54-3.
76. "Forget Me Not . . . say it best" from 78th Street/American Greetings, Cleveland, OH 44144.
77. Ibid.
78. Scott Adams, *Dilbert*, April 18, 1998, United Feature Syndicate, Inc.
79. Ramada Inn TV ad, February 1992.
80. Ramada Inn ad; seen on NBC *Today Show*, 1992.
81. Sent by Bert Hoff, May 26, 1998: "New Medicines for Men," submitted by K. Lawson.
82. A. C. Nielsen ratings, 1984.
83. Glynnis Walker, *Solomon's Children* (New York: Arbor House, 1986), p. 27, pp. 84–85. Twenty-four percent of the children said both parents spoke badly of each other; 10% said neither parent said anything derogatory about the other.
84. Paper Moon Graphics, Inc., Los Angeles, CA 90034; RET 78-125.
85. The teacher is Barbara Wilder-Smith. John Leo wrote of this response in his *US News & World Report* column on May 11, 1998. Also mentioned in Carey Goldberg's "Saving Our Sons," *New York Times*, June 30, 1998.

7. MAN BASHING (CONT'D)

86. "He Said; She Said: Personal Math for the '90s" section, *Scholastic Math,* September, 1992, p. 4.
87. This paragraph is from Chris Willman, "A Valentine's Day Massacre: Women Put the Rap on Men," Pop Beat article, *Los Angeles Times,* February 16, 1991.
88. Noble Works, PO Box 1275, Hoboken, NJ 07030.
89. Randy Lewis, "Men, Stand Up and Take It," *Los Angeles Times,* March 22, 1987, Calendar section, p. 2.
90. *Glamour,* November 1983; *Seventeen,* December 1984; *Teen,* December 1984.
91. "Tastefully Yours," op cit.
92. Movie review by Gene Shalit, *Today Show,* November 3, 1998.
93. Assorted cartoons in section called "Power Failure," *Cosmopolitan,* May 1988, p. 174.
94. Forwarded by Bert Hoff, May 25, 1998: "From a post on MSN Men's Forum, from a woman."
95. Don Addis, *Bent Offerings,* March 13, 1989, Creators Syndicate, Inc.
96. The print ad was in *USA Weekend,* September 4–6, 1998, p. 16. The Direct TV television commercial ran during September 1998.
97. Yolanda © Richard Stine 1985; RS1018-100; Paloma Press, Ojai, Ca. 93023.
98. David Hiltbrand review of *Home Improvement* in Picks & Pans section, *People,* September 17, 1991.
99. Review of Tim Allen's *Home Improvement* in "10 Stars Ready to Soar This Season," *TV Guide,* September 17, 1991.
100. "New Fall Lineup Includes Lots of Three-Kid Sitcoms," *San Diego Union-Tribune,* in TV directory section for August 22–28, 1993, p. 7.
101. Tomato © Cards/Cornerstone Productions, a division of Recycled Paper Greetings.
102. Jon Pielemeier, "Gender & Justice in Washington State," *The Backlash,* December 1994, p. 8. Jon Pielemeier is the founder of the Men's Information Network, 206-328-0356.
103. Reuters, "Demand for Silence Jolts Defendant," *Los Angeles Times,* July 10, 1998.
104. Leo, op. cit.
105. "One-on-One" by Russ Berrie and Company, Inc., Oakland, NJ.
106. The 1920 statistics are from the National Center For Health Statistics, *Monthly Vital Statistics Report,* Vol. 38, No. 5, Supplement, September 26, 1989, p. 4. In 1920, the life expectancy for men was 53.6 years; for women, 54.6 years. Lifespan statistics from the National Center for Health Statistics, *Monthly Vital Statistics Report,* Vol. 39, No. 13, August 28, 1991, p. 17. In 1990, women's average length of life was 78.8 years; men's, 72.0.
107. "Too Bawdy at the Bundy's," Business Notes section, *Time,* March 13, 1989.
108. The awards were called "The Good, the Bad, and the Ugly Awards." See Courtney Kane, "Advertising," Media Business section, *New York Times,* September 23, 1998, p. C5.
109. Lewis, op. cit. Fred Hayward is the director of Men's Rights, Inc.
110. From Men's Rights, Inc., op. cit. Their newsletter of September 30, 1988, lists the best and worst in advertising.

8. MEN-IN-THE NEWS (LACE CURTAIN)

1. Term coined by Nicholas Davidson, author of *The Failure of Feminism* (Buffalo, NY: Prometheus, 1988).
2. James W. Boyce, "Manufacturing Concern: Headline Coverage of Male and Female Victims of Violence in Canadian Daily Newspapers, 1989 to 1992," 1994. MA Thesis, Wilfrid Laurier University, Waterloo, Ontario.
3. Ibid.
4. See, for example, Laura Sydell, "How the Media Slants the Message," *On the Issues,* Summer 1992, pp. 33–36.
5. Junetta Davis, *Journalism Quarterly,* 1982, No. 59, pp. 456–60, as cited in Jack Kammer, "On Balance: The Journalism of Gender," *Quill,* May 1992, p. 29.
6. Warren Farrell, *Why Men Are the Way They Are* (New York: Berkley, 1994).
7. Steven Svoboda, private correspondence, January 19, 1997.
8. I interviewed David Thomas, author of *Not Guilty,* on December 16, 1998, and Neil Lyndon, author of *No More Sex War: The Failures of Feminism* (Sinclair-Stevenson, 1992), on January 17, 1999.
9. Poll taken mid-May 1998, and mentioned on *CNN & Company.*
10. Gail Ann Schlachter, *Directory of Financial Aids for Women, 1997–1999,* biannual edition *Directory of Financial Aids for Women, 1999–2001* (El Dorado Hills, CA: Reference Service Press, 1999).
11. Phyllis Schlafly, "Feeding Their Personal Bias," *Washington Times,* March 1, 1991.
12. Michael Brenson, "Of Male Desires and Their Effects on Women's Lives," *New York Times,* May 21, 1990, p. B1.
13. The women in this survey reported receiving between 55% and 83% of their awards, similar to the Census Bureau reports, Freya L. Sonenstein and Charles Calhoun, "The Survey of Absent Parents/Pilot Results," July 1988, U.S. Department of Health and Human Services [hereinafter USDHHS].

14. This is documented in a memorandum from Robert Helms (Assistant Secretary, USDHHS) to Wayne Stanton (administrator, the Family Support Administration), October 1, 1988. The complete letter can be obtained from the National Council for Children's Rights, 202-547-6227.

15. The censorship is discussed in Murray A. Straus, "Physical Assaults by Wives: A Major Social Problem," in *Current Controversies on Family Violence* (Newbury Park, CA: Sage, 1993), Richard Gelles and Donileen Loseke, eds., pp. 72–73.

16. U.S. Department of Justice, Bureau of Justice Statistics, *Special Report—Murder in Families* (Washington, D.C.: U.S. Department of Justice, Bureau of Justice Statistics, 1994), Table 2.

17. U.S. Department of Justice, Bureau of Justice Statistics, *Special Report—Violence against Women: Estimates from the Redesigned Survey* (Washington, DC: U.S. Department of Justice, Bureau of Justice Statistics, 1995), p. 4.

18. When contract killing is discovered, the Department of Justice registers it as a "multiple-offender" killing—*it never gets recorded as a woman killing a man*. U.S. Department of Justice, Federal Bureau of Investigations, *Crime in the United States* (Washington, DC: USGPO, 1990), p. 11, table titled "Victim Offender Relationship by Race and Sex." The notes adjoining the tables state that "Multiple-Offender" killings are not broken down into gender categories. Only "Single Victim & Single Offender" crimes are broken down into gender categories. For various real-life examples of these types of killings, see my *The Myth of Male Power* (New York: Simon & Schuster, 1993; New York: Berkley, 1994), chapter 12.

19. National Council on Economic Education, 1998–99 test of 1,010 adults and 1,085 high school students.

20. Announced by Al Gore on April 3, 1998. Equal Pay Day in 1999 was April 8.

21. Associated Press, "Clinton Goes After Gender Gap in Wage," *San Diego Union-Tribune*, January 31, 1996.

22. These percentages come from an interview July 14, 1992, with Vivian W. Pinn, M.D., director of the Office of Research on Women's Health, National Institutes of Health. I also asked whether heart research, if it were done only on men, would be considered nongender specific (heart) or gender specific (only men). They had it categorized as part of the research *on men. There is no government agency focused on health that spends as much on men's health as on women's health.*

23. In a Medline computer search of over 300,000 articles on women's and men's health research for 1993, women's health research exceeded men's by 22 percent. See Steven L. Collins, Ph.D, of Nitro, WV: "The Amount of Biomedical Research Pertaining to Men, Women, and Both Sexes, 1985 through 1993," dated March 25, 1994. Women's health research exceeded men's each year, always by at least 14 percent.

24. R. N. Anderson, K. D. Kochanek, and S. L. Murphy, "Advance Report of Final Mortality Statistics, 1995," *Monthly Vital Statistics Report* (Hyattsville, MD: National Center for Health Statistics, 1997), Vol. 45, No. 11, Suppl. 2, p. 19.

25. Dr. David Gunnell, et. al., "Sex Differences in Suicide Trends in England and Wales," *The Lancet*, No. 13, February 1999, p. 557. Dr. Gunnell is with the Department of Social Medicine at the University of Bristol, U.K.

26. Centers for Disease Control and Prevention, *National Vital Statistics Report*, Vol. 47, No. 9, November 10, 1998, p. 5, Table B.

27. In 1997, 17.6% of males and 14.8% of females had no health insurance. The gap is widening. Data is from the U.S. Census Bureau, *Health Insurance Coverage: 1997*, Table 2.

28. The latest figures available as of July 1998 (as verified on March 26, 1999, by Cynthia Clark of CFOI) are from the website for the U.S. Department of Labor, Bureau of Labor Statistics, *Census of Fatal Occupational Injuries, 1997*, Table 4.

29. U.S. Census Bureau, *Health Insurance Coverage: 1997*, op. cit.

30. Edward E. Bartlett, Ph.D., "Alert! 'Healthy People' May Be Hazardous to Men!" *Transitions*, January/February 1999, p. 11. Dr. Bartlett is senior health advisor, Men's Health Network, Washington, DC. Their website is www.menshealthnetwork.org.

31. See "For Men Only," a publication of the American Cancer Society. Call 800-ACS-2345.

32. USDHHS, National Center for Health Statistics, Center for Disease Control, Statistical Resources, *Vital Statistics of the United States* (Washington, DC: USGPO, 1991), Vol. 2, Part A, Mortality, p. 51, Tables 1–9, "Death Rates for 72 Selected Causes by 5-Year Age Groups, Race, and Sex: U.S., 1988." The 25,000% figure is derived by comparing the 0.1 suicides for boys under the age of nine to the 25.8 suicides for boys between ages twenty and twenty-four.

33. USDH&HS/NCHS, Center for Disease Control, Statistical Resources, *Vital Statistics of the United States* (Washington, DC: 1987) Vol. II, Mortality, Part A. Here is the breakdown:

SUICIDE RATES BY AGE AND SEX PER 100,000 POPULATION

Age	Male	Female
85+	66.9	4.6

34. Pamela Newkirk; "A Mother's Nightmare: The Shocking Story of DES Sons," *McCall's*, February 1993, pp. 93–164. See also the *New England Journal of Medicine*, May 25, 1995; Vol. 332,

8. MEN-IN-THE NEWS (LACE CURTAIN) (CONT'D)

pp. 1411–16. For a review of the long-term effects of DES, see the *Annals of Internal Medicine,* May 15, 1995; Vol. 122, pp. 777–88.

35. We usually think of chlamydia as a woman's disease, but between the ages of thirty and sixty, men are three times as likely as women to actually have chlamydia. Preliminary findings suggest that chlamydia may be far more responsible than cholesterol, salt, or even lack of exercise in creating heart attacks among men in this age group. Hans-Udo Eickenberg. "Androtropia: Diseases Leading to Early Death in Men," paper presented at the seventh World Meeting on the Aging Male, February 1998.

36. Ibid.

37. Ibid.

38. USDHHS, "Healthy People 2010 Objectives: Draft for Public Comment," September 15, 1998, pp. 25-16 to 25-17.

39. AP, "Rate of Leading Types of Cancer," April 20, 1999, from AOL News. The incidence for prostate cancer is 135.7 per 100,000; for breast cancer, 110.7 per 100,000.

40. Prostate and breast cancer are funded by about twenty agencies of the National Institutes of Health (NIH) plus the Department of Defense (DOD). NIH data is from the National Cancer Institute's Budget Office, DOD data is from the Medical Research Programs Office. As of April 1999, total budget allocations (in millions of dollars) for fiscal year 1998 were:

	NIH	DOD	Total
Breast	$430.1	$135.0	$565.1
Prostate	113.6	38.0	151.6
Ratio	3:79	3:55	3:73

41. AP, "More Cancer Stamps To Be Printed," January 21, 1999. Two hundred eighty million special stamps at 7 cents above the normal cost are printed as of January 1999, and will be on sale until July 2000. The first sixty-one million raised $4.9 million.

42. See N. P. Roos, "Mortality and Recuperation After Open and Transurethral Resection of the Prostate for Benign Prostatic Hyperplasia," *New England Journal of Medicine,* Vol. 320, No. 17, April 27, 1989, pp. 1120–24.

43. Written correspondence to me from Charles P. McDowell, Ph.D., M.P.A., M.L.S., Supervisory Special Agent of the U.S. Air Force Office of Special Investigations, March 20, 1992. This is based on an Air Force study of 556 rape allegations, the methodology and details of which are explained in my *The Myth of Male Power* (New York: Simon & Schuster, 1993; New York: Berkley, 1994), p. 322.

44. Speech by Norma Juliet Wikler, founding director of the National Judicial Education Project, on its decision to be sponsored by the NOW Legal Defense & Education Fund and the National Association of Women Judges. See Norma Juliet Wikler, "Water on Stone: A Perspective of the Movement to Eliminate Gender Bias in the Courts," keynote address, National Conference on Gender Bias in the Courts, Williamsburg, VA, May 18, 1989.

45. Most have a ratio of about three or four women to one man. They usually include no men's activists and approximately half women's activists. See, for example, Bruce Hight, "Male Group Says Too Many Women on Panel," *Austin American-Statesman,* January 31, 1992.

46. Allan R. Gold, "Sex Bias Is Found Pervading Courts," *New York Times,* July 2, 1989.

47. Ibid.

48. Title IX states, "No person in the United States shall, on the basis of sex, be excluded from participation in, be denied the benefits of, or be subjected to discrimination under any education program or activity receiving Federal financial assistance."

49. *Chronicle of Higher Education Almanac Issue, 1997,* pp. 18 and 22.

50. National Center for Education Statistics, *Digest of Education Statistics, 1996* (Washington, DC: U.S. Department of Education, 1996), NCES, pp. 96-133.

51. Frederick R. Lynch, *The Diversity Machine* (New York: The Free Press/Simon & Schuster, 1997), p. 320.

52. The numbers in this paragraph are the best estimates of San Diego State University's Bonnie Zimmerman, president, National Women's Studies Association, interviewed February 11, 1999.

53. Young America Foundation, *Comedy and Tragedy: College Course Descriptions and What They Tell Us About Higher Education Today, 1998–99* (Herndon, VA: YAF, 1998).

54. Ibid.

55. See my *The Myth of Male Power* (New York: Simon & Schuster, 1993; New York: Berkley, 1994), chapter 1.

56. David G. Savage, "Forbidden Words on Campus," *Los Angeles Times,* February 12, 1991, front page.

57. Ibid.

58. George F. Will, Washington Post Writers Group, *Washington Post,* October 20, 1991.

59. Asa Baber, "Feminist U," in the Men column, *Playboy,* September 1988.

60. Sam Femiano, a leader in feminist men's studies, estimates 400 courses to have been taught in recent years, perhaps 100 in any given year. D. Scott Campbell finds about three to include male

positive required reading. (E-mail at campbell@alberti.unh.edu.) Perhaps the most pioneering curriculum in the world is at Manakau Institute of Technology in Auckland, New Zealand, headed by Doug Stevens, chair, Department of Social Sciences.

61. At Hobart and William Smith Colleges (two colleges combined on one campus), in Geneva, NY.
62. E-mail on February 10, 1999 from Rocco "Chip" Capraro (capraro@hws.edu), who teaches the overview theories of masculinity course for the men's studies minor at Hobart and William Smith Colleges, Geneva, NY.
63. Ben Dobbin, Associated Press, "Male Studies—Not Just a Guy Thing," *Los Angeles Times,* July 20, 1997, pp. E1 and E4.
64. Two attorneys who have begun to look into this are Cindy McNeely in Tallahassee, Florida, and Steven Svoboda in Berkeley, California.
65. Larry Gordon, "Mills College Will Begin Admitting Men," *Los Angeles Times,* May 4, 1990, p. A3.
66. Richard Driscoll, Ph.D., *The Stronger Sex* (Rocklin, CA: Prima Publishing, 1998), p. 283. Driscoll received figures for Episcopal, Methodist, Presbyterian, and Unitarian seminaries.
67. Mary Daly, *Beyond God the Father* (Boston: Beacon, 1973), p. 13.
68. The most-widely used Bible is the New Revised Standard Version. See John Dart, "Revised Bible Tones Down References to 'Man'," *Los Angeles Times,* May 27, 1989, p. 8J.
69. In San Francisco, 96% of the adult homeless are men; in other cities, there are fewer—a median of 85% men. Richard H. Ropers, "The Rise of the New Urban Homeless," *Public Affairs Report* (Berkeley: University of California/Berkeley, Institute of Governmental Studies, 1985), October/December 1985, Vol. 26, Nos. 5 and 6, p. 4, Table 1.
70. Adam Bromberg, "Data In: Multiculturalism Gaining Ground," *Campus,* Spring 1992, p. 9.
71. John Leo, "The Professors of Dogmatism," On Society page, *US News & World Report,* January 18, 1993, p. 25; and George F. Will, 'The Tempest'? It's 'Really' About Imperialism. Emily Dickinson's Poetry? Masturbation," Literary Politics column, *Newsweek,* April 22, 1991, p. 72.
72. At Brooklyn College's Department of Sociology; in psychology at the California School of Professional Psychology; at Rutgers University in political science; at American University in public administration, and then in the Department of Women's Studies at San Diego State University.
73. American Association of University Women, *How Schools Shortchange Girls: A Study of Major Findings on Girls and Education,* (Washington, DC: AAUW Educational Foundation, The Wellesley College Center for Research on Women, 1992). The updated study is American Association of University Women, *Gender Gaps: Where Schools Still Fail Our Children* (Washington, DC: AAUW Educational Foundation, The Wellesley College Center for Research on Women 1998).
74. See, for example, Julie N. Lynem, "Bay Area Academies Stress Learning and Self-Esteem," *San Francisco Chronicle,* December 8, 1998, front page.
75. Tamar Lewin, "Amid Equity Concerns, Girls' Schools Thrive," *New York Times,* Sunday, April 11, 1999, p. 1.
76. It is the Young Women's Leadership School. Ibid.
77. Study released on November 10, 1998. See Linda Perlstein, "Kids Draw a Blank on Arts Test," *Washington Post,* November, 11, 1998, p. D1.
78. Test was administered by William Pollack, Harvard Medical School psychologist, to 150 teenage boys. See Donna Laframboise, "Why Boys Are in Trouble," *National Post* (Canada), January 5, 1999.
79. Ibid.
80. Tamar Lewin, "American Colleges Begin to Ask, Where Have All the Men Gone?" *New York Times,* Sunday, December 6, 1998, pp. 1–28.
81. Adapted from AAUW/Greenberg-Lake, *Expectations and Aspirations: Gender Roles and Self-Esteem* (Washington, DC: Greenberg-Lake, 1990), Data Report and Banners, p. 18, as cited in Judith S. Kleinfeld, "The Myth that Schools Shortchange Girls: Social Science in the Service of Deception," a Women's Freedom Network Executive Report, 1998, p. 29, Table 16.
82. National Center for Education Statistics, *Digest of Education Statistics, 1997* (Washington, DC: U.S. Department of Education, 1997), NCES 97-338, Tables 107, 113, 118, and 126. Cited in Kleinfeld, ibid., p. 9, Table 4.
83. Adapted from J. Sanders, J. Koch, and J. Urso, *Gender Equity Right from the Start* (Mahwah, NJ: Lawrence Erlbaum, 1997), p. 12, and based on U.S. Department of Education, National Center for Education Statistics, *The Condition of Education 1996* (Washington, DC: U.S. Department of Education, 1996), p. 100. Cited in Kleinfeld, ibid., p. 13, Table 7.
84. National Center for Education Statistics, *Digest of Education Statistics, 1997,* op. cit.
85. Sanders, et. al., op. cit. p. 12, and based on *The Condition of Education, 1996,* op. cit. Cited in Kleinfeld, ibid., p. 13, Table 7.
86. The study is AAUW/Greenberg-Lake, *Expectations and Aspirations,* op. cit., p. 25, Table 14. "Boys and Girls Believe Teachers Give More Attention to Girls."
87. Kleinfeld, op. cit. p. 24. Paragraph two describes the difficulties she, as well Christina Hoff Sommers (author, *Who Stole Feminism?*), had in obtaining the full data reports.
88. Cathy Schoen, Karen Davis, Karen Scott Collins, Linda Greenberg, Catherine DesRoches, and Melinda Abrams, *The Commonwealth Fund Survey of the Health of Adolescent Girls* (New York: The Commonwealth Fund, 1997). Data tabulations, as cited in Kleinfeld, ibid., p. 28, Table 15.

8. MEN-IN-THE NEWS (LACE CURTAIN) (CONT'D)

89. L. Harris, *The Metropolitan Life Survey of the American Teacher, 1997: Examining Gender Issues in Public Schools* (New York: Louis Harris and Associates, 1997).
90. Lewin, "American Colleges Begin to Ask," op. cit.
91. Ibid.
92. Tamar Lewin, "How Boys Lost Out to Girl Power," *New York Times*, December 13, 1998.
93. "How the Poll Was Taken," *New York Times*, August 20, 1989, Section Y, p. 16, regarding front page article by Lisa Belkin, "Bars to Equality of Sexes Seen As Eroding, Slowly," *New York Times*, August 20, 1989.
94. Ibid.
95. "The 1995 Virginia Slims Opinion Poll—An Overview," news release/Judy Tenzer, Cohn & Wolfe, September 12, 1995, p. 1. The sample was 3,000 women and 1,000 men.
96. Gary Langer, "Survey Has Message for Men: Shape Up, You Oversexed Pigs," *Daily Camera* (Denver), April 26, 1990.
97. Associated Press, "Women: More Men Are Pigs," *San Francisco Chronicle*, April 26, 1990, p. B3.
98. Ibid.
99. The Gallup Organization, "Gender and Society: Status and Stereotypes, an International Gallup Poll Report," March 1996.
100. June 27, 1994 covers: O. J. Simpson Covers: "Trail of Blood," *Newsweek*: "An American Tragedy," *Time*; and December 1, 1997 covers: "Miracle in Iowa," *Time*, "We're Trusting in God," *Newsweek*.
101. Paul Bedard, "Syphilis Survivors Get Late Apology: Clinton Responds to 'Racist' Testing," *Washington Times*, May 17, 1997, p. A2.
102. For example, see M. Junior Bridge, "Marginalizing Women: Front-Page News Coverage of Females Declines in 1996," a publication of Women, Men, and Media, copyright © 1996 by Unabridged Communications.
103. Cover Story: "Nicole Kidman bares all—about her daring Broadway debut, marriage to Tom Cruise, and their fight for privacy," *Newsweek*, December 14, 1998.
104. See Bob Sipchen, "The Worried Women Block Prefers Clinton," *Los Angeles Times*, April 29, 1996, pp. A1 and A12.
105. Associated Press, "Couple's Makeup Kiss Gets a Bit Nippy for Husband," *St. Louis Post-Dispatch*, August 5, 1994.
106. Jerry Cassidy complained about this headline to Kathy Richardson, the chief copy editor of the *St. Louis Post-Dispatch* and was told, "It was supposed to be an upbeat story."
107. "Another Biological Clock," *Newsweek*, February 15, 1999, p. 6.
108. Lloyd Shearer, "Short End of the Stick," *Parade*, June 10, 1990, p. 20.
109. "Women Look to Gain Power in Bosnia," *Parade*, June 21, 1998, p. 10.
110. Tracy Wilkinson, *Times* staff writer, "Women of Bosnia Try to Rebuild," *Los Angeles Times*, May 16, 1996, front page. The subtitle reads: "The war has robbed many communities of their husbands, fathers and sons. In this patriarchal society, those left behind must learn to handle money, deal with authorities and survive bitter loneliness."
111. Ibid.
112. Front Cover: "The Truth About Women's Bodies," *Time*, March 8, 1999.
113. Front Cover: "What Every Woman Needs to Know," Special Edition: Health for Life issue, *Newsweek*, Spring/Summer 1999.
114. Front Cover: "From WWI to Vietnam: The Grunts and the Great Men—In Their Own Words. Americans at War," Voices of the Century issue, *Newsweek*, March 8, 1999.
115. I will be specific about all these differences in a book to be published in 2000 or 2001 (*25 Ways to Higher Pay*).
116. See this book's chapter on domestic violence.
117. Jack Kammer, *Good Will Toward Men* (New York: St. Martin's Press, 1994).
118. In-person interview, April 21, 1999, in Encinitas, California.
119. *New York Times*, June 22, 1997. A twenty-eight-page special section. Nothing on men's health.
120. Natalie Angier, "Men. Are Women Better Off with Them, or Without Them?" *New York Times*, June 21, 1998.
121. Ibid.
122. These lines are the front-page teaser for the articles by Gina Kolata, "No Sex Please, We're Female," *Los Angeles Times*, June 21, 1998, p. 3.
123. *New York Times*, Men's Health Special Section, Section D, February 17, 1999.
124. Natalie Angier, "Why Men Don't Last: Self-Destruction as a Way of Life," in ibid., p. 8.
125. Front-page teaser titled "Nasty Habits," for Angier, ibid.
126. William Grimes, "When It Comes to Food, Guys Have All the Luck," Men's Health Special Section, *New York Times*, op. cit., p. 6.
127. Robert Lipsyte, "Don't Take Your Medicine Like a Man: As Patients, Men Are Impatient, or Uneasy, or Both. They Need to Get a Grip, Like Women," Men's Health Special Section, *New York Times*, op. cit., main article on front page of section.
128. "New Cancer Cases Decreasing . . . But Minorities and Women Are Still Particularly at Risk," *New York Times*, March 13, 1998.

129. Natalie Angier (New York Times), "Report Finds Males Weak Link in the Evolution of Species," San Francisco Chronicle, May 17, 1994.
130. Natalie Angier, "Men, Women, Sex, and Darwin," New York Times Magazine, February 21, 1999, pp. 48–53.
131. Robert Lipsyte, "Violence Translates at Home," New York Times, January 31, 1993, p. L5.
132. See Christina Hoff Sommers, Who Stole Feminism? (New York: Simon & Schuster, 1994), especially chapter 9, "Noble Lies," pp. 188–208. This "Super Bowl hoax," as Sommers called it, was perpetrated in many major newspapers and other media. Here is a summary of some of Hoff Sommers's findings.

   Fairness and Accuracy in Reporting (FAIR), quoted in their literature a 40% rise in abuse during the Super Bowl, a statistic cited by Sheila Kuehl of the California Women's Law Center, and warned women: "Don't remain at home with him during the game." FAIR's Linda Mitchell later acknowledged that Sheila Kuehl had misrepresented the 40% figure since, when double-checked with the principal author, Janet Katz, Katz said she did not find a rise in abuse during the Super Bowl.

   Similarly, Lenore Walker, author of The Battered Woman, claimed on Good Morning, America (January 28, 1993) that she compiled a ten-year record of sharp increases in violent incidents against women on Super Bowl Sundays. When pressed, Walker said the findings were "not available." She explained, "We don't use them for public consumption . . . we use them to guide us in advocacy projects."
133. "Mothers Can't Win," cover of New York Times Magazine, April 5, 1998.
134. Nan Robertson, The Girls in the Balcony: Women, Men and the New York Times (New York: Fawcett Books, 1993).
135. Ibid., p. 231.
136. Isabelle de Courtivron, ". . . And with Good Reason," a review of Marilyn French's The War Against Women, New York Times, July 5, 1992.
137. New York Times, December 27, 1987 and Time, February 14, 1994, quoting from Marilyn French's The Women's Room (New York: Ballantine Books, 1988 and 1993).
138. Robert Towers, "Don't Expect Too Much of Men," New York Times Book Review, March 11, 1990; a review of Amy Hempel's At the Gates of the Animal Kingdom (New York: Alfred A. Knopf, 1990).
139. The Women's Room by Marilyn French was reviewed in the New York Times by Ann Tyler on October 16, 1977.
140. Ibid. Reviewed by Christopher Lehmann Haupt, October 27, 1977.
141. de Courtivron, op. cit.
142. Wendy Steiner, "Declaring War on Men," New York Times Book Review, September 15, 1991, p. 11, in a review of Andrea Dworkin's Mercy: A Novel About Rape (New York: Four Walls Eight Windows, 1991).
143. Ellen Willis's review of Pornography by Andrea Dworkin appeared in the New York Times on July 12, 1981.
144. Interview on January 28, 1999, with Andrew Kimbrell, author of The Human Body Shop (New York: HarperCollins, 1993) and The Masculine Mystique (New York: Ballantine Books/Random House, 1995).
145. Ibid.
146. Warren Farrell, The Liberated Man (New York: Random House and Bantam, 1975; Berkley, revised 1993).
147. Gloria Steinem, Revolution from Within (New York: Little Brown & Company, 1993). The examples in this paragraph inspired by John Ellis, "The Takeover of the New York Times Book Review," Heterodoxy, November 1993.
148. Daly, Beyond God the Father, op. cit.
149. Fred Strebeigh, "Defining Law on the Feminist Frontier," New York Times Magazine, October 6, 1991, cover page.
150. MacKinnon's exact words are, "Women, as a survival strategy must ignore or devalue or mute desires, particularly lack of them, to convey the impression that the man will get what he wants regardless of what they want. In this context, to measure the genuineness of consent from the individual assailant's point of view is to adopt as law the point of view which creates the problem." See Catharine MacKinnon, Toward a Feminist Theory of the State (Cambridge: Harvard University Press, 1989), p. 181.
151. Andrea Dworkin, Letters from a War Zone (New York: E. P. Dutton, 1989), p. 21.
152. Steiner, op. cit.
153. Robert D. McFadden, "New York Nightmare Kills a Dreamer," New York Times, January 5, 1999, front page.
154. Elisabeth Rosenthal, "Women's Suicides Reveal Rural China's Bitter Roots," New York Times, January 24, 1999, front page.
155. Ibid., p. 8. Figures are from World Mental Health: Problems and Priorities in Low-Income Countries; Culture, Medicine and Psychiatry; World Bank.
156. In the eighty-five-plus range, there are 46 female suicides and 66.9 male suicides per 100,000 population. Latest data available as of 1992. From USBH&HS/NCHS, Vital Statistics of the United States, Vol. II, "Morality," Part A, 1987.

8. MEN-IN-THE NEWS (LACE CURTAIN) (CONT'D)

157. Rosenthal, "Women's Suicides Reveal Rural China's Bitter Roots," op. cit., p. 8.
158. Jack C. Smith, James A. Mercy, and Judith M. Conn, "Marital Status and the Risk of Suicide," *American Journal of Public Health,* Vol. 78, No. 1, January 1988, p. 79, Figure 3.
159. John F. Burns, "Unforeseen, Strife Eases for Algeria," *New York Times,* March 7, 1999, front page.
160. Jennifer Steinhauer, "A Rise in Allergies to Latex Threatens Medical Workers," *New York Times,* March 7, 1999, front page.
161. Robin Finn, "Growth in Women's Sports Stirs Harassment Issue," *New York Times,* March 7, 1999, front page.
162. Elisabeth Rosenthal, "Police Abuses Start to Get Attention in China," *New York Times,* March 8, 1999, front page.
163. Richard A. Shweder, "A Few Good Men? Don't Look in the Movies," *New York Times,* January 25, 1998, Section 2/Arts & Leisure, front page.
164. Marilyn Vos Savant, "Ask Marilyn," *Parade,* March 1, 1998, p. 6.
165. Steve Lopez, "Hide and Seek," *Time,* May 11, 1998.
166. Lance Morrow, "Are Men Really That Bad?" *Time,* February 14, 1994.
167. Peter Brimelow, "Save the Males?" *Forbes,* December 2, 1996, pp. 46–47.
168. If you are a teacher or parent, have your students or children do such a comparison.
169. Graham Masterton, "How to Seduce Your Boss," *Woman's Own,* October 1995, pp. 42–44. All quotes in this bulleted list are from this article.
170. Susan Forward, "Next Oprah: Men Who Waste Money and the Women Who Love Them," *Money,* July 1994, p. 13.
171. Mark McDonald, writer for the *Dallas Morning News,* in *Sunday Camera* (CO), April 29, 1990.
172. Xaviera Hollander, "Xaviera," *Penthouse,* December 1989, p. 64.
173. Al Martinez and Joanne Cinelli Martinez, "He Said; She Said," *Modern Maturity,* January/February 1996, p. 26.
174. Martha Duffy, "The Almighty to the Rescue," *Time,* Vol. 146, No. 20, November 13, 1995, p. 105.
175. Literary agent Ellen Levine estimates a 3:1 ratio of female-to-male editors handling books on relationships.
176. Interview with Andrew Kimbrell, January 28, 1998. The first edition, of 11,000 hardcovers, is about twice the total average book sale in hardcover.
177. Joseph Sobran, "The Story of the Real Titanic," Universal Press Syndicate, April 1998.
178. AP & Nando Times, "New Fight Over Film Version of Titanic Tragedy," April 9, 1998.
179. Ibid.
180. Ibid.
181. Shweder, op. cit.
182. Sobran, op. cit.
183. AP & Nando Times, op. cit.
184. Joe Queenan, "For Members Only," *Movieline,* September 1993, p. 85.
185. Credit for this example to the National Center for Men's *Media Watch,* No. 5, June 6, 1994.
186. This figure was part of the radio address by President Clinton to the nation in 1996 and comes from the Office of the Press Secretary, the White House, for immediate release, March 2, 1996.
187. *TV Guide,* December 2, 1998. On USA cable, prime time.
188. *Liberator,* November 1992, p. 18, reviewing the overall TV section appearing in the *Boston Herald,* September 9, 1992.
189. Harry F. Waters, "Whip Me, Beat Me, and Give Me Great Ratings . . . ," *Newsweek,* November 11, 1991, as cited in Charles J. Sykes, *A Nation of Victims* (New York: St. Martin's Press, 1992), p. 177.
190. CBS TV, 1987.
191. From a news brief titled "Captivity, From the Outside Looking In," *News & Observer* (Raleigh, NC), January 14, 1994, p. 2D.
192. Darin F. Detwiler, "E. coli Isn't Dramatic, But It Can Be Deadly," *News & Observer* (Raleigh, NC), January 13, 1994, p. 11A.
193. Credit to Stuart Pederson.
194. Credit for this example to the National Center for Men's *Media Watch,* No. 9, September 28, 1995.
195. Waters, "Networking Women," op. cit.
196. Ibid.
197. A. C. Nielsen ratings, 1984.
198. Waters, "Networking Women," op. cit.
199. Tom Post, "The Convergence Gamble," *Forbes,* February 22, 1999, p. 116.
200. Ibid., pp. 114–15.
201. Dennis Kneale, "Will a Fat Woman Who Ridicules Men Be TV's Next Hero?" *Wall Street Journal,* July 27, 1988, p. 1.
202. Ibid., pp. 1 and 13.
203. Ibid., p. 1.
204. Ibid., p. 1.

205. Both are 1987–1990 *Geraldo Rivera* shows.
206. The last three are 1988–1990 *Sally Jessy Raphael* shows.
207. *CNN Headline News,* October 25, 1994.
208. Aired June 24, 1998.
209. *CNN Headline News,* September 9, 1994. The book is by Karen Salmansohn, *How to Make Your Man Behave in 21 Days or Less Using the Secrets of Professional Dog Trainers* (New York: Workman Publishing, 1993).
210. A myriad of articles reported, and followed up on, his firing, including "Names in the News," a Sports section of the *Los Angeles Times,* February 21, 1991.
211. Jane Hall, *Times* staff writer, "CBS News Suspends Rooney for Remarks About Blacks; Race Relations," *Los Angeles Times,* February 9, 1990, Part A.
212. Mike Lupica, *Newsday* commentary, "It's Past Time to Stop Destroying Careers," *Los Angeles Times,* October 30, 1994, Sports section.
213. Katie Couric on *Today Show,* March 13, 1997.
214. *The Today Show,* November 25, 1997. Interview by Katie Couric of bride Nicole Contos; the groom was Tasos Michael.
215. In 1998–99, my assistant and I inquired of senior producer Michael Bass's office and were referred to Linda Finnell, to archives, and to other offices. When no one had such a women's health/men's health breakdown, we requested the raw data—asking for a log of all segments so we could do our own calculations, We met with 100 percent refusals, even when we asked for segments during just a three-month period.
216. Steven L. Collins, "Sexist Depictions of Men on *The Cosby Show,*" 1988.
217. *The Howard Stern Show* was in January 1999.
218. David Letterman's show was early February 1999.
219. Christine Montgomery, "For Men Who Are from Mars—and Lost," *Washington Times,* September 11, 1997, p. C10.
220. According to International Data Corporation, a market research firm, in a report released the week of January 24, 1999, and cited in the *New York Times,* January 31, 1999, p. 20.
221. E-mail on April 2, 1998 and November 26, 1998 from Mike McDermott, founder of the Men's Equal Rights folder.
222. E-mail on April 2, 1998, from WLV Pallas, Message Board Team Coordinator, Talk Women, AOL Women's Forum.
223. McDermott, E-mail, op. cit.
224. Amy Harmon, "Worries About Big Brother at America Online," *New York Times,* January 31, 1999, p. 1.
225. The website for "All Men Must Die" is: http://www.kfs.org/~kashka/ammd.html.
226. Joel Fischer, Diane D. Dulaney, Rosemary T. Fazio, Mary T. Hudak, and Ethel Zivotofsky, "Are Social Workers Sexists?" *Social Work,* November 1976, p. 430.
227. Ibid.
228. *In Health,* March/April 1990, p. 11. Study conducted by Louise Fitzgerald, University of Illinois, and John Robertson, Kansas State University. Therapists included eighteen males and twenty-nine females.
229. Armin Brott, "When Women Abuse Men," Issues section, *Washington Post,* December 28, 1993.
230. Sally Satel, MD, "The Patriarchy Made Me Do It," *The Women's Freedom Network Newsletter,* Vol. 5, No. 5, September/October 1998, p. 8. Dr. Satel is a lecturer in psychiatry at Yale University School of Medicine.
231. Ibid., front page.
232. Ibid.
233. *Minneapolis Star-Tribune,* "Why Do Mothers Kill Their Children?" September 5, 1998.
234. Amy Gage, "Clear Understanding of Media Needed to Get Women in the News," *St. Paul Pioneer Press,* June 15, 1997, p. 1D.
235. The colleague was with the National Center for Men in New York City. Unfortunately, exhausted by the general nonresponsiveness to these issues, he withdrew into more mainstream life and is fearful of reprisals should his name be in print.

APPENDIX

1. Lisa Brush analyzed the findings of the *National Survey of Families and Households,* which sampled 9,643 households with 13,017 respondents.
2. Letter from Lisa D. Brush, June 15, 1991.
3. Phone numbers were randomly generated within a suburban, middle- to upper-class neighborhood.
4. Randomly selected telephone sample from Delaware.
5. Sampling from Pennsylvania: 80% random; 20% parents of children in day care. Husbands abusive in 25% of families; wives in 29% of families.

INDEX

work (*cont.*)
  of men vs. women, 93–96, 115, 235–36, 313
  see also housework; housework, female;
    housework, male
workplace:
  double standard in, 196
  feminist version of sensitivity as dominant in,
    199–200

irony of discrimination against women in, 320
as men's emotional support system, 64–65
women's social support systems in, 64
World According to Garp, The, 291
writers, censorship by, 285–86

Yale, 249
yard work, 106

ABOUT THE AUTHOR

DR. WARREN FARRELL is the author of *The Liberated Man* plus two award-winning international bestsellers, *Why Men Are the Way They Are* and *The Myth of Male Power*. His books are in over 50 countries in eight languages.

Dr. Farrell taught in the School of Medicine at the University of California in San Diego, and has also taught psychology, sociology, and political science at Georgetown, Rutgers, and Brooklyn College. He has appeared eight times on *Donahue,* repeatedly on *Oprah* and CNN, and has been interviewed by Peter Jennings, Barbara Walters, and Larry King. He has been the subject of features in the *New York Times,* the *London Times,* the *Japan Times* and the *Australian Times,* as well as the *Wall Street Journal, Forbes, People,* and *Parade.*

Dr. Farrell lives in Encinitas, in north San Diego County. He can be reached at:

Warren Farrell, Ph.D.
103 N. Hwy. 101, PMB 220
Encinitas (San Diego), Ca. 92024-3252, or at
www.warrenfarrell.com

PERMISSIONS